*Poetics of the Pillory*

CLARENDON LECTURES IN ENGLISH

# *Poetics of the Pillory*

English Literature and Seditious
Libel, 1660–1820

THOMAS KEYMER

UNIVERSITY PRESS

# OXFORD
UNIVERSITY PRESS

Great Clarendon Street, Oxford, OX2 6DP,
United Kingdom

Oxford University Press is a department of the University of Oxford.
It furthers the University's objective of excellence in research, scholarship,
and education by publishing worldwide. Oxford is a registered trade mark of
Oxford University Press in the UK and in certain other countries

© Thomas Keymer 2019

The moral rights of the author have been asserted

First Edition published in 2019

Impression: 1

All rights reserved. No part of this publication may be reproduced, stored in
a retrieval system, or transmitted, in any form or by any means, without the
prior permission in writing of Oxford University Press, or as expressly permitted
by law, by licence or under terms agreed with the appropriate reprographics
rights organization. Enquiries concerning reproduction outside the scope of the
above should be sent to the Rights Department, Oxford University Press, at the
address above

You must not circulate this work in any other form
and you must impose this same condition on any acquirer

Published in the United States of America by Oxford University Press
198 Madison Avenue, New York, NY 10016, United States of America

British Library Cataloguing in Publication Data

Data available

Library of Congress Control Number: 2019946775

ISBN 978–0–19–874449–8

DOI: 10.1093/oso/9780198744498.001.0001

Printed and bound by
CPI Group (UK) Ltd, Croydon, CR0 4YY

Links to third party websites are provided by Oxford in good faith and
for information only. Oxford disclaims any responsibility for the materials
contained in any third party website referenced in this work.

For Hal Jackman

*nostrarum grande decus columenque rerum*

# Acknowledgements

This project began life with an invitation to give the Clarendon Lectures in English for 2014–15. I thank everyone present for their stimulating questions, and I'm especially grateful to David Womersley and Seamus Perry for their warm hospitality, and to Jacqueline Norton and Aimee Wright for their ongoing support as the monograph came to fruition. Dorothy McCarthy was a tactful and meticulous copyeditor. Generous fellowships from the John Simon Guggenheim Memorial Foundation and the University of Toronto's Jackman Humanities Institute allowed me to expand and enrich the lectures, and I thank the Warden and Fellows of All Souls College, Oxford, for hospitably giving me, as Visiting Fellow, the perfect environment in which to complete the book. Throughout this time, and to cumulatively transformative effect, numerous friends and colleagues offered advice, read drafts, arranged talks, answered questions, and wrote letters; I'm especially grateful to Paul Baines, Ros Ballaster, Paddy Bullard, Brian Cowan, Simon Dickie, Joe Hone, Paulina Kewes, Deidre Lynch, Nick McDowell, Paula McDowell, Jim McLaverty, Jon Mee, John O'Brien, Annabel Patterson, Claude Rawson, John Richetti, Pat Rogers, Michael Rossington, Valerie Rumbold, Peter Sabor, Simon Stern, Paul Stevens, Noel Sugimura, Kathryn Sutherland, David Taylor, Cindy Wall, Dan White, and Steve Zwicker. Thanks to the University of Toronto's Work-Study and Jackman Scholars in Residence programmes, I had the opportunity to involve outstanding student assistants in the project, including Shamaila Anjum, Ka Wing Chu, Graham Coulter, Angela Du, Keith Garrett, Rachel Hart, Dana Lew, Kevin Liu, Edward Sakowsky, John Siferd, Sushani Singh, Rachael Tu, and Alex Zutt; special thanks to Chris Geary, with whom I co-published a related essay on seditious libel in eighteenth-century Dublin, and Austin Long, whose astute and energetic work, not least in creating the index, was invaluable in the final stages. I also thank the Social Sciences and Humanities Research Council (Canada) for supporting my work and that of my students over time. Our research would have been impossible without the expert assistance of many University of Toronto Libraries colleagues, not least in providing access to indispensable resources such as State Papers Online, Eighteenth-Century Collections Online, and the Burney Newspapers; warm thanks too to Salvy Trojman for helping us get the best from these databases, and to special collections librarians in numerous other institutions for their prompt and generous help in particular cases. As ever, Pru, Toby, and Ben were a constant source of inspiration and love, and I could have done nothing without them.

# Contents

*List of Illustrations*     xi
*List of Abbreviations*     xv

   Introduction     1

1. 1660–1700. Faint Meaning: Dryden and Restoration
   Censorship     27
   Strange elegy: *Lachrymae musarum, Heroic Stanzas*     39
   Panegyric in print and script, *Astraea Redux* to *Mac Flecknoe*     54
   Plays and parallels: Exclusion Crisis libel and the licensing lapse     62
   Fable, history, translation: scourging by proxy     75

2. 1700–1740. Libels in Hieroglyphics: Pope, Defoe     89
   Earless in Grubstreet     100
   Wit, and punishment, and Pope: *The Dunciad* and after     106
   Irony, intention, interpretation: *The Shortest Way with the Dissenters*     121
   Defoe in the pillory     132
   Allegoric histories: *Windsor Forest, Robinson Crusoe*     148

3. 1730–1780. The Trade of Libelling: Fielding, Johnson     157
   Defeating the pillory: Mist, Curll, Shebbeare, Wilkes     165
   Performance and print under Walpole     178
   Fielding and Walpole: the art of thriving     192
   Lives of the opposition poets     201
   Johnsonian sedition: *London, Marmor Norfolciense*     207

4. 1780–1820. Southey's New Star Chamber: Literature,
   Revolution, and Romantic-Era Libel     221
   Allegories, parodies, polemics: Walter Cox, William Hone,
   and others     232
   The 'King Chaunticlere' trial: arbitrary innuendo and
   necessary sense     242
   Trumpets of sedition?     254
   Censorship, copyright, and *Wat Tyler*     261
   The most seditious book that was ever written     272

   Conclusion: England in 1820     283

*Select Bibliography*     291
*Index*     309

# List of Illustrations

0.1. *A View of the Corn Exchange London and Mr Atkinson the Contractor in the Pillory* (1785), broadside etching, © the Trustees of the British Museum. All rights reserved.   2

0.2. *This Is Not the Thing: or, Molly Exalted* (1762), illustrated broadside ballad, by courtesy of the Lewis Walpole Library, Yale University.   4

0.3. Richard Gaywood, etching of *c.*1656–60 showing the blasphemer James Nayler, by courtesy of the Lewis Walpole Library, Yale University.   10

1.1. *An Elegy on the Usurper O. C. . . . Published to Shew the Loyalty and Integrity of the Poet* (1681), by permission of the Newberry Library, Chicago.   52

1.2. Playing-card of John Culliford in the pillory (*c.*1683–4), etching on pasteboard, from a pack depicting the Rye House Plot, © the Trustees of the British Museum. All rights reserved.   66

1.3. Philopatris (Charles Blount?), *The Plot in a Dream: or, The Discoverer in Masquerade* (1681), copperplate engraving facing p. 148, © the Trustees of the British Museum. All rights reserved.   67

1.4. Earthenware tile painted in manganese over a tin glaze (1680), © the Trustees of the British Museum. All rights reserved.   68

1.5. Francis Barlow, design for a playing-card (*c.*1680), pen and brown ink drawing on paper, with grey wash over graphite, © the Trustees of the British Museum. All rights reserved.   69

2.1. *The Three Champions* (*c.*1710), engraved broadside, © the Trustees of the British Museum. All rights reserved.   105

2.2. Alexander Pope, *The Dunciad Variorum* (1729), first quarto edition (Rumbold 1729a, Vander Meulen 8, Foxon P771), p. 1, by courtesy of the William Ready Division of Archives and Research Collections, McMaster University Library.   112

## List of Illustrations

2.3. *The Works of Alexander Pope, Esq.*, ed. Joseph Warton, 9 vols (1797), 4: 356, by courtesy of the William Ready Division of Archives and Research Collections, McMaster University Library. 120

2.4. *The Scribler's Doom; or, The Pillory in Fashion* (1703), title page, © the British Library Board, 8122.b.86. 133

2.5. Daniel Defoe, *Jure Divino: A Satyr, The First Book* (*c.*1706), title page, by permission of the Beinecke Rare Book and Manuscript Library (General Collection). 135

2.6. George Bickham, *The Whigs Medly*, or *The Three False Brethren* (1711), engraved broadside, by courtesy of the Lewis Walpole Library, Yale University. 136

2.7. Robert Spofforth, playing-card of Defoe in the pillory (1705), copperplate etching on pasteboard, from a Tory pack depicting events from the first three years of Queen Anne's reign, © the Trustees of the British Museum. All rights reserved. 137

2.8. Paul Dottin, *The Life and Strange and Surprising Adventures of Daniel Defoe* (New York: Macaulay, 1929*)*, illustrated dustjacket, by permission of the New York Public Library. 139

2.9. *Allers Familj-Journal*, 14 (2 April 1924), cover illustration, © Mary Evans Picture Library. 140

2.10. Eyre Crowe, *Daniel Defoe in the Pillory* (1862), oil on canvas, by permission of Salford Museum and Art Gallery. 141

2.11. Fra Angelico (Guido di Pietro), *The Crucifixion with the Sponge-Bearer* (1442), fresco, Museo di San Marco, Florence, Italy/Bridgeman Images. 143

2.12. Petition of Daniel Defoe to Queen Anne (?November 1713), by permission of the National Archives. 147

3.1. Samuel Wale, *Egan and Salmon, the Thief-Takers, Pilloried at Smithfield* (1756), pen and grey and brown ink drawing with grey wash on paper, © the Trustees of the British Museum. All rights reserved. 162

3.2. William Hogarth, *The Times*, Plate 2 (1762–3), etching and engraving on paper, by courtesy of the Lewis Walpole Library, Yale University. 173

*List of Illustrations* xiii

3.3. Jefferyes Hamett O'Neale (?), *The Pillory Triumphant; or, No. 45 for Ever* (1765), broadside etching, by courtesy of the Lewis Walpole Library, Yale University. 174

3.4. Samuel Johnson, detail from *London* (1738), autograph manuscript, MS Hyde 50 (33), Houghton Library, Harvard University, by permission. 211

3.5. Eyre Crowe, *Dr Johnson Doing Penance in the Market Place of Uttoxeter* (1869), oil on canvas, by permission of Dr. Johnson's House Trust Ltd. 219

4.1. Samuel M. Fox, *Delaware Pillory and Whipping Post* (*c.*1889), photographic print (albumen), by permission of the Library of Congress Prints and Photographs Division. 222

4.2. Robert Harris, *The Charlottetown Pillory* (*c.*1876), ink wash and pencil on paper, gift of the Robert Harris Trust, 1965, by permission of the Confederation Centre Art Gallery, CAG H-123. 224

4.3. 'Mr. Walter Cox, on the Pillory', *Irish Magazine* (April 1811), by permission of The Board of Trinity College Dublin. 231

4.4. James Gillray, *Tom Paine's Nightly Pest* (1792), hand-coloured etching on paper, by courtesy of the Lewis Walpole Library, Yale University. 247

4.5. James Gillray, detail from *New Morality* (1798), hand-coloured etching on paper, by courtesy of Princeton University Library. 267

4.6. Charles Williams, *A Poet Mounted on the Court-Pegasus* (1817), hand-coloured etching on paper, by permission of the Library of Congress. 268

# List of Abbreviations

| | |
|---|---|
| *CCD* | D. F. McKenzie and Maureen Bell, *A Chronology and Calendar of Documents Relating to the London Book Trade, 1641–1700*, 3 vols (Oxford: Oxford University Press, 2005) |
| *CP* | Geoff Kemp and Jason McElligott (gen. eds), *Censorship and the Press, 1580–1720*, 4 vols (London: Pickering & Chatto, 2009) |
| *ODNB* | *Oxford Dictionary of National Biography* (online) |
| *OED* | *Oxford English Dictionary* (online) |
| *POAS* | *Poems on Affairs of State*, ed. George deF. Lord et al., 7 vols (New Haven: Yale University Press, 1963–75) |
| TNA | The National Archives |

If Men are forbid to speak their minds seriously on certain Subjects, they will do it ironically. If they are forbid to speak at all upon such Subjects, or if they find it really dangerous for 'em to do so; they will then redouble their Disguise, involve themselves in Mysteriousness, and talk so as hardly to be understood, or at least not plainly interpreted, by those who are dispos'd to do 'em a mischief.

> Anthony Ashley Cooper, 3rd Earl of Shaftesbury

There is freedom of speech, but I cannot guarantee freedom after speech.

> Idi Amin

# Introduction

Across the swathe of time addressed in this study, a variety of offences, some of them no longer offences at all, could land a malefactor in the uncomfortable, often dangerous, position depicted in Figure 0.1: in the pillory, that edifice which, for the historian of crime and punishment John Beattie, 'might stand as a paradigm of the old penal order'.[1] The ritual of degradation inflicted by pillorying epitomizes the theatricality of punishment in that old order: an order that lingered late and died hard. Throughout the 'long' eighteenth century (for the purposes of this book, 1660–1820), the pillory was a familiar enough feature of urban life to attract a colourful range of slang terms. You could peep through the nutcrackers or nab the stoop, you could become a surveyor of the highway or an overseer of the pavement, for several kinds of fraud, including forgery or counterfeiting, peculation, and selling adulterated goods. *A View of the Corn Exchange* (1785) is one of several graphic satires deriding the disgraced MP and corn factor Christopher Atkinson, pilloried outside the exchange after swindling the Navy Victualling Board and lying about it in an affidavit (Figure 0.1). You could look through the sheriff's picture frame, you could wear the Norway neckcloth or the wooden ruff, for subornation or perjury; a perjurer was pilloried in London as late as 1830. Official protection was often inadequate for miscreants immobilized in the pillory (typically for an hour-long spell that might be repeated over three days at different locations), and as the now dominant figurative meaning of the word indicates, the main point of the exercise was to

---

[1] J. M. Beattie, *Crime and the Courts in England, 1660–1800* (Oxford: Clarendon Press, 1986), 614.

*Poetics of the Pillory: English Literature and Seditious Libel, 1660–1820*. Thomas Keymer, Oxford University Press (2019). © Thomas Keymer.
DOI: 10.1093/oso/9780198744498.001.0001

**Figure 0.1** *A View of the Corn Exchange London and Mr Atkinson the Contractor in the Pillory* (1785), broadside etching, © the Trustees of the British Museum. All rights reserved. By this date, pillories were often designed to be rotated 90° every fifteen minutes, to maximize shaming; an official instructs Atkinson to 'Walk Round Sir'.

expose offenders to ridicule and abuse. In practice, the outcome could be worse. Informers whose perjuries led to convictions and executions were at special risk from mob violence. So were the men and occasionally women pilloried for sexual offences such as brothel-keeping and especially sodomy (or in practice attempted sodomy, a non-capital offence, and easier to prove). In *This Is Not the Thing: or, Molly Exalted*, an illustrated broadside ballad of 1762, the violence is shown only by menacing speech bubbles and the preparations of onlookers who brandish flails, reach for rotting fruit, or scoop up handfuls of filth. But on this occasion the pillory-peeper in question, the 60-year-old master of a Cheapside china shop, was pelted, beaten, and left badly injured in an orchestrated attack (Figure 0.2).[2] A similar but fatal episode in 1780 prompted the celebrated speech in which Edmund Burke called on Parliament to abolish the pillory, though the institution endured for another half-century in Britain, and longer elsewhere.

Most famously, the pillory was a tool for the retrospective censorship of print; it was, as Daniel Defoe put it when preparing to undergo his sentence for *The Shortest Way with the Dissenters* in 1703, that '*Hi'roglyphick* State *Machin*, | Contriv'd to Punish Fancy in'.[3] It was not, of course, the only contrivance for punishing fancy available to the authorities. Supplementary elements of corporal punishment (whipping at the cart's tail; officially mandated disfigurement) were rare after the Glorious Revolution, but not unheard of. The sentence of Elizabeth Cellier for writing and publishing *Malice Defeated* (1680) details excruciating further embellishments that persisted more strongly: a ruinous fine; imprisonment 'till that thousand pounds be paid'; large sureties 'for the good Behaviour during her Life'; busy locations selected to intensify humiliation (Cellier's judge wanted her first hour's exposure to happen 'as near her own House as conveniently can be . . . on the most Notorious day, I think there is a Market near that Place, let it be on that day'); exemplary destruction of the offending publications ('in every place where she shall Stand on the Pillory, some Parcels of her Books, shall, in her own view, be burnt by the Hands of the *Common Hangman*, and a Paper of the Cause, to be put upon the Pillory').[4] In 1703, Defoe was not only exhibited before three

---

[2] Rictor Norton (ed.), 'Molly Exalted, 1762', *Homosexuality in Eighteenth-Century England: A Sourcebook* (7 February 2002, updated 26 June 2008), <http://rictornorton.co.uk/eighteen/exalted.htm>.

[3] *Satire, Fantasy and Writings on the Supernatural by Daniel Defoe*, ed. W. R. Owens and P. N. Furbank, 8 vols (London: Pickering & Chatto, 2003), 1: 241 (*A Hymn to the Pillory*, lines 1–2).

[4] *The Tryal and Sentence of Elizabeth Cellier for Writing, Printing and Publishing a Scandalous Libel Called, Malice Defeated* (1680), 35–6.

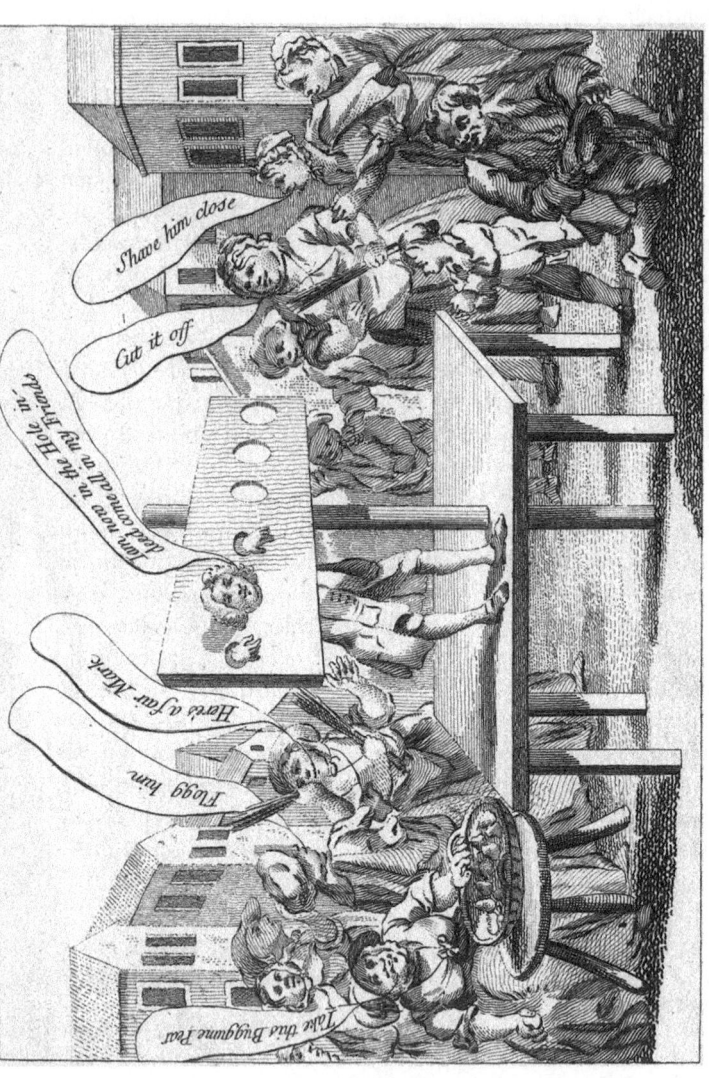

**Figure 0.2** *This Is Not the Thing; or, Molly Exalted* (1762), illustrated broadside ballad, by courtesy of the Lewis Walpole Library, Yale University. This image typifies the scapegoating of sexual offenders in the pillory, in this case a London shopkeeper named Shann.

of the city's most conspicuous landmarks (the Royal Exchange, the Cheapside Conduit, Temple Bar) but also heavily fined and imprisoned in Newgate until he could find sureties for future good behaviour. In practice, that took several months, and, it now seems, covert assistance from ministers who were planning to recruit him.

Penury could sometimes reach where the pillory couldn't, and there are numerous cases of book-trade professionals bankrupted by fines or the irreparable loss of livelihood that incarceration could entail. But the unique combination of disgrace and danger presented by the pillory gave it emblematic significance in the public mind, and special force as a deterrent. Dreading public degradation and lifelong damage to his always somewhat precarious social status, Defoe attempted, unavailingly, to plea-bargain 'for a Sentence a Little More Tollerable to me as a Gentleman, Than Prisons, Pillorys, and Such like, which are Worse to me Than Death'.[5] Even as perpetrators (following Defoe's own lead) found ways to convert the pillory into a festival of fourth-estate defiance, it continued to be viewed as a sanction outweighing all others, and came to stand as metonymic shorthand for book-trade transgression in general. Adam Smith gives an extraordinary account in his *Theory of Moral Sentiments* of the pillory as irremediable abjection. Or as a London journalist put it when the French Revolution began to raise the discursive stakes at home, fines might be the primary sanction against many crimes, 'but in the case of a libel (whether true or false), the fine is a secondary consideration, and imprisonment and pillory the first'.[6] This was, at least in theory, the most extreme form of stigmatization available under the law, the ultimate public humiliation for abusers of print publicity.

Defoe is the one major canonical author to have endured the pillory in practice for his writing, the offending text being an ironically ventriloquized mock-sermon published long before he became a novelist in 1719 with *Robinson Crusoe*. Yet Defoe is by no means the only author to have been threatened with the pillory by professional rivals,

[5] *The Letters of Daniel Defoe*, ed. George Harris Healey (Oxford: Clarendon Press, 1955), 2 (to Daniel Finch, Earl of Nottingham, 9 January 1703). One wonders, with the 'Such like', what else was on Defoe's mind; mutilation was still a theoretical possibility.

[6] *Daily Gazetteer*, 30 July 1790; for Smith, see below, pp. 163–4.

factional opponents, or government officials, or to have sensed the pillory's shadow, if not as an immediate practical hazard, then as a powerful and daunting symbol of expressive constraint. The shadow fell with equal menace over printers, publishers, and other book-trade professionals, who at some points were the targets of choice for state retribution, at others merely the simplest way for hard-pressed officials to get a result (printing and distribution being easier to prove than authorship).[7] During the Exclusion Crisis of 1679–81, with the Restoration press licensing system dangerously in abeyance, Lord Chief Justice Scroggs acknowledged that 'it is hard to find the Author, it is not hard to find the Printer'—but, he went on, '*one Author* found, is better than *twenty Printers* found'.[8] The same priorities informed Robert Harley's crackdown on the dissident press under Queen Anne, when the brunt of Harley's campaign was borne not by printers or booksellers but, a satirist protested, by Grubstreet hacks: the 'little Scriblers' for whom 'large Fines, and Pil[lori]es, by thee | Were made the base Rewards of Poetry'.[9]

For others at the forefront of eighteenth-century press control, the supply of professional writers was inexhaustible, and the real agency lay with the stationers who hired them. At the start of the Walpole era, Under Secretary Charles Delafaye wrote scathingly about the book-trade practice of commissioning 'scoundrels not worth a Groat that lived in Garretts to write at so much a sheet', and resolved that his energies 'would now fall upon printers and publishers as the more effectual way to put a stop to Libelling'.[10] Priorities shifted again

---

[7] At the start of the period Roger L'Estrange, incoming Licenser and Surveyor of the Press, produced a startlingly compendious list of potential targets: 'The *Delinquents* are the *Advisers, Authors, Compilers, Writers, Printers, Correcters, Stitchers,* and *Binders* of unlawful Books and Pamphlets: together with all *Publishers, Dispersers,* and *Concealers* of them in *General*; and all *Stationers, Posts, Hackny-Coachmen, Carryers, Boatmen, Mariners, Hawkers, Mercury-Women, Pedlers,* and *Ballad-Singers* so offending.' Among these, authors were the '*Grand Delinquents*' and '*Fountain* of our Troubles', for whom 'nothing can be too severe' (Roger L'Estrange, *Considerations and Proposals in Order to the Regulation of the Press* (1663), in *CP*, 3: 48).

[8] *The Triall of Henry Carr, Gent.* (1681), 7.

[9] *A Dialogue between Louis le Petite, and Harlequin le Grand* (1708?), p. viii.

[10] TNA, SP 43/66 (a 1723 memorandum), qtd by T. C. Duncan Eaves and Ben D. Kimpel, *Samuel Richardson: A Biography* (Oxford: Clarendon Press, 1971), 23.

during the French revolutionary decade and the socially troubled aftermath of the Napoleonic Wars, when high-profile actions were launched against metropolitan authors and booksellers, but there was also marked anxiety about low-level provincial distributors who were mediating politically disruptive content to the nation at large (see below, pp. 226 n.12, 234 n.34). Perhaps the simplest thing to say is that all the 'manufacturers of literature', in Samuel Johnson's phrase, shared a common predicament, and a predicament that endured.[11] Between the Restoration of 1660 (and of course earlier) and the last gasp of book-trade pillorying in the early 1810s, a startling number of authors, printers, and publishers endured the pillory, while many more feared its embrace, for obscene, blasphemous, and especially seditious libel, my subject in this book— though to some extent these different flavours of libel must be thought of as bleeding into one. As circumstances required, one charge could often be used as a convenient proxy for another, as was the case for the publishers Edmund Curll in 1728 and Daniel Isaac Eaton in 1812, the first prosecuted for obscene libel, the second for blasphemous libel, though in both cases the underlying motivation was political.

Hieroglyphic state machine, Defoe says—yet not, for all that, a wholly indecipherable machine. The 'pilloriable' offences itemized above are wide in range and might seem unrelated. So far as I know, there exists in official documents or legal treatises of the period no fully articulated, or even half-articulated, rationale to link them within any coherent, overarching category of transgression. However Foucauldian one might wish to be, punishment regimes were rarely so systematic in the eighteenth century, emerging over time in haphazard ways, shaped by innumerable instances of local pragmatism or sheer chance. The great common-law codifier of the 1760s, William Blackstone, has little to offer on the subject beyond mild embarrassment about a 'disgusting' punishment which, even so, pales in comparison 'with that shocking apparatus of death and torment, to be met

---

[11] Samuel Johnson, *The Rambler*, ed. W. J. Bate and Albrecht B. Strauss, 3 vols numbered 3–5 (New Haven: Yale University Press, 1969), 5: 10 (No. 145, 6 August 1751).

with in the criminal codes of almost every other nation in Europe'.[12] Perhaps Alexander Pope, a poet imaginatively preoccupied by the pillory for much of his creative life, comes closest with the witty analogies he makes between forgery, fraud, and seditious libel as comparable forms of textual crime. But Pope's ingenuity was exceptional. Understandably, Defoe had no time for that kind of analogy himself, and he hints at his own experience when deploring, in *The Consolidator* (1705), the case of a satirist exposed in the pillory who thus experiences, with gross injustice, a punishment proper only 'for *mean Criminals*, Fellows that Cheat and Couzen People, Forge Writings, Forswear themselves, and the like'.[13] Offences like this had nothing at all to do with literary authorship.

Yet it's not entirely fanciful to see a common thread running through all these various crimes—fraud, forgery, sodomy, perjury, blasphemous speech, seditious writing—in the violation or perversion of officially sanctioned norms of truth and nature. Offenders in all these categories do more than simply steal property or commit violence like common criminals. Their false words or unnatural deeds are more threatening than this; they challenge and destabilize the most basic conventions and assumptions that bind society, and the seditious libeller does so most eloquently of all. More practically, all these offences are ones that might be thought to elicit special derision: most aptly punished, then, by humiliating exhibition as an object of shame. It's for this reason that sexual 'deviants' in particular are singled out for the pillory, and it's worth repeating that the same rationale makes it the paradigmatic punishment for ideological deviants, or those whose publications simply stirred up social or political trouble.[14] For the Restoration censor Roger L'Estrange, the pillory was above all a penalty of disgrace, exactly the right one for authors

---

[12] William Blackstone, *Commentaries on the Laws of England*, gen. ed. Wilfrid Prest, 4 vols (Oxford: Oxford University Press, 2016), 4: 243.

[13] *Satire, Fantasy and Writings on the Supernatural by Defoe*, 3: 54.

[14] To the extent that clarity existed at all, this was the operative definition of seditious libel: in Blackstone's words, 'the breach of the public peace, by stirring up the objects of them to revenge, and perhaps to bloodshed'. It followed that questions of truth or falsehood, though central in a civil action, were irrelevant in political cases, where 'the tendency which all libels have to create animosities, and to disturb the public peace, is the sole consideration of the law' (*Commentaries*, 4: 99).

and stationers '*who had rather suffer any other Punishment then be made Publiquely Ridiculous*'.[15] At the end of the eighteenth century, as anxieties grew about the pillory on grounds of human dignity as well as effective deterrence, one traditionalist could still talk about 'the salutary effect of placing on an elevated pillory, a fit object for the indignant derision or honest detestation of mankind'.[16] The pilloried malefactor was shamed for ever by his, and occasionally her, exhibition to their scornful communities, or that was the theory. In his whimsical essay 'Reflections in the Pillory' (1825), Charles Lamb imagined the 'wooden cravat', 'thou younger brother to the gallows', as an exquisitely managed combination of spectacular exposure and corporeal jeopardy, 'the exact point between ornament and strangulation'.[17] To be pilloried was above all to be alienated, to face an enduringly traumatizing condition of urban isolation. 'I never felt so sensibly before the effect of solitude in a crowd', Lamb's character soliloquizes as ill-aimed eggs and brickbats fly past his face (1: 356).

Two celebrated episodes frame the period covered by this book. The first is the ordeal suffered by the truculent divine William Prynne and his fellow puritans John Bastwick and Henry Burton following their conviction by Archbishop Laud's Star Chamber in 1637, at a time when pillories served not only to frame and shame the malefactor but also to facilitate a gruesome ceremony of mutilation that would render the ignominy permanent. Prynne's ears, lightly cropped on a previous occasion (1633), were now nailed to the pillory and severed; his nostrils were slit; his face was branded with the initials 'S. L.' for Seditious or Schismatic Libeller, though Prynne himself embraced the letters as a badge of honour: 'STIGMATA LAUDIS', he called them, 'LAUDS STAMPS'.[18] This was not in fact the most excruciating pillorying of the seventeenth century, and Prynne escaped the full

---

[15] L'Estrange, *Considerations and Proposals*, in *CP*, 3: 49.

[16] Thomas Macdonald, *Thoughts on the Public Duties of Private Life* (1795), 46.

[17] *The Works in Prose and Verse of Charles and Mary Lamb*, ed. Thomas Hutchinson, 2 vols (London: Oxford University Press, 1908), 1: 356, 358, 356.

[18] William Prynne, *A New Discovery of the Prelates Tyranny* (1641), 65, 66. For a Habermasian account of the episode that emphasizes performance, see Christopher B. Balme, *The Theatrical Public Sphere* (Cambridge: Cambridge University Press, 2014), 95–9.

**Figure 0.3** Richard Gaywood, etching of c.1656–60 showing the blasphemer James Nayler, by courtesy of the Lewis Walpole Library, Yale University. Nayler's punishment included whipping at the cart's tail, tongue-boring, and branding.

penalty inflicted on the Quaker James Nayler, a blasphemer whose tongue was bored through with a hot iron under Cromwell in 1656, in pure *lex talionis* style (Figure 0.3). But Prynne's was probably the most notorious episode of this kind, and in modern scholarship has been highlighted by Annabel Patterson as the quintessential case of retribution against authorship in her *Censorship and Interpretation* (1984), a classic study that has made the hermeneutics of censorship enduringly central for our thinking about the early modern period.[19]

At the other end of the period is an event no less well known to scholars of Romanticism: the pillorying in 1812 of Daniel Isaac Eaton, a radical publisher who escaped several seditious libel prosecutions in

---

[19] See Annabel Patterson, *Censorship and Interpretation: The Conditions of Writing and Reading in Early Modern England*, revised edn (Madison: University of Wisconsin Press, 1990), 113–15 and 52–127 *passim*.

the 1790s but was at last convicted, in a long-delayed act of proxy retribution, for publishing the third part of Tom Paine's *The Age of Reason*. There was no question now of state-inflicted mutilation, and the only physical danger to Eaton was from crowd violence. But the violence failed to materialize. Just a few months earlier, William Cobbett reported, two sodomites pilloried where Eaton now stood had been viciously bombarded and scapegoated, but this time a crowd of 20,000 turned out to cheer Eaton on, and the event became a politically counterproductive festival of popular disaffection. Yet not from any public attachment to Paineite deism, Cobbett adds: 'it was their attachment to the *liberty of the press*, to which they know well that they owe whatever of freedom they enjoy.'[20] At the end of Eaton's rather gratifying hour in the spotlight, one supporter placed a gamecock on the pillory, defiantly recalling John Thelwall's fable of 'King Chaunticlere' and his beheading (published, with menacing implications for George III, soon after the guillotining of Louis XVI) for which Eaton had been prosecuted in the 1790s.

On the face of it, these are very different episodes, getting on for two centuries apart. The cruel and spectacular punishment inflicted on Prynne, Bastwick, and Burton in Palace Yard is in sharp contrast with what must have been quite a heartening hour for Eaton outside Newgate Gaol. A merciless demonstration of state power in the heyday of Stuart absolutism and Star-Chamber repression contrasts with an inadvertent dramatization of official impotence in the face of nineteenth-century public opinion. Yet there are common threads, and already in Prynne's martyrdom (as he adroitly represented it thereafter) we may foresee the pillory's demise in legislation passed following Eaton's triumph. Prynne was an insightful analyst of Laudian strategies of intimidation (the three were to be 'deprived of their ears...to the publike terror of all others', he later wrote)[21] and realized that a spectacle of exemplary punishment could be turned around as one of exemplary resistance. When the time came, all three sufferers performed their ordeal by analogy with the crucifixion, though also with a careful eye on the risk of presumptuous impiety.

---

[20] *Cobbett's Political Register* 21 (January–June 1812), 751 (13 June 1812).

[21] William Prynne, *Sad and Serious Politicall Considerations* (1650), 2.

'Shall I be ashamed of a Pillory for *Christ*, who was not ashamed of a Crosse for me?', Burton cried on approaching the scaffold. He later refused a drink held up to him in the pillory for fear of seeming to pastiche the Passion, and declared his nailed ears 'nothing to that my Saviour suffered for me, who had his hands and feet nayled to the Crosse'.[22] Popular sympathy, indeed veneration (spectators dipped handkerchiefs in Burton's blood as it ran down the scaffold), was just as much a factor in their case as it was to become in Eaton's.

So was the boost given by the episode to the dissident speech and writing it was intended to crush. A later actor in the history of seditious libel (Robert Southey, whose career path from Jacobin zealot to Tory laureate was to produce the delicious ironies described in my final chapter) was struck by Laud's outrage 'that Prynne and his fellows should be suffered to talk what they pleased while they stood in the pillory and win acclamations from the people, and have notes taken of what they spake, and those notes spread in written copies about the city; and that when they went out of town to the several imprisonments, there were thousands suffered to be upon their way to take their leave and God knows what else!'[23] Nor was Laud alone in recognizing the severity of the public-relations misstep that had just been committed. Writing with a few years' hindsight, the Earl of Clarendon was only the first of many historians to remember the mutilations, the sympathy they elicited, and the sufferers' triumphant procession into internal exile, as directly contributing to the abolition of Star Chamber, the execution of Laud, and even the course of the war that was now raging. Spectators looked on 'with anger and indignation', Clarendon wrote, 'and treasured up wrath for the time to come'.[24] Already, censorship and the pillory were starting to look counterproductive: own goals that irreversibly awakened public opinion, and destabilized established authority instead of securing it. Prynne's own judgment was that he (a lawyer) and his fellow sufferers (a physician and a cleric) had lost their ears that the professions they

---

[22] William Prynne, *New Discovery*, 48, 60.

[23] *Southey's Commonplace Book*, ed. John Wood Warter, 4 vols (1849–51), 2: 176, quoting Laud's letter to Thomas Wentworth, Earl of Strafford, 28 August 1637.

[24] Edward Hyde, Earl of Clarendon, *The History of the Rebellion and Civil Wars in England*, ed. W. Dunn Macray, 6 vols (Oxford: Clarendon Press, 1888), 1: 126 (i. §197).

represented might 'heare better'.[25] In a proto-Whig history first published as press control broke down during the Exclusion Crisis, another observer frankly represented the episode as the wake-up call for a downtrodden people. When Star Chamber 'began to swell big, and was delighted with Blood...and nothing would satisfy the revenge of some Clergy-men but *cropt Ears*, *slit Noses*, *branded Faces*... Then began the *English* Nation to lay to heart the slavish condition they were like to come unto'.[26]

In this context, it would be relatively easy for the following chapters to tell a story about emergent freedom of expression that already has its germ in the pillorying of Prynne, and to some extent that story—clarified recently by Trevor Ross for the decades after 1760—is impossible to avoid.[27] Between the legislative landmarks that frame the extended period, the Press Licensing Act of 1662 and the 1819 Act for the More Effectual Prevention and Punishment of Blasphemous and Seditious Libels, press control certainly became harder to exert, even as the resources of the executive expanded. Restoration England never achieved the kind of monolithic or absolutist state apparatus constructed in France under Louis XIV, and despite the formidable energies of individual regulators from Licenser and Surveyor Roger L'Estrange under Charles II to Lord Chancellor Eldon in the Regency years, censorship across the extended period was always a somewhat ramshackle affair, brutally effective in particular cases, a leaky sieve in general. For most of the eighteenth century it's implausible to speak in terms of a unified executive power, and as early as the Exclusion Crisis, competing authorities and rival interests—at this point the Tory court and the Whig city—could and did frustrate one another's efforts to convict and punish partisan writers and stationers. The totalitarian fallacy is always a temptation for historians of censorship before the bureaucratic age, but it's a temptation to be resisted. Just how hard it is to conceive, even a century later, of an

---

[25] Prynne, *New Discovery*, p. 1 ('To the Courteous Reader').

[26] John Rushworth, *Historical Collections of Private Passages of State*, 8 vols (1721), 2: 475; the passage is from Rushworth's second part, published in 1680 following licensing obstacles in 1677.

[27] Trevor Ross, *Writing in Public: Literature and the Liberty of the Press in Eighteenth-Century Britain* (Baltimore: Johns Hopkins University Press, 2018).

efficient, single-minded state apparatus is beautifully illustrated by the case of the poet, philologist, and lawyer William Jones in 1783, whose republican pamphlet *The Principles of Government, in a Dialogue between a Scholar and a Peasant* was under prosecution by one branch of government as a 'seditious, treasonable, and diabolical' tract even as its author was being knighted and appointed a Supreme Court judge by another. The provincial high sheriff who launched the prosecution, Thomas Fitzmaurice, was the brother of the statesman, Prime Minister Lord Shelburne, who engineered the knighthood.[28]

Then there were juries and crowds. We may no longer subscribe without reservation to a Habermasian narrative about the eighteenth-century emergence of a public sphere characterized by critical-rational reflection and debate and the increasing influence over politics of public opinion. But it was clearly the perception of ministers and their officials, brought home to them by recurrent experience of defeat, that juries, sometimes even packed special juries, could not be counted on to issue the desired 'guilty' verdict, and that urban crowds could not be prevented from honouring instead of shaming the pilloried writer. Other processes and mechanisms contributed to a weakening of control over politically inflected literature across the period, from the self-perception of the eighteenth century as polite and enlightened (Shaftesbury and Hume are telling voices here) to the irrepressible commercial energies of a book trade in which seditious libels were hot commodities and, as Samuel Johnson observed, to prosecute a book was also to promote it.[29]

Yet this progressive, if jaggedly erratic, loss of official control over print is very far from being the whole story. Instead, given the powerful inhibitions and forces just mentioned, we must ask about the decline and fall of literary censorship on political grounds, and about the decline and fall of the pillory as a sanction against seditious libel, the question Gibbon famously asks about the Roman empire:

---

[28] Michael J. Franklin, *Orientalist Jones: Sir William Jones, Poet, Lawyer, and Linguist, 1746–1794* (Oxford: Oxford University Press, 2011), 2; see also 163–204 *passim*.

[29] See Johnson's commentary on Milton's *Areopagitica* in *The Lives of the Poets*, ed. Roger Lonsdale, 4 vols (Oxford: Clarendon Press, 2006), 1: 252: 'this punishment, though it may crush the author, promotes the book.'

not why did it end, but why, and how, did it last so long?[30] Because last it did, in powerful and pervasive ways, though ways we continue to underestimate. Patterson and the many scholars to have developed, modified, or contested her arguments have, since the 1980s, kept censorship in our minds as a crucial determinant of individual works, and indeed of the very nature of the literary, in early modern England. More recently, the scholarship of John Barrell, Jon Mee and others on treasonable utterance and its prosecution during the revolution panic of the 1790s has put the same topic fruitfully on the map for Romanticists (see below, pp. 242–53). Yet despite important work, much of it cited in the chapters to follow, on individual writers of the intervening period such as Delarivier Manley or Jonathan Swift, or particular episodes such as the legislative intervention for which Fielding's farces became a catalyst in the 1730s, there persists an assumption that the collapse of pre-publication licensing in 1695 marks an end to political censorship as a major factor for literature thereafter, except during certain periods of special crisis. The assumption is an old one, fully formed in the Whig historiography of the nineteenth century, and finds its classic statement in Thomas Macaulay's declaration, in 1835, that press emancipation after the Glorious Revolution (specifically the 1695 lapse of the Licensing Act) released the English from the 'great practical evil' of Tudor and Stuart censorship, and did 'more for liberty and for civilisation than the Great Charter or the Bill of Rights'.[31]

In mid to late twentieth-century scholarship, Macaulay's view persisted, albeit with qualifications, in influential monographs and standard textbooks like F. S. Siebert's *Freedom of the Press in England, 1476–1776* (1952) and John Feather's *A History of British Publishing* (1987), which sideline censorship, or at least political censorship, as a relative non-issue after the Walpole era. In scholarship since then, the implications of Patterson's work on the seventeenth century,

[30] 'The story of its ruin is simple and obvious; and instead of inquiring why the Roman empire was destroyed, we should rather be surprised that it had subsisted so long' (Edward Gibbon, *The Decline and Fall of the Roman Empire*, ed. David Womersley (London: Allen Lane, 1994), 2: 509).

[31] *The Works of Lord Macaulay, Complete*, ed. Lady Trevelyan, 8 vols (1866), 6: 130; 4: 124.

though rapidly and richly pursued by early modernists, have been slow to filter through into eighteenth-century studies. Even the best new authorities on Elizabethan, Stuart, and Commonwealth censorship such as Geoff Kemp and Jason McElligott, though keen in principle to debunk the Whiggish grand narrative of steadily emergent press freedom, continue to treat 1700 as an approximate watershed beyond which far less constraint exists for authors, or for the printers and booksellers who frequently carried the can for dissident expression. In their important anthology *Censorship and the Press, 1580–1720*, Kemp and McElligott explain their decision to go some years beyond the traditional end-point of 1695 on the grounds that the licensing lapse did not mean that 'state censorship of the press ceased' (a claim by J. A. Downie from which they distance themselves). Even so, they see state censorship as fatally weakened by the 1695 lapse—as having, in their own metaphor, 'lost the limb of pre-publication censorship'— and as limping on thereafter in relatively ineffectual ways.[32]

It's certainly true that after 1695 the licenser's imprimatur—that mark of censorship requiring, as Milton protested under an earlier dispensation, that even 'unoffensive books must not stirre forth without a visible jaylor in their title'[33]—became a thing of the past. Yet there's little scope to view the licensing lapse as the conscious achievement of a liberalizing consensus in Parliament, and numerous efforts were made over the next few years, and at critical later junctures, to restore pre-publication censorship of one kind or another. Most were failures, but there were significant rearguard successes along the way, and powerful alternative schemes were devised to achieve the broad purpose of licensing—containment of the wayward energies of print—by other means. It was not for want of parliamentary effort at the turn of the century that no new statute emerged to replace the Licensing Act and so restore, as Defoe wrote in 1704, 'this Padlock to

---

[32] Geoff Kemp and Jason McElligott, 'General Introduction: The Constitution of Early Modern Censorship', *CP*, 1: xvi, citing J. A. Downie, *Robert Harley and the Press: Propaganda and Public Opinion in the Age of Swift and Defoe* (Cambridge: Cambridge University Press, 1979), 1. For Siebert and Feather, see below, p. 91.

[33] *Complete Prose Works of John Milton*, gen. ed. Don M. Wolfe, 8 vols (New Haven: Yale University Press, 1953–82), 2: 536.

the Press'.[34] During the reign of Queen Anne, new revenue and copyright legislation established other methods of restraint, the first by taxing print, the second by making it more easily traceable to source.[35] The last printer to be executed in England, a teenage journeyman caught red-handed with the Jacobite tract *Vox Populi, Vox Dei* in 1719, died as a result of hideously effective further legislation, the Succession to the Crown Act of 1707, with its specific provisions against supporting the Pretender's claims in either manuscript or print. And although licensing was never restored for printed books, under Walpole the Stage Licensing Act of 1737 brought drama under stricter pre-performance regulation than ever before, and involved a ban on improvisation to ensure conformity with the pre-approved text. Under Pitt, the Treasonable and Seditious Practices Act of 1795 was just one among several Romantic-period measures—more came with the notorious (though in the case of print, dubiously effective) Six Acts of 1819—aimed at perpetuating or toughening press control. In this context, no simple narrative of progressive statutory liberalization can be sustained.

Most important of all is the shift of emphasis after 1695 from pre-publication inspection to post-publication prosecution, without any sense on the part of book-trade professionals that this new regime—a regime based not on the Licensing Act but on the common law of seditious libel—provided greater latitude for free or safe expression. For eighteenth-century jurists, who typically take censorship to begin and end with prior restraint, the new dispensation could of course be celebrated as one in which 'the *liberty of the press*, properly understood, is by no means infringed or violated', as Blackstone sonorously declared. Blackstone offered a simple contrast with the benighted past: 'To subject the press to the restrictive power of a licenser, as was formerly done...is to subject all freedom of sentiment to the prejudices of one man, and make him the arbitrary and infallible judge

---

[34] *Political and Economic Writings of Daniel Defoe*, ed. W. R. Owens and P. N. Furbank, 8 vols (London: Pickering & Chatto, 2000), 8: 150.

[35] On the 1710 Copyright and the 1712 Stamp Acts as restraints on the press that inhibited anonymous publication and cheap print, see Thomas Keymer, 'Circulation', in Nicholas McDowell and Henry Power (eds), *The Oxford Handbook of English Prose, 1640–1714* (Oxford: Oxford University Press, forthcoming).

of all controverted points in learning, religion, and government.'[36] It was in no sense an erosion of this freedom—on the contrary, it was a necessary defence of freedom—to make authors who misapplied it accountable after the fact: 'to punish (as the law does at present) any dangerous or offensive writings, which, when published, shall on a fair and impartial trial be adjudged of a pernicious tendency, is necessary for the preservation of peace and good order, of government and religion, the only solid foundation of civil liberty.' For Blackstone, the free will of individuals was guaranteed in their right to unrestricted expression; 'the abuse only of that free will is the object of legal punishment' (p. 100). At risk of summarizing crudely, the message here, and the message of Lords Chief Justice from Sir William Scroggs during the first (1679–85) licensing lapse to Lord Ellenborough in the run-up to Peterloo, was that authors now had freedom of speech; freedom after speech was another matter.[37]

Of course, the happy picture presented by Blackstone makes sense only if one credits eighteenth-century ministers and judges with strenuous impartiality of the kind he denies to the licensers they replaced: a confidence not borne out by several episodes analysed in the following chapters, with Scroggs and Ellenborough among the protagonists. All too often, seditious libel judges of the period seem to step fresh from the pages of *Albion's Fatal Tree*, that classic work of Marxist historiography, like caricatures of shameless *raison d'état*, not rigorous, impartial upholders of the rule of law.[38] More important, Blackstone's picture makes sense only if one takes a severely attenuated view of censorship, its definition, and its scope and operation in

---

[36] Blackstone, *Commentaries*, 100. Blackstone somewhat elides the dispersed (and in practice very patchy) nature of Restoration censorship, in which different categories of book were licensed by different authorities; for the various agents and their remits, see Margaret J. M. Ezell, *The Oxford English Literary History, Volume 5: 1645–1714: The Later Seventeenth Century* (Oxford: Oxford University Press, 2017), 127–30.

[37] For a sinister modern restatement of the message, see Bankole Ola, 'Introduction', in Akindele Orimolade, *Close Shaves: Diary of a Journalist* (Osogbo: Frontpage Media, 2015), p. xv, quoting a speech by Idi Amin in 1970s Uganda.

[38] Douglas Hay, Peter Linebaugh, John G. Rule, E. P. Thompson, and Cal Winslow, *Albion's Fatal Tree: Crime and Society in Eighteenth-Century England* (London: Allen Lane, 1975).

practice. To take a broader view, and to recognize print expression as curtailed not only by *a priori* restraint but also by *a posteriori* retribution, and by a less conspicuous range of drags and duresses short of prohibition or prosecution—to say nothing of the internalized check on all discourse that Bourdieu terms 'constitutive' censorship—is to see that the freedom hailed by Blackstone was really a mirage.[39] The wave of criminal prosecutions in which Defoe was caught under Queen Anne gives an early indication of the rigour with which print would henceforward be controlled by other means. In the aftermath, Defoe himself was just one of many writers to argue that the new regime of seditious libel made authorship more, not less, hazardous and insecure than before. The world of Restoration licensing was erratic and unsystematic enough, but at least it was navigable, and left authors reasonably confident of where they stood. Now, Defoe asked, when there was no longer a fixed mark, how could one know not to overstep it? Laws, he wrote, were like buoys 'set upon dangerous Places under Water, to warn Mankind, that such Sands or Rocks are there, and the Language of them is, *Come here at your Peril*'. With licensing defunct and seditious libel undefined, however, no author could know his crime until after committing it, 'and I think verily no Book can be wrote so warily, but that if the Author be brought on his Tryal, it shall be easy for a cunning Lawyer...to put an *Innuendo* upon his Meaning, and make some Part of it Criminal'.[40]

The same objection was still being voiced a century later. When a French correspondent congratulated Jeremy Bentham on English liberty of the press, Bentham sourly replied that 'the liberty which *you* want *we* have: it consists in the *absence* of that *security*, which would be afforded to authors by a licenser: the assurance of not being punished for any thing they write'. Bentham adds, with a telling parenthesis, that 'what we possess is (subject to being punished for the use of it) the full liberty of publishing whatever we please'—the punishment being 'if not pillory imprisonment for a few months or years, *fine* a few hundreds of pounds, besides costs of prosecution, to

---

[39] On constitutive censorship, see below, p. 254.

[40] *Political Writings of Defoe*, 8: 154. On innuendo, see below, pp. 249–50.

the amount of a few hundreds more: this last *item* attaching upon a man whether he is convicted or acquitted.'[41]

If not pillory. Bentham was writing two years after the Eaton affair, and though formal abolition still lay ahead, he probably intuited that Defoe's hieroglyphic state machine would never again be used for seditious libel. Yet it remained a potent symbol of the restrictive conditions of authorship for earlier generations, and one made all the more intimidating at the time by the sheer unpredictability of its use. Every so often, as Voltaire might have said, the English would pillory an author or a printer to encourage the others—but no one could be quite sure when, or what for. And though we may already have seen, as early as the pillorying of Prynne in the 1630s, the writing on the wall for retributive literary censorship by the state in a world of ungovernable public opinion, the same struggle played out repeatedly for more than a century after the punishment of Defoe; protagonists included the journalist Nathaniel Mist (1721), the printer Edmund Curll (1728), the novelist and pamphleteer John Shebbeare (1758), a printer of John Wilkes's *North Briton* (1765), and on through several revolution-era cases to the Dublin journalist Walter Cox (1811), and Eaton for publishing Paine (1812).

Such episodes are the tip of the iceberg, moreover. Beneath the surface lie not only the invisible prior processes that sent book-trade professionals to jail, the pillory, ruin, or all three, but also a range of informal and formal actions from extra-legal harassment, cautionary arrests, and *ex officio* informations, through the exquisite humiliation of being required to kneel before Parliament in expiation, to the sleazily pecuniary methods that characterized eighteenth-century politics, including both sticks (notably, crippling sureties for future good conduct) and carrots (secret bribes, public pensions). Our long view, in which censorship now looks to have been in a state, albeit glacial in pace, of terminal decline, was the perspective of very few at the time, and though no offending writer was now going to suffer like Prynne and his fellows, that didn't mean no suffering at all. When Swift told Pope in 1725 that he would only be able to publish *Gulliver's Travels*

[41] *The Correspondence of Jeremy Bentham, Volume 8: 1809–1816*, ed. Stephen Conway (Oxford: Clarendon Press, 1988), 429–30 (to Jean Antoine Gauvin Gallois, September 1814).

'when a Printer shall be found brave enough to venture his Eares', he used a teasing figure of speech. But it remains the case that arrest and prosecution, if no longer the exotic additional flourish of mutilation, were occupational hazards for Swift's printers and publishers, at least two of whom (John Barber in 1714, John Harding in 1724) had already spent time in prison on Swift's account.[42]

Partly, then, I want to argue a historical case about the persistence and residual power of censorship, even while we can see it as on the wane—a historical case in which, rather than resort to grand narratives about the inevitable triumph of free-expression ideology, I emphasize instead the cumulatively overwhelming practical difficulty involved for the authorities as they sought to control an exuberant, diverse, endlessly innovative print culture. No less important is the critical case, for our slowness to make censorship central to our understanding of literature across the long eighteenth century is not a merely historical blind spot. To underestimate the ongoing place of censorship in the post-licensing world, specifically as exerted via the ever-present threat of seditious libel action, is also to miss a crucial determinant of eighteenth-century authorship and a condition, I argue, to which the complexities and energies of the period's writing are often directly owing. That optimistic conclusion is not, of course, the most obvious one to draw from the regime of seditious libel, and important voices to the end of the period represent it instead as a crippling inhibition. In 1814, Cobbett was drawn to the same metaphors as Defoe a century beforehand. In the absence of both press licensing and clear legal definition of seditious libel, he deplored the lack of observable '*boundaries*' and 'land-marks to guide the writer'— boundaries within which, in consequence, the writer 'would, as far as the law permitted him to go, be *free* to write'. In the old system, for Cobbett, the licenser's imprimatur leaves an author 'certain of impunity for what he may write and submit to the censors', and is thus preferable to the arbitrary dictum of a seditious libel judge. In the new system, the ever-present threat of legal retribution instead leaves an author

---

[42] Swift's remark is from his letter to Pope of 29 September 1725 (*Gulliver's Travels*, ed. David Womersley (Cambridge: Cambridge University Press, 2012), Appendix C, p. 592). For the stationers in question, see Mary Pollard, 'Who's for Prison? Publishing Swift in Dublin', *Swift Studies*, 14 (1999), 37–49.

'constantly under the influence of fear, which...destroys the beauty and force of his writing'. Cobbett's paradoxical, but by now quite familiar, conclusion is that the absence of formal pre-publication censorship could damage the creative process more than its presence—for 'while there is no boundary; while all is left to the opinions and the taste of others [the Attorney General in the first instance, trial judges in the next], can any man be said to be *free* to write?'[43]

Yet there's a no less compelling alternative view, in which the pressures described by Cobbett constitute not disabling constraint but enabling discipline—a discipline in which writers cultivate complex literary strategies of indirection, or even on occasion misdirection, in order to communicate dissident meaning while also rendering it deniable. On this count I align my argument with Patterson's in *Censorship and Interpretation*, a book of its moment that challenged poststructuralist celebrations of aporia and emphasized instead the intentionalist category that Patterson termed 'functional ambiguity'.[44] In her view, there was something frivolous, and historically lazy, about teasing contradiction or indeterminacy from a literary work and then comfortably attributing these properties to the insurmountable bind of language or the textual condition. Ambiguity was indeed a pervasive characteristic of early modern writing, but not incompatible with authorial agency. It could be read instead as a calculated and often powerful strategy for addressing and circumventing censorship: a strategy, Patterson proposed, to which we owe our notion of literature itself as a mode of writing characterized by complexity, polyvalence, and openness to interpretation. In this light, censorship was not only an instrument of control or suppression, but also a powerful stimulus to literary creativity and rhetorical complexity—and, it might be added, to book-trade innovation throughout the period. While regulating what could be said, and how, it could foster ingenious strategies

---

[43] *Cobbett's Political Register*, 26 (July–December 1814), 196–8; Kevin Gilmartin contextualizes this passage alongside other contemporaneous objections to the legal indeterminacy of seditious libel as an offence (*Print Politics: The Press and Radical Opposition in Early Nineteenth-Century England* (Cambridge: Cambridge University Press, 1996), 114–21).

[44] Patterson, *Censorship and Interpretation*, 18.

of circumvention, from clandestine presses and decoy imprints to the strictly literary techniques of functional ambiguity.

Aspects of Patterson's argument have been cogently challenged, including the picture she presents of a generally recognized, albeit constantly renegotiated, borderline between tolerable indirection and actionable provocation, and her notion of press control as an elite game played out between authors and authorities, governed by unstated but understood conventions that made the cautious insinuation of dissent possible and safe. In this view, cases of victimization like that of Prynne epitomize not an overarching, monitory theatre of intimidation but moments of exceptional breakdown in codes and conventions governing literary production that authors for the most part found navigable enough. Here is a picture that bears interesting comparison with Robert Darnton's account of an often sympathetic, even productively collaborative, licensing system in Enlightenment France, though other scholars of early modern England have emphasized, as I do here, the arbitrary, and in general alarmingly unpredictable, nature of state action, which imposed on the producers of politically inflected literature an enduring condition of anxiety and suspense.[45]

More relevant to my purposes, and as useful as ever, is Patterson's overall emphasis on literary ambiguity as the outcome not of inherent discursive indeterminacy but of a widely shared and understood need to shroud or disavow dissident content. This emphasis is richly applicable to the later period, when in creative terms the institutions and mechanisms of press regulation, after 1695 no less than before, energized the production of politically inflected literature as much as they also constrained it. To compare the crass and obvious anti-Walpole dramas that were banned from the stage after 1737 with the subtle, insidious provocations of Gay or Fielding is to see the close

---

[45] See Robert Darnton, *Censors at Work: How States Shaped Literature* (New York: Norton, 2014), 49 and 23–86 *passim*; for counter-arguments to Patterson, see Kemp and McElligott in *CP*, 1: xxiii–xxix. A notable alternative account is that of Cyndia Susan Clegg, *Press Censorship in Caroline England* (Cambridge: Cambridge University Press, 2008), who here and in related studies of Elizabethan and Jacobean censorship stresses the distributed, unsystematic, often arbitrary nature of early modern regulation (pp. 1–43).

relationship between practical censorship and the technical ingenuity of the period's cleverest, most incisive satires. Again, it's where Pope moves closest to the perilous zone of anti-Hanover innuendo that his verbal duplicities are at their most brilliant: the strategic confusion between asses, dunces, and kings that opens *The Dunciad*, for instance, or the grammatical subterfuge that allows him to insinuate seditious hints into the *Epistle to Bathurst*. For Jonathan Swift, libel amounted to a genre with rules of its own, 'suppos'd to be writ with Caution and double Meaning, in order to prevent Prosecution', and these rules reached every corner of the period's satire.[46]

A primary purpose of the chapters that follow is to argue this case about irony, indirection, and censorship in its new post-licensing form through contextualized readings of oppositional verse, and to a lesser extent fiction and drama, with particular emphasis on satirical techniques of indirection and encoding. Each chapter surveys an approximately forty-year period, combining historical analysis with critical and interpretative focus on telling examples: works such as Defoe's *Shortest Way*, with its insufficiently muted provocations; works also such as Johnson's *London*, where fragmentary manuscript evidence reveals crucial variants between an incautious draft version and a more circumspect published text. In every case, the aim is to specify the distinctive characteristics and dynamics of literary censorship and the pressures it exerted at different junctures, and to analyse the creative responses of authors who wrote, in all their different ways, under the sign of seditious libel: Dryden in the shifting sands of Restoration politics, and the mixed regime of Restoration censorship, between the collapse of Cromwellian rule and the aftermath of the Glorious Revolution; Defoe and Pope in an era of great self-consciousness about seditious libel and the pillory between the pamphlet wars of Queen Anne's reign and the literary campaign against Walpole; Fielding and Johnson, who cut their teeth as satirists during the height of that campaign, with enduring creative consequences for their later careers; Southey, like Dryden a Tory poet laureate with seditious skeletons in the cupboard, whom I read alongside a range of ingenious

[46] *Swift vs. Mainwaring: The Examiner and The Medley*, ed. Frank H. Ellis (Oxford: Oxford University Press, 1985), 431 (*Examiner* 42, 17 May 1711).

provocateurs under Pitt in the 1790s and Lord Liverpool in the 1810s. The intention throughout is to clarify our sense of the most distinctive features of eighteenth-century writing—ellipsis, indirection, innuendo, irony, periphrasis—by relating their use to the persistence of censorship, and to the knowingness and virtuosity with which constraints on expression were negotiated by writers of politically inflected literature.

A further intention is to remember a theory articulated throughout the period by some of the most adroit exponents of literary indirection: a theory in which, for the licenser turned libeller L'Estrange in 1692, the best way to activate the readerly mind was by 'a Train of Mystery and Circumlocution'. Or one in which, as Blake put it a century later, implication was the technique 'fittest for Instruction, because it rouzes the faculties to act'.[47] The hermeneutics of suspicion—Ricoeur's coinage, recently reanimated by Rita Felski to denote a style of critique in which texts become scenes of crimes to be unmasked by quasi-forensic deciphering of their silences and falsifications—may often be an aggressive, or even a supercilious, practice.[48] Yet there's a sense in which eighteenth-century writers were soliciting from their readers a comparable hermeneutic vigilance, or a comparable suspicion of surface meaning, though one they hoped would work with, not against, a consciously embedded grain of dissident signification. We might almost think in terms of a distinctively Augustan hermeneutics of suspicion, an unmasking of criminal subtexts in which the author's own complicity is deeply knowing.

Yet reading, of course, is never quite as predictable as such a scenario would suggest: a point Fielding recognizes when declining to act as narrator, in *Tom Jones*, like a '*jure divino* Tyrant' who constrains the interpretative liberties of his readers.[49] Readers will go their own

---

[47] Roger L'Estrange, *Fables, of Aesop and Other Eminent Mythologists* (1692), sig. A2; *The Letters of William Blake*, ed. Geoffrey Keynes, 3rd edn (Oxford: Clarendon Press, 1980), 8 (to Dr Trusler, 23 August 1799).

[48] Rita Felski, *The Limits of Critique* (Chicago: University of Chicago Press, 2015), esp. 30–51.

[49] Henry Fielding, *Tom Jones*, ed. Martin C. Battestin and Fredson Bowers (Oxford: Clarendon Press, 1975), 77 (II.i).

way, according to their own desires, and according to their time and place. It's not least for this reason that the strategies with which writers immunized themselves from prosecution—the poetics of the pillory—in practice do the opposite of confining their works to the historical circumstances that first produced them. In the chapters that follow, my project is to recover these circumstances in order to illuminate the feats of literary subtlety and rhetorical complexity that they served to bring forth. The resulting texts compel, and by the same token liberate, their readers to imagine and interpret, and in so doing they open themselves endlessly up to future contexts, unforeseen meanings, and new ways of understanding.

# 1
# 1660–1700
# Faint Meaning: Dryden and Restoration Censorship

At first sight, Dryden's verse might seem an unpromising lens through which to view the pressures exerted on Restoration writing by official censorship: a term used broadly in these chapters to include pre-publication licensing, post-publication retribution, and the subtler, less visible, less documented range of drags and duresses, typically extra-legal in kind, that operated short of outright prohibition or formal prosecution. After all, Dryden had his feet firmly under the table in Restoration England. In 1660 he wrote the standout poem among scores of instant panegyrics lavished on the returning king, and within a decade the bravura loyalism of *Annus Mirabilis* (1667) and other works propelled him into the twin offices of poet laureate (1668) and historiographer royal (1670). Established from that point on as almost the literary mouthpiece of the restored Stuart monarchy, Dryden was also close enough in practice to Charles II's licenser and surveyor of the press, Roger L'Estrange, nicknamed 'Towser' for his ferocious harassment of dissident printers, to be lampooned as 'Towser the Second, A Bulldog' in a 1681 poem of that title by Henry Care. Care's malicious squib berates Dryden for running with L'Estrange as a Tory attack dog ('The Currs had got | Between them in their Mouthes a new Sham-Plot') and urges that he be hanged for his 'sawcy Satyr' and 'Venom'd Tongue' in *Absalom*

---

*Poetics of the Pillory: English Literature and Seditious Libel, 1660–1820*. Thomas Keymer, Oxford University Press (2019). © Thomas Keymer.
DOI: 10.1093/oso/9780198744498.001.0001

*and Achitophel*.¹ Yet it was Care himself, lacking not only Dryden's court connections but also his literary guile, who was arraigned no fewer than five times between 1679 and 1685 for seditious libel or the proxy charge of unlicensed newsbook printing. *Canis a non canendo*, one might say of reckless Care. Meanwhile, Towser the Second continued to enjoy his royal pension, albeit with erratic payment in that earlier age of budget shortfalls and austerity drives.²

It is instructive to compare the post-1660 careers of the two great poets with whom the young Dryden processed in Cromwell's funeral cortege in November 1658, just eighteen months before the Stuart monarchy was restored. Dryden was conspicuously the junior partner on this occasion, and official accounts allow us to calibrate his relative unimportance: fifteen yards of mourning cloth for Milton, enough to kit out a servant as well as himself; fifteen yards for Marvell; nine for Dryden, who must have had to walk unattended.³ But the tables were soon turned. In 1660 Milton escaped being listed among the 102 individuals excluded from the Act of Free and General Pardon, Indemnity and Oblivion (though his name was considered), and he may have thought himself technically absolved of complicity in the regicide. But by that time *Eikonoklastes* (1649) and the first *Defence* (*Pro populo Anglicano defensio*, 1651) had already been condemned to the flames for 'sundry Treasonable passages' justifying the execution of Charles I. A proclamation was issued calling for Milton's 'Legal Tryal, and...condigne punishment', or at least regretting the difficulty of locating and apprehending him for this purpose.⁴ The

---

¹ Henry Care, *Towser the Second, A Bull-Dog; or, A Short Reply to Absalon and Achitophel* (1681), [2], [1], [2]. For Care's protracted struggles with L'Estrange and Lord Chief Justice Scroggs, see Lois G. Schwoerer, *The Ingenious Mr. Henry Care, Restoration Publicist* (Baltimore: Johns Hopkins University Press, 2001), esp. 104–33. For L'Estrange as Towser, bloodhound of the press, see Helen Pierce, 'The Devil's Bloodhound: Roger L'Estrange Caricatured', in Michael Cyril William Hunter (ed.), *Printed Images in Early Modern Britain: Essays in Interpretation* (Farnham: Ashgate, 2010), 237–54.

² James Anderson Winn, *John Dryden and His World* (New Haven: Yale University Press, 1987), 552.

³ Winn, *Dryden and His World*, 557.

⁴ *A Proclamation for...Suppressing of Two Books*, TNA, SP 45/11, p. 14, qtd by Barbara K. Lewalski, *The Life of John Milton: A Critical Biography* (Oxford: Blackwell, 2000), 401 (and see pp. 398–404 *passim*).

tradition that Milton was saved by the intercession of Marvell now looks doubtful, and it may be nearer the truth that he was saved by the example of William Prynne. To persecute a blind, vanquished intellectual would have been to repeat, egregiously, Archbishop Laud's public-relations misstep of the 1630s (see above, pp. 11–13). Even so, Milton was lucky to get off with just a few weeks in prison that autumn.

Few now accept the Addisonian assumption that in the epics Milton went on to publish, political commitment evaporates in the religious sublime. But the politics certainly had to assume indirect or subtextual forms. These include Milton's presentation of blank verse (in a headnote added to *Paradise Lost* in 1668) as inherently republican, a formal recovery of 'ancient liberty... from the troublesome and modern bondage of rhyming'—in which context Dryden's *The State of Innocence, or Fall of Man* (1677), which reworks *Paradise Lost* in heroic couplets, looks like an exercise in royalist recuperation.[5] Later passages in *Paradise Lost* associate Milton's epic voice with the ailing, thwarted author of the regicidal tracts, 'On evil days though fallen, and evil tongues; | In darkness, and with dangers compassed round'. The closing book brings in a trenchant account of biblical divine-right kingship as mere arrogation, a case of 'Authority usurped, from God not given'.[6]

Then there is the presentist rhetoric with which *Samson Agonistes* (1671), echoing Milton's last-gasp pre-Restoration tract *The Readie and Easie Way to Establish a Free Commonwealth* (1660), deplores the decadence of a people who comfortably acquiesce in absolute power: 'But what more oft in nations grown corrupt, | And by their vices brought to servitude, | Than to love bondage more than liberty, | Bondage with ease than strenuous liberty.'[7] As press licenser, L'Estrange paid close personal attention to Milton's *History of Britain* (1670), but the volume containing *Samson Agonistes* was licensed by the episcopal chaplain

---

[5] John Milton, *Paradise Lost*, ed. Alastair Fowler, revised 2nd edn (Harlow: Longman, 2007), 55.

[6] Milton, *Paradise Lost*, 391 (vii.26–7), 650 (xii.65–6).

[7] John Milton, *The Complete Shorter Poems*, ed. John Carey, revised 2nd edn (Harlow: Longman, 2007), 367–8 (*Samson Agonistes*, lines 268–71). On this pattern, see Blair Worden's reading of *Samson Agonistes* in his *Literature and Politics in Cromwellian England: John Milton, Andrew Marvell, Marchamont Nedham* (Oxford: Oxford University Press, 2007), 358–83.

Thomas Tomkyns, and as Nicholas von Maltzahn writes, 'actionable material was difficult to isolate in poetry of such complexity'.[8] Even so, the implication was clear enough for the early reader who responded to the 'bondage with ease' passage by adding the grim marginalium 'Englands Case'.[9] Milton's right hand, it would seem, could circumvent censorship more deftly and effectively than his left. Tomkyns also licensed *Paradise Lost*, presumably as a work in the category of divinity. But he did so only after worrying about passages of 'imaginary Treason' scattered through the poem, or so John Toland scoffed a generation later. The example Toland gives is the solar eclipse of Book I, which 'disastrous twilight sheds | On half the nations, and with fear of change | Perplexes monarchs'.[10]

The political animus of Marvell's Restoration verse lay nearer the surface, but a different kind of subterfuge was in play. Recent attention to his satires of the 1660s and 1670s reveals qualities remote from the serene ambiguities and unworldly detachment on which T. S. Eliot and William Empson founded Marvell's modern reputation, and they return us to his much earlier public image as direct, even strident, to a fault. To contemporaries he was a pugnacious Whig controversialist, not a languid connoisseur of paradox. It's worth recalling that as late as 1726, when the publisher Edmund Curll found himself in trouble with the authorities (and eventually in the pillory), among the publications Curll cited as making him a target was what he called his 'Revival of MARVELL's *Works*': a new edition, prepared for Curll by Thomas Cooke, in which the most important thing about Marvell was his 'Real Character' as 'a sincere

---

[8] Nicholas von Maltzahn, 'L'Estrange's Milton', in Anne Dunan-Page and Beth Lynch (eds), *Roger L'Estrange and the Making of Restoration Culture* (Aldershot: Ashgate, 2008), 27–54 (40). On the division of labour between civil and ecclesiastical authorities in Restoration licensing, see Ronan Deazley, *On the Origin of the Right to Copy: Charting the Movement of Copyright Law in Eighteenth-Century Britain (1695–1775)* (London: Bloomsbury, 2014), 1–29.

[9] Laura Lunger Knoppers, '"England's Case": Contexts of the 1671 Poems', in Nicholas McDowell and Nigel Smith (eds), *The Oxford Handbook of Milton* (Oxford: Oxford University Press, 2009), 571–88 (572, citing a first edition held at the University of Illinois, Urbana-Champaign).

[10] John Toland, *The Life of John Milton* (1699), 130; Milton, *Paradise Lost*, 97 (i.598–9) and n.

and daring Patriot'.[11] By the same token, when on Marvell's death in 1678 L'Estrange identified him with infuriated admiration as 'a great Master of Words' (albeit one who displayed 'rather the Suppleness and Address of a Tumbler, than the Force and Vigor of a Man of Business'), it was not delicate lyricism that L'Estrange had in mind. Marvell's mastery was in the belligerent arts of invective and polemic.[12]

L'Estrange was describing the political dynamite of Marvell's *Account of the Growth of Popery and Arbitrary Power* (1677). But the gritted-teeth compliment (made without explicitly naming his target) applies just as well to the 'Advice to a Painter' poems in which Marvell and his imitators wittily excoriated the cowardice and corruption of leading courtiers during the Second Dutch War of 1665–7. The subterfuge was in the medium, not the message—or, as we might say in the language of Jerome McGann, the linguistic coding was clear enough, the bibliographic coding studiously opaque.[13] In the absence, relatively speaking, of literary indirection, it was through practical ruses of textual transmission—manuscript circulation, spurious attribution, surreptitious printing, clandestine publication—that Marvell's 'cat-and-mouse relationship with L'Estrange', as Martin Dzelzainis calls it, could be prolonged until Marvell's death, with no success at all for L'Estrange, though he may have been closing in at the end.[14] There's a sense in which the game lasted even longer, for as L'Estrange was quick to understand in 1678, new opportunities for misdirection were now available to purveyors of clandestine satire, who could 'cast the whole on Mr. Marvell, who is lately dead, and there the enquiry ends'.[15] Just

---

[11] *The Case of Seduction* (1726), p. v, qtd by Paul Baines and Pat Rogers, *Edmund Curll, Bookseller* (Oxford: Oxford University Press, 2007), 160; *The Works of Andrew Marvell Esq.*, ed. Thomas Cooke, 2 vols (1726), I, [vi].

[12] Roger L'Estrange, *An Account of the Growth of Knavery, under the Pretended Fears of Arbitrary Government, and Popery* (1678), 4.

[13] Jerome J. McGann, *The Textual Condition* (Princeton: Princeton University Press, 1991), 56–62.

[14] Martin Dzelzainis, 'L'Estrange, Marvell and the *Directions to a Painter*: The Evidence of Bodleian Library, MS Gough London 14', in Dunan-Page and Lynch (eds), *L'Estrange and Restoration Culture*, 53–66 (54).

[15] L'Estrange to Joseph Williamson, 23 August 1678 (*CCD*, 2: 204); see Nicholas von Maltzahn, 'Marvell's Ghost', in Warren Chernaik and Martin Dzelzainis (eds), *Marvell and Liberty* (Basingstoke: Macmillan, 1999), 50–74.

as Marvell had been protected by false attribution of the second and third 'Painter' poems to the superannuated royalist Sir John Denham (an implausible but sufficient smokescreen), so posthumous ascription to him of later satires would shield future writers.[16]

This was no small benefit. Throughout the Restoration, scriptorial production and manuscript circulation were the default means of publication for Whig or proto-Whig satire, as was the case after 1688 for Jacobite verse. But although manuscript libels seemed quite as dangerous to L'Estrange as printed texts—'not one in forty ever comes to press, though, by the help of transcripts, they are well nigh as public'[17]—remediation into print aroused special alarm, with consequences for authors as well as stationers. In 1671 the bookseller Thomas Palmer was fined and pilloried for his role in publishing a collection of 'Painter' poems: 'Not to be granted', L'Estrange briskly notes on Palmer's petition for clemency.[18] But apprehension of the author was the ultimate prize, the holy grail of political press control. As Lord Chief Justice Scroggs declared during Henry Care's trial of 1680: 'It is hard to find the Author, it is not hard to find the Printer: but *one Author* found, is better than *twenty Printers* found.'[19] Of course, book-trade professionals could tell what they knew, if they knew, and

---

[16] On the complex functions of the Denham ruse, see Randy Robertson, *Censorship and Conflict in Seventeenth-Century England: The Subtle Art of Division* (University Park: Pennsylvania State University Press, 2009), 135–46.

[17] 'Mr L'Estrange's Propositions concerning Libels, &c.', 11 November 1675 (*CCD*, 2: 94–5); L'Estrange calls in this document for scribal publications to be made subject to the same legal regime as libels in print.

[18] *CCD*, 2: 6. For this episode and the 1670 indictment on a similar charge of Elizabeth Calvert (widow of Giles Calvert, a prolific Interregnum publisher of blasphemy and sedition), see Martin Dzelzainis, 'Andrew Marvell and the Restoration Literary Underground: Printing the Painter Poems', *The Seventeenth Century*, 22.2 (2007), 395–410 (esp. 401–5); Nicholas von Maltzahn, *An Andrew Marvell Chronology* (Basingstoke: Palgrave Macmillan, 2005), 121, 126; Robertson, *Censorship and Conflict*, 140 and 238 n. 49.

[19] *The Triall of Henry Carr, Gent.* (1681), 7. On the relative liability of authors as opposed to booksellers and printers, see Jody Greene, *The Trouble with Ownership: Literary Property and Authorial Liability in England, 1660–1730* (Philadelphia: University of Pennsylvania Press, 2005), esp. 63–88; also Harold Weber, *Paper Bullets: Print and Kingship under Charles II* (Lexington: University Press of Kentucky, 1996), 172–208.

were routinely pressured to do so. But in 1664 the printer John Twyn went to a gruesome death under treason legislation—hanging, drawing, and quartering—rather than give up the anonymous author of a treatise he had printed, laced with topical import, on the godly duty to rebel against unjust rulers. 'His Answer was, *That it was not his Principle to betray the Authour*', the Newgate chaplain reported—a principle we should interpret as traditional guild solidarity, not freedom-of-speech ideology of a modern kind.[20] It goes without saying that Marvell was never in danger of the severities risked by Twyn's author, even when his handiwork was recognized. He steered clear of outright extremism, he enjoyed some protection as a Member of Parliament, and in many ways he drew creative energy from press control. As Annabel Patterson puts it, 'censorship was the kind of shade in which he peculiarly flourished'.[21] Yet it was also a shade in which, Marvell well knew, hostile hands were always busy, some of them equipped with impious steel.

The points of contrast with Dryden look stark, and might suggest a view of him as a poet immune to the constraints and hazards that enmeshed his dissident contemporaries: an establishment poet enjoying the privilege of discursive freedom while Milton was pushed into strategic indirection, Marvell lurked in the literary underground, and noisy controversialists like Henry Care were in constant fear of arrest. Yet no such account can withstand scrutiny, at least without extensive modification. For a start, Dryden's lengthy publishing career spans several very different political dispensations. We think of him as the quintessential Restoration poet, but he made his name with a precocious elegy of 1649, at which time a decade of Cromwellian rule still lay in the future. He was writing as late as 1700, more than a decade after the Glorious Revolution, when he signs off at last, in the 'Secular Masque', with a wry farewell to history. For Steven N. Zwicker, in this late work, first performed weeks before Dryden's death and published weeks after it, Dryden rises above the particulars of his age 'to see in the futility and change and disappointment of his own life a pattern

---

[20] *An Exact Narrative of the Tryal and Condemnation of John Twyn* (1664), in *CP*, 3: 79.

[21] Annabel Patterson, 'Andrew Marvell: Living with Censorship', in Andrew Hadfield (ed.), *Literature and Censorship in Renaissance England* (London: Palgrave, 2001), 187–203 (187).

more beautiful than its frustrations'.[22] The lyric at issue, written with limpid minimalism, certainly marks a point of achieved serenity. That said, the age it foresees is closed off to Dryden, and the past is a barren continuum of strife and betrayal:

> All, all of a piece throughout;
> Thy chase had a beast in view;
> Thy wars brought nothing about;
> Thy lovers were all untrue.
> 'Tis well an old age is out,
> And time to begin a new.[23]

It might be added that, throughout this lifetime of hunting, warfare, and broken allegiance, Dryden himself was often alleged to be the most faithless lover of all: a poet who twisted and turned with each shift of the political wind. Mobile and unprincipled, he was a writer 'hired to Lye and Libel' in the service of power, no matter who held that power, one adversary insisted. His early output showed it with embarrassing plainness: 'Now farewel wretched Mercenary *Bayes*, | Who the *King* Libell'd, and did *Cromwel* praise.'[24]

The fact is that Dryden's literary career spans five decades of extreme, perhaps even unequalled, political turbulence, and if we think of him as a Stuart loyalist—the right place to start, though too crude a category for a poet of his agility, complexity, and inveterate irony—he was in opposition for two of the five. These were decades of heavy censorship, moreover, in which even well-connected writers had to tread with care. The first was marked by especially intensive press regulation following the regicide of 1649 and the emergency provisions of the Printing Act later that year, and then again as cracks formed in the Protectorate in the later 1650s; the second by a campaign against Jacobite writing that saw L'Estrange arrested at least

---

[22] Steven N. Zwicker, *Politics and Language in Dryden's Poetry: The Arts of Disguise* (Princeton: Princeton University Press, 1984), 176.

[23] *The Poems of John Dryden*, ed. Paul Hammond and David Hopkins, 5 vols (Harlow: Longman, 1995–2005), 5: 605. Hereafter *Poems*.

[24] Thomas Shadwell (?), *The Medal of John Bayes* (1682), in *The Complete Works of Thomas Shadwell*, ed. Montague Summers, 5 vols (London: Fortune Press, 1927), 5: 247, 261.

three times, while new work by Dryden was scrutinized for seditious hints, not least by his nemesis Thomas Shadwell.[25]

Nor, in the absence of a monolithic, bureaucratic state of the kind being built in France by Louis XIV, can we count on Stuart hegemony in the remaining decades as a force ensuring the security of royalist writers or the silence of their adversaries. Instead, censorship was erratic, unpredictable, and far from unidirectional. The Licensing Act of 1662 aimed to establish comprehensive mechanisms for press control, but the great majority of books went unlicensed in practice, and roughly half flouted the Act by bearing no printer's name.[26] In his capacity as surveyor, L'Estrange maintained a costly network of 'Spyes and Instruments', but he can scarcely be said to have enjoyed the resources of totalitarian surveillance. For all his formidable energy, he often felt overwhelmed by the chaos and fecundity of print, locked in Sisyphean struggle with the '*Vagabond License* of the *Press*'.[27] In this context, press control was an oxymoron, and opposition writing hydra-headed. On the other hand, court favour offered no free passes. The inability of Thomas Hobbes to publish any work on politics, history, or religion after 1662 shows the real difficulties

---

[25] For the censorship campaigns of 1649–51 and 1656–59, see *CP*, 2: xviii; also, for the 1640s background, Joad Raymond, 'Censorship in Law and Practice in Seventeenth-Century England: Milton's *Areopagitica*', in Lorna Hutson (ed.), *The Oxford Handbook of English Law and Literature, 1500–1700* (Oxford: Oxford University Press, 2017), 507–28. For the post-regicide emergency specifically, see Martin Dzelzainis, '1649', in Joad Raymond (ed.), *The Oxford History of Popular Print Culture, Volume 1: Cheap Print in Britain and Ireland to 1660* (Oxford: Oxford University Press, 2011), pp. 609–18. For the 1690s, see below, pp. 78–82.

[26] D. F. McKenzie, *Making Meaning: 'Printers of the Mind' and Other Essays*, ed. Peter D. MacDonald and Michael F. Suarez (Amherst: University of Massachusetts Press, 2002), 109–25; see also D. F. McKenzie, 'Printing and Publishing 1557–1700: Constraints on the London Book Trades', and Michael Treadwell, 'The Stationers and the Printing Act at the End of the Seventeenth Century', both in John Barnard and D. F. McKenzie, with Maureen Bell (eds), *The Cambridge History of the Book in Britain, Volume 4: 1557–1695* (Cambridge: Cambridge University Press, 2002), 553–67 and 755–76.

[27] L'Estrange to Lord Arlington, 17 October 1665, TNA, SP 29/134, fo. 168; L'Estrange, *Observator*, 9 January 1683, qtd by Peter Hinds, *'The Horrid Popish Plot': Roger L'Estrange and the Circulation of Political Discourse in Late-Seventeenth-Century London* (Oxford: Oxford University Press, 2010), 9.

that Restoration censorship could pose for an author who, for all the complexities of Hobbes's prior output, was now quite close to Charles II, and in receipt of a royal pension. On the prospect of *Behemoth* getting into print, the king made encouraging noises but urbanely feigned deference to church authorities. As Aubrey later reported (to Locke), Hobbes's manuscript was one 'which the King has read and likes extreamly, but tells him there is so much truth in it he dares not license for feare of displeasing the Bishops'.[28]

The situation was at its most tangled during the Exclusion Crisis and its aftermath of 1679–85, when the licensing system collapsed for a period, the Whig metropolis exerted its jurisdiction against that of the Tory court, and legal action against authors and stationers could emanate from either position (to say nothing of extra-legal action: Dryden was badly beaten up in the so-called Rose-Alley ambush of 1679). Under the later Stuarts 'it tends to be assumed that the Whigs never achieved power', writes Mark Goldie, 'yet for four years, from 1679 to 1682, the Whigs *were* in power, for they controlled the streets, juries, newspapers, coffee houses and the City of London'. Until the City's charter was revoked in 1682, Whig control meant installation of Whig sheriffs, who in turn selected Whig juries, so that 'progovernment writers were presented by the grand jury and suffered imprisonment, the pillory, and fines, while ignoramus juries protected opposition writers and leaders'.[29] For a while, it was nonconformist hardliners or borderline republicans like Slingsby Bethel, the villainous Shimei of *Absalom and Achitophel*, who controlled the sheriff's picture frame. In 1680 even L'Estrange, who temporarily lost his offices as licenser and surveyor when the Licensing Act lapsed in 1679, found himself under investigation by the Privy Council and then the House of Lords. At this point Towser turned tail, absconding to Scotland and later The Hague, that favourite refuge of Restoration

---

[28] Noel Malcolm, *Aspects of Hobbes* (Oxford: Oxford University Press, 2002), 24, 348–9, quoting a letter dated Shrove Tuesday 1673.

[29] Mark Goldie, 'Roger L'Estrange's *Observator* and the Exorcism of the Plot', in Dunan-Page and Lynch (eds), *L'Estrange and Restoration Culture*, 73; Schwoerer, *Ingenious Henry Care*, 144. 'Ignoramus' verdicts (professing not to know) were a standard tactic of Exclusionist juries, notably in closing down the 1681 treason trial of the Earl of Shaftesbury.

libellers of any stripe. 'I am to be question'd for my Books, and that concludes the Story', he bitterly wrote.[30] Gloating lampoons threatened L'Estrange with the pillory himself; one especially menacing broadside makes him worry about having to wear 'th'old-fashion'd Wooden Ruff', now that power lies with 'Judges turn'd Phanaticks' and their 'damn'd Whiggish Laws'.[31]

It was during such moments of uncertainty and hazard that many of Dryden's greatest poems appeared. *Heroic Stanzas* (1659), *Absalom and Achitophel* (1681), and *The Hind and the Panther* (1687) were all written on the cusp of regime change, whether merely anticipated, as in the second case, or dramatically fulfilled, as in the first and third. These were historical junctures—the death of Cromwell, the Exclusion Crisis, James II's Declaration of Indulgence—that forced writers to consider, as Milton had refused to consider when writing *Eikonoklastes* and the *Defensio*, future as well as present scrutiny of a work, or the possibility of retrospective incrimination in changed conditions. And though Dryden's surviving correspondence is relatively slender, we have direct evidence at other politically fraught times of the anxiety he felt when transgressing, or fearing he might have transgressed, the always uncertain boundaries of acceptable expression. Having slipped a topical innuendo into a historical translation of 1684, he was relieved 'that the History of the League is commended; & I hope the onely thing I feard in it, is not found out'. A few months after his politicized translation of Virgil appeared in 1697, he writes in a nervous postscript that 'I hear Tom Brown is comeing out upon me'. He cannot have been reassured when Brown, imprisoned at the time for seditious libel, gleefully observed that more eminent authors than Dryden had committed the same offence: 'For if Poets

---

[30] L'Estrange, *L'Estrange's Case in a Civil Dialogue betwixt Zekiel and Ephraim* (1680), 34; for this episode see George Kitchin, *Sir Roger L'Estrange: A Contribution to the History of the Press in the Seventeenth Century* (London: Kegan Paul, 1913), 250–9.

[31] *The Pillory; or, A Dialogue betwixt Roger L'Estrange and Nat. Thompson* (1682), [1]; see also *Trincalo Sainted* (1682), a lampoon on the recently pilloried Tory printer Nathaniel Thomson, published 'for the Encouragement of Towzer and Heraclitus, To Proceed till They Obtain the Like Exaltment' (1682); *Heraclitus Ridens* was a Tory journal often linked with L'Estrange's *Observator*.

are punish'd for Libelling Trash, | *John Dryden*, tho' Sixty, may yet fear the Lash.'[32]

Viewed in such contexts, it is an obvious fact that for all his celebrated powers of lucid exposition, many of Dryden's major poems were written when circumstances allowed no such thing. We might detect, indeed, a correlation between the richness and complexity of Dryden's verse and the context of expressive constraint from which it emerged. In their different ways, most of his major poems take on the delicate project of analysing a contested present from viewpoints—sometimes unstable or kaleidoscopic viewpoints, rich in evasive uncertainties and juxtaposed contradictions—that could not be articulated without 'the strategies and arts of disguise', in Zwicker's phrase.[33] In the process, the poems develop intricate, polyvalent discursive modes that not only cloud topical meaning but also lend each work an amplitude reaching beyond the mere occasion. At some points Dryden uses guileful encoding of the kind that allowed Milton to insinuate critique of Stuart absolutism into his religious epics; at others the ruses of transmission through which Marvell and his imitators kept up the flow of 'Painter' poems in the face of L'Estrange's efforts to suppress them. Sometimes he exploits both strategies in tandem, with effects that were practical and aesthetic at once, protecting his personal position as author while also enriching the grain and texture of his verse. As a body, the poems demand to be read as products of a shifting and perilous historical environment that Dryden negotiated with exquisite skill, and certainly with far greater circumspection than his ally L'Estrange, though at key moments he too experienced calls for his prosecution on grounds of seditious libel or *scandalum magnatum*.[34] If in the end Dryden suffered nothing more than the private retribution of Rose-Alley, when he was cudgelled senseless

---

[32] *The Literary Correspondence of the Tonsons*, ed. Stephen Bernard (Oxford: Oxford University Press, 2015), 88, 129 (Dryden to Jacob Tonson, August/September 1684 and November 1697); *The Works of Mr. Thomas Brown, in Prose and Verse*, 2 vols (1707), 1: 94 ('To the Lords in Council Assembled, The Petition of Thomas Brown, by which he received his Enlargement from Prison').

[33] Zwicker, *Politics and Language*, 34.

[34] On these calls, and for an account of *Absalom and Achitophel* attributing Dryden's anonymity to fear of attention from a Whig grand jury, see Robertson, *Censorship and Conflict*, 146–62, 241–2.

as the supposed author of a manuscript lampoon,[35] one reason is that he was not only a consummate navigator of literary censorship in its broadest sense, but also, in the writings of his last decade, a sophisticated theoretician of its workings and limits.

## Strange elegy: *Lachrymae musarum, Heroic Stanzas*

Linguistic and bibliographic wiles mingle in Dryden's first publication, though without heavy disguise in either case. *Lachrymae musarum* ('Tears of the Muses') was a lavish volume of verse bewailing the death of Henry, Lord Hastings, a rather obscure 19-year-old nobleman who died of smallpox on the eve of his wedding in June 1649. The collection represented the work of thirty-five poets, varying in competence, but united almost always by royalist sympathies, with just the odd anomalous presence to temper the effect.[36] Cotton, Denham, and Herrick were all there, as was Marvell in his pre-Cromwellian mode: the mode that makes the opening of his 'Nymph Complaining', with its wanton troopers and purple-grained sin, such a plangent, albeit fleeting, moment of royalist lament.[37] Poem after poem stresses Hastings's royal lineage (which was distant at best), his innocence and greatness, the cruelty and injustice of his death, his status as a victim of evil in the fallen world of men. Hyperbole is everywhere. One poet wonders about the 'excessive Wo' poured out in the volume, as though acknowledging that the woe goes beyond the proximate need; another wonders why the 'sad stroke of Fate' that killed Hastings did not provoke the heavens to assume 'Prodigious forms, | To groan

---

[35] On this episode and its implications for Restoration authorship, see John Mullan, 'Dryden's Anonymity', in Steven N. Zwicker (ed.), *The Cambridge Companion to John Dryden* (Cambridge: Cambridge University Press, 2004), 156–80.

[36] Nicholas McDowell emphasizes the presence of John Hall, who moved in royalist literary circles but became a salaried Commonwealth propagandist shortly before Hastings died (*Poetry and Allegiance in the English Civil Wars: Marvell and the Cause of Wit* (Oxford: Oxford University Press, 2008), 209–15).

[37] However, for the resistance of this and other Marvell lyrics to totalizing political explanation, see Steven N. Zwicker and Derek Hirst, 'Marvell and Lyrics of Undifference', in Martin Dzelzainis and Edward Holberton (eds), *The Oxford Handbook of Andrew Marvell* (Oxford: Oxford University Press, 2019).

in Thunder, and to weep in Storms'.[38] Several expatiate on larger ills—'*Great Britains* curse, whose sinful, shameful State | Makes all Heroick Vertue soon decay' (p. 21)—as though Hastings's death both illustrates and completes a national misery. In one of the collection's lumpier offerings, 'Not perfect Bankrupt was this Land till now, | Nor her sick lapsed desp'rate state below | The hopes of all recovery: till His fall, | We could not justly say we had lost All' (p. 28). In Denham's more accomplished formulation, Hastings's death constitutes a national punishment or atonement: 'What Sin unexpiated in this Land | Of Groans, hath guided so severe a hand? | The late Great Victim that your Altars knew, | You angry gods, might have excus'd this new | Oblation' (p. 41).

It needs no very strenuous effort of decoding to grasp the agenda here, at a time when public mourning for the king executed a few months earlier was forbidden, and when *Eikon Basilike*, the primary vehicle for private mourning, was at the centre of a punitive campaign against royalist stationers.[39] *Lachrymae musarum* was an act of covert lament for the regicide, even in some of its gestures an expression of defiance towards the new regime.[40] In case we miss the point, Samuel Bold is on hand to remind us how much better things are in the royalist, Laudian afterlife to which young Hastings is bound: 'Fly then from *Babylon* up to *Sion*; there's | In Heaven both Monarch, and an House of Peers; | Yea, there are Bishops too, with grave aspect, | The Churches Nobles, all with glories deckt' (p. 34). Passages like this make clear that Richard Brome, the veteran playwright who orchestrated *Lachrymae musarum* and initialled the title page, saw little practical need for deep disguise. Unlike a cheap broadside or newsbook, and unlike mass-produced, pocket-sized *Eikon Basilike*, this was a lavish,

[38] Richard Brome (ed.), *Lachrymae musarum* (1649), 40, 13.

[39] Robert Wilcher, '*Eikon Basilike*: The Printing, Composition, Strategy, and Impact of "The King's Book"', in Laura Lunger Knoppers (ed.), *The Oxford Handbook of Literature and the English Revolution* (Oxford: Oxford University Press, 2012), 289–308; Jason McElligott, *Royalism, Print and Censorship in Revolutionary England* (Woodbridge: Boydell, 2007), 127–49.

[40] See Michael Gearin-Tosh, 'Marvell's "Upon the Death of Lord Hastings"', *Essays and Studies*, 34 (1981), 105–22; John McWilliams, '"A Storm of Lamentations Writ": *Lachrymae Musarum* and Royalist Culture after the Civil War', *Yearbook of English Studies*, 33 (2003), 273–89.

prestigious volume beyond the means of non-elite readers. The new Council of State's searchers—'State-Ferrets' and 'Parliament Beagles', one newsbook called them—had more than enough popular royalist print on their hands.[41] Although in several poems Hastings becomes merely a cipher, a surrogate for the real focus of lament, it was enough that the volume as a whole was bibliographically marked as mourning a private individual, not so far in this respect from *Justa Edouardo King naufrago* (1638), the collection of elegies in which *Lycidas* first appeared before Milton reframed it in 1645 as an anti-prelatical poem.[42] Material features of the volume suggest something more, including an ornamental headpiece of royal insignia on the opening text page. But Hastings, not Charles, remained the ostensible subject. A second edition of *Lachrymae musarum* was published without apparent consequence on or near the first anniversary of the regicide, 30 January 1650, the date on which the habitually prompt George Thomason obtained his copy.[43]

Dryden was among a group of younger poets, represented in a postscript to *Lachrymae musarum*, who found their way into the book at a late stage, presumably attracted by the opportunity to keep company with leading poets of the Denham generation. Also included in this section were a circumspect poem by Marvell and a reckless one by Marchamont Nedham, both then still in their twenties. Marvell opens at some distance from the prevailing analogy with Charles I by finding Hastings's case unique, one for which 'we must finde a Store | Of Tears untoucht, and never wept before' (p. 78). But he does then associate Hastings's death, in a cryptic passage, with 'State-Jealousie' and the rise of '*Democratick* Stars'. Nedham, then in his ill-timed royalist phase, embraces the political analogy more firmly by finding it 'decreed, we must be drain'd (I see) | Down to the dregs of a *Democracie*'.[44] Here

[41] *Mercurius Pragmaticus*, 20–27 February 1649, qtd by McElligott, *Royalism, Print and Censorship*, 165.

[42] A poem that 'by occasion foretells the ruin of our corrupted clergy then in their height' (Milton, *Complete Shorter Poems*, 243).

[43] *The Poems of Andrew Marvell*, ed. Nigel Smith, revised edn (Harlow: Pearson Longman, 2007), 23.

[44] This image seems to have lodged in Dryden's mind; it returns in *Absalom and Achitophel*, where 'Kingly Power, thus ebbing out, might be | Drawn to the dregs of a Democracy' (i. 226–7), and again in *The Hind and the Panther* (i. 210–11): see Aaron

Hastings becomes a 'tender Sapling' whose death, after the felling of 'well-grown Oaks, and Pillars of the Crown', cruelly serves to 'inhanse the Kingdoms Funeral' (p. 81).

Dryden was still in his teens at this point, younger than Hastings himself, and keen to make a splash. When scholars pay any attention to his contribution, it is usually to regret its qualities as 'overwrought and underfelt' (Earl Miner's phrase) or to find in it promise, albeit callow in execution, of greater future achievement, as James Winn does.[45] The poem is certainly epideictic, a display piece that seems more interested in staging elaborate effects of ingenuity and wit than in consoling the bereaved, most notably the grieving '*Virgin-Widow*' addressed in the poem's close (p. 92). One startling passage, in which Hastings shifts bewilderingly between the roles of Ganymede and Venus while the fatal smallpox pustules are figured first as jewels, then flowers (a momentary Marvellian touch), and finally tears, adds up to a howling failure of poetic tact:

> Replenish'd then with such rare Gifts as these,
> Where was room left for such a Foul Disease?
> The Nations sin hath drawn that Veil, which shrouds
> Our Day-spring in so sad benighting Clouds.
> Heaven would no longer trust its Pledge; but thus
> Recall'd it; rapt its *Ganymede* from us.
> Was there no milder way but the Small Pox,
> The very Filth'ness of *Pandora*'s Box?
> So many Spots, like *næves*, our *Venus* soil?
> One Jewel set off with so many a Foil?
> Blisters with pride swell'd, which th'row's flesh did sprout
> Like Rose-buds, stuck i' th' Lily-skin about.
> Each little Pimple had a Tear in it,
> To wail the fault its rising did commit:
> Who, Rebel-like, with their own Lord at strife,
> Thus made an Insurrection 'gainst his Life.
> Or were these Gems sent to adorn his Skin,

Santesso, '*Lachrymae Musarum* and the Metaphysical Dryden', *Review of English Studies*, 54 (2003), 615–38 (632).

[45] Earl Miner, *Dryden's Poetry* (Bloomington: Indiana University Press, 1967), 4; James A. Winn, 'The Promise of Dryden's Elegy for Hastings', *Modern Language Review*, 79.1 (1984), 21–31.

> The Cab'net of a richer Soul within?
> No Comet need foretel his Change drew on,
> Whose Corps might seem a *Constellation*.

(p. 90; see *Poems*, 1: 5–6)

Here is an early instance of the 'wild and daring sallies of sentiment' or 'irregular and excentrick violence of wit' that Johnson thought second only to argument as Dryden's distinctive mode.[46] But Dryden, who probably had access to the main body of *Lachrymae musarum* when composing his eleventh-hour contribution, was not just seeking to outdo more senior poets in metaphysical conceit and elegiac amplification. He was seeking to outdo them in the art of political encoding, of communicating dissident meaning within a framework of permissible or deniable utterance. He treats his elegy, selected by Brome to close the volume, as an almost abstract exercise in that vein, as though the technical challenge mattered as much as the kind of allegiance implied. In so doing, he provides an arresting solution, unachieved by any other poet in *Lachrymae musarum*, to two problems that haunt the collection throughout: first, the problem of solidifying an inherently tenuous analogy between a king's decollation and a nobleman's disease, which he does by figuring the pustules assailing Hastings's body as rebel troops; second, the problem of registering a complexity of response to the regicide that was widely felt in the nation but not otherwise articulated in the volume, which he does by figuring the agents of Charles I's defeat as weeping even as they rebel. At this moment, if nowhere else in the poem, metaphorical encoding allowed Dryden to articulate not only transgressive meaning but also a vision of political trauma that transcends mere partisanship.

Over the ensuing decade, Marvell's trajectory from the enigmatic balance of the *Horatian Ode* to the heartfelt commitment of his 1658 elegy to Cromwell is easier to trace than that of Dryden, who wrote little else of significance until (to give the poem its full title) *Heroic Stanzas, Consecrated to the Glorious Memory of His Most Serene and Renowned Highness Oliver, Late Lord Protector of This Commonwealth, etc. Written after the Celebration of His Funeral* (1659). There is no mischief to be read into

---

[46] Samuel Johnson, *The Lives of the Poets*, ed. Roger Lonsdale, 4 vols (Oxford: Clarendon Press, 2006), 2: 149.

'celebration' here, which unambiguously means the performance of a solemn ceremony, with no connotation of dancing on graves. Nor should one make too much of a slight contraction of the title between manuscript and print versions of the poem, from 'glorious & happy memorie' to just 'Glorious Memory' (*Poems*, 1: 533). Yet this adjustment, made in the surviving autograph fair copy, indicates the high stakes operating in a volume that was projected by the publisher Henry Herringman after Cromwell's death in September 1658, entered in the Stationers' Register in January 1659, and then published at an unknown date the following spring.[47] Three changes in the interim are significant, the larger context being a progressive erosion of support in both parliament and the army for Richard Cromwell, who fell from power in May 1659.[48]

First, Herringman dropped the project some time after registering it with the Stationers, and it devolved to the printer and occasional publisher William Wilson. Second, the title registered by Herringman, *Three Poems to the Happy Memory of the Most Renowned Oliver, Late Lord Protector of This Commonwealth*, became Wilson's more neutral published title *Three Poems upon the Death of His Late Highnesse Oliver Lord Protector of England, Scotland and Ireland*. Note the removal of 'Commonwealth' as well as 'Happy'; even the prepositional change ('upon' Cromwell's death in place of 'to' Cromwell's memory) makes a difference, suggesting mere description or analysis as opposed to loyal dedication. Third, the most sincere and straightforward of the elegies announced in the Stationers' Register, Marvell's *A Poem upon the Death of His Late Highness the Lord Protector*, was either withdrawn by Marvell or purged by Wilson; it was not to appear in print until three years after Marvell's death, and then only by accident, when a last-minute decision to cancel all three Cromwell poems from his *Miscellaneous Poems* (1681) was unsystematically implemented, leaving uncancelled

---

[47] The best account of this indistinct episode is by Steven N. Zwicker, ' "He seems a king by long succession born": The Problem of Cromwellian Accession and Succession', in Paulina Kewes and Andrew McRae (eds), *Stuart Succession Literature: Moments and Transformations* (Oxford: Oxford University Press, 2018), 60–74.

[48] On the rapidly shifting political situation and the pressures it exerted on the volume, see David Norbrook, *Writing the English Republic: Poetry, Rhetoric and Politics, 1627–1660* (Cambridge: Cambridge University Press, 1999), 379–96.

pages in certain copies.[49] Inserted in Marvell's place was Edmund Waller's more guarded and evasive 'Upon the Late Storm, and of the Death of His Highnesse Ensuing the Same', which crucially avoided Marvell's move of treating Cromwell as a *principe nuovo* whose political dynasty must now be extended by his son Richard.

Yet even the reticence of Waller's encomium was insufficient in retrospect. When first published as a standalone broadside in 1658, 'Upon the Late Storm' was subjected to hostile close reading from both republican and royalist standpoints. The radical George Wither disparaged Waller as a tyrant's lackey who 'takes much more care then I, | What will best please, and wherewith to complie'. The royalist Richard Watson looked forward to 'his *Penitentiall Palinode... sigh'd* and *wept* out at $y^e$ two Tribunals of Heaven & Earth, where I as heartily wish him pardon, as I do $y^e$ rigour of justice and revenge, if he perseveres, as he promiseth, $y^e$ *Panegyrist* of *rebellion*'.[50] The Restoration brought with it an exquisite twist to Waller's predicament, if a much-repeated anecdote is to be believed. In the account of Voltaire (citing Bayle as his authority), Waller was directly challenged about his Cromwell elegy by Charles II. 'This King, to whom *Waller* had a little before, (as is usual with Bards and Monarchs) presented a Copy of Verses embroider'd with Praises; reproach'd the Poet for not writing with so much Energy and Fire as when he had applauded the Usurper (meaning *Oliver*,)', Voltaire records: '*Sir*, reply'd *Waller* to the King, *we Poets succeed better in Fiction than in Truth.*'[51] It's hard to know with what degree of levity or menace the question might have been posed, and hard to say whether Waller's quick wit saved him from mere transient embarrassment or enduring disfavour. Even so, the anecdote is a good reminder of the rhetorical challenge faced by all three contributors to

[49] The evidence is reviewed in Niall Allsopp, 'A Surreptitious State of Marvell's *Miscellaneous Poems* (1681)?', *Notes & Queries*, 62.2 (2015), 268–70; see the alternative hypothesis of Stephanie Coster, 'Robert Boulter and the Publication of Andrew Marvell's *Miscellaneous Poems*', *Review of English Studies*, 69 (2018), 259–76.

[50] Richard Watson, *The Panegyrike and The Storme, Two Poëtike Libells by Ed. Waller, Vassall to the Usurper, Answered by More Faythfull Subjects* (?Bruges, 1659), sigs $B2^v$–$C^r$; George Wither, *Salt upon Salt, Made out of Certain Ingenious Verses upon the Late Storm and the Death of His Highness Ensuing* (1659), 5.

[51] Voltaire, *Letters Concerning the English Nation*, ed. Nicholas Cronk (Oxford: Oxford World's Classics, 1999), 105.

the Cromwell volume—the third was the young Thomas Sprat—at a time when Stuart restoration no longer looked inconceivable, alongside other possible outcomes including hard republicanism. Pragmatically, the situation required each poem to be armed against equal and opposite potential readings, as sincere lament or as ironic deflation, and to keep both interpretative options in play as viable, yet also doubtful. Expressively, all three poets avoid the heartfelt style of Marvell's engagement with Cromwell's memory, and seek a rhetoric that transcends personal utterance in order to articulate or channel a public—and thus inevitably a vexed, uncertain—response.

Sprat's strategy—a successful one, to judge by his thriving career after 1660—was to voice the problem explicitly. On the face of it, his poem is the bold, forward-looking expression of Cromwellian allegiance described by Edward Holberton, for whom Sprat celebrates the Protectorate as 'the triumph of Oliver's intelligence, moderation, and valour against other political forces' and looks to Richard and his allies to protect its legacy.[52] Yet this is also a poem of questions and apprehensions, most of all as Sprat casts around for a secure language of encomium. 'What shall I say, or where begin?' he asks himself at one point. At another, 'We know, to praise thee is a dangerous proof | Of our Obedience and our Love: | For when the Sun and Fire meet, | Th'one's extinguish't quite'.[53] Here *proof* means not confirming evidence but experimental test, leaving open the possibility for royalist readers—an audience Sprat courted the same year in his ode *The Plague at Athens*, with its hints about sinful, regicidal England—that this is a test the poem fails or refuses. At the same time, the language of danger and extinction, though resolved as the stanza continues into a point about poetic reputation, also suggests a surrounding atmosphere of coercion and risk. Sprat is remembered now for his advocacy of transparent, referential style in *The History of the Royal Society* (1667). But here he knew better, and prudently exploits the very manoeuvres—

---

[52] Edward Holberton, *Poetry and the Cromwellian Protectorate: Culture, Politics, and Institutions* (Oxford: Oxford University Press, 2008), 196.

[53] *Three Poems upon the Death of His Late Highnesse Oliver, Lord Protector of England, Scotland, and Ireland* (1659), 14, 12–13.

'these specious Tropes and Figures... these seeming Mysteries... this trick of Metaphors'—that he would later proscribe.[54]

Dryden employs similar gambits, but within a more complex and ingenious larger context. First, he adopts a halting, syntactically compressed verse form, lacking the lucid fluency of the heroic couplets he would resume at the Restoration, which constantly throws meaning into doubt. He would later defend this so-called 'Gondibert' stanza for its dignity of sound and number (*Poems*, 1: 115–16), but here the effect is of inhibition, even confusion—an effect scarcely alleviated by the ever-present echo of royalist epic inherent in his chosen form.[55] Several stanzas float alternative, even opposite, meanings at once, in ways that have been deftly disentangled by Zwicker, for whom the poem is an unresolved mingling of 'open praise, praise qualified by ironies, and something like troubled disenchantment'.[56] Second, Dryden concentrates his celebration, especially in the phase of the poem devoted to the Protectorate years, on the qualities of 'glory' and 'highness' announced in the poem's title, seeking common ground among a broad constituency of readers, including royalist sympathizers, who might value Cromwell's achievements of orderly government, maritime pre-eminence, and foreign conquest. Yet even in this fairly straightforward section of *Heroic Stanzas*, Dryden's wording is sometimes guarded. A declaration that 'Peace was the prize of all his toils and care' (1: 23; st. 16) gestures towards an established poetic tradition of praising Cromwell, in line with his personal motto *pax quaeritur bello*, as only waging war for the sake of peace.[57] Yet Dryden quietly withholds assent from this standard answer to the warmongering charge that had dogged Cromwell, and with 'prize', which stresses not intention but merely effect, stops short of the more unequivocal alternatives available to him (spur, aim, goal, end). He's certainly far

---

[54] Thomas Sprat, *The History of the Royal-Society of London, for the Improving of Natural Knowledge* (1667), 112 (pt II, sect. xx).

[55] On the politics of William Davenant's *Gondibert* (1651), see Kevin Sharpe, *Criticism and Compliment: The Politics of Literature in the England of Charles I* (Cambridge: Cambridge University Press, 1990), 101–8.

[56] Zwicker, *Politics and Language*, 84.

[57] See Laura Lunger Knoppers, *Constructing Cromwell: Ceremony, Portrait, and Print, 1645–1661* (Cambridge: Cambridge University Press, 2000), 103–4 and *passim*.

from the warm endorsement of Marvell's 'he whom Nature all for peace had made'.[58]

This indicates a third technique, most pronounced in the congested opening stanzas of the poem, which is to introduce uncertainties that never quite open into full-blown irony, though cumulatively they tend that way. While studiously omitting to name its dedicatee, the poem begins in Sprat-like mode by noting the difficulty of the poet's expressive task and doubting his capacity to fulfil it: 'How shall I then begin, or where conclude, | To draw a fame so truly circular?' (1: 19; st. 5). The attempt soon goes off on peculiar tangents. When Dryden writes that 'our best notes are treason to his fame' (1: 18; st. 2), this master of the *mot juste* makes at best an infelicitous choice of words, whatever the immediate referent of 'treason', for an encomium to a regicidal leader. When he adds that 'in [Cromwell's] praise no arts can liberal be' (1: 19; st. 3), he seems to go awry again, opening up equal and opposite options (is Cromwell too good, or too bad, for generous praise?) without confirming either. And then if these arts are not liberal (freely given; made without holding back), does that mean they are coerced? The possibility is scarcely dispelled by Dryden's dour declaration that building a poetic monument to Cromwell is 'our duty and our interest too' (1: 19; st. 4): an act Marvell presents by contrast as one of 'Love and Grief'.[59]

Typically, the doubts Dryden raises with these superficially tactless, profoundly calculated verbal choices are resolved into less disquieting meanings by the end of each stanza. Arts are not liberal when praising Cromwell because they constitute the poet's own grab for reflected glory; it is the duty and interest of English poets to praise Cromwell because otherwise foreign rivals will get in first. But these belated resolutions never fully erase the disconcerting first impression. At the same time, while the tendency of the poem's early stanzas to begin on notes of concession or even denial ('Though', 'Though', 'Yet', 'How', 'No' in the first seven stanzas alone) reinforces the sense, unstated but pervasive, of expressive reluctance or constraint.

Things grow murkier still when Dryden announces that 'wars, like mists that rise against the sun, | Made him but greater seem, not greater grow' (1: 19; st. 6). On the face of it, the lines celebrate an

---

[58] *Poems of Marvell*, 304 (*Poem upon the Death of the Lord Protector*, line 15).

[59] *Poems of Marvell*, 305 (*Poem upon the Death of the Lord Protector*, line 21).

inherent stature that nothing changes, but they end on an oddly negative note, and flirt with an unsettling idea of Cromwellian greatness as a trick of the light. This image also commits another of the poem's now suspiciously frequent lapses in tact, this time by recalling a familiar royalist trope, used several times in *Lachrymae musarum* and indeed in Dryden's own poem on Hastings, in which the sun of divine-right kingship is extinguished by clouds of rebellion;[60] here the choice of 'rise against' intensifies the hint. Then comes a further misstep, if misstep is the word, in a botched compliment on Cromwell's stage-managed refusal of the crown: 'Nor was his virtue poisoned soon as born, | With the too early thoughts of being king' (1: 20; st. 7). The emphasis on timing here—soon as born, too early—leaves open the widely suspected possibility that thoughts of being king did indeed poison Cromwell's virtue: just somewhat later, and without fulfilment only because conquered by caution. As John Evelyn alleged in 1657, 'the Protector *Oliver*, now affecting *King-ship*, is petition'd to take the Title on him, by all his new-made sycophant Lords &c: but dares not for feare of the *Phanatics*, not thoroughly purged out of his rebell army'.[61]

At this point Dryden's method starts to shift, and having opened stanzas with off-key notes that he then resolves too late to prevent interpretative damage, he now moves to an alternative pattern in which seemingly innocuous compliments are retrospectively weakened. 'And yet dominion was not his design; | We owe that blessing not to him but heaven' (1: 20; st. 10): here denial of the royalist (indeed also republican) allegation against Cromwell as would-be dictator continues to stand. But it starts to look like providential intervention despite Cromwell, not through him—if design here means not just a plan or stratagem but, as it could in the seventeenth century, the plan's actual fulfilment (*OED*, s.v. Design, 5).

Samuel Johnson wrote of Dryden as a poet who 'delighted to tread upon the brink of meaning, where light and darkness begin to mingle'.[62]

---

[60] See above, pp. 30, 42. For Dryden, 'The nation's sin hath drawn that veil which shrouds | Our dayspring in so sad benighting clouds'; in Toland's report, it was Milton's potentially republican version of the same trope ('disastrous twilight') that alarmed the episcopal censor.

[61] Knoppers, *Constructing Cromwell*, 118, quoting Evelyn's report of 22 March 1657.

[62] Johnson, *Lives of the Poets*, 2: 149–50.

In this poem he does it several times in quick succession, though without ever quite taking the plunge. The meanings in question are left unconfirmed, and sometimes they're even denied. But they leave a residue on the mind. By the end of *Heroic Stanzas*, Dryden seems to be commenting on this curious process himself, though with an opacity of expression that by now is firmly established as the poem's mode:

> His ashes in a peaceful urn shall rest,
> His name a great example stands, to show
> How strangely high endeavours may be blessed,
> Where piety and valour jointly go.

(1: 29; st. 37)

More than one question is begged in this closing but scarcely conclusive stanza, including the long-running question of why Dryden seems unable to bring himself, throughout the poem, to indicate Cromwell by more than a cool pronoun. Marvell had no such inhibition in the *Horatian Ode* with 'restless Cromwell', or in his funerary poem with 'Cromwell, Heaven's favourite'; even Waller and Sprat affect less detachment from their subject.[63] The more immediate question is what to make of the free-floating adverb 'strangely', which in the period can be a neutral intensifier, but which Dryden elsewhere tends to use in the modern sense (unaccountably, oddly). What does this adverb modify as the line goes on, the adjective or the verb phrase? In other words, is Cromwell's high endeavour the strange thing here, or is it the equivocal nature of Dryden's blessing? After so much poetic strangeness in the previous stanzas, it's hard not to detect a self-reflexive hint in this final flourish, and with it an invitation to understand the poem as one that problematizes Cromwell's achievements more than it praises them. This is the direction in which Dryden's autograph manuscript points by inserting an interruptive comma ('How strangely, high Endeavours may bee blest') that disconnects 'strangely' from 'high'—a telling piece of rhythmic punctuation that was omitted by Wilson's compositor in the published text.[64]

---

[63] *Poems of Marvell*, 273 (*Horatian Ode*, line 9), 308 (*Poem upon the Death of the Lord Protector*, line 157).

[64] Dryden, *Poems*, 1: 538; see Paul Hammond, 'The Autograph Manuscript of Dryden's *Heroique Stanza's* and Its Implications for Editors', *Publications of the Bibliographical Society of America*, 76 (1982), 457–70.

None of this is to call *Heroic Stanzas* a work of sustained irony, a systematic covert critique tricked out as overt praise. But it is a work of recurrent interrogation, thoughtfully and skilfully so, too quiet to be objectionable in its immediate context, but studded with get-out clauses in case of future awkwardness in another. Just how much such nuances, ambiguities, and juxtapositions of competing attitude might matter becomes clear with the reception of *Heroic Stanzas* after the Restoration. The simplest remedy was of course to bury the poem, and that, understandably enough, was Dryden's preference. It may even have been in an attempt to expunge or overwrite *Heroic Stanzas* that he resumed its distinctive 'Gondibert' stanza in *Annus Mirabilis* (1667), a work of unimpeachable loyalty which, in an elaborate manoeuvre involving Marvell's then unpublished *Horatian Ode*, compares Cromwell's devastation of church and state to the ruinous fire of London (*Poems*, 1: 181–2; sts 213–15). Only after the Whig Revolution of 1688–9, when there was no harm at all in complicating his reputation as a Stuart panegyrist, did Dryden authorize a reprint for Jacob Tonson's quarto series of his major works.[65] Until then, the poem remained a clanking skeleton in Dryden's closet, and the general view of it is probably reflected by the reader of the first edition who angrily scrawled 'Heroique Stanza's, Consecreated to the infamous Memory of Oliver Cromwell, Late Lord Destroyer of this Common-Wealth/Kingdom' over the original title.[66] At least fourteen manuscript copies of *Heroic Stanzas* are now known as well as the fair copy in Dryden's hand, and the motivation for circulating these manuscripts may have been hostile. That was certainly the case with several unauthorized reprints produced at the height of Dryden's career as a Tory polemicist, three in 1681–2 in the wake of *Absalom and Achitophel*, and another following *The Hind and the Panther* in 1687 (*Poems*, 1: 17). One reprint, a malicious half-sheet entitled *An Elegy on the Usurper O. C. by the Author of Absalom and Achitophel, Published to Shew the Loyalty and Integrity of the Poet* (Figure 1.1), was followed by a bogus verse postscript attributed to Dryden. Here 'J. D.' regrets the evidence that '*my nauseous Mercenary*

[65] See Paul Hammond, *The Making of Restoration Poetry* (Woodbridge: D. S. Brewer, 2006), 15.

[66] I am grateful to Steven Zwicker for this point, from a copy of the 1659 volume in his possession.

# AN ELEGY ON THE USURPER O. C.
## BY THE AUTHOR OF
## Absalom and Achitophel,

*published to shew the Loyalty and Integrity of the POET.*

AND now 'tis time for their Officious haft,
Who would before have born him to the Sky
Like eager *Romans* e're all rites were paft,
Did let too foon the facred Eagle fly.

Though our beft Notes are Treafon to his Fame,
Joyn'd with the lowd Applaufe of publick Voice,
Since Heaven the praife we offer to his Name,
Hath rendred too Authentick by its Choice.

Though in his Praife no Arts can lib'ral be,
Since they whofe Mufes have the higheft flown,
Add not to his Immortal Memory,
But do an Act of Friendfhip to their own.

Yet 'tis our Duty and our Intereft too,
Such Monuments as we can build to raife,
Leaft all the World prevent what we fhould do,
And claim a title in him by their praife.

How fhall I then begin or where conclude,
To draw a Frame fo truly circular?
For in a Round what Order can be fhew'd,
Where all the parts fo equal perfect are?

His Grandeur he deriv'd from Heaven alone;
For he was great e're Fortune made him fo,
And Wars like Mifts that rife againft the Sun;
Made him but Greater feem, not Greater grow.

No borrow'd Bays his Temples did adorn,
But to our Crown he did frefh Jewels bring;
Nor was his Vertue poifon'd foon as born,
With the too early thoughts of being King.

Fortune (that eafie Miftrefs of the young,
But to her Antient Servants coy and hard;)
Him at that Age her Favorites rank't among,
When fhe her beft Lov'd *Pompy* did difcard.

He private, mark't the Faults of others fway,
And fet as Sea-marks for himfelf to fhun,
Not like rafh Monarchs who their youth betray
By Acts, their Age too late would wifh undone.

And yet Dominion was not his defign,
We owe that Bleffing not to him but Heaven,
Which to fair Acts rewards unfought did joyn;
Rewards which lefs to him than us were given.

Our former Cheifs like Sticklers in the War,
Firft fought t'enflame the Parties, then to poize,
The Quarrel lov'd, but did the Caufe abhor,
And did not ftrike to hurt, but make a noife.

War, our Confumption, was their gainful Trade,
We inward bled whilft they prolong'd our pain,
He fought to end our Fightings, and Effaid
† *To ftanch the Blood by breathing of a Vein.*

Swift and refiftlefs through the Land he paft,
Like that bold *Greek* who did the *Eaft* fubdue,
And made to Battle fuch Heroick hafte,
As if on Wings of Victory he flew.

He fought feeure of Fortune as of Fame,
'Till by new Maps the Ifland might be fhown,
Of Conquefts which he ftrew'd where e're he came;
Thick as the Galaxy with Stars is fown.

His Palmes though under weights, they did not ftand,
Still thriv'd, no Winter could his Lawrels fade,
Heaven in his portraict fhew'd a Workmans hand,
And drew it perfect yet without a fhade.

Peace was the Price of all his Toyls and Care,
Which War had banifht and did now reftore,
*Bolognia's* Wall thus mounted in the Air,
To feat themfelves more furely than before.

Her

**Figure 1.1** *An Elegy on the Usurper O. C. ..... Published to Shew the Loyalty and Integrity of the Poet* (1681), by permission of the Newberry Library, Chicago. This belated piracy of *Heroic Stanzas* is one of several published to embarrass Dryden during his laureateship.

Her safety rescued, Ireland to him owes,
And treacherous Scotland to no In'trest true:
Yet blest that Fate which did his Arms dispose,
Her Land to civilizeas to subdue.

Nor was he like those Stars which only shine,
When to pail Mariners they Storms portend,
He had his calmer Influence, and his Mein
Did Love and Majesty together blend.

'Tis true, his Count'nance did Imprint an Awe,
And Nat'rally all Souls to his did bow,
As wands of Divination downward draw,
And point to Beds where Sovereign Gold does grow.

When past all Offerings to Pheretrian Jove,
He Mars depos'd, and Arms to gowns made yeild;
Successful Councels did him soon Approve,
As fit for close Intreagues, as open field.

To suppliant Holland he vouchsaft a Peace,
Our once bold Rival in the Brittish Main,
Now tamely glad her unjust claim to cease,
And buy our Friendship with her Idol gain.

Fame of th'asserted Sea through Europe blown,
Made France and Spain ambitious of his Love,
Each knew that side must Conquer he would own,
And for him fiercely as for Empire strove.

No sooner was the Frenchman's Cause embrac't,
Then the light Monsieur the grave Don outweigh'd,
His Fortune turn'd the Scale where it was cast,
Though Indian Mines were in the other laid.

When absent, yet we conquer'd in his right
For though some meaner Artists Skill were shown,
In mingling Colours or in placing right,
Yet all the fair designment was his own.

For from all Tempers he could Service draw,
The worth of each with its allay he knew,
And as the Confident of Nature saw,
How the Complexions did divide and brew.

Or he their single Vertues did survey,
By intuition in his own large Breast;
Where all the rich Ideas of them lay,
That were the Rule and Measure to the rest.

When such Heroick Vertue Heaven sets out,
The Stars like Commons sullenly obey;
Because it dreyns them when it comes about,
And therefore is a Tax they seldome pay.

From th is high Spring our Forreign Conquests flow,
Which yet more Glorious Triumphs do portend,
Since their Commencement to his Arms they owe,
If Springs as high as Fountains may ascend.

He made us Freemen of the Continent,
Whom Nature did like Captives treat before,
To nobler Preys the English Lyon sent,
And taught him first in Belgian walks to roar.

That old unquestion'd Pirate of the Land,
Proud Rome with dread the fate of Dunkirk heard,
And trembling, wisht behind more Alps to stand,
Although an Alexander were her Guard.

By his Command we boldly crost the Line,
And bravely fought where Southern Stars arise,
We trac'd the far fetcht Gold unto the Mine,
And that which brib'd our Fathers made our Prize.

Such was our Prince yet own'd a soul above,
The highest Acts it could produce to shew;
Thus poor Mechanick Arts in publick move,
Whilst the deep Secrets beyond Practice go.

Nor Dy'd he when his ebbing Fame went less,
But when fresh Laurels courted him to live,
He seem'd but to prevent some new success,
As if above what Tryumphs Earth could give.

His latest Victories still thickest came,
As, near the Center, motion doth encrease,
Till he, prest down with his own weighty Name
Did like the Vessal under Spoils decrease.

But first the Ocean as a Tribute sent,
The Gyant Prince of all her watry herd,
And th'isle when her protecting Genius went,
Upon his obsequies lowd sighs conferr'd.

No Civil Broils have since his Death arose,
But Faction now by habit does obey;
And Wars have that respect for his repose,
As Winds for Halcyons when they breed at Sea.

His Ashes in a peaceful Urn shall rest,
His Name and great example stand to show
How strangely high endeavours may be blest,
Where Piety and Valour Joyntly go.

---

# POSTSCRIPT.

THe Printing of these Rhimes Afflicts me more
    Than all the Druts I in Rose-Alley bore.
This shews my nauseous Mercenary Pen
Would praise the vilest and the worst of men.
A Rogue like Hodge am I, the World will know it,
Hodge was his Fidler, and I John his Poet.
This may prevent the pay for which I write;
For I for pay against my Conscience fight.
I must confess so infamous a Knave
Can do no Service, though the humblest Slave.

Villains I praise, and Patriots accuse,
My railing and my fawning Talents use;
Just as they pay I flatter or abuse.
But I to men in Power a Turd am still,
To rub on any honest Face they will.
Then on I'le go, for Libels I declare,
Best Friends no more than worst of Foes I'le spare,
And all this I can do, because I dare.
He who writes on, and Cudgels can defie,
And knowing hee'l be beaten still writes on, am I.

J. D.

---

LONDON, Printed for J. Smith. MDCLXXXI.

*Pen | Would praise the vilest and the worst of Men*', yet resolves to continue writing libels even in the face of setbacks like the Rose-Alley ambush: 'He who writes on, and Cudgels can defie | And knowing hee'l be beaten still writes on, am I.'[67]

Prompted by these embarrassing piracies, Whig antagonists combed through *Heroic Stanzas* for unguarded moments, and seized on lines that could not be explained away as ironic subversion. The good physician trope of Stanza 12, 'He fought to end our fighting, and essayed | To stanch the blood by breathing of the vein' (1: 21), was aggressively interpreted as justifying the regicide: Milton's crime in the tracts burned by the hangman in 1660. And indeed, it's hard to say what else this passage might mean. Had Charles II followed his father to the scaffold, writes Robert Gould, 'Even thou hadst prais'd the Fact; his Father Slain, | Thou call'dst but gently breathing of a Vein'.[68] An anonymous attack on Dryden's emphatically royalist opera *Albion and Albanius* (1685) combined the same notorious phrase with a nasty sideswipe about lack of ears, on the surface suggesting deafness to music, but also dropping a menacing hint about pillories and Prynne-style mutilation: 'Leave making operas and writing of lyricks, | Till thou hast ears, and can alter thy strain; | Stick to thy talent of bold panegyricks, | And still remember—*breathing the vein*.'[69]

## Panegyric in print and script, *Astraea Redux* to *Mac Flecknoe*

A century later even Johnson, for all his alertness in general to Dryden's brinkmanship with meaning, seems to have taken *Heroic Stanzas* at face value. It is a well-known passage, but one that bears close examination:

> When the king was restored, Dryden, like the other panegyrists of usurpation, changed his opinion, or his profession, and published ASTREA REDUX, *a poem on the happy restoration and return of his most sacred*

---

[67] *An Elegy on the Usurper O. C. by the Author of Absalom and Achitophel* (1681), 2.

[68] Robert Gould, *The Laureat* (1687), 1.

[69] *The Raree-Show, from Father Hopkins* (1685); see also Charles Sackville, Earl of Dorset (?), 'To Mr. Bays', in *POAS*, 4: 81.

*Majesty King Charles the Second.* | The reproach of inconstancy was, on this occasion, shared with such numbers, that it produced neither hatred nor disgrace; if he changed, he changed with the nation.[70]

There is little trace here of the 'contempt and indignation' that Johnson expresses when writing about Waller's *volte-face* at the same juncture.[71] After the caustic 'panegyrists of usurpation', the tone is indulgent, with touches of verbal air-brushing worthy of Dryden himself. Yet while refusing to pass judgment, Johnson is also tentative about the underlying fact; his wording leaves open the possibility that perhaps Dryden didn't change at all, or that, in one or both poems of 1659–60, opinion and profession might diverge. There are several grounds, as outlined above, for reading *Heroic Stanzas* as a poem that ironically disrupts its surface propositions, but *Astraea Redux* is not quite straightforward either, for all its air of free and fluent expression. It's as though, for later readers of Dryden's Restoration panegyrics, the reproach of inconstancy obscures his constancy of approach. Johnson's words are usually cited to explain a simple transfer of allegiance from Cromwell to Charles. Yet it would be truer to the nuances of his statement to read both poems as cultivating as much detachment as the rhetoric of encomium would allow, to achieve a sophisticated if unstable mingling of praise and blame.

*Astraea Redux* is a seminal work in the history of panegyric, the *locus classicus* for poetic tropes that were to dominate the genre for three decades: the language of divine right and sacred unction, linking Charles with the biblical David as 'God's anointed' (*Poems*, 1: 42; line 80); the celebratory analogies with Rome at the dawn of empire, promising 'times like those alone | By Fate reserved for Great Augustus' Throne' (1: 54; lines 320–1); the pervasive Stuart iconography of roses, oaks, and suns; the rightful convergence of divine and popular wills.[72] The poem's ease and expansiveness give formal expression to a sense of harmony restored, a sense intensified when moments of exaggerated metrical disruption—'Madness the pulpit, faction seized the

---

[70] Johnson, *Lives of the Poets*, 2: 80.    [71] Johnson, *Lives of the Poets*, 2: 40.

[72] This iconography, as inherited in Jacobitism, is usefully itemized in Murray G. H. Pittock, *Material Culture and Sedition, 1688–1760: Treacherous Objects, Secret Places* (Basingstoke: Palgrave Macmillan, 2013), 159–69.

throne' (1: 39; line 22)—evoke the chaos before. Yet *Astraea Redux* also withholds unconditional endorsement from Charles and his policies, which centred officially on clemency and reconciliation for the sake of future peace, but in the eyes of opposition figures masked a vengeful reality of 'lust and rage'.[73] 'How shall I then my doubtful thoughts express | That must his sufferings both regret and bless!' (1: 41; lines 71–2), Dryden exclaims in a couplet reminiscent of *Heroic Stanzas* ('How shall I then begin...'). He goes on to resolve the paradox by analogy with the Fortunate Fall. But as in *Heroic Stanzas*, the damage is done before this resolution, and the 'doubtful thoughts' that precede it are never quite dispelled.

Oddly, Dryden's doubt comes across most clearly in the poem's distinctive use of indicatives, which function several times as disguised warnings or imperatives. By pointedly attributing to Charles the very qualities he was feared to lack, they urge these qualities on him in the public interest. 'Inured to suffer ere he came to reign, | No rash procedure will his action stain' (1: 42; lines 87–8): at a time when rash procedure was exactly the danger, Dryden's statement asks to be read as something else, poised between hope and fear, with the effect of rendering conditional the welcome of the poem. 'Not tied to rules of policy, you find | Revenge less sweet than a forgiving mind' (1: 51; lines 260–1): too early for confident statement, this couplet must be read contextually as prediction at best, or as kid-glove instruction— as a sly version, in effect, of the *laudando praecipere* tradition.[74] When Dryden adds that 'Your power to justice doth submit your cause, | Your goodness only is above the laws' (1: 52; lines 266–7), he not only compliments Charles but also issues a tactful prohibition on political absolutism. Royal power and royal goodness become distinct things at

[73] Worden finds this phrase in both Edmund Ludlow and Algernon Sidney (*Literature and Politics*, 374); for hopes and fears more broadly at this juncture, see Matthew Jenkinson, *Culture and Politics at the Court of Charles II, 1660–1685* (Woodbridge: Boydell, 2010), 21–47.

[74] 'A form due in civility to kings and great persons, *laudando praecipere*; when by telling men what they are, they represent to them what they should be' (Francis Bacon, *The Essays or Counsels, Civil and Moral*, ed. Brian Vickers (Oxford: Oxford University Press, 1999), 118).

this point, the former not included in the latter and thus, crucially, subordinate to rule of law.

In this respect, Elliott Visconsi is not quite right to represent Dryden as ignoring a reality of violent retribution in order to flatter the king as 'a virtuoso of therapeutic equity...an agent of princely mercy'.[75] Rather, Dryden plays quietly, but obviously enough, on the alarming potential mismatch between words and deeds. Later poems pursue panegyric with the same guile, notably Dryden's coronation poem *To His Sacred Majesty* (1661), with its pointed reminder, explicitly indicative, implicitly imperative, not to renege on the Act of Indemnity and Oblivion: 'Among our crimes oblivion may be set, | But 'tis our King's perfection to forget' (*Poems*, 1: 59; lines 87–8).[76] In a beautiful opening image of the receding Flood, Dryden pulls off the trick of praising Charles by analogy with divinely favoured Noah as he disembarks, while also warning him to watch his step in the perilous, ravaged environment he now repossesses—for 'when that flood in its own depths was drowned, | It left behind it false and slippery ground' (1: 55; lines 5–6). This mode of insinuating warning within praise would be bold and demanding even in a mature poet, and Dryden mastered it early. Yet his relationship to panegyric was more complicated still, for as well as being the most accomplished exponent of this quintessentially Restoration genre, he was also the wiliest parodist of its tropes and tricks.

At one level there is nothing incongruous at all about *Mac Flecknoe*, composed in 1676, a superbly excessive lampoon on Thomas Shadwell, the Whig rival who was to supplant Dryden as poet laureate on the regime change of 1688–9. Beyond this immediate personal agenda, the poem builds from its attack on Shadwell a satirical account of professional authorship and commercial print culture that anticipates Pope's *Dunciad*, albeit without such clear emphasis

---

[75] Elliott Visconsi, *Lines of Equity: Literature and the Origins of Law in Later Stuart England* (Ithaca: Cornell University Press, 2008), 18–19.

[76] On the disintegration of this ideal following the coronation, see Paulina Kewes, 'Acts of Remembrance, Acts of Oblivion: Rhetoric, Law, and National Memory in Early Restoration England', in Lorna Clymer (ed.), *Ritual, Routine, and Regime: Repetition in Early Modern British and European Cultures* (Toronto: University of Toronto Press, 2006), 103–31.

on broader cultural decay. The complication is that Dryden casts his satire in a mode of mock panegyric that ironically resumes the idiom of *Astraea Redux* and *To His Sacred Majesty* while pointing mischievously forward to the succession struggle, already smouldering, that was to flare up in the Exclusion Crisis.[77] With the conceit of the poem, in which the acknowledged master of bad verse (Flecknoe) canvasses the rising generation for a worthy successor, Dryden skilfully targets Shadwell for his unerring consistency as a writer of nonsense: 'The rest to some faint meaning make pretence, | But Shadwell never deviates into sense' (*Poems*, 1: 315; lines 19–20). The problem is the ulterior meaning, by no means faint, that accompanies this attack. As Dryden presents him, Flecknoe here is not merely a byword for authorial incompetence, but in his literary influence a figure awkwardly reminiscent of Charles II, whose failure to sire a legitimate heir while filling the court with bastard offspring, notably the still-favoured Duke of Monmouth, was storing up political trouble. 'Blessed with issue of a large increase', Flecknoe now must select from this issue an official heir and 'settle the succession of the state' (1: 314; lines 8, 10).

When he does so, the avalanche of bad poetry that accompanies Shadwell's coronation cannot but recall the extended outpour of panegyric to which Dryden himself contributed fifteen years earlier, as Charles II came to the throne:

> From dusty shops neglected authors come,
> Martyrs of pies, and relics of the bum.
> Much Heywood, Shirley, Ogilby there lay,
> But loads of Shadwell almost choked the way.
>
> (1: 323; lines 100–3)

This is not only an early instance of what Leah Price has called 'the waste paper trope', or a distant antecedent of Philip Larkin's 'Books are a load of crap'—capped by Dryden with the felicitous expedient

---

[77] For this context (alternatively the Restoration Crisis) and Dryden's poetry more broadly, see Philip Connell, *Secular Chains: Poetry and the Politics of Religion from Milton to Pope* (Oxford: Oxford University Press, 2016), 98–130; for the plays, see Susan J. Owen, *Restoration Theatre and Crisis* (Oxford: Oxford University Press, 1996), 110–56, 200–38.

(when he finally authorized a printed version in 1684) of gutting Shadwell's name to read simply 'Sh—'.[78] It's also a self-implicating moment that mocks the very business of coronation panegyric as spearheaded by Dryden himself in 1660–1—not least when he follows the lines quoted above by nominating the bookseller Herringman, who among much else had published *Astraea Redux* and *To His Sacred Majesty*, as captain of the guard of stationers at the coronation procession. In effect, *Mac Flecknoe* sends up its own author's public, professional self, and incidentally establishes a playful but deeply tactless association between the hackney targets of his satire here and the royal patrons of his panegyric elsewhere.

In this context, we might detect in the satirical energies of *Mac Flecknoe* an exuberant moment of release: a return of the repressed on the laureate's part, and a gleeful spoof of the very genre from which his Restoration career had taken off. In a poem unlike anything he had written before—'vituperative, scatological and riddlingly allusive', Harold Love calls it[79]—there is a palpable sense of liberation from public duty, an imaginative throwing off of the cares of office. Yet the spoof also does collateral damage to the usual beneficiaries of panegyric in Dryden's hands. All the tropes and trappings of the genre reinforce an implied parallel between the inglorious Flecknoe/Mac Flecknoe dynasty and the reigning Stuart line, from the Flecknoe–Augustus parallel of the opening to the invocations of 'monarch oaks' (line 27), 'anointed dulness' (line 63), 'sacred unction' (line 118), and much else that pervade the body of the poem. Even the coronation oath is subject to parody, when Shadwell vows 'That he till death true dullness would maintain, | And in his father's right, and realm's defence | Ne're to have peace with wit, nor truce with sense'

---

[78] Leah Price, *How To Do Things with Books in Victorian Britain* (Princeton: Princeton University Press, 2012), 219–57; Philip Larkin, 'A Study of Reading Habits', in *The Whitsun Weddings* (London: Faber, 1964), 31. Hammond cautions that 'modern critics who comment on the poem's association of "Sh—" with shit are basing their interpretation on a typographical convention not encountered by the poem's first readers, and almost certainly not in the original manuscript' (*Making of Restoration Poetry*, 51). They base this interpretation, it seems fair to say, on an opportunity created by Dryden in manuscript for later exploitation in print.

[79] Harold Love, *Scribal Publication in Seventeenth-Century England* (Oxford: Clarendon Press, 1993), 147.

(lines 115–17). But Dryden too breaks truce with sense here, not by descending like Shadwell into 'nonsense absolute', but by courting double or divided meaning: an ambiguity that mischievously links his immediate targets, Shadwell and other professional enemies, with his official Stuart patrons. In one of *Mac Flecknoe*'s parting insults, Dryden has Flecknoe urge Shadwell to take up writing acrostics 'And torture one poor word ten thousand ways'. Yet he himself was torturing a whole genre.

That is not to say that Dryden was now crossing the indistinct, mobile line—the 'brink', to recall Johnson's term—between tolerable jest and seditious earnest. It was all more delicate and indefinable than that, a matter of incidental association, not explicit analogy; it may not even have been fully conscious or controlled. Pope probably came closer to the boundary half a century later, when he borrowed Dryden's ploy in early versions of *The Dunciad* (1728, 1729) soon after the death of George I and the coronation of George II. 'Still Dunce the second reigns like Dunce the first', Pope writes at this juncture, a few lines after vowing to bring the Smithfield muses to the ear of Kings and visually glossing his vow in a printer's headpiece depicting asses' ears.[80] Yet Pope was by that time a firmly oppositional poet; Dryden was poet laureate, though not the only one (as Southey's case would later demonstrate) whose verse could be drawn into the realm of sedition.

Most scholars explain the fact that Dryden refrained from publishing *Mac Flecknoe*, and instead used manuscript circulation, with reference to the virulence of its lampoon against Shadwell in an environment where violent reprisals from the libelled were commonplace: certainly more common than legal retribution.[81] Yet manuscript circulation of *An Essay upon Satire* (mainly the Earl of Mulgrave's work, though Dryden's authorship was widely assumed) was not enough to spare his

---

[80] *The Poems of Alexander Pope, Volume III: The Dunciad (1728) and The Dunciad Variorum (1729)*, ed. Valerie Rumbold (Harlow: Longman, 2007), 177 (*Dunciad Variorum*, i.6); for analysis, see below, pp. 111–12.

[81] See Winn, *Dryden and His World*, 326; Hammond, *Making of Restoration Poetry*, 140. Winn notes several contemporaneous cases of violent physical retaliation (see also p. 382); for Hammond, anonymity 'may also be attributable to a form of delicacy in not forcing an open, public breach with Shadwell'.

bruises in Rose-Alley three years later, and Shadwell would have known well enough—indeed, he did know—about a manuscript poem that now survives in at least seventeen early copies.[82] In the court of opinion that mattered, scribal publication, to use Love's term, was no less effective or damaging than print, and indeed Love cogently argues that seventeenth- and eighteenth-century constraints on the press could give manuscript the greater air of authority and truth.[83] By circulating the poem in scriptorial copies, anonymously at first, Dryden was avoiding the need to license a work that was not only personally abusive but also in its subtext politically mischievous, or to commit himself to a work so much in tension with his print panegyrics and his office as poet laureate. The effect was to confine the poem within a small, sophisticated metropolitan milieu of perhaps one or two hundred readers, of whom only some would know the secret of authorship.[84]

Dryden may even have seen manuscript circulation as thematically fitting, the proper fulfilment of *Mac Flecknoe*'s meaning, in two ways. Scriptorially produced, typically with fine calligraphy suggesting elite circulation, the poem inhabited just the right medium for a satire on print: the dull, proliferating, choking commodity that degrades the world of the poem. Second, it materially entered the category of clandestine satire, and became kin in its very mode of transmission, not with Dryden's official print output, but with unprintable lampoons and libels on affairs of state. In practice, *Mac Flecknoe* rubbed shoulders with this kind of verse in several scriptorial miscellanies that now survive. For Love, the poem constitutes a 'holiday from print' in which Dryden brilliantly invades and possesses a hitherto alien mode, that of manuscript satire in the style of Whig wits and court lampooners of the Buckingham circle. It's a poem in which, Patterson

---

[82] On the authorship of *An Essay on Satire*, see Edward L. Saslow, 'The Rose Alley Ambuscade', *Restoration*, 26 (2002), 27–49; also *Poems*, 5: 684. Harold Love is unusual in assigning a significant role to Dryden (*English Clandestine Satire, 1660–1702* (Oxford: Oxford University Press, 2004), 83–4, 178–9). On scriptorial manuscripts of *Mac Flecknoe*, see *Poems*, 1: 306, 310.

[83] Love, *Scribal Publication*, esp. 177–95, 297–310.

[84] These are Hammond's informed estimates, *Making of Restoration Poetry*, 151–2; for the handsome production values of some copies, see his p. 52 (reproducing Brotherton Collection MS Lt 54).

adds, he shows signs of having the underground 'Painter' satires 'on his mind, or under his skin'.[85]

More significantly for present purposes, *Mac Flecknoe* also constitutes a holiday from allegiance: in no sense a practical move into opposition, but an imaginatively vigorous adoption, in the heat of composition, of the signature methods and postures of dissident satire. It's surprising that so few scholars have recognized the sheer political awkwardness of *Mac Flecknoe* in this respect: its lingering air of witty disaffection, as though Dryden had written a Whig poem in his sleep, or on his day off. Michael McKeon comes closest when wondering about early reception: 'did some read it as a libel on figures of state?' McKeon's suggestion is that Dryden foresaw or even invited this reading, and 'may well have seen fit to hide the ultimate referent of his mock epic under the allegorical cover of "literary" satire'.[86] Certainly, the waywardness of implication in the poem, its capacity to bleed out from the rivalries of poets to affairs of state, cannot be discounted. Dryden did not go into print with *Mac Flecknoe* until a piracy of 1682 forced his hand, and did not acknowledge authorship until after being fired as poet laureate.[87] At that point, there was little to lose, and perhaps even something to gain, by blurring his reputation as loyal Stuart panegyrist.

## Plays and parallels: Exclusion Crisis libel and the licensing lapse

If Dryden became increasingly self-conscious about the hermeneutics of censorship in his last years, it was above all because of *The Duke of Guise* (performed 1682, published 1683), a topical application tragedy that landed him, with his collaborator Nathaniel Lee, in trouble from all sides. This was a play of unusual political vehemence and

---

[85] Love, *Scribal Publication*, 147, and see also his *English Clandestine Satire*, 83, 178; Annabel Patterson, 'Dryden, Marvell, and the Painful Lesson of Laughter', in Claude Rawson and Aaron Santesso (eds), *John Dryden (1631–1700): His Politics, His Plays, and His Poets* (Newark: University of Delaware Press, 2004), 198–216 (206).

[86] Michael McKeon, *The Secret History of Domesticity: Public, Private, and the Division of Knowledge* (Baltimore: Johns Hopkins University Press, 2005), 409.

[87] Dryden, *Poems*, 1: 306, 310; Hammond, *Making of Restoration Poetry*, 152–3.

transparent meaning, and Dryden may have miscalculated because of the increasingly outspoken norms of discourse during the Exclusion Crisis, a period to which historians routinely date the origins of modern partisanship, and to which we owe the party labels 'Tory' and 'Whig'.[88] As he wrote in *Absalom and Achitophel*, satire was now a weapon of factional duelling—the swordplay metaphor is unmistakable—in which 'he who draws his pen for one party must expect to make enemies of the other' (*Poems*, 1: 450). And though at this point Dryden strikes a splendidly disingenuous pose of moderation, one in which his pen/sword is prevented 'from carrying too sharp an edge' (1: 451), this is a pose he abandons by the time of *The Medal: A Satire against Sedition* (1682). There Dryden calls frankly for the execution of the Whig leader the Earl of Shaftesbury, the 'restless' (and so by implication Cromwellian) Achitophel of the earlier poem.[89] Of the commemorative medal struck by the Whigs to celebrate the failure of Shaftesbury's indictment for treason, he provocatively writes that 'the head would be seen to more advantage if it were placed on a spike of the Tower, a little nearer to the sun' (*Poems*, 2: 10).

This was also a period (1679–85) when licensing was in abeyance, and there is ample evidence that booksellers and authors saw the lapse as an opportunity to test the boundaries of the publishable, not least in the briefly vibrant field of proto-pornography.[90] Randy Robertson estimates that across Charles II's reign as a whole, licensers suppressed

---

[88] See Abigail Williams, *Poetry and the Creation of a Whig Literary Culture, 1681–1714* (Oxford: Oxford University Press, 2005), 56–7; also her account of *Absalom and Achitophel* and *The Medal* in this context, 58–74.

[89] 'Restless, unfixed in principles and place, | In power unpleased, impatient of disgrace' (*Poems*, 1: 467; *Absalom and Achitophel*, lines 154–5); cf. *Poems of Marvell*, 273 (*Horatian Ode*, line 9). For Dryden's many echoes of the *Horatian Ode*, before as well as after its first printing, see *Poems*, 1: 64 n.

[90] See Thomas Keymer, 'Obscenity and the Erotics of Fiction', in Robert L. Caserio and Clement C. Hawes (eds), *The Cambridge History of the English Novel* (Cambridge: Cambridge University Press, 2012), 131–46 (133–5). Title counts depend on vagaries of survival, but book production appears to have increased quite sharply with the licensing lapse, and then dropped by almost 50% when licensing resumed (*Cambridge History of the Book in Britain*, 4: 783–4).

about 3 per cent of all publications excluding serials and periodicals, but this check to their activities in the reign's last years seemed to open up new possibilities for print.[91] Plays censored in performance could now flaunt their controversial status on the page by restoring cancelled lines to print editions and adding typographic emphasis: 'all that was expunged is Printed in the Italick Letter', as Shadwell explained to readers of *The Lancashire Witches*.[92] Yet if anything the lapse of licensing intensified risk for political writers, as competing authorities, the Whig city as much as the Tory court, turned to retrospective prosecution as the best alternative means of press control.[93]

The pillories were busy in these years, as indeed was the execution block in the case of Algernon Sidney, who was arraigned on a practical treason charge (a plot of 'killing the king and altering the government'), but whose Whig-republican *Discourses upon Government*, then still in manuscript, were enlisted as a decisive witness against him.[94] All kinds of heterodoxy, religious as much as political, were unleashed in print, while a rogues' gallery of conspirators, perjurers, and suborners joined various categories of book-trade offender in the sheriff's picture-frame. It was with an inspired flourish of urban pastoral that John Oldham imagined pillories sprouting up all over the city, yet somehow without deterring blasphemous libellers: 'No shame, nor loss of Ears can frighten these, | Were every Street a

---

[91] Robertson, *Censorship and Conflict*, 198; see also Robertson's *The British Index*, a catalogue of books and pamphlets censored between 1641 and 1700 (<http://www.academia.edu/1598680/The_British_Index>).

[92] Thomas Shadwell, *The Lancashire Witches* (1682), sig. A2; see Owen, *Restoration Theatre and Crisis*, 13.

[93] For the variety of charges used during this legally uncertain period (not only seditious libel and *scandalum magnatum* but also the proxy charge of unlicensed newsbook printing, still an available option as grounded in royal prerogative), see Philip Hamburger, 'The Development of the Law of Seditious Libel and the Control of the Press', *Stanford Law Review*, 37 (1985), 661–765 (682–90). Other makeshift strategies are described by Timothy Crist, 'Government Control of the Press after the Expiration of the Printing Act in 1679', *Publishing History*, 5 (1979), 49–77.

[94] Jonathan Scott, *Algernon Sidney and the Restoration Crisis, 1677–1683* (Cambridge: Cambridge University Press, 1991), 292, quoting Richard Stretton's letter of 31 March 1683; see also 313 and 329 for Judge Jeffreys's notorious ruling, of the *Discourses Concerning Government*, that 'scribere est agere' (to write is to act).

Grove of Pillories.'[95] A satire was devoted by Thomas Otway to seditious libel in the abstract, represented by Otway as a sinister mutant—'A Beast of Monstrous guise, and *LIBELL* was his name'— with inherent physical immunity to the fate of Prynne: 'Behold its Head of horrid form appears: | To spight the Pillory, it had no Ears.'[96] Topically minded consumers could buy commemorative prints of celebrity pilloryings like that of Titus Oates, fabricator-in-chief of the Popish Plot, when the law at last caught up with him in 1685. Partisan playing-cards for use in coffee-houses and taverns featured other egregious miscreants like Nathaniel Reading, a lawyer convicted of subornation during the Popish Plot investigations of 1679, and John Culliford, printer of, among other libels, an incendiary sequel to Marvell entitled *The Second Part of The Growth of Popery and Arbitrary Government* (1682) (Figure 1.2).[97] There were related book illustrations, even a tasteful range of ceramic ware (Figures 1.3, 1.4).

Women were not exempt from spectacular punishment, even when pleading their sex. Jane Curtis was imprisoned and fined, though she may have escaped the pillory, for publishing *A Satyr against In-justice: or, Sc[rog]gs upon Sc[rog]gs* (*c.*1679), a ballad probably composed by Stephen College, a Whig incendiary who was hanged for treason two years later (in part as author of another broadside, *A Ra-Ree Show* (1681), which ridiculed the king as a tricksy puppeteer and advocated pulling down the show).[98] Less fortunate than Curtis was

---

[95] *The Poems of John Oldham*, ed. Harold F. Brooks with Raman Selden (Oxford: Clarendon Press, 1987), 177 ('The Thirteenth Satyr of Juvenal, Imitated' (1682), lines 137–8).

[96] Thomas Otway, *The Poet's Complaint of His Muse, or, A Satyr against Libells* (1680), 9, 13.

[97] On Culliford or Cullyford, see von Maltzahn, *Marvell Chronology*, 232, 236–9; *The Second Part* is usually attributed to Robert Ferguson, though Culliford is named as author in one record (*CCD*, 2: 410). On playing-cards, see Tim Harris, *London Crowds in the Reign of Charles II: Propaganda and Politics from the Restoration until the Exclusion Crisis* (Cambridge: Cambridge University Press, 1990), esp. 108–13.

[98] For Curtis, see Paula McDowell, *The Women of Grub Street: Press, Politics, and Gender in the London Literary Marketplace, 1678–1730* (Oxford: Clarendon Press, 1998), 71–2, 91; for College, see Weber, *Paper Bullets*, 172–208, and the headnote to *A Ra-Ree Show* (1681) in *POAS*, 2: 425, quoting Narcissus Luttrell's note on his copy: 'A most scandalous libel against the government, for which and other things College was justly executed.'

**Figure 1.2** Playing-card of John Culliford in the pillory (c.1683–4), etching on pasteboard, from a pack depicting the Rye House Plot, © the Trustees of the British Museum. All rights reserved. Culliford printed *The Second Part of The Growth of Popery and Arbitrary Government* (1682), shown burning at his feet.

Elizabeth Cellier, a Catholic agitator who was acquitted of treason following the so-called Meal-Tub Plot of 1679, but convicted of libel soon afterwards for *Malice Defeated* (1680), a self-published pamphlet celebrating the brief triumph of her release (Figure 1.5).[99]

This is the period in which Dryden himself, his bruises fresh from Rose-Alley, came to be threatened with the pillory, albeit in the virtual arena of opposition diatribe and lampoon, not the real world of courts and prisons. In a retaliatory lampoon of 1682, a satirist who was almost certainly Shadwell moves on from gloating about the private retaliation of Rose-Alley to speculating about public retribution for

[99] See Penny Richards, 'A Life in Writing: Elizabeth Cellier and Print Culture', *Women's Writing*, 7.3 (2000), 411–25.

**Figure 1.3** Philopatris (Charles Blount?), *The Plot in a Dream: or, The Discoverer in Masquerade* (1681), copperplate engraving facing p. 148, © the Trustees of the British Museum. All rights reserved. The lower panels show the execution of William Staley, first victim of the Popish Plot trials, and the pillorying of Nathaniel Reading.

**Figure 1.4** Earthenware tile painted in manganese over a tin glaze (1680), © the Trustees of the British Museum. All rights reserved. Based on a playing-card illustration, the tile shows the attorney Nathaniel Reading being pilloried in Palace Yard, Westminster.

*The Medal*, specifically for the poem's attack on Whig jurymen who had defeated Tory efforts to convict Shaftesbury. Now Dryden was no more nor less than a 'Libeller' whose insolence, 'in comparing the Jury (that gave in *Ignoramus* to the Bill against our Noble Peer) to a Jury taken out of *Newgate*, deserves the Pillory'.[100] Shadwell can hardly have expected this outcome in practice, but punitive fantasies about

---

[100] Thomas Shadwell (?), *The Medal of John Bayes*, in *Complete Works of Shadwell*, 5: 250.

**Figure 1.5** Francis Barlow, design for a playing-card (*c.*1680), pen and brown ink drawing on paper, with grey wash over graphite, © the Trustees of the British Museum. All rights reserved. Sentenced to stand 'on' as opposed to 'in' the pillory, Elizabeth Cellier shields herself from projectiles.

privileged wits had an imaginative power of their own, laced with class antagonism. As Etherege's citizen shoemaker retorts when threatened with the pillory by Dorimant in *The Man of Mode* (1676), 'some of you deserve it, I'm sure, there are so many [libels], that our journeymen nowadays... sing nothing but your damned lampoons'.[101] For Shadwell, it was damaging enough to associate Dryden so relentlessly with sedition and shame, and to cast his verse as the epitome of prostituted truth and inverted justice. 'There is not so vile an employment, as that

---

[101] *The Plays of Sir George Etherege*, ed. Michael Cordner (Cambridge: Cambridge University Press, 1982), 229 (*The Man of Mode*, I.i).

of a Hired Libeller, an Executioner of mens Reputations', he protests: 'the Hangman is an Office of greater Dignity.'[102]

Dryden also seems to have underestimated the rapidly shifting sands of Exclusion Crisis politics: a miscalculation he shared with Aphra Behn, who was arrested (though not prosecuted) for the royalist epilogue she contributed to *Romulus and Hersilia*, an anonymous tragedy of August 1682.[103] The paradox is that from the court point of view the Toryism of *The Duke of Guise* was too assertive, as Dryden grew increasingly extremist while Lee overcompensated for his back catalogue of Whig tragedy, notably *Lucius Junius Brutus*, prohibited after a few performances in 1680 for the relish with which it dramatized the defeat of tyranny by republican virtue.[104] *The Duke of Guise* was even more emphatic in application, beginning with a forthright announcement that 'Our Play's a Parallel'.[105] It represents in unyieldingly hostile terms the disloyalty and sedition of powerful urban interest groups and the civic authorities they control, makes clear analogies between rebellious Guisards and Exclusionist Whigs, and ends by celebrating the assassination of a would-be usurper backed for the throne by the city. By the time the play entered rehearsal in July, reconciliation between Monmouth and the king seemed to be on the cards and the play was refused a performance licence, apparently at Monmouth's instigation. But there was also a sound political motive in keeping provocative Tory drama from the stage (not only *The Duke of Guise* but also its comic counterpart, John Crowne's *City Politiques*)

---

[102] *Complete Works of Shadwell*, 5: 249.

[103] Janet Todd, *The Secret Life of Aphra Behn* (New Brunswick: Rutgers University Press, 1997), 288–9.

[104] J. M. Armistead, 'Lee, Nathaniel (1645x52–1692), Playwright and Poet', *ODNB*.

[105] *The Works of John Dryden*, ed. E. N. Hooker and H. T. Swedenberg et al., 20 vols (Berkeley and Los Angeles: University of California Press, 1956–2002), 14: 210. The fullest account of this complex episode is still that of Vinton A. Dearing and Alan Roper in the California Dryden; see also Paulina Kewes's reading of *The Duke of Guise* as a work of Tory propaganda that 'explores the phenomenon to which it belongs' ('Dryden and the Staging of Popular Politics', in Paul Hammond and David Hopkins (ed.), *John Dryden: Tercentenary Essays* (Oxford: Clarendon Press, 2000), 57–91 (74)).

while the government tried to fix London's shrieval election in its favour.[106] Then Monmouth over-reached again and was briefly imprisoned in September, while the disputed election was settled and Shaftesbury went into hiding, at which point the play was on again by order of the Lord Chamberlain. In a phenomenon familiar to historians of censorship—Geoff Kemp notes 'the timeless paradox that censorship tends to increase interest and demand'[107]—it was now subject to avid public interest, alongside violent counter-attacks from the opposition press.

The pamphlet war that followed is a strange blend of no-holds-barred political polemic and literary-theoretical speculation. For Thomas Hunt, a radical lawyer who turns up again among the heroes of Defoe's *Hymn to the Pillory* (see below, p. 145), there was in fact nothing French, and nothing sixteenth-century, about *The Duke of Guise*, despite its ostensible setting. It was a frontal attack on modern Whiggism and the claims laid to autonomy by the municipal authorities, in which Dryden (Hunt assumes a single playwright) and the Tories for whom he speaks 'have already condemned the Charter and City, and have executed the Magistrates in Effigie upon the Stage, in a Play...intended most certainly to provoke the rabble into tumults and disorder'. In particular, Hunt emphasizes the line crossed by the play in not only staging but also recommending political assassination: 'Untill this age, never before, was an assassination invited, commended and encouraged upon a publick Theatre.'[108] This was not all, and here Hunt plays a lawyer's trick of surpassing cynicism. Since the logic of historical parallelism escapes authorial control, and any individual parallel contextually brings with it others, a play comparing Monmouth with the Duke of Guise could not be absolved of comparing Charles II with weak, murderous Henri III, or the future James II

[106] See Elaine M. McGirr, *Heroic Mode and Political Crisis, 1660–1745* (Newark: University of Delaware Press, 2009), 99–101; Owen, *Restoration Theatre and Crisis*, 12, 99.

[107] *CP*, 3: xvii. L'Estrange encountered the same problem as both censor and journalist, denying accusations that 'there may be some *Ill-Books*: But if you'd *let 'em alone*, they'd *Dye of themselves*: And besides; your taking *Notice* of them in the *Observator*, helps them off' (*Observator*, 11 December 1682).

[108] Thomas Hunt, *A Defence of the Charter, and Municipal Rights of the City of London* (1683), Appendix A in *Works of Dryden*, 14: 607.

with ambitious, unprincipled Henri of Navarre ('an unlucky and disastrous representation'). *The Duke of Guise* was thus objectionable from Tory as well as Whig standpoints. Dryden should be prosecuted by whatever means were to hand—and by singling out a couplet about 'pious fools' (written, as it happens, by Lee), Hunt in effect proposed a proxy charge of impiety, as easier to contrive than sedition: 'Such public Blasphemies against religion, never went unpunished in any Country or Age but this' (*Works of Dryden*, 14: 608, 609).

When Hunt's pamphlet was itself declared a libel (under pressure from L'Estrange's periodical the *Observator*, for its general case about City politics, not its local attack on *The Duke of Guise*), Hunt evaded the pillory by fleeing to Holland. The attack on Dryden was carried forward more directly in *Some Reflections upon the Pretended Parallel in the Play Called The Duke of Guise*, written in the first person singular, but apparently co-authored. Dryden may have been correct in attributing the lead role to Shadwell, who sets about his task of making points about both intention and meaning (first, that Dryden intends a parallel with modern politics; second, that the parallel is invalid) by undertaking close analysis of the play 'even to the very line'.[109] In practice, this must have meant repeat attendance at the play in performance, since the play-text was not yet printed. Lee is absolved as being Dryden's unwitting gull, a co-author deluded by 'the *old Serpent Bays*' (14: 612), so that when Shadwell seconds Hunt's call for prosecution, the proposed victim is emphatically Dryden alone: 'For certainly most exemplary Punishment is due to him for this most devilish Parallel [meaning the whole play]; and methinks Magistrates (that respect their Oaths and Office) should put the Law in Execution against this lewd Scribler' (14: 612). Before the end of Shadwell's pamphlet, the charge against Dryden has escalated to one of treason for likening Charles to the famously depraved Henri III, even if the parallel failed to stick: 'does not this Villain deserve to be hang'd, drawn, and quartered for his Intention?' (14: 617).

Lined up on the Tory side were L'Estrange and Dryden, the 'vile Observator' and 'renegade rhymer' whose names were now inseparable

---

[109] Thomas Shadwell (?), *Some Reflections upon the Pretended Parallel in the Play Called The Duke of Guise*, Appendix B in *Works of Dryden*, 14: 611.

in opposition satire.[110] L'Estrange devotes seven numbers of the *Observator* and a separate, free-standing response to Hunt's pamphlet, so inadvertently boosting Hunt's sales, it was alleged, by thousands of copies.[111] He concentrates his fire, however, on Hunt's case about municipal rights, and has little to say about *The Duke of Guise* beyond attacking Hunt's attempt to extend its analogies in unwelcome directions ('his unmannerly application of the Characters, and his framing of Parallels where little or no similitude can be found').[112] Developing this line, Dryden's sixty-page *Vindication* of *The Duke of Guise* is a masterpiece of equivocation which explicitly denies, while implicitly reinforcing, the analogy central to the play. Winn calls this pamphlet 'overlong and unwise', but if imprudent it is also ingenious, and it wastes few words.[113] Even on the title page, Dryden makes nuances of expression work for him by representing the play's parallel as 'Turn'd into a Seditious Libell against the KING and his ROYAL HIGHNESS, BY *Thomas Hunt* and the Authors of the *Reflections*' (*Works*, 14: 308). Seditious meaning, in other words, has not been written into the play by Dryden and Lee; it has been read into the play by Hunt and Shadwell, in which sense they, not he, were the authors of sedition—a move anticipating the so-called 'Gurney defence' of the 1790s, which located treasonable meaning in the interpretative acts of prosecuting lawyers, not in the text itself (see below, pp. 250–3).

In the body of the pamphlet, with a wiliness that is almost deconstructive, Dryden insists on the inaccessibility of authorial intention, on the responsibility of readers, not authors, for the meanings they find, and on the contingency of allegorical patterns that arise from natural historical recurrence as opposed to authorial agency. In any case, the Duke of Monmouth was a boy of 11 when Dryden first drafted the play, and personally unlike the Duke of Guise in ways Dryden rehearses at length, while simultaneously letting slip a range of contrary insinuations. The blasphemous couplet was by Lee, not

---

[110] Goldie, 'L'Estrange's *Observator*', 87, quoting *POAS*, 4: 318. See also *The Medal of John Bayes*, alleging that Dryden simply 'turn'd the *Observator* into Rime' (*Complete Works of Shadwell*, 5: 255).

[111] See *Works of Dryden*, 14: 497–8; Goldie, 'L'Estrange's *Observator*', 82.

[112] Roger L'Estrange, *The Lawyer Outlaw'd* (1683), 9.

[113] Winn, *Dryden and His World*, 383.

himself; it was placed in the mouth of the devil, so was not blasphemous at all but dramatically authentic; and more besides. All this is couched in phrasing of transcendent evasiveness, a pattern inaugurated when (on the charge of attacking Monmouth by analogy with Guise) Dryden finds it 'almost unnecessary to say, *It was not in my Thought*'—which on inspection is no denial at all, only a statement about whether or not he should make one (4: 310). It hardly helps when he then adds that 'as far as any one man can vouch for another, I do believe it was as little in Mr. Lee's', a comment rendered meaningless by three simultaneous dodges: the comparison with Dryden's thought about Monmouth, still not denied; the focus on Dryden's belief about Lee's thought, not the thought itself; the qualification about whether the thoughts of others can be known at all. Winn calls the *Vindication* 'the clearest instance of lying in his career', yet Dryden also seems keen to exhibit the lies to anyone capable of enjoying them.[114] Alongside this kind of dexterity, the standard defence mechanisms also invoked in the *Vindication*—joint authorship with another, the play as historical not fictional, the Monmouth–Guise parallel as incomplete—were child's play.

Deniability of political innuendo was at last being put to the test, and in a high-stakes context: a context in which, as Dryden alleges in his dedication to the play, literary attack-dogs of the Whig party were seeking to punish him and Lee as nothing less than substitutes for the King and Monmouth, since 'the greatest and the best of men are above their reach' (*Works*, 14: 209). In the *Vindication*, Dryden was ready with adroit and sophisticated, albeit supremely disingenuous, arguments to support his case. He was also ready with mocking counter-accusations, fortified no doubt by the fact that Hunt was already a fugitive, and he turns the allegation of seditious libel back against his opponents. As the debate proceeds, indeed, the term *seditious* becomes wholly unstable in signification, pulled between Whig and Tory interpretations, with Dryden insisting that work his enemies call seditious is in fact written 'for a *lawful establish'd Government* against *Anarchy*, *Innovation*, and *Sedition*'. More specifically, it's written against Whig dramatists who have 'made a *Play-house* more Seditious than a *Conventicle*' (14: 326, 312).

---

[114] Winn, *Dryden and His World*, 384; see also, on the 'not in my Thought' dodge, 383.

Punishment for these playwrights and their cheerleaders must not be escaped. Hunt's pamphlet was a catchpenny effort, a speculative foray into marketable political controversy in which Hunt 'is contented to expose the *Ears representative* of your *Party* [the Whigs] on a *Pillory*' (14: 328). As for Shadwell's account of Dryden as a lewd scribbler (*lewd* meaning base, ignorant, unprincipled), here the pot was calling the kettle black: 'let them put the Law in execution, against *leud Scriblers*, the *Mark* will be too *fair* upon a *Pillory*, for a *Turnip* or a *rotten Egg* to *miss* it'. Dryden continues with sneering mock-solicitude for the threat not only of crowd violence but also of official mutilation, being without 'Malice enough, to wish him so much harm; not so much as to have a Hair of his head perish, much less, that one whole side of it should be dismantled' (14: 345). Here is a beautifully menacing use of the word 'dismantled', one that looks forward to the disfigurement of the Lapith Celadon in Dryden's Ovid translations of the 1690s: 'His eyeballs rooted out are thrown to ground, | His nose dismantled in his mouth is found, | His jaws, cheek, front, one undistinguished wound' (*Poems*, 5: 445; 'The Twelfth Book of Ovid His *Metamorphoses*', lines 352–4). At the end of all this, it's hard to find much benevolence in Dryden's parting shot about mutilation, an anecdote about a Jacobean libeller who escapes hanging by charming the king in his final distich: '*Now God preserve our King, Queen, Prince and Peers,* | *And grant the Author long may wear his Ears*'.[115]

## Fable, history, translation: scourging by proxy

The self-consciousness is most pronounced in *The Hind and the Panther*, a nested sequence of Aesopian fables that Dryden prefaces with images of violent transformation and unregulated conflict: 'The nation is in too high a ferment for me to expect either fair war, or even so much as fair quarter, from a reader of the opposite party' (*Poems*, 3: 39). In this ferment, a condition of radical, perhaps even explosive, chemical change, Dryden adopts a mode which, for all its potential polyvalence, was associated especially with royalist political

[115] *Works of Dryden*, 14: 354. Dryden's source, unidentified by the California editors, is probably a letter of 8 October 1621 by James Howell (*Epistolae Ho-Elianae*, 2nd edn (1650), pt 2, p. 68).

encoding under Cromwellian censorship, and would become so again after the Glorious Revolution with L'Estrange's inescapably Jacobite *Fables, of Aesop* (1692).[116] Yet of course, when Dryden wrote, the Revolution had not yet happened, and in this respect the historical situation of the poem repeats that of *Heroic Stanzas*, with a constraint on expression that had less to do with present conditions than with anticipated future eventualities. As in 1659, regime change might be, and indeed would turn out to be, just around the corner, with retrospective incrimination a threat to consider. As one journalist bluntly put it after another such historical turn, that of 1714, 'What might lawfully be printed in Queen Anne's Reign is become Treason now'.[117]

Just this possibility was floated at the expense of both Dryden and L'Estrange in *Pendragon*, a hudibrastic lampoon that seems to have been written near the end of James II's reign, though it did not appear in print until 1698. In doggerel verse, the poem imagines the retribution that will follow the impending Whig revolution, when freedom blows in from Holland:

> For on so great an Alteration
> The Whipping-posts throughout the Nation,
> The Rods and Axes, Pill'ry, Gibbet,
> Will change their Side too, and distribute
> Due Punishments for old Abuses,
> On those who put them to wrong Uses.
> All this may come to pass, and rotten
> Eggs for a little may be gotten.[118]

---

[116] See Annabel Patterson, *Fables of Power: Aesopian Writing and Political History* (Durham: Duke University Press, 1991), esp. 85–94 (on John Ogilby's 1651 *Fables of Aesop Paraphras'd in Verse*), 95–105 (on *The Hind and the Panther*), 139–46 (on L'Estrange).

[117] P. B. J. Hyland, 'Liberty and Libel: Government and the Press during the Succession Crisis in Britain, 1712–1716', *English Historical Review*, 101 (1986), 863–88 (888), quoting the Jacobite author and printer Isaac Dalton in *Robin's Last Shift*, 31 March 1716. Dalton was warning Addison and Steele against complacent Whig triumphalism lest the Hanoverian settlement fail.

[118] *Pendragon; or, The Carpet Knight His Kalendar* (1698), 135. This lampoon is sometimes attributed to Thomas D'Urfey.

Here L'Estrange ('*Pendragon* with his Pen *dragoon'd*') is the main target of a punitive fantasy in which his past life supplying the pillory with libellers comes back to haunt him: an egg for an egg, a turnip for a turnip. But Dryden ('Old *Bays*') is also in play, specifically the mystifying fabulist of *The Hind and the Panther*, a poet who never quite spells out his meaning: 'But when he 'ad giv'n the Character | Of Hind and Panther, Fox and Bear, | And all sufficiently were seen, | He wisely shut them up again.'[119]

Throughout *The Hind and the Panther*, which concerns theological as well as political questions, Dryden emphasizes the vagaries of interpretation, and at one point worries about the stability of religious meaning under Protestantism, 'As long as words a different sense will bear, | And each may be his own Interpreter' (*Poems*, 3: 81; *HP*, i.462–3).[120] Yet in the poem's crucial third and final book, announced as an exercise in 'mysterious writ' (*Poems*, 3: 121; *HP*, iii.2), Dryden turns his poem over to just these vagaries. The concluding fable of the pigeons and the buzzard has none of the clarity with which L'Estrange would invest his analogous fable of 'The Kite, Hawk and Pigeons', published five years later, in which 'the *Pigeons* finding themselves Persecuted by the *Kite*, made Choice of the *Hawk* for their Guardian'; the hawk then chases off the harmless kite and devours the pigeons. This fable, L'Estrange concludes in a reflection far longer than the narrative itself, 'was never more Exactly Moralized than in our Broils of Famous Memory': a standard formulation for the civil wars, behind which L'Estrange uses pointed formulations like 'Enemy-Prince' to suggest William of Orange in 1688, not Cromwell in the 1640s.[121] Dryden writes in clear anticipation of this event, just as Behn so ominously did in *Oroonoko* (1688), where a flawed but noble divine-right king suffers judicial murder in a scene recalling the regicide while

---

[119] *Pendragon*, 6, 87, 88.

[120] It was 'a compleat Abstract of sixteen thousand Schoolmen from *Scotus* to *Bellarmin*', in Swift's famous jibe (*A Tale of a Tub and Other Works*, ed. Marcus Walsh (Cambridge: Cambridge University Press, 2010), 43). On Dryden's marked departure here from *Religio Laici* (1682), with its emphasis on the clarity of scripture, see Zwicker, *Politics and Language*, 127.

[121] Roger L'Estrange, *Fables, of Aesop and Other Eminent Mythologists* (1692), 21.

also suggesting the danger of imminent repetition.[122] Yet Dryden also renders his fable impossible to decode with specificity. In some respects the buzzard connotes William III, but in others his ambitious henchman Gilbert Burnet, and in others still a more generalized figure of usurpation without clear identifying features.[123] It's even impossible to tell what finally happens, for Dryden cleverly arrests the fable before its denouement unfolds, just as history itself was unresolved. The killing and eating are merely potential events, though all too likely, Dryden's wording suggests: 'Already he has tasted Pigeons' blood, | And may be tempted to his former fare | When this indulgent lord [James II] shall late to heaven repair' (*Poems*, 3: 180; iii.1280–2).

When it came, the bloodshed was on the Boyne and at Glencoe, not in Grubstreet. But the one book-trade execution of the 1690s, that of a Jacobite printer named William Anderton, sent out a sanguinary message, and throughout the decade press control was far more intensive than the Whig mythology of the Glorious Revolution as liberty triumphant would suggest. There was an especially marked crackdown in 1692–3.[124] In a notable anticipation of press control under Walpole in the 1720s and 1730s, when bribery sometimes replaced or at least sweetened intimidation, the most potentially damaging royalist writers were offered both sticks and carrots. L'Estrange was obviously incorrigible, and the early days of the Revolution saw him imprisoned in Newgate in 1688 for 'writing and dispersing treasonable papers against the government'. Excluded from the 1690 Indemnity Act, he was arrested again in 1691, and he still seemed worth arresting yet again in 1696, at the age of 80.[125] On the other hand, an attempt was clearly made to recruit Behn,

---

[122] See Richard Kroll, '"Tales of Love and Gallantry": The Politics of *Oroonoko*', *Huntington Library Quarterly*, 67.4 (2005), 573–605.

[123] See Zwicker, *Politics and Language*, 156–7, 229–30.

[124] See *CP*, 4: ix–x; Paul Monod, 'The Jacobite Press and English Censorship, 1689–95', in Eveline Cruickshanks and Edward Corp (eds), *The Stuart Court in Exile and the Jacobites* (London: Hambledon Press, 1995), 125–42; Paul Hopkins, 'Anderton, William (1663–1693), printer', *ODNB*.

[125] Harold Love, 'L'Estrange, Sir Roger (1616–1704), Author and Press Censor', *ODNB*, citing Kenyon MSS, 211. 'Sir *Roger* suffer'd for his Principles, bad as they were', as the novelist Samuel Richardson recalled when uneasily

whose last work, 'A Pindaric Poem to the Reverend Doctor Burnet, on the Honour He did Me of Enquiring after Me and My Muse', offers the new King's propaganda chief a rebuke of surpassing dignity. Burnet is praised for his 'Seraphick Quill! | That can by unperceptable degrees | Change every Notion, every Principle | To any Form', without Behn specifying whether the compliment indicates Burnet's power to sway readers, or merely the plasticity of his own principles. By contrast, Behn's own muse 'would endeavour fain to glide | With the fair prosperous Gale, and the full driving Tide | But Loyalty Commands with Pious Force, | That stops me in the thriving Course.'[126] She will not budge for Burnet, or for Burnet's cash.

Dryden lay somewhere between L'Estrange and Behn: less provocative and relentless than the former, but too fully committed to the outgoing regime, not least after his ill-timed conversion to Catholicism in 1685, for overtures of the kind made to Behn to be worth pressing far. Behn was merely a Tory extremist of a freelance, even loose-cannon, kind; Dryden's situation more closely resembled Milton's in 1660, as the mouthpiece of a defeated regime in some of its most controversial commitments. A panegyric did indeed appear as *The Address of John Dryden, Laureat to His Highness the Prince of Orange*, in which the poet renounces '*Rome* my Religion half an hour ago'. But this was of course a spoof, perhaps by Shadwell.[127] And though Dryden refers in one place to a political offer made to him with which he felt unable to comply, if any deal at all was struck, it was merely for quietism on his own part in exchange for security from the state: a deal he tested to the limit over the next few years.[128] Almost inevitably, he was stripped

---

justifying, in 1740, his admiration for L'Estrange's Aesop (*Early Works*, ed. Alexander Pettit (Cambridge: Cambridge University Press, 2012), 107).

[126] *The Works of Aphra Behn*, ed. Janet Todd, 7 vols (London: William Pickering, 1992), 1: 309 ('A Pindaric Poem to the Reverend Doctor Burnet', lines 70–3, 49–52).

[127] *Complete Works of Shadwell*, 5: 349.

[128] In a passage cancelled from the dedication to *King Arthur* (1691), and surviving by chance, the new regime is 'a Government which has hitherto protected me (and by a particular Favour wou'd have continued me what I was, if I could have comply'd with the Termes which were offered me)', qtd by Winn, *Dryden and His World*, 434. In this decade Dryden takes several opportunities to define his posture in terms of passive obedience and non-resistance. Though 'adhering to a lost Cause', he was 'no disturber of the Government', he writes in

of his offices as poet laureate and historiographer royal (to be replaced by Shadwell in both roles), constrained thereafter in his ability to write original verse on affairs of state, and closely watched as he resumed his theatrical career. At the instigation of the implacable Shadwell, a prologue of 1690 in which he compared expensive, unpredictable opera productions with expensive, unpredictable overseas wars was suppressed for seeming 'to have a double Meaning, and that Meaning to reflect on the Revolution'.[129] Which may have been vindictive on Shadwell's part, but looks fair enough as interpretation. Some of the prologue's meanings, indeed, are downright single, notably with reference to William III's war in Ireland, the taxes raised to fund it, and the slim prospects of troops getting paid 'Till rich from vanquished rebels you return; | And the fat spoils of Teague in triumph draw, | His firkin butter, and his usquebaugh' (*Poems*, 3: 233; 'Prologue to *The Prophetess*', lines 27–9).

Shadwell also seems to have been behind efforts to prohibit *Cleomenes* (1692), a Sparta-themed tragedy that Dryden freights with Jacobite innuendo, though in ways he sought to distinguish from the provocative directness of *The Duke of Guise*. 'Here is no Parallel to be found', his preface claims. *Cleomenes* was eventually approved without alteration by the Lord Chamberlain, whose complicated posture towards Dryden (as both private patron and official censor) is a reminder that backroom negotiation as much as outright confrontation remained part of the dynamics of censorship throughout the period. But *Cleomenes* was then 'garbled ... by the Superiours of the Play-House', whose 'Zeal for the Government is such, that they had rather lose the best Poetry in the World, than give the least Suspicion of their Loyalty'. Dryden called the effect on his text a kind of

---

his 1690 dedication to *Amphitryon* (*Works of Dryden*, 15: 224); in a letter of 1699, officials must be 'content with my acquiescence under the present Government, & forbearing satire on it' (*Letters of John Dryden*, ed. Charles E. Ward (Durham, NC: Duke University Press), 123).

[129] *Works of Dryden*, 3: 508, quoting Shadwell's words as reported in John Oldmixon's *Muses Mercury*, January 1707; for the plausibility of the anecdote, see Winn, *Dryden and His World*, 444 n.

castration, tending 'to geld it so clearly in some places, that they took away the very Manhood of it' (*Works*, 16: 79).[130]

While pushing the envelope in these ways, however, Dryden was also very plainly biting his lip. Just how much further he might have gone, and decided against going, may be measured by the limit case of *Tarquin and Tullia* (1689), an anonymous, illicitly published broadside that was attributed to Dryden in print soon after his death, though in fact it was the work of a young Jacobite hothead, Arthur Maynwaring.[131] Several things are remarkable about Maynwaring's poem, which excoriates William and Mary by analogy with the usurper Tarquin and his parricidal wife as they overthrow her father Tullius, the legitimate Roman king. The first is Maynwaring's deft mimicry of Dryden's satirical mode, from emphatic use of interspersed triplets to extended character assassinations on the model of *Absalom and Achitophel*. One victim is John Churchill, the future Duke of Marlborough, whose defection to William was a defining moment of the Revolution; another is Burnet, 'A prophet deep in godly faction read; | A sycophant that knew the modish way | To cant and plot, to flatter and betray'.[132] The most striking feature of *Tarquin and Tullia* is the full-blooded directness of its assault on the incoming monarchs, with nothing to cloud or qualify present application of a past world 'When children used their parents to dethrone, | And gnawed their way like vipers to a crown' (*POAS*, 5: 47). This distich was a startling reflection on Tullia/Mary, but the poem reserves its most scathing tones for Tarquin/William: 'Too hard to melt, too wicked to repent; | Cruel in deeds, more merciless in will, | And blest with natural delight in ill' (5: 53). Like *The Hind and the Panther*'s predatory buzzard, he sows groundless fears of tyranny by Tullius/James in order to establish the real thing himself.

---

[130] On the politics of *Cleomenes*, see Howard Erskine-Hill, *Poetry of Opposition and Revolution: Dryden to Wordsworth* (Oxford: Clarendon Press, 1996), 24–8; also David Bywaters (who sees the play as conciliatory), *Dryden in Revolutionary England* (Berkeley and Los Angeles: University of California Press, 1991), 93–100.

[131] For the attribution to Dryden in the 1704 volume of *Poems on Affairs of State*, see Dryden, *Poems*, 5: 287, 686. With adroit footwork, Maynwaring would later reinvent himself as a strident Whig propagandist and leading Kit-Kat.

[132] Arthur Maynwaring, *Tarquin and Tullia* (1689), in *POAS*, 5: 48.

It can be no surprise that this poem attracted official notice when first published, though it took the authorities two years to catch up with the printer, William Cannyn or Canning, who was said to have gone unmolested for so long 'upon the consideration of some tokens and gratuities' to the new inspector of printing presses, Robert 'Hog' Stephens, a notorious former henchman of L'Estrange.[133] In 1691 an informant listed *Tarquin and Tullia* among the 'treasonable pamphlets' and 'seditious bookes' printed by Canning at his official premises and a secret press elsewhere, and he was locked up in Newgate by the end of the year.[134] Reckless but well-connected Maynwaring appears to have escaped attention for both this and *The King of Hearts* (1690), another verse libel that sounded enough like Dryden for the normally well-informed Tonson to suspect him as author.[135] The fact that poems of this kind called Dryden so readily to mind leaves no doubt of his closeness to the mode of verse sedition in the 1690s, not least in the eyes of contemporaries. Yet at the same time, these forthright libels define for us a line that Dryden occasionally touched but never crossed. Instead, he could subtly exploit the precedents set by poems like *Tarquin and Tullia*, as when he slips into his great Virgil edition of 1697 a passage about the justice of Tarquin's fall that draws silently on Maynwaring's now notorious parallel with William III.[136]

Dryden's remaining creative outlet was translation, where meaning was deniable as the preserve of an ancient or medieval poet as opposed to his modern conduit: an argument Dryden had already rehearsed for the tendentious final fables of *The Hind and the Panther*, 'at which I hope no reader of either party will be scandalized, because they are not of my invention, but as old...as the times of Boccace

---

[133] *CCD*, 3: 108. For the appalling Stephens, see Leona Rostenberg, 'Robert Stephens, Messenger of the Press: An Episode in 17th-Century Censorship', *Papers of the Bibliographical Society of America*, 49.2 (1955), 131–52.

[134] *CCD*, 3: 114. At this point Canning, 'about 23 years old...of a fresh coulourd round face and smileing looks', disappears from the historical record.

[135] 'This Poem was said to be Mr. Dryden's, and He was charg'd with it by Mr. Tonson, but he disown'd it...and Nam'd Mr. Maynwaring' (John Oldmixon (ed.), *The Life and Posthumous Works of Arthur Maynwaring, Esq.* (1715), 14).

[136] See Zwicker, *Politics and Language*, 182–3, 231; also, for Dryden's *Aeneid* as Jacobite epic, Murray G. H. Pittock, *Poetry and Jacobite Politics in Eighteenth-Century Britain and Ireland* (Cambridge: Cambridge University Press, 1994), 101–5.

and Chaucer' (*Poems*, 3: 45). This explanation may not cover the concentrated gloom with which, probably in 1689, he translated a neo-Latin epitaph on the fallen Jacobite leader Viscount Dundee, where 'New people fill the land now thou art gone, | New gods the temples, and new kings the throne' (*Poems*, 3: 219). But 'Upon the Death of the Viscount Dundee' remained in manuscript until 1704, albeit with wide circulation (or so an unusually large number of scribal witnesses—twenty, even more than for *Mac Flecknoe*—would suggest).[137] In print, Dryden consistently stresses the antiquity of seditious meaning, and this seems to have been the legitimating assumption behind his 1692 translation of Juvenal's third satire, a controlled rant about corruption and misrule in imperial Rome. This translation proceeds without the flamboyant topicality of Oldham's 1682 version of Satire 3 (which targets the conspiratorial politics of the Exclusion Crisis) or Johnson's anti-Walpole adaptation of 1738 (see below, pp. 208–13). Even so, the relish with which Dryden evokes ancient evils that were now also staple themes of Jacobite protest—the power, especially, of self-serving, self-enriching grandees 'who in full assemblies have the knack | Of turning truth to lies, and white to black'—has unmistakable contemporary resonance. Moreover, couplets with no textual basis in Juvenal's Latin crop up from time to time, not least to voice the scorn of a discarded poet for usurping, duplicitous rulers: ''Tis time to give my just disdain a vent, | And cursing, leave so base a government' (*Poems*, 4: 23, 22; iii.54–5, 43–4). As a whole, Dryden's rendering of his original source stops short of what he elsewhere calls the 'libertine' mode of imitation, the mode in which Oldham had openly satirized Whiggish London a decade earlier: its noisy 'Factions' and artful 'Plot-mongers', its devious 'City-Traders', its mutinous 'Silk-Weavers'.[138] But this was certainly what Dryden referred to on the same occasion as 'translation with... latitude' (*Poems*, 1: 387, 390); it was also translation with attitude.

Those careful distinctions about modes of translation and their varying degrees of freedom and creative surplus are from Dryden's 1680 preface to *Ovid's Epistles*. In the Juvenal edition, his prefatory 'Discourse Concerning the Original and Progress of Satire' is a more

---

[137] Love, *English Clandestine Satire*, 178.

[138] *Poems of Oldham*, 247, 248, 250, 252 ('A Satyr, in Imitation of the Third of Juvenal' (1682), lines 11, 38, 114, 183).

elaborate and sophisticated essay, long seen as a founding document of modern literary criticism. Significant for present purposes is the extent to which the theory of satire outlined in the 'Discourse' not only functions locally to encourage a reading of the translation to follow as politically charged, but also becomes inextricable in Dryden's hands from a theory of censorship and functional ambiguity. Something similar was attempted by L'Estrange in the preface to his Aesop edition the same year, when he recommends literary indirection or 'a Train of Mystery and Circumlocution' not only as a strategy for conveying forbidden meanings but also on grounds of rhetorical impact.[139] Earlier, at the onset of his career as licenser, L'Estrange had expressed special anxiety about open polemics 'written in times of *Freedom*, and Menag'd by great *Masters* of the Popular Stile, [which] speak *playner*, and strike *homer* to the *Capacity* and *Humour* of the *Multitude*; whereas they that write in the fear of a *Law*, are forc'd to cover their Meaning under *Ambiguities*, and *Hints*, to the greater Hazzard of the *Libeller*, than of the *Publique*'.[140] But in his new post-Revolution guise as a libeller himself—as gamekeeper turned poacher—he privileges instead a mode of indirection that will satisfy licensers and activate readers at a single stroke: 'For there's Nothing makes a Deeper Impression upon the Minds of Men, or comes more Lively to their Understanding, then Those Instructive Notices that are Convey'd to them by Glances, Insinuations, and Surprize; and under the Cover of some *Allegory* or *Riddle*.'[141] Readers become imaginatively complicit in the construction of seditious meaning, which thus impresses itself on the mind—or, as Blake was to put it with reference to Aesop a century later, rouses the faculties to act.[142] In the fables themselves, L'Estrange resumes this emphasis on interpretative challenge, cognitive activation, and the enduring rhetorical gains.

---

[139] L'Estrange, *Fables, of Aesop*, sig. A2.

[140] L'Estrange, *Considerations and Proposals in Order to the Regulation of the Press* (1663), in *CP*, 3: 34.

[141] L'Estrange, *Fables, of Aesop*, sig. A2v.

[142] 'The wisest of the Ancients consider'd what is not too Explicit as the fittest for Instruction because it rouzes the faculties to act. I name Moses, Solomon, Esop, Homer, Plato' (*Complete Poetry and Prose of William Blake*, ed. David V. Erdman, revised edn (Berkeley and Los Angeles: University of California Press, 2008), 702 (to John Trusler, 23 August 1799).

'The very Study to Unriddle a Mystery, furnishes the Memory with more Tokens to remember it by', he writes in his reflection on 'A Father and Sons': 'A Tale in Emblem sinks Deeper, where the Life and Spirit of it is Insinuated by a kind of Biass [i.e. obliqueness] and Surprize.'[143]

This is very much the process that Dryden too seeks to engineer in practice, and it's no doubt relevant to the strategy that his Tonson-published Juvenal volume—the same goes for L'Estrange's folio Aesop—was a lavish, expensive production, aimed at a sophisticated, leisured readership. With their elite implied audience, moreover, these works were as far as could be from the street pamphleteering that preoccupied anxious officials during the crackdown that claimed Anderton's life (and also involved arrest for Charles Leslie, Defoe's main Tory antagonist in the next decade). Two things especially should be pulled out of the 'Discourse' in this context. The first is Dryden's awareness of censorship as a historical fact about imperial Rome, and his desire to keep it in the minds of the modern reader. In a passage drawing heavily on Tacitus,[144] he explains the historical circumstances that required Augustus to control lampoons, libels, and satires by reinstituting a censorship regime backed by capital punishment; he makes this explanation, moreover, in terms that connote William III and his new subjects as much as Augustus and the Romans, a 'conquered people [who] could not possibly have forgotten the usurpation of that prince upon their freedom, nor the violent methods which he had used in the compassing of that vast design' (*Poems*, 3: 416–17). For Dryden, it's in this context of Augustan censorship, and not only as a matter of personal disposition, that Horace's focus on 'the ridiculing of petty vices and common follies', in preference to 'the lashing of greater crimes', is best explained (*Poems*, 3: 419).

This emphasis on historical conditions, not innate temperament, applies no less to Juvenal, and as he develops his famous distinction between laughing Horace and railing Juvenal, Dryden represents

[143] L'Estrange, *Fables, of Aesop*, 102.
[144] For the relationship between the 'Discourse' and the Jacobite-inflected *Annals and History of Cornelius Tacitus* (1698) on which Dryden collaborated with L'Estrange and others, see Steven N. Zwicker and David Bywaters, 'Politics and Translation: The English Tacitus of 1698', *Huntington Library Quarterly*, 52.3 (1989), 319–46.

Juvenal as driven to resist and circumvent censorship, where Horace had largely acquiesced. Part of the difference in tone and target is that Augustus, for all his severities against authors, understood the need to rule Rome with moderation, in which context 'Horace was a mild admonisher, a court satirist, fit for... gentle times'. For Juvenal, by contrast, the reign of Domitian 'was an age that deserved a more severe chastisement. Vices were more gross and open, more flagitious, more encouraged by the example of a tyrant; and more protected by his authority' (*Poems*, 3: 420–1). Juvenal's strategy in response, as Dryden represents it, is an affectation of historical focus that renders the topicality of his satire deniable, yet at the same time inevitable through the force of implied analogy: 'Therefore, wheresoever Juvenal mentions Nero he means Domitian, whom he dares not attack in his own person, but scourges him by proxy' (*Poems*, 3: 421).

The question begged here, and implicitly answered, is why Dryden, having translated Horace under Charles II, should now be turning his own attention to Juvenal under William III. He reinforces the answer in two ways. First, if Juvenal is the great prototype of satire under tyranny and in defiance of censorship, his usefulness to modern writers lies in the ambiguities he was forced to cultivate, and the interpretative possibilities he offers. Where meaning is 'crabbed' in Persius (the third great exemplary poet of the 'Discourse'), it is 'copious' in Juvenal, and here Dryden quotes a telling *bon mot* from the Jacobean translator Barten Holyday: 'in Persius the difficulty is to find a meaning, in Juvenal to choose a meaning' (*Poems*, 3: 427). Second, Dryden ends by acknowledging that the terms in which he renders Juvenal will often seem incongruously modern. Stylistically, he and his fellow translators have sought to make Juvenal 'speak that kind of English which he would have spoken had he lived in England, and had written to this age'; semantically, 'if sometimes any of us... make him express the customs and manners of our native country rather than of Rome; 'tis either when there was some kind of analogy betwixt their customs and ours, or when... we give him those manners which are familiar to us' (*Poems*, 3: 449–50). By this late stage of the 'Discourse', it can fool no one that Dryden presents these forays into translation with latitude as occasional unfortunate lapses, in need of apology. Instead, we've been conditioned to read the translation that follows as one in which, wheresoever Juvenal mentions Nero, we must now take him to mean

William III, and to scourge William by proxy. From there it becomes a simple matter to read the satires as always on the verge of topical reflection, a tendency Dryden encourages further with jarring forays into modern parlance. In Satire 3, the corrupted senators who specialize in 'turning truth to lies, and white to black' also turn out, with more specifically anachronistic implication, to 'rent the fishery' and 'oppress the poor | By farmed excise'. Unmistakably, the senators suggest the most modern and modernizing of Williamite targets, the Whiggish engineers of financial revolution, with their innovative instruments and kleptocratic schemes: 'All this for gain: for gain they sell their very head' (*Poems*, 4: 23; iii.55–60).

It's in this layering of implication that the genius of Dryden's Juvenal translation lies, just as it's in the discipline of writing under the sign of censorship that his political poetry more broadly achieves its complexity and power. Whether stopping short at the brink of meaning, or rendering it strategically faint or double, or turning meaning into something that readers have to choose, Dryden navigated an environment of fluctuating constraints on expression with great technical virtuosity and formidable rhetorical impact. In this respect, Voltaire was gloriously wrong in the celebrated letter he wrote against censorship in 1733, just a year before his *Lettres philosophiques* (the French version of *Letters Concerning the English Nation*) was publicly burned by the hangman: 'Had there been a literary censorship in Rome, we should have had to-day neither Horace, Juvenal, nor the philosophical works of Cicero. If Milton, Dryden, Pope, and Locke had not been free, England would have had neither poets nor philosophers; there is something positively Turkish in proscribing printing; and hampering it is proscription.'[145] For Dryden, there emphatically *was* a literary censorship in imperial Rome, as there was again in Restoration and Williamite England. Yet this censorship

---

[145] 'S'il y'avait eu une inquisition littéraire à Rome, nous n'aurions aujourd'hui ni Horace, ni Juvénal, ni les œuvres philosophiques de Cicéron. Si Milton, Dryden, Pope, et Locke n'avaient pas été libres, l'Angleterre n'aurait eu ni des poètes ni des philosophes: il y a je ne sais quoi de turc à proscrire l'imprimerie; et c'est la proscrire, que la trop gêner' (Voltaire, *Lettre à un premier commis*, ed. Pierre Rétat, in *Œuvres de 1732–1733* (*Œuvres complètes*, Vol. 9), ed. O. R. Taylor et al. (Oxford: Voltaire Foundation, 1999), 319.

was of a kind to energize poets and enrich their verse as much, perhaps indeed more, than it hampered or proscribed literary creativity. In this sense—taking poetry to be a delicate, complex art of indirection and implication—we might legitimately turn things around. Had Dryden, and for that matter Milton or Pope, been free, England would have had no poets.

# 2
# 1700–1740
# Libels in Hieroglyphics: Pope, Defoe

Voltaire's assumption that the England of Dryden and Pope was a zone of authorial freedom and safety—if his point was more than a rhetorical flourish—should be seen in comparative context: comparative in both time and place. It's true that in seditious libel and related cases the severities experienced in the pillory by Star Chamber victims of the 1630s like Prynne or Lilburne, or for that matter Cromwell-era dissidents like Nayler, were rare after the Restoration—though the odd printer continued to be executed for treason (*pour encourager les autres*, Voltaire might have said). Corporal punishment persisted into the eighteenth century in extreme cases of forgery, that other textual perversion of official truth.[1] But the last book-trade mutilation was probably in 1678, when 'the translator of the gazette into French [had] his ears cut off in the Pillory for misrendering his Majesty's proclamation'. Authorial floggings were rare after the Glorious Revolution, when the 1686 ordeal of the Whig propagandist Samuel 'Julian' Johnson—whipped at the cart's tail from Newgate to Tyburn—was retrospectively declared 'illegal and cruel'.[2] Courts occasionally flouted this precedent: a pamphleteer was whipped in 1702; another, a

---

[1] See below, p. 107, for Pope's malicious jokes about the forger Japhet Crook. Earlier, it may have been Defoe who applauded the 'wholesome severity' recently used in Ireland on two malefactors who 'stood in the Pillory, and had their Ears cut off, and their Noses slit for Forgery' (*Mercurius Politicus* (August 1717), 520; for Defoe's role in this newspaper, see P. N. Furbank and W. R. Owens, *A Political Biography of Daniel Defoe* (London: Pickering & Chatto, 2006), 159–61, 169–71).

[2] *CCD*, 2: 215–16; 3: 64.

---

*Poetics of the Pillory: English Literature and Seditious Libel, 1660–1820.* Thomas Keymer, Oxford University Press (2019). © Thomas Keymer.
DOI: 10.1093/oso/9780198744498.001.0001

nonjuring cleric, had to petition for remission of whipping in 1717.[3] Several times during Queen Anne's reign, mob violence against seditious libellers proved more injurious in practice than judicially directed mutilation. Yet at least the optics of the pillory were changing in its role as an instrument of press control, with corporal punishment informally outsourced to the crowd.

It's also true that eighteenth-century Britain was nothing like the centralized, censoring absolutist state described in Robert Darnton's studies of *ancien-régime* France, with its meticulous oversight of literary production and its vast trade in smuggled print from Switzerland or Holland. Pre-publication licensing, always a leaky sieve, was now a thing of the past in England, whereas in France elaborate mechanisms remained at work for controlling print, albeit not, Darnton contends, in ways that were always malign.[4] Both these reference points—the English past, the French present—came into play as writers extolled the liberty of the press in eighteenth-century Britain. In his urbane argument for authorial freedom of raillery and wit, the third Earl of Shaftesbury—grandson of Dryden's factious Achitophel—sees censorship as beneath the dignity of a civilized modern government, and as a clumsy, counter-productive means of addressing dissent. Suppose we were to prohibit the excesses of love poetry or amatory fiction, Shaftesbury muses: 'we might perhaps see a new *Arcadia* arising out of this heavy Persecution: Old People and Young wou'd be seiz'd with a versifying Spirit: We shou'd have Field-Conventicles of Lovers and Poets.'[5] In the Elizabethan and Stuart volumes of his *History of England*, Hume emphasizes the brutalities inflicted on dissident writers, though he also warns (in the case of Prynne) against projecting enlightened values back on times when freedom of the press was an

---

[3] C. E. A. Cheesman, 'Fuller, William (1670–1733)', *ODNB*; Robert D. Cornwall, 'Howell, Laurence (c.1664–1720)', *ODNB*.

[4] See especially Robert Darnton, *The Forbidden Best-Sellers of Pre-Revolutionary France* (New York: Norton, 1995), and his *The Corpus of Clandestine Literature in France, 1769–1789* (New York: Norton, 1995). Darnton emphasizes the sometimes supportive role of *ancien-régime* censors in *Censors at Work: How States Shaped Literature* (New York: Norton, 2014), 23–86.

[5] Anthony Ashley Cooper, 3rd Earl of Shaftesbury, *Characteristicks of Men, Manners, Opinions, Times*, ed. Philip Ayres (Oxford: Clarendon Press, 1999), 1: 16 ('A Letter Concerning Enthusiasm', 1708).

alien concept. Now, by contrast, 'nothing is more apt to surprize a foreigner, than the extreme liberty, which we enjoy in this country, of communicating whatever we please to the public, and of openly censuring every measure, entered into by the king or his ministers'.[6] Hume's enthusiasm was eroded by the ferocity of Wilkes, Junius, and other radical journalists of the 1760s, but even in the final (posthumous) version of the essay just quoted, in which 'the unbounded liberty of the press' becomes an 'evil' in need of 'suitable remedy', this liberty remains an inherent component of a polity predicated on balanced powers.[7]

The assumption has stuck, above all in the Whig historical tradition, though not only there. For Macaulay, the public of 1695 was only 'beginning dimly to perceive how closely civil freedom and freedom of conscience are connected with freedom of discussion', and he was dismayed that parliamentary debates at the time turned on petty questions of interest and privilege, not liberty in the abstract. Yet the lapse of licensing was momentous nonetheless, a watershed in which 'English literature was emancipated, and emancipated for ever, from the control of the government'.[8] This liberalization narrative was influentially restated in the postwar years by F. S. Siebert, and it underpins influential textbooks such as John Feather's *A History of British Publishing*, in which, following the Glorious Revolution, free access to oppositional print became 'an important birthright to the Briton'. Constraints persisted, but their exercise was infrequent and mild, and 'publishers operated in a free market and in an intellectual and political atmosphere which generally favoured freedom of expression'.[9]

---

[6] David Hume, *The History of England from the Invasion of Julius Caesar to the Revolution in 1688*, intr. W. B. Todd, 6 vols (Indianapolis: Liberty Fund, 1983), 5: 240; *Essays Moral, Political, and Literary*, ed. Eugene F. Miller, revised edn (Indianapolis: Liberty Fund, 1985), 9 ('Of the Liberty of the Press', 1741).

[7] See Donald Thomas, *A Long Time Burning: The History of Literary Censorship in England* (New York: Praeger, 1969), 2.

[8] *The Works of Lord Macaulay, Complete*, ed. Lady Trevelyan, 8 vols (1866), 3: 633; 4: 126.

[9] F. S. Siebert, *Freedom of the Press in England, 1476–1776: The Rise and Decline of Governmental Controls* (Urbana: University of Illinois Press, 1952); John Feather, *A History of British Publishing* (London: Routledge, 1988), 87, 88. More specifically and

The story takes another form in Jürgen Habermas's classic account of the origins of the public sphere, a central component of which is the absence of licensing, or an 'elimination of the institution of censorship' that made possible the 'influx of rational-critical arguments into the press'. Recent scholarship has emphasized the rowdy, factious incivility of the spaces and organs on which Habermas bases his narrative, and his serene view of coffee-houses would have startled officials who fretted at the time about what went on inside them. Overall, however, Habermas's account of the salutary consequences for print of public opinion and its institutions, and his emphasis on the 'unique liberties' of authors and the press in eighteenth-century Britain, has lost little traction.[10] Darnton is more measured and alert to counter-currents within censorship systems, but he too emphasizes the permissiveness of press control in Britain by contrast with Bourbon France. 'The English enjoyed something close to freedom of the press, despite the repressive effect of prosecution for seditious libel', Darnton writes, 'while prepublication censorship and the book police inhibited the French trade, despite the opening up of legal loopholes such as *permissions tacites* (permission to publish books without official approbation by a censor).'[11]

Yet celebratory narratives of emergent liberty of expression miss much of the story, resting as they do on a definition of censorship that

---

persuasively, a new study by Trevor Ross dates the entrenchment of liberty of expression as a national value to the period after 1760: see his *Writing in Public: Literature and the Liberty of the Press in Eighteenth-Century Britain* (Baltimore: Johns Hopkins University Press, 2018).

[10] Jürgen Habermas, *The Structural Transformation of the Public Sphere*, trans. Thomas Burger with Frederick Lawrence (Cambridge: Polity Press, 1989), 58, 59. Anxiety about London coffee-houses became acute in the 1690s, which saw a crackdown on 'seditious Newsmongers and Incendiaryes' who 'dayly resort to Coffee houses within the City of London...on purpose to spread false and seditious reports' (SP 44/99, fo. 19, 17 February 1691). For recent challenges to Habermas, see Brian Cowan, 'Making Publics and Making Novels', in J. A. Downie (ed.), *The Oxford Handbook of the Eighteenth-Century Novel* (Oxford: Oxford University Press, 2016), 55–70.

[11] Robert Darnton, '"What is the History of Books?" Revisited', *Modern Intellectual History* 4:3 (2007), 495–508; see also Darnton's reinforcement of this contrast in *Censors at Work*, 96 and *passim*.

limits the term to the mere provision or refusal of a publication licence, with or without expurgation, and excludes the crucial role of post-publication retribution. The alternative view is one in which 1695 marked not an abolition of press control, merely a shift in method. As Mark Goldie insists in his account of the period to 1720, in practice 'the lapse of licensing is something of a mirage, or distraction, in the history of press liberty': one best viewed as a tactical retreat by public authorities who could trust instead to extensive powers of post-publication restraint.[12] So yes, press licensing did indeed cease in 1695, and over time what seemed at first to be a temporary lapse became a permanent state by default. Yet it would be hard to explain the lapse as a matter of conscious, liberal-minded abolition, and it was hostility to monopolistic privilege, not commitment to free expression, that motivated most criticism of the 1662 legislation.[13] At least nine legislative attempts were made to reintroduce licensing between 1695 and 1704, and it was one such bill that provoked Defoe's *Essay on the Regulation of the Press*.[14] To judge from a manuscript in Shaftesbury's hand, a draft clause targeting Jacobite print following the 1701 Act of Settlement (which lined up the Hanoverian succession), even he seems to have countenanced censorship legislation in times of need.[15]

Powers of proscription and general warrants could still be employed after 1695, as they vigorously were by Secretary of State Bolingbroke during his 1711 campaign against the Whig press,[16] and new legislation was framed to inhibit dissident print by other means. This includes not only obvious measures like the new statutes passed concerning blasphemy (1698) and treason (1707), the latter of which explicitly targeted the printed expression of Jacobitism, and was used

---

[12] *CP*, 4: xv.

[13] Ian Higgins, 'Censorship, Libel and Self-Censorship', in Paddy Bullard and James McLaverty (eds), *Jonathan Swift and the Eighteenth-Century Book* (Cambridge: Cambridge University Press, 2013), 179–98 (180).

[14] *CP*, 4: xii; on Defoe's *Essay*, see below, pp. 121–2.

[15] Anthony Ashley Cooper, 3rd Earl of Shaftesbury, 'For the Further Prevention of Printing Seditious Books and Pamphlets' (1702), in *CP*, 4: 283.

[16] P. B. J. Hyland, 'Liberty and Libel: Government and the Press during the Succession Crisis in Britain, 1712–1716', *English Historical Review*, 101 (1986), 863–88 (865).

to hang a printer in 1719.[17] Also of importance were the Copyright Act of 1710, which required identification of ownership in literary property, and the Stamp Act of 1712 (Bolingbroke's brainchild), which stipulated that pamphlets carry printers' or publishers' names, and imposed disproportionate taxation on popular print, always a prime concern in the official mind.[18] These were not simply commercial or fiscal statutes, in other words. Insofar as they made print more expensive and its source more traceable, they were instruments of censorship. 'Grubstreet is dead and gone', wrote Swift in the wake of the Stamp Act, though he wasn't complaining.[19]

In the second quarter of the century, a further challenge to liberalization narratives comes with Walpole's Stage Licensing Act of 1737, which established formal pre-censorship of drama, including a prohibition on improvisation, and remained in force until the Theatres Regulation Act of 1843, which in turn carried forward certain 1737 provisions into the 1960s. One reason why this legislation aroused such alarm is that it was widely suspected to be a stalking-horse for reintroduced press licensing, with the satire of Fielding again a leading provocation (see below, pp. 184–91). The move never came, Walpole fell from power, and plays banned from the stage continued to appear in print; some were even planned as publishing ventures, contrived to elicit performance prohibition and so boost print sales.[20]

---

[17] *CP*, 4: xvii; on the printer John Matthews, see below, p. 168. Strictly speaking (though anything would do), the statute Matthews fell foul of was not the Treason Act (7 Ann. c. 21), as is sometimes stated, but the Succession to the Crown Act (6 Ann. c. 41), which makes guilty of treason anyone who 'by writing or printing' supports the claims of 'the pretended prince of Wales, who now styles himself... James the Third'.

[18] John Feather, 'The English Book Trade and the Law, 1695–1799', *Publishing History*, 12 (1982), 51–75 (52–6); Hyland, 'Liberty and Libel', 864. For the immediate damage done to newspapers, see J. A. Downie, *Robert Harley and the Press: Propaganda and Public Opinion in the Age of Swift and Defoe* (Cambridge: Cambridge University Press, 1979), 159.

[19] Higgins, 'Censorship, Libel', 181, citing Swift's *Journal to Stella*, 7 August 1712.

[20] See Matthew J. Kinservik, 'The Dialectics of Print and Performance after 1737', in Julia Swindells and David Francis Taylor (ed.), *The Oxford Handbook of the Georgian Theatre, 1737–1832* (Oxford: Clarendon Press, 2014), 123–39.

Press licensing would never again emerge as a serious prospect, and later authorities like William Blackstone could celebrate the 1695 lapse as a permanent state of affairs.[21] In this respect the Glorious Revolution does indeed mark a watershed—but not a watershed between censored press and free press. Rather, it marks a watershed between one prevailing method of press control and another, perhaps more effective, method. More important than any new statute was the existing common law of libel, used with increasing intensity in the new world ushered in by the licensing lapse, in which the primary difficulty encountered by writers was no longer pre-publication approval but post-publication retribution, whether in the shape of formal prosecution or informal harassment.

Even before 1695, both threatened and actual prosecutions for seditious and related kinds of libel were essential means of plugging holes in the licensing system, which was erratic, accident-prone, and often overwhelmed by the sheer volume of Restoration print. These methods came to the fore during the brief licensing hiatus of 1679–85, which saw a spike in book-trade arrests and trials under various pretexts (more often, technically speaking, for violating the royal prerogative to license news than for seditious libel as such, though prosecutors tended to conflate the issues rhetorically). After 1695 such methods became the norm, as prior restraint on publication under the Licensing Act gave way to prosecution after the fact, and clarification of seditious libel doctrine reduced the need for reliance on proxy charges.[22] Additional mechanisms continued to operate, not least via Parliament in its role as a summary court, as in the sensational case of Henry Sacheverell, impeached in 1710 for a sermon denouncing sections of the Whig establishment as 'False Brethren'.[23] Extra-legal methods provided useful short cuts, especially in the case of street ballads and other low-end productions. In one of many such

---

[21] William Blackstone, *Commentaries on the Laws of England*, ed. Wilfrid Prest et al. (Oxford: Oxford University Press, 2016), 4: 100.

[22] See Philip Hamburger, 'The Development of the Law of Seditious Libel and the Control of the Press', *Stanford Law Review*, 37 (1985), 661–765 (682–90, 725–43).

[23] See Brian Cowan (ed.), *The State Trial of Doctor Henry Sacheverell* (Oxford: Wiley-Blackwell, 2012).

memoranda to survive from the early Hanoverian years, a zealous official congratulates himself on silencing a balladeer ('I have spoyl'd his singing for the present haveing comited him to the house of Correction') and identifies the source of the trouble ('Osborne the printer of them is just sett up in y$^e$ Minoryes & his principle buisnes is to print such low seditious stuff'). He then asks Charles Delafaye, the under-secretary responsible for press control from 1717, 'whether sending the Messinger of the Press to rumidge his house may not in some measure prevent it for the future'.[24]

In this case the rummaging did the trick, and serves to remind us that now as much as in earlier centuries, press control remained unsystematic in character and opportunist in application, involving casual raids and interrogations as much as formal prosecutions and trials. To a marked extent, albeit with differences of emphasis and means, censorship still had much in common with the 'crazy quilt' of proclamations, ordinances, and precedents, emanating from 'a disarray of entities, interests, and occasions', that Cyndia Susan Clegg describes in the early modern period.[25] Government may now have played a more active and co-ordinated role than in the world of dispersed authority described by Clegg, but it drew on a range of mechanisms and operated through different conduits, from the ancient offence of *scandalum magnatum* to the humiliating sanction of kneeling in apology at the Bar of either House of Parliament.

That said, within a few years of the 1695 lapse, prosecution for seditious libel had become central as never before, and with it the shame and hazard of the pillory. Of seventy crown prosecutions against print, writing, or speech during the last seven years of William III's reign and the first five of Anne's, sixty focused on 'seditious libel' or cognate terms (the remaining ten were for 'treasonous' or 'heretical' publications).[26] In the volume of his *History of*

[24] TNA, SP 36/26/2, fo. 60 (Joseph Bell to Charles Delafaye, 14 April 1732).

[25] Cyndia Susan Clegg, *Press Censorship in Elizabethan England* (Cambridge: Cambridge University Press, 1997), p5; *Press Censorship in Caroline England* (Cambridge: Cambridge University Press, 2008), 41.

[26] Wendell Bird, *Press and Speech under Assault: The Early Supreme Court Justices, the Sedition Act of 1798, and the Campaign against Dissent* (New York: Oxford University Press, 2016), 38–9.

*England* covering the reign of Queen Anne, Tobias Smollett describes the intensification of exemplary punishment that accompanied this process:

> As many severe and sarcastic writings had lately appeared, in which the Whigs and Ministry were reviled, and reflections hinted to the prejudice of the Queen's person, the government resolved to make examples of the authors and publishers of these licentious productions. Dr. Joseph Browne was twice pilloried for a copy of verses, intituled "The Country Parson's Advice to the Lord-Keeper," and a letter which he afterwards wrote to Mr. Secretary Harley. William Stephens, rector of Sutton in Surrey, underwent the same sentence, as author of a pamphlet, called, "A Letter to the Author of the Memorial of the Church of England." Edward Ward was fined and set in the pillory, for having written a burlesque poem on the times, under the title of "Hudibras Redivivus;" and the same punishment was inflicted upon William Pittes, author of a performance, intituled "The Case of the Church of England's Memorial fairly stated."[27]

A more colourful version of Smollett's narrative survives in an official record of Crown Office prosecutions that was compiled in 1760 or thereabouts.[28] Disproportionate space is occupied in this document by the efforts of Robert Harley, Secretary of State from 1704 to 1708, to control disruptive print from either political extreme, notably in the aftermath of *The Memorial of the Church of England*, a High-Tory tract (with its viral 'Church in Danger' slogan) that was published and quickly suppressed in 1705.[29] Harley was assiduous in these efforts, cultivating a network of book-trade informers, authorizing frequent searches of printing houses, and employing as Messenger of the Press a man who could take in the meaning of standing type ('I can read the

---

[27] Tobias Smollett, *The History of England, from the Revolution to the Death of George the Second*, new edn, 5 vols (1791), 2: 113–4.

[28] TNA, KB 15/54, fos. 1–17; information and quotations below are from fos. 2–5 of this document.

[29] On this controversy and Harley's pursuit of the authors named by Smollett, see Downie, *Harley and the Press*, 80–100; also D. D. Gibbs, 'Browne, Joseph (*bap.* 1673, *d.* in or after 1721)', Bridget Hill, 'Drake, James (*bap.* 1666, *d.* 1707)', Stuart Handley, 'Stephens, William (1649/50–1718)', James Sambrook, 'Ward, Edward (1667–1731)', Philip Carter, 'Pittis, William (1673/4–1724)', all in *ODNB*.

Metal as well as the Print') as easily as a printed page.[30] Yet like Scroggs in the 1680s, Harley was not content with apprehending printers or publishers. Though harder to trace, authors were his targets of choice, and as one satirist later protested, the brunt of his campaign was born by those 'little Scriblers' for whom 'large Fines, and Pil[lori]es, by thee | Were made the base Rewards of Poetry'.[31]

In the case of the *Memorial*—publicly burned but often reprinted, in one instance disguised as a refutation that quoted the original in full— it's a measure of Harley's priorities that stationers complicit in the volume were offered large rewards as well as the usual pardon for naming the author or authors. No author was convicted (the original printer claimed to have had the manuscript from 'a Woman in a Mask'), but the chief suspect, James Drake, was prosecuted instead for his serial *Mercurius Politicus* (1705). Drake's case was adjourned following a bizarre episode of courtroom close reading that turned on a clerical mistranscription of 'not' as 'nor', and he succumbed to a fever with action still pending. As the compiler of KB 15/54 records, 'it was the general opinion that the severe Prosecution he underwent on Account of Mercurius politicus occasioned the Distemper of which he died'.

Browne was another Tory extremist, fined and pilloried 'for a scandalous & malicious Libel in Verses on the Lord Keeper Cowper & several other Lords', and for compounding the offence in 'another scandalous & seditious Libel' that ventured foolhardy glosses on the original poem.[32] Stephens, a radical Whig who had outraged politicians some years earlier by preaching borderline republicanism in a 30 January sermon at Westminster, was fined and sentenced to be pilloried for his riposte to the *Memorial*. As a clergyman, Stephens was spared the pillory in practice, but only after an exquisitely calibrated

---

[30] Henry L. Snyder, 'The Reports of a Press Spy for Robert Harley: New Bibliographical Data for the Reign of Queen Anne,' *The Library*, 5th ser., 22, no. 4 (1967), 326–45 (334).

[31] *A Dialogue between Louis le Petite, and Harlequin le Grand* (1708?), p. viii; on this 'very scurrilous pamphlet', to which Browne also contributed preliminary verses, see *POAS*, 7: 322–3.

[32] The original poem is in *POAS*, 7: 151–9; for discussion, see below, pp. 123–5.

ritual of intimidation. Reprieve was delayed until the last possible moment, 'with this mortifying Circumstance, that M<sup>r.</sup> Stephens was brought to a public House at Charing Cross from whence he saw the Scaffold & Multitudes of People gathering to be Spectators of his Disgrace'.

Ward was an opportunist more than an ideologue, twice pilloried 'cum Papyro &c.' (the formula for a paper fixed above the offender's head announcing his crime) for early instalments of *Hudibras Redivivus*, a serialized verse satire of 1705–7. Later instalments were more circumspect, and Ward replaced the offending lines when he later reissued the first few parts.[33] Pittis, a ferocious Tory loose cannon, 'was fined 100 Marks—Pillory on the Morrow at Charing Cross cum Papyro &c.—Pillory again Die Sabb prox at the Royal Exchange ut supra, & Security for his Good Behaviour for 2 years'. Good behaviour was not Pittis's forte, however. He fired back with *A Hymn to Confinement* (1705), in which he adds himself to a truly eclectic line of martyrs, stretching from the biblical Job to Sir Roger L'Estrange. In sprawling doggerel, the hymn welcomes imprisonment as denying Pittis the worldly temptations for which government ministers have been selling their souls: 'The Times will come, and I those Times foresee, | When the Imperious and the Great | Shall wish too late, | That they had been confin'd with me: | That they had been witheld from the Pursuit | Of private Interest, and of publick Sin...'[34]

Yet for all Harley's reputation as 'President of the Pillory', J. A. Downie suggests, the remarkable thing in view of the fraught atmosphere of 1705–6 is that so few authors were pilloried in the wake of the *Memorial*.[35] All were egregious, provocative instances that can help us measure the limits of acceptable discourse at this delicate juncture. Browne made rudimentary gestures of functional ambiguity, but what he took for protective irony was blatant sarcasm, and his strategy backfired (see below, pp. 123–5). Stephens was more

---

[33] Howard William Troyer, *Ned Ward of Grub Street: A Study of Sub-Literary London in the Eighteenth Century* (Cambridge, MA: Harvard University Press, 1946), 95–7.

[34] William Pittis, *A Hymn to Confinement* (1705), 9; see also Theodore F. M. Newton, 'William Pittis and Queen Anne Journalism', *Modern Philology*, 33.2–3 (1935–6), 169–86 and 279–302.

[35] Downie, *Harley and the Press*, 89, 100.

proficient in disguise, a writer credited by one contemporary with 'a peculiar Knack at wounding with a Slie, Oblique, and Paltry Suggestion; at Stabbing and yet looking another way, as if he were wholly Innocent and Unconcern'd'.[36] But Stephens, like Browne, was too confident for his own good, and mistakenly thought himself protected by Shaftesbury and other Whig grandees, who melted away when he moved into open invective. Ward was the most talented writer of the group, but with more imaginative flair than he was able to control. He was brought down by the vividness of his writing: by verse 'in w$^{ch}$ he lays open some sort of People in a little too lively Colours', as one contemporary put it.[37] As for Pittis, the outdoor voice was his only mode, and as he admitted in his journal the *Whipping Post*—named for the retribution it seemed to invite—he had written a work in which 'the Author, like an unskilful Rider...begins his Race full speed to be distanc'd at the end of it'.[38] We may think of these authors as a control group, defiant in their refusal of functional ambiguity, or incompetent in their exercise of it.

## Earless in Grubstreet

At this point neither Smollett nor the compiler of KB 15/54 mentions the most conspicuous pillory victim of Queen Anne's reign—but there was no need. In one of *The Dunciad*'s richest, most corrosive lines, Pope lodged Defoe enduringly in the public mind not as the author of *Robinson Crusoe* (a work he privately admired) but instead as a libeller in the pillory.[39] As in his notorious portrait of Eliza Haywood some lines later, 'With cow-like udders, and with ox-like eyes',[40] Pope's line of attack begins with the body. But it's not the breast or the eyes that

[36] *POAS*, 7: 161, quoting Thomas Rogers, *A True Protestant Bridle* (1694), 15.

[37] *Remarks and Collections of Thomas Hearne*, ed. C. E. Doble and D. W. Rannie, 11 vols (1885–1921), 1: 179–80.

[38] *Whipping Post*, 2 October 1705.

[39] Joseph Spence, *Observations, Anecdotes, and Characters of Books and Men*, ed. James M. Osborn, 2 vols (Oxford: Clarendon Press, 1966), 1: 213 (No. 498).

[40] *The Poems of Alexander Pope, Volume 3: The Dunciad (1728) and The Dunciad Variorum (1729)*, ed. Valerie Rumbold (Harlow: Longman, 2007), 58 (*Dunciad Variorum*, ii.146). Further references are given parenthetically (*D* for the original *Dunciad*, *DV* for *The Dunciad Variorum*).

he has in view when contemplating Defoe. It's that feature on which his great epic of the asinine most often dwells, the ears, or in this case their absence. 'Ear-less on high, stood pillory'd *D—*' is the original version (*D*, p. 55; ii.127), and in *The Dunciad Variorum* Pope brilliantly refines the line to read 'Earless on high, stood un-abash'd Defoe' (*DV*, p. 231; ii.139). The implied layers of insult are hard to exhaust. Defoe's ears were not of course severed in the pillory, but by pretending to think they were, Pope deftly associates him with puritan agitators of the seventeenth century, above all Prynne. The point is reinforced when elsewhere in the poem the Goddess of Dulness 'saw old Pryn in restless Daniel shine' (*D*, p. 28 n.; i.91), with a note added in *The Dunciad Variorum* (*DV*, p. 186; i.101 and n.) to explain exactly what links them: a toxic blend, Pope suggests, of bad poetry and bad politics.[41] Deafened by fanaticism, they lack an ear for the first and lose their ears for the second.

Beneath all these insinuations, Pope evokes a long tradition in which the earless pillory victim suffers a symbolic emasculation: a milder version of the castration literally endured by zealots like Thomas Harrison, the godly regicide whose gruesome execution was compared with Defoe's pillorying by Ned Ward in a lampoon of 1703.[42] Decades earlier, the verse libeller John Bond put the point with eye-watering succinctness when he begged the pillory, in a desperate poem, not to 'geld mine eare'.[43] Alternatively, but with the same emphasis on shameful unmanning, the libeller's cropped ears linked him with the collapsed nose of the love-poxed libertine. As a Shadwell character says in one of many syphilis/sedition jokes in Restoration comedy, 'I hear he writ a Libel, I shall have him scrible away his ears, or write himself so far into the Ladies favours, to lose his Nose... these are the fruits of Wit'.[44] In long-established contexts like

---

[41] For the Defoe/Prynne analogy as pursued by other satirists, see Thomas Keymer, 'Defoe's Ears: *The Dunciad*, the Pillory, and Seditious Libel', *The Eighteenth-Century Novel*, 6–7 (2009), 159–96.

[42] Edward Ward, *In Imitation of Hudibras, The Dissenting Hypocrite, or Occasional Conformist* (1703), 16–17. On Harrison and the execution rituals of 1660, see N. H. Keeble, *The Restoration: England in the 1660s* (Oxford: Blackwell, 2002), 54–7.

[43] John Bond, *The Poets Recantation* (1642), 4.

[44] Thomas Shadwell, *A True Widow* (1679), in *Complete Works of Thomas Shadwell*, 3: 298; see also *POAS*, 1: 336, for a broadside targeting syphilitic

this, Defoe's earlessness connotes disempowerment in the broadest sense, while visually enshrining him as the very type of the seditious libeller, the mutilated embodiment of Grubstreet transgression.

Pope's association of Defoe with the libeller's proverbial earlessness was so emphatic that some have mistaken it for fact. In 1763 an anonymous attack on Wilkite pamphleteering savaged the clergyman-poet Charles Churchill as the Defoe of his age, a 'sower of sedition' who 'like *Defoe*... has left his own proper employment to follow the lampooning trade; heaven grant, like Defoe, he may not lose his ears'.[45] In his 'Chapter on Ears', a Shandean excursus first published as a magazine item in 1820, Charles Lamb's Elia rejoiced that he personally had never risked the pillory, 'neither have I incurred... with Defoe, that hideous disfigurement, which constrained him to draw upon assurance—to feel "quite unabashed"'.[46] A century later Sir Charles Firth, glossing Swift's joke that *Gulliver's Travels* would only appear 'when a Printer shall be found brave enough to venture his Eares', still seems to take *The Dunciad* at face value: 'this reference to the printer's ears', Firth patiently explains, 'is an acknowledgement that the book contained political allusions which might... draw upon [Swift] the fate which befell Defoe.'[47] Not quite fearless but only earless, Defoe is defined here not by attributes he possesses but by those he lacks, or is thought to lack. A further twist comes with Pope's quiet play on Milton, for in his earless condition Defoe also recalls the revolutionary prisoner of *Samson Agonistes*, 'Eyeless in Gaza at the mill with slaves'. A negative prefix at the end of the line mirrors a negative suffix at the start (*un*-abashed, ear*less*), and here Pope craftily echoes a well-known stylistic signature in Milton, in John

---

Sir William Davenant as author of a seditious play, for which 'the pill'ry should crop off his ears | And make them more suitable unto his nose'.

[45] *A Letter from a Member of Parliament in London to His Friend in Edinburgh* (Edinburgh, 1763), 11 n.

[46] Charles Lamb, *Elia and The Last Essays of Elia*, ed. Jonathan Bate (Oxford: Oxford University Press, 1987), 43.

[47] Sir Charles Firth, 'The Political Significance of *Gulliver's Travels*', *Proceedings of the British Academy*, 9 (1919–20), 237–59 (239). Swift's remark is from his letter to Pope of 29 September 1725 (*Gulliver's Travels*, ed. David Womersley (Cambridge: Cambridge University Press, 2012), Appendix C, p. 592).

Leonard's words 'a Latin idiom in which past participles with a negative prefix signify the strongest possible negation'.[48] In this context, Defoe's unabashed state becomes a burlesque version of Samson's heroism, 'patient but undaunted'. He is risibly unlike the 'unmoved', 'untroubled', 'unshaken' Christ of *Paradise Regained*.[49]

Negative formulations like this bode ill in the satirical world of *The Dunciad*, where they connect Defoe with larger targets of the poem's derision like 'supperless' Theobald (Cibber in later versions) and 'dauntless' Curll (*DV*, pp. 191, 216; i.109, ii.54). The primary link, however, is with other pamphleteering incendiaries of Queen Anne's reign, all of whom bring to mind humiliating corporal punishment. In the group portrait in tapestry that Pope imagines at this point, Defoe is paired with 'Tutchin flagrant from the scourge, below: | There Ridpath, Roper, cudgell'd might ye view; | The very worsted still look'd black and blue' (*DV*, p. 231; ii.140–2). We know him by the company he keeps, the suggestion is. Defoe's political stablemate but personal enemy John Tutchin had been publicly whipped for joining the Monmouth rebellion in 1685 (Pope is unlikely to have known of Defoe's own involvement and subsequent pardon). As author of the Whig *Observator*, jeeringly named after L'Estrange's Tory vehicle of the 1680s, Tutchin was found guilty in 1704 of libelling the government after prosecutors 'Muster'd *Innuendo*'s' to refute his defence, which was that only mid-ranking officials had been attacked. The verdict was annulled on a technicality, but three years later Tutchin was badly beaten up, perhaps at the Duke of Marlborough's instigation, and died in prison from his injuries.[50] George Ridpath was a firebrand Scots Presbyterian who later took over the *Observator* and ran it alongside his existing journal the *Flying Post*, a pioneering disseminator

---

[48] John Leonard, 'Self-Contradicting Puns in *Paradise Lost*', in Thomas N. Corns (ed.), *A Companion to Milton* (Oxford: Blackwell, 2001), 393–410 (408).

[49] John Milton, *The Complete Shorter Poems*, ed. John Carey, revised 2nd edn (Harlow: Longman, 2007), 409 (*Samson Agonistes*, line 1623); 488, 501, 502 (*Paradise Regained*, iv.109, iv.401, iv.421).

[50] Lee Sonsteng Horsley, 'The Trial of John Tutchin, Author of the *Observator*', *Yearbook of English Studies*, 3 (1973), 124–40 (134, quoting Tutchin's preface to Volume 3 (1704) of the *Observator*); see also 138, quoting Marlborough's remark to Harley (1–11 October 1706) that 'if I can't have justice done me, I must find some friend that will break his and the printer's bones'.

of fake news that Defoe liked to call the 'Lying Post'.[51] He was soon notorious enough to feature in an illustrated broadside (Figure 2.1) intended to implicate Richard Steele's *Tatler* in the scurrilous factionalism of Ridpath's *Observator* and Defoe's *Review*: 'Him with *the Brittish Libellers* I join; | Nor envy him the Company of Fellows | That have *the Pillory* disgraced and may *the Gallows*.'[52]

Ridpath escaped the pillory in 1713 by flying to Holland when at last convicted for a seditious number of his *Flying Post*; the can was carried instead by Ridpath's printer William Hurt, who was reportedly feted at his first pillorying—'very handsomely dressed', with 'not so much as an egg or bit of dirt thrown at him'—but nearly killed on the second occasion by a Tory mob. The mob included, it was alleged, men in the livery of Bolingbroke, then Secretary of State.[53] This context may have prompted Pope to remember Abel Roper, a malignant Tory journalist and printer whose output got him arrested at least three times between 1695 and 1714, for Hurt's injuries resulted from an inflammatory notice placed by Roper in his rival journal the *Post Boy*.[54] The *Post Boy* was a tawdry, rabble-rousing organ, though one issue was elevated by a contribution from Swift, which Swift joked about making 'as malicious as possible, and very proper for Abel Roper th[e] Printer of it'. A contribution may even have been made by Defoe, who in a little-known and still mysterious episode was targeted by an official warrant 'to apprehend Dan$^l$. Defoe for bringing a scandalous and seditious Paragraph to be inserted in y$^e$ Post boy of 19 Aug$^t$ 1714 N$^o$. 3010'.[55] Again, Pope can have known nothing

---

[51] Maximillian E. Novak, *Daniel Defoe: Master of Fictions* (Oxford: Oxford University Press, 2001), 431; see, for example, Defoe's *Review* for 19 July 1712.

[52] *The Three Champions* (*c*.1710).

[53] Hyland, 'Liberty and Libel', 867, quoting W. Wilbey to White Kennet, 2 July 1713. The allegation about Bolingbroke is made by John Oldmixon in *The History of England . . . Being the Sequel of the Reigns of the Stuarts* (1735), 536.

[54] Hyland, 'Liberty and Libel', 867; for Roper's career and reputation as a polemicist for hire, see G. A. Aitkin, rev. M. E. Clayton, 'Roper, Abel (bap. 1665, d. 1726)', *ODNB*.

[55] Jonathan Swift, *Journal to Stella: Letters to Esther Johnson and Rebecca Dingley, 1710–1713*, ed. Abigail Williams (Cambridge: Cambridge University Press, 2013), 460 (17 November 1712); Hyland, 'Liberty and Libel', 872, quoting TNA, SP 44/79A, fo. 13.

# The Three Champions.

*The British Censor*

*Isaac Bickerstaff*

*The British Libellers*

*Reviewer*   *Observator*

VIEW here Three Brethren in Iniquity,
That vex *the Church*, and fpight *the Monarchy*,
Cry up *Refiftance to the Power Supreme*,
And Men of Loyal Principles Defame;
Lefs valuing the brighteft Characters,
Than other Libellers wou'd fuch as theirs:
Refuteing all their bare-fac'd Calumnies,
A Thoufand Shams and Stories they devife,
Which Reputations Stab in that difguife.
Nor do they in their Zeal or Fury ftick,
To Scandalize ev'n Bodies Politick,
But make't a Crime (than Treafon little lefs)
For thofe they've wrong their Sovereign to Addrefs.
High Treafon to pull Meeting Houfes down,
But not to ftrike at openly *the Crown*,
Denying *ANNA's Title by Defcent*,
Tho' recogniz'd *by Acts of Parliament*:
Yet *thofe* that have all this Confufion wrought
Affect the beft of Subjects to be thought;
Tho' (in Schifmatical Academies
Train'd up) they *evil fpeak of Dignities*,
And others teach *Dominion to defpife*.
Their *Aiders* and *Abettors* preach up Law,
Yet never were by any kept in Awe;
But with God's Law, *to ferve a turn*, difpenfe;
Yet to do fo by Man's, will not allow their Prince.

Let Whiggs but have their Will, they'd quickly all
Th' *Apoftle's Writings* vote Apochryphal,
That fquare not with their Intereft, and inftead,
*Milton*'s and *Hoadley*'s to the Canon add.

But oh, that *Ifaac* that Romantick 'Squire,
Shou'd proftitute the Sciences for hire!
Queftion that Right *the QUEEN* by Birth receives,
When She th' Ingrate both Place and Penfion gives!
That One that's thought *a Cunning Man* fhou'd fneak,
To *a Wrong Intereft* when his All's at Stake!
*The Conventicle* to *the Church* prefer!
A certain Sign the Man's no Conjurer!
Yet our top Whiggs, confcious that their *De Foes*,
And *Redpaths*, to contempt their Caufe, expofe,
That their forg'd Letters, Queries, Libels fail,
And Serious Arguments grow Flat and Stale.
*The Church and her True Sons* to ridicule,
Have chofen *Britain's Cenfor* for their Tool.
In nothing like the Cenfor of Old *Rome*,
But Siding with *the Party overcome*.
Embark'd in the fame laudable Defign,
Him with *the Brittifh Libellers* I join;
Nor Envy him the Company of Fellows,
That have *the Pillory* difgrac'd and may *the Gallows*.

*London*: Printed for *J. Baker* at the *Black-Boy* in *Pater-Nofter-Row*.

**Figure 2.1** *The Three Champions* (*c*.1710), engraved broadside, © the Trustees of the British Museum. All rights reserved. Defoe and his fellow libellers are surrounded by emblems of spectacular punishment including scourges, pikes, and the pillory.

about these murky events, but it's a measure of his unerring instincts that the libellers he names were so closely intertwined in practice with Defoe's extended career in literary sedition.

## Wit, and punishment, and Pope: *The Dunciad* and after

Pope's insistence on this aspect of Defoe's identity was shared by Swift, whose best-known notice of Defoe comes in a faux-casual remark of 1709 about 'the Fellow that was *pilloryed*, I have forgot his Name'—a name, Claude Rawson observes, 'we know Swift did not forget, because in 1735, when reprinting his works, he added Defoe's name in a footnote without deleting the remark about having forgotten it'.[56] A high/low binary is deployed by both these satirists, in which they look down with impunity, as elite authors, on the quintessential Grubstreet fate of disgrace in the pillory. Rhetorically, there could be no more effective way of obscuring what really brings Pope, Swift, and Defoe together: their shared condition as writers forever navigating the vexed, indistinct boundaries of seditious libel.

It's impossible, of course, to imagine a well-connected celebrity poet like Pope degraded in the pillory, as Defoe had been. Authors of his public stature and social rank were handled in subtler ways. Yet Pope clearly saw a need for special caution in the fraught years following the Hanoverian accession, when the 1715 rebellion and the Atterbury plot of 1721 intensified the scrutiny to which all literary production was subject, from lowbrow journalism to highbrow epic. He delayed publishing the second volume of his *Iliad* translation when the first came under attack as implicitly Jacobite ('*HOMER for the Use of the PRETENDER*', Oldmixon screamed). He destroyed the manuscript of his juvenile poem *Alcander*, in which a usurped prince seeks to recover his throne, on advice from Atterbury himself.[57] In an

---

[56] Claude Rawson, *Satire and Sentiment, 1660–1830* (New Haven: Yale University Press, 2000), 251; the remark comes in *A Letter Concerning the Sacramental Test* (1709).

[57] J. V. Guerinot, *Pamphlet Attacks on Alexander Pope, 1711–1744: A Descriptive Bibliography* (New York: New York University Press, 1969), 40, quoting Oldmixon's *The Catholick Poet; or, Protestant Barnaby's Sorrowful Lamentation* (1716), 5; Joseph Hone, 'Pope's Lost Epic: *Alcander, Prince of Rhodes* and the Politics of Exile', *Philological Quarterly*, 94 (2015), 245–66.

obscure but significant episode of 1723, he was taken into custody and questioned following the seizure as 'a seditious and scandalous Libel' of a publication he had edited for the Jacobite bookseller John Barber, *The Works of John Sheffield, Duke of Buckingham*.[58] Thereafter Pope reportedly went back to his handiwork 'to expunge all those Passages which have given Offence', though several copies now survive with the cancelled passages intact.[59] Pope never came so close again to the rigours of prosecution, but literal and metaphorical pillories continued to fascinate his imagination, not least as the occupational hazard of Grubstreet life: as part of the professional author's ever-present 'fears | Of hisses, blows, or want, or loss of ears' (*D*, p. 23; i.35–6). Elsewhere Pope recollects not only Defoe but also Curll, pilloried for seditious libel in 1728, whose protest that the first *Dunciad* misrepresented the episode gave him an irresistible opportunity to elaborate further. The notes he now adds, Pope suggests, should be seen as functioning in the poem like the *cum-papyro* placards worn by miscreants in the pillory 'to mark the Enormities for which they suffer'd' (*DV*, p. 123).

Pope was also interested in those other categories of scandal and falsehood for which the pillory stood sanction, with a conscious sense of satire as a punitive mode that redoubled the punishments described: lash upon lash. There was 'Mother' Needham, a brothel-keeper fatally injured in the pillory in 1731, and thus an inevitable presence in the final versions of *The Dunciad* in 1742–3. There was Japhet Crook, a forger whose 1731 pillorying was accompanied, exceptionally at this late date, by ear-cropping and nose-slitting; hence the *Epistle to Bathurst*'s merciless jibe about 'Japhet, Nose and Ears'. There was John Ward of (felicitously) Hackney, an MP and high-level fraudster whose 1727 pillorying gives rise to a gloating footnote in the *Epistle to Bathurst* and a memorable simile in *The*

---

[58] Maynard Mack, *Alexander Pope: A Life* (New Haven: Yale University Press, 1985), 396–7; Howard Erskine-Hill, 'Under Which Caesar? Pope in the Journal of Mrs. Charles Caesar, 1724–1741', *Review of English Studies*, 33 (1982), 436–44.

[59] Pat Rogers, *A Political Biography of Alexander Pope* (London: Pickering & Chatto, 2010), 140, quoting the *London Journal* for 9 March 1723. With characteristic chutzpah, Curll then pirated the cancellanda, as *The Castrations*.

*Dunciad*, where volumes of disposable poetry accumulate 'As thick as eggs at *W—d* in pillory' (*D*, p. 83; iii.26).[60]

Whatever the underlying offence, Pope typically brings it back to seditious libel, insistently associating hack writing with forgery and fraud as analogous offences against truth. Having first established Ward of Hackney as the referent for his line about eggs, he then adds a note wondering whether he might not in fact have meant 'Mr. *Edward Ward* the Poet' (*DV*, p. 269 n.). As Paul Baines observes, by recalling one Ward's seditious verses alongside the other Ward's forged documents, he installs in the poem a characteristic link 'between degraded white-collar crime and Grub Street journalism'.[61] A similar link is proposed in the *Epistle to Arbuthnot* between venal literature and venal politics: between being

> *Sporus* at Court, or *Japhet* in a Jayl,
> A hireling Scribler, or a hireling Peer,
> Knight of the Post corrupt, or of the Shire;
> If on a Pillory, or near a Throne,
> He gain his Prince's Ear, or lose his own.[62]

With scathing parallelism, Pope alleges a continuity of knavery in politics, commerce, and literature alike, and notes the giddy proximity of power to disgrace. Corrupt writers, statesmen, and financiers become undifferentiated targets of poetic scorn, and scorn intended to do damage. It was even alleged that Pope had previously been bribed by the Duchess of Buckingham, victim of Ward of Hackney's boldest scam, to write a satire inciting mob violence against Ward— who, though protected by a body of constables, was taken down from

---

[60] For Elizabeth Needham, see Alexander Pope, *The Dunciad in Four Books*, 139 (lines 323–4 and n.); for Japhet Crook and John Ward, see *The Twickenham Edition of the Works of Alexander Pope*, ed. John Butt et al., 11 vols (London: Methuen, 1938–68), 3.ii: 95; 3.ii: 83 (*Epistle to Bathurst*, line 88 and n.; line 20 n.).

[61] Paul Baines, 'Crime and Punishment', in Pat Rogers (ed.), *The Cambridge Companion to Alexander Pope* (Cambridge: Cambridge University Press, 2007), 155; see also Baines's *The House of Forgery in Eighteenth-Century Britain* (Aldershot: Ashgate, 1999), 61–80.

[62] *Twickenham Edition of Pope*, 4: 122 (*Epistle to Arbuthnot*, lines 363–7).

the pillory bleeding and senseless.[63] No such broadside is known, though several earlier examples survive of this unlovely subgenre of instant verse (see below, p. 144 and n. 151).

If Pope was never, like Ward of Hackney or Ward the hack, a candidate for the pillory himself, he was certainly concerned about retribution of one kind or another. Several *Dunciad*-era anecdotes report the precautions he took against assault when going out: a Great Dane named Bounce, an Irish bodyguard, loaded pistols. For John Mullan, his case indicates a trend in which personal, not state, retribution was now the primary hazard faced by satirists.[64] But Pope also had directly legal anxieties, shared by the booksellers and printers with whom he worked. His circumspect handling of *The Dunciad Variorum* is revealing in terms of both literary guile and publishing practice: like Dryden decades earlier, he manipulated linguistic and bibliographic codes to obscure both meaning and provenance. Anxious to establish 'if there be anything in these sheets...which an Action may be grounded upon', Pope had a Tory lawyer named Nicholas Fazakerley review the poem for actionable passages and 'mark or alter them' as necessary. Fazakerley was shortly to gain prominence when defending the printer of the *Craftsman*, a leading opposition journal, against charges of seditious libel arising from a contribution probably by Bolingbroke (who, once the scourge of libellers, was now a libeller himself, albeit of an upmarket kind).[65] We have no details of Fazakerley's advice to Pope, though we can infer a good deal about it from his line of defence in the *Craftsman* trial, and we know that Pope waited to hear it. Without 'the Decisive opinion of Mr Fazakerly', he told Burlington, he would not move

---

[63] Guerinot, *Pamphlet Attacks*, 113, 157; Romney R. Sedgwick, 'Ward, John (d.1755), of Hackney', *History of Parliament Online*, <https://www.historyofparliamentonline.org>.

[64] John Mullan, *Anonymity: A Secret History of English Literature* (London: Faber, 2007), 167.

[65] A previous *Craftsman* prosecution had failed in 1729, courtesy of a jury packed with opposition sympathizers by John Barber, a leading Tory printer who was then in shrieval office; the episode led to Walpole's Juries Act of 1730, which created a mechanism for empanelling compliant 'special juries'.

forward to publication.[66] It speaks volumes about the uncertainties faced by poets in the post-licensing era that the most accomplished ironist of the day felt compelled, even so, to take professional advice.

Pope's strategies of transmission and circulation were no less considered and complex than his actual text. The original *Dunciad* came out under a false Dublin imprint, as though published without authorial sanction, in a gesture of subterfuge that was partly, but only partly, a matter of play. For *The Dunciad Variorum*, Pope avoided declaring ownership in the Stationers' Register, and instead vested copyright in three opposition peers (Bathurst, Burlington, and Oxford) whose rank placed a further obstacle in the way of legal action. Perhaps his most brilliant strategy of legitimation was to have Prime Minister Walpole, who liked to keep the most dangerous satirists within personal reach, present a pre-publication copy of *The Dunciad Variorum* to George II, the famously philistine Hanoverian king who had recently come to the throne.[67] With this move, the two most powerful men in the country were in effect made complicit in the poem, even before formal publication. A week later, it was drily reported to Swift by John Arbuthnot that the king had 'perused' *The Dunciad Variorum*, and thought its author 'a very honest man'.[68]

How far did the new king get with his perusal, and how deep did he probe? Over the years, there are many anecdotes about powerful figures enjoying satires written one way or another at their own expense: Charles II and *The Rehearsal Transpros'd*; Walpole and *The Beggar's Opera*; Bonnie Prince Charlie and *Tom Jones*.[69] But this may

---

[66] *The Correspondence of Alexander Pope*, ed. George Sherburn, 5 vols (Oxford: Clarendon Press, 1956), 3: 4 (to the Earl of Burlington, 1728/9). For Fazakerley's virtuoso performance in the *Craftsman* trial of 1731, which in key moves anticipates the celebrated 'Gurney defence' of the 1790s, see T. B. Howell, *A Complete Collection of State Trials*, 21 vols (1816), 17: 625–76.

[67] On these and other ruses, see Jody Green, *The Trouble with Ownership: Literary Property and Authorial Liability in England, 1660–1730* (Philadelphia: University of Pennsylvania Press, 2005), 150–94.

[68] Mack, *Pope: A Life*, 501, quoting Arbuthnot to Swift, 19 March 1729.

[69] For Walpole and Gay, see below, pp. 181–3; for Charles II on Marvell, see Annabel Patterson, *Censorship and Interpretation: The Conditions of Writing and Reading in Early Modern England*, revised edn (Madison: University of Wisconsin

well be the extreme case. The mockery starts early, with an ornamental headpiece to the opening book in which the royal motto *Nemo me impune lacessit*—brilliantly, this is the motto of the Order of the Thistle—is flanked not by the unicorn of Scotland and the lion of England but by a pair of asses with protuberant ears, alongside their favourite food (Figure 2.2).[70] Then come the opening couplets of the poem, in which Pope twice reinforces the dunce/king analogy, first by juxtaposing his line about 'the Ear of Kings' with the asses' ears of the headpiece, and then with the deadpan question: 'Say from what cause, in vain decry'd and curst, | Still Dunce the second reigns like Dunce the first?' (*DV*, pp. 176–7; i.2, i.5–6). The allusion is in the first place to Dryden's verses to Congreve on *The Double Dealer*: 'For Tom the Second reigns like Tom the First.'[71] But in case anyone misses the point, Pope helpfully brings *Mac Flecknoe* into play by adding a note denying that *Mac Flecknoe* is in play. This is textbook apophasis, and the device makes inescapable, so soon after George II began reigning like George I, *The Dunciad*'s reanimation of *Mac Flecknoe*'s most transgressive move: the association made in the poem between dynasties of bad poets and bad kings. The additional twist is the unmentionable cause, decried and cursed, why Hanoverian monarchs are now on the throne, which turns the allegation of stupidity into something approaching an expression of Jacobite regret. One further twist is made in editions of *The Dunciad* after 1735, which, with an intrusive, legalistic parenthesis, invite readers to picture George II poised to start reading about himself in his guise as Dunce II. Pope even supplies an exact date: 'We are willing to acquaint Posterity that this Poem (as it here stands) was presented to King

---

Press, 1990), 31; for the Young Pretender and Fielding, see Frank McLynn, *Charles Edward Stuart* (Oxford: Oxford University Press, 1991), 520.

[70] On the visual cues at work in this passage (the headpiece was probably by William Kent), see J. Paul Hunter, 'From Typology to Type: Agents of Change in Eighteenth-Century English Texts', in Margaret J. M. Ezell and Katherine O'Brien O'Keeffe (eds), *Cultural Artifacts and the Production of Meaning: The Page, the Image, and the Body* (Ann Arbor: University of Michigan Press, 1994), 41–69 (61–5). Originally Stuart, the motto was retained in the version of the Royal Arms used in Scotland in the Hanoverian era.

[71] *The Poems of John Dryden*, ed. Paul Hammond and David Hopkins, 5 vols (Harlow: Longman, 1995–2005), 4: 333 (line 48) and n. (Thomas Rymer having succeeded Thomas Shadwell as Historiographer Royal).

# THE
# DUNCIAD.

BOOK the FIRST.

**B**OOKS and the Man I sing, the first who brings
The Smithfield Muses to the Ear of Kings.

REMARKS ON BOOK the FIRST

\* THE *Dunciad, Sic* M. S. It may be well disputed whether this be a right Reading? Ought it not rather to be spelled *Dunceiad,* as the Etymology evidently demands? *Dunce* with an *e,* therefore *Dunceiad* with an *e*. That accurate and punctual Man of Letters, the Restorer of *Shakespeare,* constantly observes the preservation of this very Letter *e,* in spelling the Name of his beloved Author, and not like his common careless Editors, with the omission of *one,* nay sometimes of two *ee*'s [as *Shak'spear*] which is utterly unpardonable. Nor is the neglect of a *Single Letter* so trivial as to some it may appear; the alteration whereof in a learned language is an *Atchievement that brings honour* to the Critick who advances it; and Dr. *B.* will be remembered to posterity for his performances of *this sort,* as long as the world shall have any Esteem for the Remains of *Menander* and *Philemon.*
THEOBALD.

I have a just value for the Letter E, and the same affection for the Name of this Poem, as the forecited Critic for that of his Author; yet cannot it induce me to agree with those who would add yet another *e* to it, and call it the *Dunceiade;* which being a French and foreign Termination, is no way proper to a word entirely English, and Vernacular. One *E* therefore in this case is right, and two *E*'s wrong; yet upon the whole I shall follow the Manuscript, and print it without any *E* at all; mov'd thereto by Authority, at all times with Criticks equal if not superior to Reason. In which method of proceeding, I can never enough praise my very good Friend, the exact Mr. *Tho. Hearne;* who, if any word occur which to him and all mankind is evidently wrong, yet keeps he it in the Text with due reverence, and only remarks in the Margin, *see* M. S. In like manner we shall not amend this error in the Title itself, but only note it *obiter,* to evince to the learned that it was not our fault, nor any effect of our own Ignorance or Inattention.
SCRIBLERUS.

VERSE 1. *Books and the Man I sing, the first who brings*
*The* Smithfield *Muses to the Ear of Kings.*
Wonderful is the stupidity of all the former Criticks and Commentators on this Poem! It breaks forth at the very first line. The Author of the Critique prefix'd to *Sawney,* a Poem, *p.* 5. hath been so dull as to explain *The Man who brings,* &c. not of the Hero of the Piece, but of our Poet himself, as if he vaunted that *Kings* were to be his Readers (an Honour which tho' this Poem hath had, yet knoweth he how to receive it with more Modesty.)

F
We

**Figure 2.2** Alexander Pope, *The Dunciad Variorum* (1729), first quarto edition (Rumbold 1729a, Vander Meulen 8, Foxon P771), p. 1, by courtesy of the William Ready Division of Archives and Research Collections, McMaster University Library. The engraved headpiece, perhaps from a design by William Kent, playfully mixes the asinine with the royal.

George the Second and his Queen, by the hands of Sir R. Walpole, on the 12th of March 1728/9' (*DV*, p. 174).

*Nemo me impune lacessit*: no one attacks me with impunity. Yet this was nothing like frontal attack or the lash of Juvenalian satire; it was something defter and funnier. As Roger D. Lund has shown, an underlying objection to raillery and wit throughout the period was that it was so hard to refute without seeming pompous, stupid, or flat-footed—without confirming oneself, in effect, to be a proper target of ridicule.[72] Wit was certainly a difficult quality to prosecute, even though, as several journalists discovered, to move from mocking a ministry and attacking its policies to mocking royalty and questioning its legitimacy was to cross a red line.[73] The danger became more acute when wit gave way to invective. A verse example of startling incaution is a broadside entitled *Nero the Second* which used a recent urban conflagration (the Thames Street fire of January 1715) to develop an undisguised parallel between Nero and George I. Both tyrants laugh as their capital burns, and both oppress their subjects with illegal edicts. Both, crucially, lack inherited legitimacy: '*NERO* possest *BRITANNICUS*'s Crown; | *GEORGE* has usurp'd our royal *JAMES*'s Throne.' *Nero the Second* also demonstrates another failsafe route to arrest, which was to shift out of the indicative and into the imperative mood: 'O Free-born *Brittons!* since a Tyrant reigns, | Assert your Liberties, shake off your Chains: | Let us in Justice rival ancient *ROME*; | Let *NERO*'s Vices meet with *NERO*'s Doom, | And speed'ly call King *JAMES* from Exile Home.'[74]

---

[72] Roger D. Lund, *Ridicule, Religion and the Politics of Wit in Augustan England* (Farnham: Ashgate, 2012), esp. 187–218.

[73] See Michael Harris, *London Newspapers in the Age of Walpole: A Study of the Origins of the Modern English Press* (Rutherford: Fairleigh Dickinson University Press, 1987), esp. 134–54.

[74] I quote the printed broadside copy of *Nero the Second* (1715) in the Bodleian Library, where it survives without date or imprint in a volume mainly composed of government reports on Jacobite activity, with print and manuscript copies of Jacobite texts (MS Rawl. D 383, fo. 111). A presentation manuscript, with some variants, survives at the University of Leeds (Brotherton Collection, MS Lt q 6), dated 29 August 1714 (before the fire that occasioned the poem, perhaps to match the date of the Pretender's Plombières Declaration claiming the throne).

These incendiary verses came to notice on being reprinted in the West Country by Philip Bishop, proprietor of the *Exeter Mercury*, against whom an information was filed quoting the lines about usurping thrones and shaking off chains.[75] Bishop died in prison after being convicted, and there is no evidence to support the gloating claim of a local rival that among other punishments he was to have had, in Elizabethan *lex-talionis* style, 'his Ears (if not his Hands also) cut off and nail'd to the [Pillory]'.[76] That being said, *Nero the Second* was certainly viewed by officials as an exceptional problem. A copy found its way to Dublin, where Edmund Bingley, a young Jacobite who later worked for *Mist's Weekly Journal*, was convicted for uttering treasonable words ('ye Prince of Orange & Princess Ann, were Usurpers') and publishing a seditious libel (*Nero the Second*); he was pilloried for the latter offence.[77] On further investigation the author turned out to be a former mayor of Leeds named William Cookson, who, under pretence of taking the waters in Bath, was allegedly conspiring with West Country Jacobites to raise a rebellion. Cookson spent the winter in Newgate, and was lucky to return to normal life the following year (after intercessions from, among others, his cousin Ralph Thoresby).[78]

This poem was of course the work of a bungling amateur, a consideration that in the end may have saved Cookson. No professional or worldly-wise author would have violated the conventions of disguise so blatantly—or, if tempted to do so, he would have stuck to manuscript circulation, like the young Richard Savage in his Jacobite

---

[75] TNA, KB 15/54, fo. 8; W. H. Hart, ' "Nero the Second": A Jacobite Ballad', *Notes & Queries*, 4th series 6 (15 October 1870), 322.

[76] Geoffrey Alan Cranfield, *The Press and Society: From Caxton to Northfield* (London: Longman, 1978), 181–2, quoting the *Protestant Mercury* for 21 December 1716: 'A Sentence indeed too mild for his inexorable Villany', the *Mercury* cheerfully adds. For the amputation of a seditious libeller's writing hand in 1579, see Patterson, *Censorship and Interpretation*, 33–4, 53–4.

[77] Paul Michael Chapman, *Jacobite Political Argument in England, 1714–1766* (London: Jacobite Studies Trust, 2013), 185–6; *Journals of the House of Lords*, 22 (1722), 177.

[78] TNA, KB 15/54, fo. 8; David Thornton, *The Story of Leeds* (Stroud: History Press, 2012), 82.

poems at the same juncture.[79] For print authors in the decades that followed, even quite rudimentary techniques of encoding were normally enough to inhibit prosecution. From the point of view of officials, the underlying problem is well documented in sedition and treason trials of the 1790s, when prosecutors struggled with the difficulty of asserting the presence of a satirical analogy while not thereby seeming to confirm it as valid. A radical journalist encapsulated their dilemma in a mock-Aesopian fable called 'What Makes a Libel', in which an incautiously litigious man sues Aesop for defaming him as an ass; when Aesop denies the charge, the man patiently goes through numerous details that show the exact match.[80]

This defensive strategy was by no means the invention of Romantic-era journalists and lawyers, however. In the 1731 *Craftsman* trial, about a Bolingbroke essay that nominally concerned criminal ministers in France and Spain, Fazakerley rang rings round the prosecution with his poker-faced insistence that Britain had no such thing as a criminal minister: on what grounds, and on whose head, did his learned colleagues think the cap might possibly fit? He still lost the case, and the defendant (neither Bolingbroke nor Nicholas Amhurst, the *Craftsman*'s editor, but its hapless printer Richard Francklin) was lucky to get off on technical grounds. But Fazakerley scored a rhetorical victory nonetheless. Playing to a gallery packed with the nation's elite, he established a powerful deterrent against future prosecution of encoded texts by smoothly ridiculing crown lawyers and the ministers they served. For the ministry, the risk of self-inflicted reputational damage was now clear. In the larger controversy about functional ambiguity provoked by the *Craftsman*'s methods (which Lord Hervey intensified with a pamphlet insisting that historical sobriquets—Sejanus for Walpole, say—were no defence), a Tory jurist posed the problem with embarrassing directness: 'that a Person entirely innocent of any Crime should be ruffled at the mention of any Villain who had happened Ages before to be in the same Post with

---

[79] See *The Poetical Works of Richard Savage*, ed. Clarence Tracy (Cambridge: Cambridge University Press, 1962), 15–25; one poem, 'The Pretender', features George I as Nero (p. 19).

[80] See Jon Mee, *Print, Publicity, and Popular Radicalism in the 1790s: The Laurel of Liberty* (Cambridge: Cambridge University Press, 2016), 41–2.

himself, and construe every Reflection upon him as a Satyr upon himself, must... make [readers] imagine that he is conscious to himself of the secret Guilt.'[81]

In this context, the delicate mischief of Pope's anti-Hanoverian touches is clear to see. He was a virtuoso exponent of the insulting sobriquet, which he could turn on court politicians with brazen specificity (Hervey as Sporus) or teasing indeterminacy (Timon in the *Epistle to Burlington*), as circumstance demanded. When it came to royalty and the underlying question of fitness to rule, however, his feints and dodges had to operate in subtler, more localized ways. As Pat Rogers has demonstrated, the 'Ear of Kings' passage was only the start of a thread that runs through *The Dunciad* and deftly implicates the royal family in further corruptions.[82] Perhaps most beautifully immune to objection is a couplet Pope inserted a few years later in the *Epistle to Bathurst*, where he imagines a loyal Hanoverian subject toasting George II: "Tis GEORGE and LIBERTY that crowns the cup, | And Zeal for that great House which eats him up.'[83] What does Pope mean here, with this odd grammatical infelicity—infelicity of a kind nicely diagnosed, though without grasping the reason, by the contemporary who thought Pope's style 'too often obscure, ambiguous & uncleanly'?[84] The distich is ambiguous indeed, and certainly ungainly, with the awkward *that–that–which* sequence, and the referent left unspecified in the final dependent clause. What exactly is it that eats up Young Cotta here: is it the zeal, or is it the great house? The allegation that Hanoverian kings were devouring the substance of their English subjects was a standard opposition trope, best remembered now for the way Fielding puts it in the mouth of Squire Western, his ludicrous Tory backwoodsman in *Tom Jones*. But in the

---

[81] *The Doctrine of Innuendo's Discuss'd, or the Liberty of the Press Maintain'd* (1731), 7–8. For the surrounding debate, see Roger Lund, '"An Alembick of Innuendos": Satire, Libel, and *The Craftsman*', *Philological Quarterly*, 95.2 (2016), 243–68. The so-called 'Hague Letter' at the centre of the trial (*Craftsman* 235, 2 January 1731) is traditionally attributed to Bolingbroke, but like many *Craftsman* attributions cannot be proved.

[82] Rogers, *Political Biography of Pope*, 165–73.

[83] *Twickenham Edition of Pope*, 3.ii: 107 (*Epistle to Bathurst*, lines 207–8).

[84] *The Literary Correspondence of the Tonsons*, ed. Stephen Bernard (Oxford: Oxford University Press, 2015), 165 (John Dennis to Tonson, 4 June 1715).

*Epistle to Bathurst*, the trope is perfectly deniable, even though Pope, unlike Fielding, deploys it in his own voice. We all know what he really means, but strictly speaking his lines mean two things at once, one of them innocent: that Young Cotta is consumed by his own laudable zeal, not by a predatory monarch. The objectionable further hint is for readers to find if they choose. The king's own term, 'honest man', seems exactly wrong for this splendidly duplicitous poetic technique—unless, of course, George II was speaking in code himself at a time when 'honest man' was widely used to mean a secret Jacobite.[85]

In the end, the only trial provoked by *The Dunciad Variorum* was a somewhat arcane dispute about copyright infringement.[86] Remarkably, however, Pope's increasingly strident satire of the 1730s was co-opted by Jacobitism when armed rebellion against the House of Hanover erupted after his death. In 1745, one of the Pretender's proclamations alluded unmistakably to *One Thousand Seven Hundred and Thirty Eight* (Pope's original title for the *Epilogue to the Satires*) when invoking a characteristically Popean association between the Hanoverian establishment and the culture of corruption over which it presided: 'It could never be said justly, till of late Years, that *not to be corrupted is the shame.*'[87] This was not the squeaking baby trumpet of sedition that Coleridge disavowed at the age of 24; it was the resonant, penetrating blast of Pope's maturity: 'Hear her black Trumpet thro' the Land proclaim, | That "Not to be corrupted is the Shame."'[88] Yet for just this reason it was also the last blast of the trumpet. As Pope shifted away from the deft insinuations of his earlier verse into a mode of explicit polemic, he also made attempts to silence him inevitable. Though more or less untouchable himself, he could be touched by proxy, and the manoeuvres that effectively ended his career as a writer

---

[85] Pittock, *Material Culture and Sedition*, 66–8.

[86] David Foxon, *Pope and the Early Eighteenth-Century Book Trade*, revised and ed. James McLaverty (Oxford: Clarendon Press, 1991), 111–14.

[87] Howard Erskine-Hill, 'Alexander Pope: The Political Poet in His Time', *Eighteenth-Century Studies*, 15.2 (1981–2), 123–48 (148, quoting *An Address to the People of England*).

[88] *Twickenham Edition of Pope*, 4: 309 (*Epilogue to the Satires*, i.159–60); for Coleridge, see below, p. 260.

of anti-ministerial satire nicely illustrate the sophistication with which censorship worked in the Walpole era, often serving to obviate the need for unpredictable or embarrassing trials.

The exemplary victim was a minor satirist named Paul Whitehead, who in his poem *Manners* (1739) comments thus on Pope's immunity in an increasingly dangerous environment for smaller fry:

> *Pope* writes unhurt—but know, 'tis different quite
> To beard the Lion, and to crush the Mite.
> Safe may he dash the Statesman in each Line,
> Those dread his Satire, who dare punish mine.[89]

Right on cue, Whitehead was arraigned and his poem condemned as scandalous by the House of Lords, the pretext being his failure to disguise the name of a bishop (Thomas Sherlock) mentioned in the text. For Samuel Johnson, who had a ringside seat, this was a move 'intended rather to intimidate Pope than to punish Whitehead'.[90] Johnson was clearly right, and it seems significant that the most conspicuous casualty of the episode was not Whitehead but Robert Dodsley, publisher of both *Manners* and the second part of *One Thousand Seven Hundred and Thirty Eight*, who had to undergo ten days' detention and a demeaning ritual of admonition in the House of Lords. It has plausibly been suggested that the whole affair was an elaborate charade in which Whitehead was complicit himself, having been bribed by the ministry to write, and publish with Dodsley, a punishable poem that incidentally raised the issue of punishing Pope.[91]

Whatever the truth, it's clear that Pope no longer felt invulnerable, and he was moved to withdraw from the fray of political satire. The opening of the second part ('"Tis all a Libel—Paxton (Sir) will say') jokes about possible prosecution, but matters had now progressed beyond joking.[92] A posthumous note to *One Thousand*

---

[89] Paul Whitehead, *Manners: A Satire* (1739), 16.

[90] Johnson, *Lives of the Poets*, 4: 47.

[91] John D. Baird, 'Literary Politics and Political Satire: Paul Whitehead and Alexander Pope', *Lumen*, 35 (2016), 19–36.

[92] *Twickenham Edition of Pope*, 4: 313 (ii.1). Treasury Solicitor Nicholas Paxton assumed responsibility for press control on Delafaye's retirement in 1734, and outdid his predecessor for paranoia and zeal.

*Seven Hundred and Thirty Eight* explains Pope's resolution to publish no further poems of this kind because 'Ridicule was become as unsafe as it was ineffectual'. It was even alleged that Dodsley's arrest for *Manners* 'struck Mr. *Pope* with such a Pannic, and trembling in his Nerves, that he has not since been able to hold a Pen'.[93] The widely expected follow-up to *One Thousand Seven Hundred and Thirty-Eight*, which Pope had implicitly promised with that poem's reference to 'the Sins of *Thirty-nine*', never materialized.[94] A fragment entitled *One Thousand Seven Hundred and Forty* turned up decades later, in Joseph Warton's 1797 edition of Pope, and though this may have been an uncompleted draft, it looks more like a completed display of constraint, meaningful precisely for its failure to articulate meaning. Pope 'left many blanks for fear of the Argus Eye of those who, if they cannot find, can fabricate treason', wrote Warton's source for the manuscript, a scholar named Thomas Wilson (who had it in the first place from Bolingbroke): wording that seems intended to connect Pope under Walpole with the radicals prosecuted for constructive treason under Pitt in the 1790s.[95] Some passages were a baffling mix of dashes, ellipses, and what Wilson called 'hieroglyphics', as though Pope was evoking the *Craftsman*'s use of pictograms, or more specifically the prosecution of a minor pamphleteer who had decoded these pictograms as political satire.[96] Pope's manuscript no longer survives, but to judge from Warton's edition he seems to have contrived it in graphic demonstration that after *Manners* functional ambiguity was no longer enough; scarcely penetrable obscurity was the only option (Figure 2.3).

---

[93] *Twickenham Edition of Pope*, 4: 327; *The Tryal of Colley Cibber, Comedian* (1740), 30 n.

[94] *Twickenham Edition of Pope*, 4: 313 (ii.5).

[95] *Twickenham Edition of Pope*, 4: 330. On the hieroglyphics, see Pat Rogers, 'The Symbols in Pope's *One Thousand Seven Hundred and Forty*', *Modern Philology*, 102.1 (2004), 90–4.

[96] See *The Tryal of William Rayner, for Printing and Publishing ... an Explanation of Mr. Danvers's Seven Ægyptian Hieroglyphics* (1733); also *State Hieroglyphicks: or, Caleb Decipher'd* (1731).

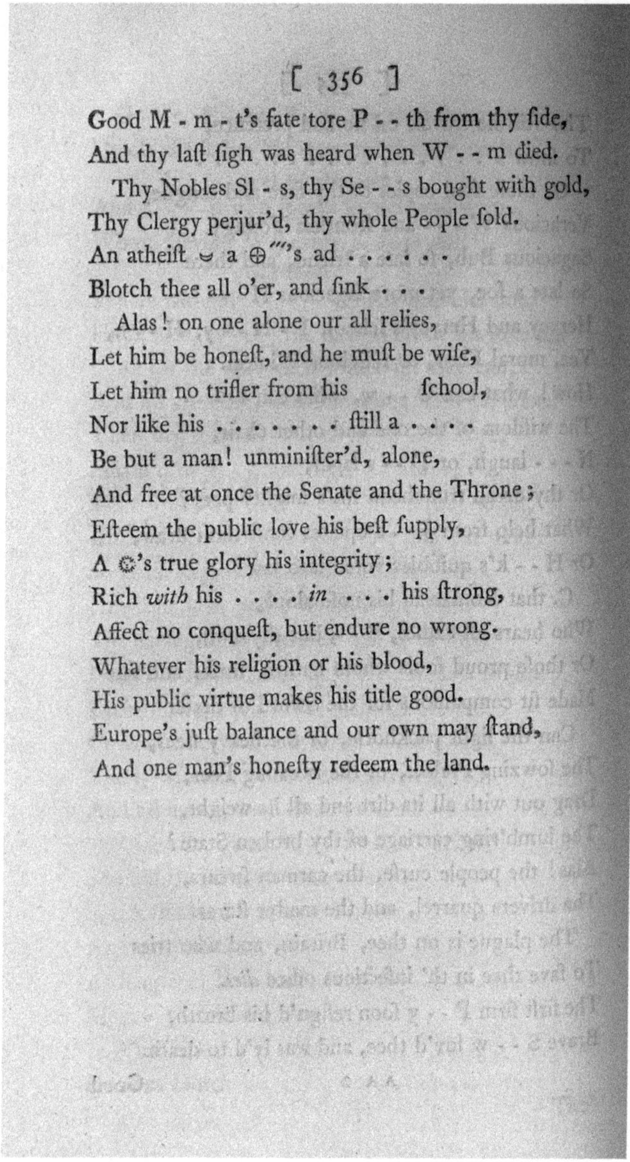

[ 356 ]

Good M - m - t's fate tore P - - th from thy side,
And thy last sigh was heard when W - - m died.

Thy Nobles Sl - s, thy Se - - s bought with gold,
Thy Clergy perjur'd, thy whole People sold.
An atheist ⌣ a ⊕""'s ad . . . . . . .
Blotch thee all o'er, and sink . . .

Alas! on one alone our all relies,
Let him be honest, and he must be wise,
Let him no trifler from his         school,
Nor like his . . . . . . . still a . . . .
Be but a man! unminister'd, alone,
And free at once the Senate and the Throne;
Esteem the public love his best supply,
A ☉'s true glory his integrity;
Rich *with* his . . . . *in* . . . his strong,
Affect no conquest, but endure no wrong.
Whatever his religion or his blood,
His public virtue makes his title good.
Europe's just balance and our own may stand,
And one man's honesty redeem the land.

**Figure 2.3** *The Works of Alexander Pope, Esq.*, ed. Joseph Warton, 9 vols (1797), 4: 356, by courtesy of the William Ready Division of Archives and Research Collections, McMaster University Library. This edition prints, for the first time, '1740, A Poem', which disintegrates in its final page into dashes, ellipses, and unexplained typographic emblems.

## Irony, intention, interpretation: *The Shortest Way with the Dissenters*

So what of Defoe? Queen Anne's reign was a tougher environment for authors than the Walpole era, and more hinged on the fundamental question that Pope was to grapple with in *The Dunciad* (and Swift in *Gulliver's Travels*) in the 1720s. How far might one go? Where was the line? Was there even an identifiable line, a question Defoe asks in *An Essay on the Regulation of the Press* (1704), and if so, was it fixed or moving? For Defoe, an inveterate uncertainty infests both prepublication licensing and post-publication prosecution as methods of censorship, but especially the latter. Under the pre-1695 regime, it was always open to licensers to find grounds for objection against any book, 'tho' Penn'd with never so much caution'. But under the common law of seditious libel, things were still harder for political writers in one important respect. If new proposals to reintroduce licensing were to be enacted, at least 'all Men will know when they Transgress, which at present they do not; for as the Case now stands, 'tis in the Breast of the Courts of Justice to make any Book a Scandalous and Seditious Libel... and the Jury being accounted only Judges of Evidence, Judges of Fact, and not of the Nature of it, the Judges are thereby Unlimited'.[97] Defoe compares good laws with buoys marking dangerous sands or rocks, 'and the Language of them is, *Come here at your peril*', whereas no such specificity applies with retrospective press control. Uniquely, 'the Crime of an Author is not known; and I think verily no Book can be wrote so warily, but that if the Author be brought on his Tryal, it shall be easy for a cunning Lawyer, ay for a Lawyer of no great Cunning, to put an *Innuendo* upon his Meaning, and make some Part of it Criminal'.[98]

---

[97] *Political and Economic Writings of Daniel Defoe*, ed. W. R. Owens and P. N. Furbank, 8 vols (London: Pickering & Chatto, 2000), 8: 148, 153.

[98] *Political Writings of Defoe*, 8: 154. *Innuendo* is used here, in its longstanding legal sense, to mean the parenthetical explanation inserted in a prosecutor's indictment to decode a seditious hint; only later does it come to mean, as its primary sense, the raw encoded hint (*OED*). On the changing functions of innuendos, see Alan Roper, 'Innuendo in the Restoration', *JEGP*, 100.1 (2001), 22–39; Annabel Patterson, 'Defeating Innuendos: Thomas Rosewell (1684) and Daniel Isaac Eaton (1794)', in

At this point Defoe cites several capital cases (including those of Algernon Sidney and the printer William Anderton) to reinforce his claim that punishment is no less unpredictable than conviction: 'if a Man robs a House, counterfeits the Coin, or kills a Man, he knows what he has to trust to, but Authors have never known their Punishment.' Merely on judicial whim, the same offence might generate anything from a manageable fine to public execution. There was a terrifying scale of harm, which suspended writers in a permanent, expressively disabling state of anxiety and intimidation: '*Fines, Whippings, Pillories, Imprisonment for Life, Halters and Axes.*'[99]

The context for Defoe's complaint about the absolute discretion of judges is an influential common-law ruling made during the 1679–85 licensing lapse by Lord Chief Justice Scroggs, in the case (among others) of Henry Care. Scroggs limited the role of the jury to deciding the mere fact of authorship: whether the defendant had or had not written any given piece. Whether or not the piece constituted seditious libel in substantive terms (Defoe's judgment about the 'nature' of it as opposed to mere 'evidence' or 'fact') was the judge's prerogative, and this anomaly was not resolved by legislation until Fox's Libel Act of 1792 brought content within the remit of the jury.[100] Moreover, after licensing ended in 1695, a possibly concerted series of judicial interpretations was expanding the practical definition of seditious libel, a term originally encompassing publications offensive to, or subversive of, monarchs or prelates, but now steadily extended to include the Crown's ministers, government, or the constitution in general, and

*The State Trials and the Politics of Justice in Later Stuart England*, ed. Brian Cowan and Scott Sowerby (Woodbridge: Boydell & Brewer, forthcoming).

[99] *Political Writings of Defoe*, 8: 156.

[100] See William T. Mayton, 'Seditious Libel and the Lost Guarantee of a Freedom of Expression', *Columbia Law Review* 84 (1984), 91–142 (106–7); for *Rex v. Care*, see Schwoerer, *The Ingenious Mr. Henry Care, Restoration Publicist* (Baltimore: Johns Hopkins University Press, 2001), 104–33. For pragmatic reasons, Scroggs's ruling blurred the boundaries between unlicensed newsbook printing and seditious libel, but was applied thereafter in both areas, notably, in Defoe's time, by Lord Chief Justice Holt in the trial of James Drake for *Mercurius Politicus* (Hamburger, 'Development of the Law of Seditious Libel', 687–90, 736–8).

most broadly of all the peace of the realm, again at the judge's determination.[101] For Lord Chief Justice Holt as he directed Tutchin's jury in 1704, it was 'strange Doctrine' to limit libel to reflections on individuals when spreading disaffection in general was the crime that mattered—for if authors 'cou'd not be call'd to Account for possessing People with an ill Opinion of the Government, no Government cou'd subsist'.[102] Libel law was now at risk of becoming a matter of mere *raison d'état*.

In this decade, the marked rise in seditious libel prosecutions, not least Defoe's own, made the interpretative monopoly of judges a pressing question, and with it the question of whether ambiguity, irony, and other forms of indirection might render authors safe.[103] Most often, authors were on the losing side of the argument, and pro-government lawyers strenuously upheld the principle that no mystery or obscurity of literary style, including irony or allegory, should be allowed to frustrate the law. As one Whig jurist summed up the tradition in 1730, 'from the Reasons of the Law, a Libel in Hieroglyphicks, is as much a Libel, and as highly punishable, as an open Invective'. Encoding must not be assumed to constitute protection. 'If it be really unintelligible to any one, it will pass for Nonsense with every one, and, as such, meet with Impunity', this commentator continued: 'But if there be only a thin Veil, or aukward Disguise thrown over it, thro' which those who can see and observe may perceive the lurking Satyr within, a Court of Law will examine it narrowly, and judge of it according to the Intention of the Maker, and the Influence it may have.'[104]

A landmark case on the issue was Joseph Browne's in 1706, which established that irony was libellous if the court so interpreted it, or if the defendant failed to refute the charge of underlying 'ill Intent'.[105]

---

[101] *CP*, 4: xvii–xviii; Jeffrey K. Walker, 'A Poisen in Ye Commonwealthe: Seditious Libel in Hanoverian London', *Anglo-American Law Review*, 26 (1997), 341–66 (esp. 342–9).

[102] *CP*, 4: 117 ('The Trial of John Tutchin, on an Information for a Libel').

[103] See Mark Knights, *Representation and Misrepresentation in Later Stuart Britain: Partisanship and Political Culture* (Oxford: Oxford University Press, 2005), 261–6.

[104] *State Law: or, The Doctrine of Libels, Discussed and Examined*, 2nd edn (c. 1730), 74.

[105] *A Report of Cases Argued, Debated, and Adjudged in B. R. in the Time of the Late Queen Anne* (1737), 86.

The poem in question was *The Country Parson's Honest Advice*, a rudimentary exercise in ironic epideixis—or, really, plain-vanilla sarcasm—that praised assorted Whig grandees for exactly the virtue that each most notoriously lacked. Double-dealing Godolphin is singled out for 'Probity', promiscuous Devonshire for 'Chastity', arrogant Halifax for 'Modesty'. Gilbert Burnet, now Bishop of Salisbury and a bête noire of the Anglican elite for his pro-Dissenter views, gets a couplet to himself: 'Like *Sarum* I wou'd have thee love the Church; | He scorns to leave his Mother in the Lurch.'[106] At trial, Browne rested his defence on the poem's patently untenable surface meaning, and after conviction dug himself in deeper with a pamphlet that upheld 'the natural and genuine sense' of the poem, not the 'harsher Meaning' alleged by the court. Now Browne tests each compliment to breaking point. If any doubt were to be cast on Devonshire's chastity, surely his grace had too much good nature, or good sense, to ask the reason—and then how could anyone doubt Godolphin's probity when his lordship controlled such enormous sums of public money?[107]

Inevitably (though he failed to see the inevitability himself), Browne received a fresh sentence to the pillory for compounding his offence: for 'Writing *Ironies*, and then Expounding them *Ironically*', Defoe cheerfully wrote.[108] The episode in effect criminalized subtextual meaning, and in the original trial, Holt was careful to spell out the precedent being set: the 'Manner of Speaking' was to be noted, and 'an Information will lie for speaking ironically'.[109] Over the next few years, prosecutors seized on the precedent to clamp down on functional ambiguity more broadly, for as Attorney General Northey observed in 1713, when securing the conviction of George Ridpath despite his evasive wording, 'if Libellers were suffer'd to dress up Persons and things in seeming Disguise, but in such Terms as may be understood by every body but a Judge and Jury, we are in a sad Case'.[110] The same legal clarity did not extend to allegory, but similar assumptions were routinely applied, and pro-government jurists

---

[106] *POAS*, 7: 157–8 (*The Country Parson's Honest Advice*, 1706).

[107] Joseph Browne, *A Letter to the Right Honourable Mr. Secretary Harley* (1706), 5; see also 15–16.

[108] *Review*, 8 April 1706.  [109] *Report of Cases*, 86.

[110] *Evening Post*, 21 February 1713.

insisted that with this kind of text 'a Court shall, notwithstanding its Obscurity and Perplexity, be allowed to judge of its Meaning'. Meaning was no longer necessarily the literal surface; it was the sense in which (as we might now put it) the interpretative community addressed by a work might reasonably be expected to construe it.[111]

This pragmatic understanding of inherent meaning was crucial in a range of contexts. Among the most widely publicized was Steele's expulsion from the Commons when his pro-Hanover tract *The Crisis* (1713) was voted a seditious libel—as too, in a nice display of the period's political to-and-fro, was Swift's no-holds-barred riposte of 1714, *The Public Spirit of the Whigs*, this time by the House of Lords. Shortly afterwards, on the Hanoverian accession, *The Crisis* earned Steele a knighthood, but at the time he made no headway with his argument that the most innocent potential meaning of an ambiguous text should prevail in law over other possible constructions. Or, as he put it, 'that if an Author's Words, in the obvious and natural Interpretation of them, have a Meaning which is Innocent, they cannot without great Injustice be condemned of another Meaning which is Criminal'.[112] Legal textbooks were clear thereafter 'that such Scandal as is expressed in a scoffing and ironical Manner, makes a Writing as properly a Libel, as that which is expressed in direct terms'. The same applied to the use of dashed, gutted, or otherwise disguised names, for example by anagram or rebus, 'for it brings the utmost Contempt upon the Law, to suffer its Justice to be eluded by such trifling Evasions'.[113] This particular source, William Hawkins's influential *Treatise of the Pleas of the Crown* (1716–21), helpfully adds 'That it is far from being a Justification of a Libel, that the Contents thereof are true'.[114] If anything, it was an aggravation.

---

[111] *State Law*, 75.

[112] Richard Steele, *Mr. Steele's Apology for Himself and His Writings* (1714), 54. For context, see Charles A. Knight, *A Political Biography of Richard Steele* (London: Pickering & Chatto, 2015), 145–58.

[113] William Hawkins, *A Treatise of the Pleas of the Crown*, 2nd edn, 2 vols (1724), 1: 193–4. On the legal status of gutted names, see Andrew Bricker, 'Libel and Satire: The Problem with Naming', *ELH*, 81.3 (2014), 889–921.

[114] Hawkins, *Treatise*, 1: 194. As C. R. Kropf notes, this explains why lampooned ministers preferred seditious libel prosecutions to *scandalum magnatum* suits: questions of truth need not be debated, and acquittal would not seem to validate a

In this context, there might seem to be a case for setting aside, as irrelevant in practice, the longstanding critical debate about the pamphlet that landed Defoe in the pillory, *The Shortest Way with the Dissenters* (1702). Is it a work of irony of the kind most famously exemplified in the 1720s by Swift's *Modest Proposal*, in which explicit meaning is undermined, discredited, and replaced by implicit counter-argument? Or is it merely a hoax, a malicious act of mimicry, hostile in motivation but not in terms of ulterior meaning, since no subtextual hints or irony markers are there to subvert the surface case?[115] If irony (in this case the use of a persona whose words collapse from within when properly scrutinized) is no defence, the question, legally speaking, goes away. Yet things on the ground were messier than legal textbooks of the day suggest, and the landmark ruling against Browne that brought ironic discourse within the purview of the common law of seditious libel was not yet in place. Even afterwards, it was still assumed that well-executed irony could constitute adequate protection, alongside more extreme forms of indirection as the stakes grew higher. In Shaftesbury's words, 'if Men are forbid to speak their minds seriously on certain Subjects, they will do it ironically'. If forbidden absolutely, 'they will then redouble their Disguise, involve themselves in Mysteriousness, and talk so as hardly to be understood, or at least not plainly interpreted, by those who are dispos'd to do 'em a mischief'.[116] Moreover, though the role of juries was formally limited by Scroggs's ruling to facts of publication as opposed to interpretation of texts, juries sometimes pushed back in practice, and were encouraged by pro-jury writers who thought it legitimate to question, above all in

---

defamation ('Libel and Satire in the Eighteenth Century', *Eighteenth-Century Studies*, 8.2 (1974–5), 153–68, esp. 156–8).

[115] On modern approaches to *The Shortest Way* as either irony or hoax, see Ashley Marshall, 'The Generic Context of Defoe's *The Shortest-Way with the Dissenters* and the Problem of Irony', *RES*, 61 (2010), 234–58. On irony markers, see Linda Hutcheon, *Irony's Edge: The Theory and Politics of Irony* (London: Routledge, 2004), esp. 141–58.

[116] Shaftesbury, *Characteristicks*, 1: 43 ('Sensus Communis', 1709).

seditious libel cases, the judicial allocation of duties between jury and bench.[117]

For this reason, *The Shortest Way* is of peculiar interest, because it coincided with, indeed played a major role in instigating, a period of intense debate in and beyond courtrooms about the legitimacy of functional ambiguity, and specifically about irony, to which Defoe made vigorous appeal not only in this case but also in that of three similarly provocative pamphlets published a decade later, on the cusp of the Hanoverian accession. However desperate or pragmatic, Defoe's arguments for immunity as ironist or ventriloquist constitute the period's most powerful defence of the early modern conventions described by Patterson—the conventions allowing tolerable indirection when expressing political dissent—just as ministers under Queen Anne seemed determined to roll them back.[118]

Further complicating the uncertain status of *The Shortest Way* as either irony or hoax is Defoe's own inconsistency about the pamphlet, which advocates ruthless, even genocidal, suppression of the confessional minority to which he belonged himself. In one account, he wrote the pamphlet as *agent provocateur*, studiously imitating the extremist rhetoric of Tory rabble-rousers like Sacheverell, but shifting their hints and insinuations into frank calls for action. Sacheverell was beautifully mimicked in tone. All that changed was the degree of explicitness, so that, as Defoe later asked,

> When [Sacheverell] tells us, *Every Man that wishes the Welfare of the Church, ought to hang out a Bloody Flag and Banner of Defiance against the Dissenters* ... What can any Man suppose he means, but *the Shortest Way*? What's the Difference between Mr. *Sachevrel's Bloody Flag*, and *De Foe's Gallows* and *Galleys*? Only that One is an *Oxford* Modern Dialect, and the Other put into Downright Plain *English*.[119]

This, then, was hoax with a practical purpose, designed to make High-Church Tories publicly embrace measures that until now they

---

[117] Thomas A. Green, *Verdict According to Conscience: Perspectives on the English Criminal Trial Jury, 1200–1800* (Chicago: University of Chicago Press, 1985), 318–55.

[118] Patterson, *Censorship and Interpretation*, esp. 3–31.

[119] *Political Writings of Defoe*, 3: 195 (*A New Test of the Church of England's Honesty*, 1704).

had recommended only with deniable indirection, and so expose themselves as the sanguinary maniacs that Defoe took them to be. Elsewhere, Defoe gloated about a letter he claimed to have seen from a Tory reader who valued *The Shortest Way* 'next to the Holy Bible' and hoped the Queen would 'put all that is there prescribed into Execution'. There's evidence elsewhere of other instances in which the hoax succeeded in flushing out Tory extremism.[120] 'The Case the Book pointed at', Defoe summed up years later, 'was to speak in the first Person of the Party, and then, thereby, not only speak their Language, but make them acknowledge it to be theirs, which they did so openly, that confounded all their Attempts afterwards to deny it, and call it a *Scandal* thrown upon them by another.'[121]

Yet this was not Defoe's immediate explanation of *The Shortest Way*, and in a pamphlet hastily printed after his arrest he described it instead as manifest irony, 'an irony not unusual' that any alert reader would be able to decipher. As he insisted, 'If any man take the pains seriously to reflect upon the Contents, the Nature of the Thing and the Manner of the Stile, it seems Impossible to imagine it should pass for any thing but an Irony.'[122] There was the surface meaning, objectionable enough, indeed seditious in the broad sense of tending to subvert the peace of the realm. But this was trumped by a deeper and more authentic textual stratum, 'the Native Genuine Meaning and Design of the Paper'.[123] And indeed if we go back to *The Shortest Way* in this spirit, it's not difficult to find several quite conspicuous irony markers: moments that discredit Defoe's persona and explicit argument, and point instead to an implicit layer of authorial contradiction or counter-argument. The text goes awry at the very start, when Defoe's churchman opens not with the usual scriptural source but with an Aesopian fable by Sir Roger L'Estrange, that indestructible

---

[120] *Review*, 11 August 1705; for other hoodwinked Tories, see Paula R. Backscheider, *Daniel Defoe: His Life* (Baltimore: Johns Hopkins University Press, 1989), 99–100.

[121] Daniel Defoe, *The Present State of the Parties in Great Britain* (1712), 24.

[122] *Political Writings of Defoe*, 3: 113 (*A Brief Explanation of a Late Pamphlet, Entituled, The Shortest Way with the Dissenters*, 1703); I quote the first-edition reading recorded in the textual notes, 3: 386.

[123] *Political Writings of Defoe*, 3: 113.

elder statesman of the Tory extreme. Numerous errors follow, which Defoe's editors sometimes correct on his behalf with embarrassed footnotes. But these errors are part of the ironic pattern, and deftly indicate the frenzy of the supposed author. 'I do not prescribe Fire and Fagot, but as *Scipio* said of *Carthage, Dilenda est Carthago*':[124] here the desperate resort to classical allusion barely papers over the contradiction of a sentence that in effect says 'I do not urge destruction, but I urge destruction'. Defoe intensifies the point by getting both the orator and the Latin wrong: it was Cato the Elder who wanted Carthage destroyed (*delenda est Carthago*); Scipio, as Defoe's target audience would have known, made the case for co-existence. A few paragraphs later, with another of his insouciant transitional conjunctions, Defoe's churchman turns to the Book of Exodus to recall that '*Moses* was a merciful meek Man, and yet with what Fury did he run thro' the Camp, and cut the Throats of Three and thirty thousand of his dear *Israelites*, that were fallen into Idolatry'. Again his zeal gets the better of his accuracy, the true biblical body count being a more modest—though still, for a meek man, impressive—three thousand.[125]

All this prepares the way for the pamphlet's brilliant peroration, in which the speaker's frenzied analogies consistently get away from him and subvert, not support, his case. Berating the Dissenters for refusing to enter Anglican churches, Defoe's churchman inadvertently aligns them with the primitive Christians, with the established clergy resembling the worshippers of Baal. Then he undermines his attempt to portray Dissenters as endangering religion by saying instead that they 'endanger the utter Extirpation of Religion': in effect a double negative that reverses his intended meaning. The climax to the pamphlet comes with the following lament:

> *Alas the Church of England!* What with Popery on one Hand, and Schismaticks on the other; how has she been Crucify'd between two Thieves.
>
> Now *let us Crucifie the Thieves*. Let her Foundations be establish'd upon the Destruction of her Enemies...[126]

---

[124] *Political Writings of Defoe*, 3: 105; again I quote the first-edition reading (3: 386).
[125] *Political Writings of Defoe*, 3: 105 and n.
[126] *Political Writings of Defoe*, 3: 109.

The rhetorical incompetence of Defoe's churchman here is dizzying, but at the same time hard to miss. His words look back in the first place to Sacheverell's hysterical analogy between an unholy modern alliance of anti-Anglican factions and the cynical partnership of Herod and Pilate 'in the Same Common Design of Crucifying *Their Lord and Saviour*, betwixt *Thieves* and *Robbers*'.[127] Defoe's parody neatly draws out not only Sacheverell's failure to remember that one of the thieves—by implication, now, the Dissenters—was saved, but also his hypocrisy in advocating persecution while claiming the subject position of the persecuted. Brilliantly, Defoe makes his speaker's analogy for the Church of England lurch uncontrollably across the paragraph break from the crucified Christ to the crucifying authorities, an absurdity compounded by another basic failure of scriptural memory: that Christianity was to be founded on the rock of faith, not the destruction of enemies.

By this stage, it's hard to see what scope there could be to deny the operation of irony, irony of a kind that dissociates Defoe from his churchman's sanguinary case and embeds in the text an implicit counter-case. Yet this does not require us to reject Defoe's alternative account of the pamphlet as entrapment or hoax. *The Shortest Way* was both things at once, or rather it was each in turn. Anonymously published and casually read, it functioned first as a hoax inciting Tory readers to declare and discredit themselves. It could then function as irony when more carefully read, or in Defoe's words more seriously reflected on, as the facts of authorship emerge.

Defoe could reasonably contend, in this light, that he should not be held accountable for the arguments of the voice he wrote in. He could claim, indeed, that he was implicitly refuting these arguments, and with them more broadly '*the Cant of the Nonjuring party Expos'd*'.[128] Yet in the end the finer points of literary interpretation have limited relevance to a case that turned in practice on brute power. Several side-issues in the pamphlet, not least the speaker's scathing hostility to the impending union with Scotland, added to the broadly destabilizing effect, and all could be enlisted to secure the case against Defoe,

---

[127] Henry Sacheverell, *The Political Union* (Oxford, 1702), 52.
[128] *Political Writings of Defoe*, 3: 115 (*Brief Explanation*, 1703).

*Libels in Hieroglyphics* 131

whether he meant them literally or not.[129] Sensing the slippery nature of the text, the officials responsible for framing charges cast the net as wide as possible, invoking not only particular passages that were seditious when read at face value, but also Defoe's own personality as seditious in its nature, and the pamphlet's seditious effect in the overall sense of disturbing peace. Parliament found *The Shortest Way* a work 'tending to *promote* Sedition' (emphasis added); more colourfully, and with marked intensification of the usual formulae, the Old Bailey indictment called it 'a Seditious, pernicious and Diabolical Libel', its author 'a Seditious man and of a disordered mind', and his intention that of 'perfidiously, mischievously and seditiously contriving, practicing and purposing to make and Cause discord between ... the Queen and her ... Subjects'.[130] Here was a charge that could be made to stick however one understood *The Shortest Way*: as a non-ironic work attacking Dissenters, an ironic work attacking High-Church Tories, or some more unstable amalgam of both these things. It was seditious in the simple sense of rocking the boat.

Some observers felt that in the end *The Shortest Way* was merely a pretext for controlling Defoe more broadly, or that he was really being punished for his radical Whig agitation in earlier tracts like *Legion's Memorial* and *The Original Power of the Collective Body of the People of England* (both 1701). Others thought he ended up in the pillory because he refused or failed to supply information that ministers wished to extract concerning the larger infrastructure and sponsorship of opposition propaganda. Certainly, there were complex and protracted negotiations between Defoe and Secretary of State Nottingham over the six-month period between early January 1703, when Nottingham issued a warrant for his arrest, and late July, when the pillorying at last took place.[131] These dealings inaugurate a pattern of direct negotiation between ministers and libellers that was to intensify under Walpole, and in Defoe's case they included the monarch, before whom Defoe

---

[129] For the significance of the supposed author's anti-unionism, see Thomas Keymer, 'Fictions, Libels and Unions in the Long Eighteenth Century', in Gerald Carruthers and Colin Kidd (eds), *Literature and Union: Scottish Texts, British Contexts* (Oxford: Oxford University Press, 2018), 97–122 (105–6).

[130] Backscheider, *Daniel Defoe*, 103–4.

[131] Backscheider, *Daniel Defoe*, 101, 107–8, 114–17.

appeared at Windsor two days before his first pillorying, in a last-ditch effort to stave off execution of his sentence. The negotiations also herald the stick-and-carrot style of press control that Walpole was to perfect, for Defoe—too dangerous to be left in opposition, too talented to be wasted as a resource—was soon to be on Harley's payroll.[132]

## Defoe in the pillory

The pillorying is no simpler to decipher than the text that occasioned it, and again two rather different accounts of it come down to us. Though Pope's Defoe is unabashed, not alarmed or even embarrassed, the larger context of *The Dunciad* stresses the pillory's role as a theatre of public humiliation and physical peril. Defoe was clearly terrified, as well as abhorring a style of punishment intolerable to him 'as a Gentleman', and he admitted to Nottingham that 'Prisons, Pillorys and Such like... are Worse to me Than Death'. Only weeks before the event, he hoped to avoid his ordeal by pleading guilty in full to the florid indictment drawn up against him, 'Even to all the Adverbs, the Seditiously's, The Malitiously's'.[133] It's a striking fact that the few early images we have of the occasion emphasize abjection. The earliest is a crude woodcut on the title page of *The Scribler's Doom*, an imaginary dialogue between Defoe and William Fuller (a conspiracy theorist and seditious libeller who lost an eye when pilloried in 1702) which seems to have been hastily issued after Defoe's first spell in the pillory, and before the second and third: 'may Rotten Eggs like *March* Hail shower on thy head', the fictional Fuller wishes him (Figure 2.4).[134] Another image is from a hostile piracy of *Jure Divino*, Defoe's 1706 verse satire on patriarchal political theory, which replaces the usual grand frontispiece portrait with a woodcut of

---

[132] On the negotiations with Harley, see Backscheider, *Daniel Defoe*, 154–8.

[133] *The Letters of Daniel Defoe*, ed. George Harris Healey (Oxford: Clarendon Press, 1955), 2, 8.

[134] *The Scribler's Doom; or, The Pillory in Fashion* (1703), 7. As Joseph Hone notes (see below, n. 136), this image was clumsily customized (with superimposed 'D') from a stock woodblock.

*Libels in Hieroglyphics* 133

*The Scribler's Doom;*

OR, THE

**Pillory** IN **Fashion**

BEING

A New DIALOGUE

BETWEEN

Two Loop-Hole Sufferers,

*William Fuller* and *De Fooe*,

In their late Conference concerning *Pilloring*.

*Licensed according to Order.*

London, Printed for J. Sharp in Holbourn. 1703.

**Figure 2.4** *The Scribler's Doom; or, The Pillory in Fashion* (1703), title page, © the British Library Board, 8122.b.86. A hastily customized woodblock shows 'the chiefest Tophick now in Discourse ... *Du Foo*'s being Pillor'd'.

Defoe looking conspicuously abashed, even physically bashed, as he undergoes punishment (Figure 2.5).[135]

Then there is *The Whigs Medly* or *The Three False Brethren* (1711), an illustrated broadside by George Bickham which juxtaposes verses and portraits in collage form: 'Here's Daniel, the Pope, and the Devil well match'd | By whose Crafty Inventions all mischief is hatch'd.' Also included in *The Whigs Medly* is Defoe's restless, warty soulmate Oliver Cromwell, while at the top of the page a further blast of doggerel, attached to a headshot of Defoe as pillory-peeper, ends by urging the viewer 'pray take a Throw' (Figure 2.6). The least aggressive image, though still very partisan in context, comes in a Tory playing-card pack of 1705, engraved in copperplate by Robert Spofforth, which attaches unusual weight to the project of seditious libel; the pack also features cards showing Tutchin on trial and Fuller beating hemp in Bridewell. Here Defoe ('*The Author of $y^e$ Shortest way $w^{th}$ Dissenters Pillor$^{yd}$*') is the five of spades, still wearing his trademark full-bottomed wig. The engraving emphasizes the throng of spectators, with a guard of pikemen behind them (Figure 2.7).[136]

Of a piece with these images are remarks such as that of the Tory interlocutor in a dialogue about Sacheverell by William King, who 'never saw a *W—gg* with Satisfaction before, unless it was *D—l d'Foe* in the Pillory': a sneer that hardly suggests a happy Defoe.[137] Before the pillorying, another pamphleteer confidently predicted that the Dissenters whose interests Defoe had jeopardized would pelt him with eggs, despite the presence of armed guards ('the *Halbert Gentlemen*').[138] Several verse lampoons kept up the attack. In one, Tom Brown's 'Pleasant Dialogue between the Pillory and Daniel de Foe', Defoe humbly acknowledges the superior power of the pillory, as an organ of state, over mere hacks: 'Thou Prop of Justice, Adjutant of Law; | That keep'st the Paper-blurring World in awe.'[139] A longer, nastier poem by Pittis, *The True-Born-Hugonot* (1703), deplores the fact that Defoe

[135] The cut is reproduced as the frontispiece to Novak, *Daniel Defoe*.

[136] Joseph Hone, 'A New Portrait of Defoe in the Pillory', *Notes & Queries*, 63 (2016), 70–1.

[137] *A Vindication of the Reverend Dr. Henry Sacheverell* (1711), 2.

[138] *The Shortest-Way with Whores and Rogues* (1703), sig. a$^v$.

[139] *The Works of Mr. Thomas Brown, in Prose and Verse*, 2 vols (1707), 1: 24.

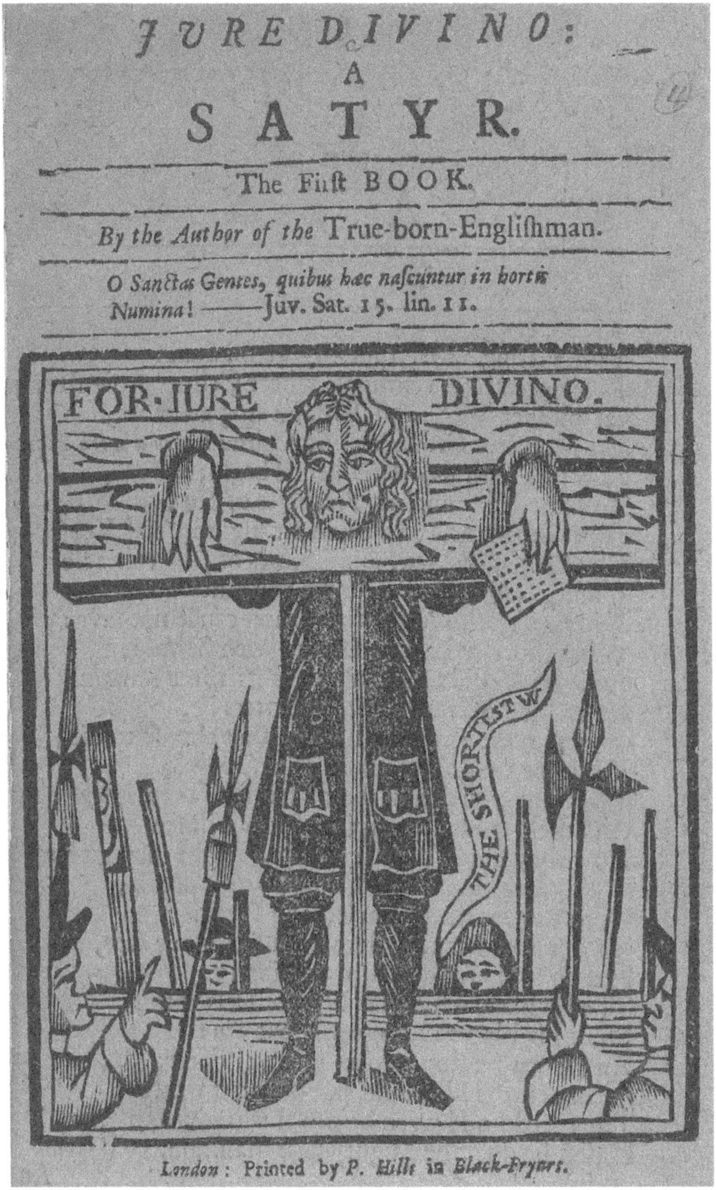

*JURE DIVINO:*
A
SATYR.

The Firſt BOOK.

*By the Author of the* True-born-Engliſhman.

*O Sanctas Gentes, quibus hæc naſcuntur in hortis*
*Numina!* ——Juv. Sat. 15. lin. 11.



*London*: Printed by *P. Hills* in *Black-Fryars*.

**Figure 2.5** Daniel Defoe, *Jure Divino: A Satyr, The First Book* (*c.*1706), title page, by permission of the Beinecke Rare Book and Manuscript Library (General Collection). This piracy replaces the usual frontispiece portrait with a demeaning woodcut.

**Figure 2.6** George Bickham, *The Whigs Medly*, or *The Three False Brethren* (1711), engraved broadside, by courtesy of the Lewis Walpole Library, Yale University. The portrait of Defoe as a seditious pillory-peeper is a hostile caricature ('With blobber Lips, & Lockram Jaws, | Warts, Wrinkles, Wens, and other Flaws'), but very recognizable.

*Libels in Hieroglyphics* 137

**Figure 2.7** Robert Spofforth, playing-card of Defoe in the pillory (1705), copperplate etching on pasteboard, from a Tory pack depicting events from the first three years of Queen Anne's reign, © the Trustees of the British Museum. All rights reserved. The caption plays on Defoe's habit of styling himself 'the Author of *The True-Born Englishman*'.

('a Villain we should brain') has escaped grave injury, but stresses that what saves him is not popular sympathy but protection organized by 'his *City Friends*', with bribes distributed to spectators from '*Faction*'s Money'. For Pittis, justice has been usurped by Whig activists, figured towards the end of the poem as heathen idolaters before Defoe's false god, 'As round him *Philistians* adoring stand, | And keep their *Dagon* safe from *Israel's Hand*'.[140] In this view, to pillory Defoe is to put things in their proper place, to 'place *Sedition* in Sedition's *Throne*'. The whole spectacle becomes a tawdry Grubstreet coronation, right down to the endless supply of incendiary waste paper. *Mac Flecknoe* is unmistakably recalled as Pittis surveys Defoe's back catalogue of fugitive propaganda: 'Loads of *Sedition* there, might also come, | Fit *Ammunition* for the *Reader*'s *Bum*.'[141] It's a nice historical irony that when Pittis was pilloried himself not long afterwards, it was for a work sharing many rhetorical similarities with *The Shortest Way*—in particular, its account of poison or contagion infesting the church, 'a *Hectick Fever* lurking in the *Bowels* of it'—but written in earnest.[142]

To put this fragmentary evidence together is to gain a sense of Defoe's pillorying as in some respects functioning as intended: as a frightening ordeal. Yet this is far from being the consensus of posterity, and again we may look to visual representations—each conditioned by its particular moment—to see the alternative view in its clearest form. On the dustjacket of Paul Dottin's classic biography, published during the rise of totalitarianism in Europe, Defoe looks serenely, almost quizzically, out from the pillory, isolated in heroic detachment by a surrounding halo (Figure 2.8). A Swedish magazine of the same era gives a calmly Nordic take on the event, in which nothing worse occurs than mild traffic congestion, while something slightly more interesting is happening off to the right (Figure 2.9).[143] The *locus*

[140] Pittis, *The True-Born Hugonot* (1703), 3, 4, 20, 19.

[141] Pittis, *True-Born Hugonot*, 19, 11.

[142] William Pittis, *The Case of the Church of England's Memorial Fairly Stated* (1705), 17; this work is sometimes attributed to the Irish Jacobite Charles Leslie, who may have assisted Pittis, and was then under investigation for *The Rehearsal* (1704–9), a newspaper opposing Defoe's *Review*.

[143] Paul Dottin, *The Life and Strange and Surprising Adventures of Daniel Defoe* (New York: Macaulay, 1929*)*; *Allers Familj-Journal*, 14 (2 April 1924).

**Figure 2.8** Paul Dottin, *The Life and Strange and Surprising Adventures of Daniel Defoe* (New York: Macaulay, 1929*)*, illustrated dustjacket, by permission of the New York Public Library.

*classicus* is Eyre Crowe's magnificent historical canvas of 1862, from which the Swedish image borrows the architectural detail of Temple Bar, scene of the third and final pillorying (Figure 2.10). Crowe's fascination with the pillory reaches beyond Defoe (see below, pp. 218–9), and in this case, in line with the dominant Whig historiography of the Victorian era, he represents Defoe as a martyr in the struggle against Stuart censorship.[144] Never mind that Defoe (like Swift and others of his day) saw censorship not as an affront to free-speech principles but as a weapon to be evaded oneself and used against others, as when he campaigned in 1712–13 to persuade

---

[144] On Crowe's painting of Johnson at Uttoxeter, see below, pp. 218–19; Crowe's earliest exhibited painting, now lost, shows earless Prynne meeting Archbishop Laud, the tables turned after Laud's arrest (J. P. Hopson, 'Crowe, Eyre (1824–1910)', *ODNB*).

**Figure 2.9** *Allers Familj-Journal*, 14 (2 April 1924), cover illustration, © Mary Evans Picture Library. The illustration shows Defoe's third and final pillorying, at Temple Bar.

**Figure 2.10** Eyre Crowe, *Daniel Defoe in the Pillory* (1862), oil on canvas, by permission of Salford Museum and Art Gallery.

the ministry to suppress the *Flying Post* and prosecute Ridpath.[145] Crowe's sense of Defoe's heroism is strong enough, indeed, to make him draw on visual elements associated with crucifixion paintings. There is not only the frontal view of Defoe in a cross-like frame, flanked by niched statues where the thieves would otherwise be (cheekily, these were Stuart monarchs), but also the evocation of other motifs: the kneeling mourner, the grouped women, the soldiers, the scuffles, the sponge-bearer. Crowe had trained and travelled in France and Italy, and seems to have had no single model in mind as he painted the scene; instead he absorbed traditional elements that are best seen in their starkest early forms (Figure 2.11).

Flowers are everywhere in the painting—littering the foreground, garlanding the pillory, held by the women, raised on the pole—and this again may arise from crucifixion iconography. But Crowe also drew on a biographical tradition in which the crowd not only refrains from pelting Defoe with refuse or stones but actively subverts the expectation of violence by decorating the pillory and tossing flowers. The interesting thing is that this now celebrated expression of popular support can be traced to no source earlier than Walter Wilson's 1830 biography of Defoe, which hesitantly mentions the garlanding ('Tradition reports') but says nothing about the flower-pelting.[146] The flowers, sometimes reported now by scholars as established fact, first seem to emerge in John Forster's tentative wording of 1858 ('nothing harder than a flower was thrown at him') and only then solidify into positive statement: 'the crowd cheered him, and drank his health, and threw flowers at him', reports *Harper's Magazine* in 1860.[147]

Enemies certainly objected at the time that Defoe turned his pillorying to advantage, but most complaints refer to his exultations after, not during, the event, and all represent the occasion as not an

---

[145] Furbank and Owens, *Political Biography of Defoe*, 125. For a good account of Swift in this vein—instigating the arrest of Whig opponents; using irony and obliquity to avoid arrest himself—see Higgins, 'Censorship, Libel'.

[146] Walter Wilson, *Memoirs of the Life and Time of Daniel De Foe*, 3 vols (1830), 2: 69. For the flower-pelting, see e.g. Backscheider, *Daniel Defoe*, 118; Furbank and Owens, *Political Biography of Defoe*, 24.

[147] John Forster, *Historical and Biographical Essays*, 2 vols (1858), 2: 50; *Harper's New Monthly Magazine*, 20 (February 1860), 412.

**Figure 2.11** Fra Angelico (Guido di Pietro), *The Crucifixion with the Sponge-Bearer* (1442), fresco, Museo di San Marco, Florence, Italy/Bridgeman Images. The fresco, designed for monastic contemplation, epitomizes the crucifixion iconography drawn on by Eyre Crowe.

irruption of spontaneous sympathy but a feat of party muscle. Most explicit was Charles Leslie, who fulminated against 'the *Party* causing his *Books* to be *Hauk'd* and Publickly *Sold* about the *Pillory*, while he stood upon it (in *Triumph!*) for *Writing* them'. Pittis blamed deep-pocketed Whig fixers for sending hired 'Scum' to the pillory, who then 'Hallow'd him down from his Wooden Punishment, as if he had been a *Cicero* that had made an Excellent Oration in it, rather than a *Cataline* that was Expos'd and Declaim'd against there'.[148] Defoe contents himself with saying, in an oblique recollection of 1705, that the mob, whom 'it was expected would have treated this Man very ill,

---

[148] Charles Leslie, *The Wolf Stript of His Shepherd's Clothing* (1704), 59; William Pittis, *Heraclitus Ridens*, 3–7 August 1703.

on the contrary *Pitied him*'.[149] We know that he emerged unscathed from all three of his spells in the pillory, unlike less fortunate Whig agitators of the day. But it's equally clear that our image of the episode owes a great deal to fanciful Victorian embellishment. A possible explanation is that later writers confused or conflated his case with the punishment of a radical Wilkite printer in 1765, probably the earliest case of pillory-garlanding as a matter of eyewitness report.[150]

The real triumph was on the page, in the poem Defoe crafted in his own defence—literally his physical defence—while awaiting execution of his sentence, and published on the day of his first pillorying (at the Royal Exchange). We know from various Restoration cases that instant broadsides were often produced to mock pillory victims or even incite violence against them, and this nasty subgenre persisted throughout Defoe's lifetime.[151] *A Hymn to the Pillory* brilliantly exploits the genre in reverse, perhaps mindful of the precedent set in 1638 by the future Leveller John Lilburne, who spoke invectives and distributed pamphlets from the pillory until finally gagged by officials.[152] Or we might think of Defoe as consciously subverting the time-honoured practice of burning copies of the offending text beneath the pilloried author—in 1633, Prynne was nearly suffocated by his massive *Histriomastix*—by instead creating and distributing yet more text.

In attacks like *The True-Born Hugonot*, Defoe is represented as a master of enigmatic words and deeds: 'There let him stand exalted with his Muse, | Himself a *Riddle*, who does Riddles *use*.'[153] But in *A Hymn to the Pillory*, he turns the allegation of cryptic meaning against the pillory itself, that '*Hi'roglyphick* State *Machin*, | Contriv'd to Punish

---

[149] *Satire, Fantasy and Writings on the Supernatural by Daniel Defoe*, ed. W. R. Owens and P. N. Furbank, 8 vols (London: Pickering & Chatto, 2003), 3: 54 (*The Consolidator*, 1705).

[150] Johann Wilhelm von Archenholz, *A Picture of England: Containing a Description of the Laws, Customs, and Manners of England* (1789), 64, and see below, pp. 172–4.

[151] See especially the broadsides targeted against Titus Oates in 1685, two of which are in *POAS*, 4: 14–23; also, for a later example, *A Trip to the Pillory* (1727), on an unidentified sodomy case.

[152] Andrew Sharp, 'Lilburne, John (1615?–1657)', *ODNB*.

[153] Pittis, *True-Born Hugonot*, 19.

Fancy in'.[154] Defoe himself might be a victim of hostile misreading, 'a poor author who has 'Embrac'd *thy Wood*, | Only because he was not understood' (lines 234–5). But at the same time he's a speaker of plain truth to power, a man 'who stands Exalted there, | For speaking what we wou'd not hear' (lines 437–8). In this respect, he resembles those earlier 'Men of unspotted Honesty' (line 42) who have endured the pillory or only narrowly escaped it, and at this point Defoe names not only Prynne and Bastwick but also Dryden's Whig antagonist over *The Duke of Guise*, Thomas Hunt, and the great Carolean jurist John Selden. The truly illegible figure is the pillory he addresses: illegible because the guilt the pillory signifies, and the shame it apportions, are void of stable signification. Justice is now an arbitrary or relative category, dependent for its meaning on those with the power to enforce it by reason of state: 'Justice with Change of Int'rest Learns to bow, | And what was Merit once, is Murther now: | Actions receive their Tincture from the Times, | And as they change are Vertues made or Crimes' (lines 27–30).

Yet for much of the poem Defoe also entertains a fantasy in which the pillory abandons its 'Masquerade' quality of making the guilty seem innocent and the innocent guilty (line 180). Instead its embrace should fall on those 'Whom present Pow'r has made too great to name: | Fenc'd from thy hands, they keep our Verse in Awe, | Too great for Satyr, and too great for Law' (lines 290–2). Potentially, the pillory is a benign agent that might one day serve authentic justice by targeting the men at the top, like some carved avenging angel sprung to life: 'Then clap *thy Wooden Wings* for Joy, | And greet the Men of Great Employ, | The Authors of the Nations discontent...' (lines 160–2).

So even as Defoe endured the pillory, he resisted learning his lesson in full, and in later years continued to provoke power with intolerable lack of reserve. A decade later, his reckless mock-Jacobite pamphlets on the intensifying succession crisis (as Queen Anne's health sharply declined) demonstrated his failure or refusal to practise irony, or other strategies of evasion, with appropriate circumspection. The irony of

---

[154] *Satire, Fantasy and Writings on the Supernatural by Defoe*, 1: 241 (*A Hymn to the Pillory*, lines 1–2).

these 1713 pamphlets—*Reasons against the Succession of the House of Hanover, And What if the Pretender Should Come?* and *An Answer to a Question that No Body Thinks of, viz., But What if the Queen Should Die?*—was more stable and transparent than in *The Shortest Way*. But the real issue was the troublesome directness of Defoe's journalism in the *Review*; the ironic pamphlets, which prosecutors affected to take at face value, were a handy pretext.[155] When arrested again (despite now residing, his enemies alleged, in a fortified house with trapdoor escapes),[156] and formally indicted, Defoe repeated his failed defence of irony, this time not in print but in a manuscript petition to the ailing queen (Figure 2.12).

In the circumstances, the defence was irrelevant, but the petition is a remarkable document nonetheless, a rare case of an author attempting to instruct his sovereign on the nature of ironic discourse and subtextual meaning, and on the distinction between authorial intention and readerly construction. Tactfully, Defoe focuses on the Hanover and Pretender pamphlets, and neglects to name *But What if the Queen Should Die?*, though this was the question now dominating the minds of all actors and observers. 'In all which books', he explains in exasperation laced with panic,

> Altho' The Titles Seemed to look as if written in Favour of the Pretender and Sundry Expressions, as in all Ironicall Writing it must be, may be Wrested Against the True Design of the whole, and turned to a Meaning quite different From $y^e$ Intencion of the Author: yet $yo^r$ Peticioner Humbly Assures $yo^r$ Maj$^{ty}$ in The Solemnest Manner Possible, That his True and Onely Design in all $y^e$ said books was by an Ironicall Discourse of Recomending The Pretender, in the strongest and Most Forcible Manner to Expose his designs, and The ruinous Consequences of his Succeeding Therein.[157]

As with many ironists before and since, Defoe's claim is that to enlist readers in the discovery of meaning is to enhance its impact: its strength and force of manner. But it was not the hermeneutic theory

---

[155] See Backscheider, *Daniel Defoe*, 322–8; Hyland, 'Liberty and Libel', 868–9.

[156] For the alleged fortifications and escape routes, see Novak, *Daniel Defoe*, 426, 430.

[157] TNA, SP 34/37, fo. 11.

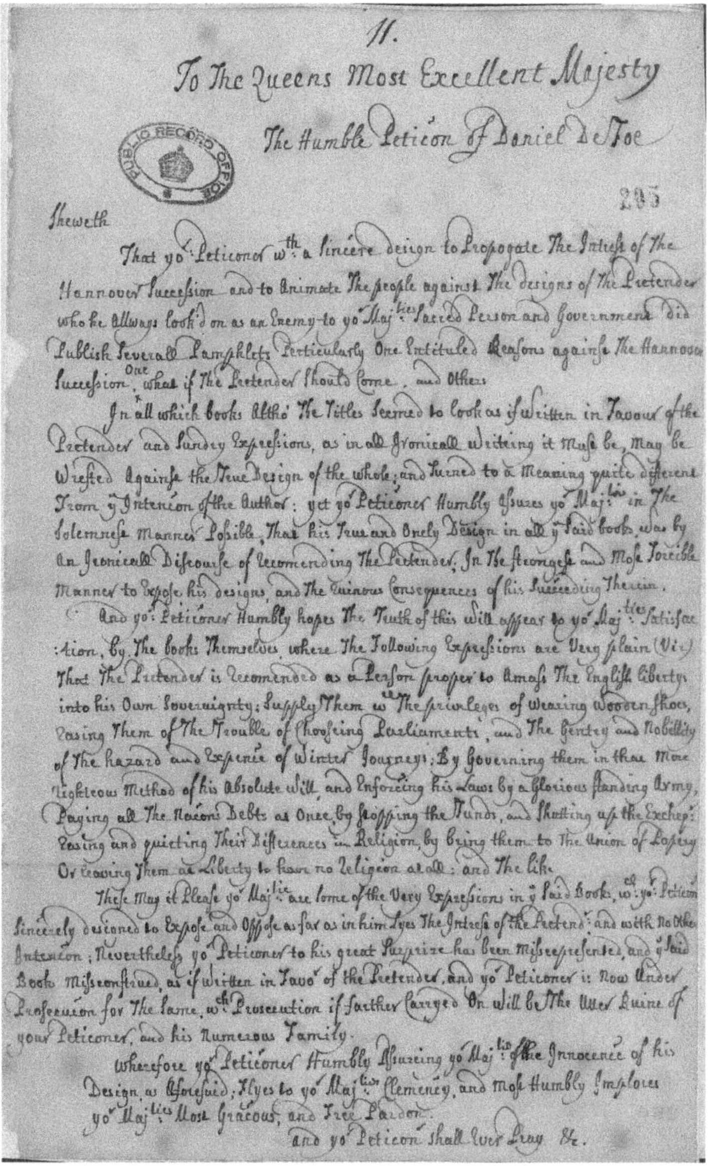

*11.*

To The Queens Most Excellent Majesty

The Humble Petition of Daniel de Foe

Sheweth

That yo.r Petitioner w.th a sincere design to Propogate The Int.rest of The Hannover Succession and to Animate The people against The designs of The Pretender who he Allways look'd on as an Enemy to yo.r Maj.ties Sacred Person and Government, did Publish Severall Pamphlets, Perticularly One Intituled Reasons against The Hannover Succession, One what if The Pretender Should Come, and Others

In all which books Altho' The Titles Seemed to look as if written in Favour of the Pretender and Sundry Expressions, as in all Jronicall writing it Must be, May be Wrested Against the True design of the whole, and turned to a Meaning quite different From y.e Intention of the Author: yet yo.r Petitioner Humbly Assures yo.r Maj.tie in The Solemnest Manner Possible, That his True and Onely Design in all y.e said books was by An Jronicall Discourse of recomending The Pretender, In The Strongest and Most Forcible Manner to Expose his designs and The ruinous Consequences of his Succeeding Therein.

And yo.r Petitioner Humbly hopes The Truth of this will appear to yo.r Maj.ties Satisfaction, By The books Themselves where The Following Expressions are Very plain (Viz) That The Pretender is recomended as a Person proper to Amass The English Liberty, into his Own Soveraignty; Supply Them w.th The priviledges of wearing wooden shoes, Easing Them of The Trouble of Choosing Parliaments, and The Gentry and Nobillity of The hazard and Expence of winter Journeys; By Governing them in Thee More Rightcrous Method of his Absolute will, and Enforceing his Laws by a Glorious Standing Army, Paying all The Nations Debts at Once, by Stopping the Funds, and Shutting up the Excheq.r Easing and quieting Their Differences in Religion, by bring them to The Union of Popery Or Leaving Them at Liberty to have no Religeon at all: and The like

These May it Please yo.r Maj.tie are some of the Very Expressions in y.e Said Book, w.ch yo.r Petitioner Sincerely designed to Expose and Oppose as far as in him lyes The Int.rest of The Pretender and with No Other Intention; Nevertheless yo.r Petitioner to his great Surprize has been Misrepresented, and y.e Said Book Misconstrued, as if written in Favo.r of the Pretender and yo.r Petitioner is Now Under Prosecution for The Same, w.ch Prosecution if further Carryed On, will be The Utter Ruine of your Petitioner and his Numerous Family.

Wherefore yo.r Petitioner Humbly Assuring yo.r Maj.tie of the Innocence of his Design as Aforesaid, Flyes to yo.r Maj.ties Clemency, and Most Humbly Implores yo.r Maj.ties Most Gracious and Free Pardon

and yo.r Peticon shall Ever Pray &c.

**Figure 2.12** Petition of Daniel Defoe to Queen Anne (?November 1713), by permission of the National Archives. Technically, in the pamphlets concerned, Defoe had committed a capital offence under the Succession to the Crown Act (1707); he pleads irony.

that counted here; it was the abject authorial grovel. Defoe was duly pardoned (not acquitted), probably with help from Harley behind the scenes, but the whole *Shortest Way* episode could easily have happened again.

Even afterwards, he remained a magnet for trouble. Within weeks of Anne's death in 1714, he was under investigation again for a paragraph in the *Flying Post and Medley* (the manuscript was found in his handwriting, or in one of his hands, since he allegedly used several) accusing a prominent pro-Hanoverian Tory peer of being a closet Jacobite. Proceedings dragged on for almost a year, but although Defoe was eventually found guilty, no sentence was passed.[158] The case remains obscure, and the particular offence may be less relevant than the broader motivation the authorities had to keep a notorious loose cannon under control in the new political era that was dawning. Defoe could not be controlled, however, and it's in these years that his reputation for wild political oscillation—for 'writing *upon, for* and *against* all manner of Subjects, Persons and Parties'—becomes most firmly entrenched. Late in the decade he was even writing for the crypto-Jacobite *Mist's Weekly Journal*, an activity he explained to Delafaye in terms of loyal infiltration, but which was probably something more devious again: a double bluff that gave him a platform to vent anti-ministerial polemics of his own, including a leader for which Nathaniel Mist was arrested in 1718, while protected by his cover as a ministerial agent.[159] These episodes speak volumes about Defoe's reputation for lighting unexpected fires wherever he went, reliant sometimes on strategies of literary encoding, at others on practical subterfuge in the ill-lit world of political pamphleteering and journalism.

## Allegoric histories: *Windsor Forest, Robinson Crusoe*

It's instructive to return finally to Pope, who, with a harder hand than Defoe to play in the run-up to the Hanoverian accession, played it

[158] Backscheider, *Daniel Defoe*, 378–80, 382; Hyland, 'Liberty and Libel', 871.

[159] Furbank and Owens, *Political Biography of Defoe*, 154 (quoting Abel Boyer in 1717) and 160–6; see also Pat Rogers, 'Nathaniel Mist, Daniel Defoe, and the Perils of Publishing', *Library*, 10.3 (2009), 298–313.

with greater dexterity. With its evidently politicized but at the same time unfathomable card game, and its delicate but relentless punning on stolen hairs and absent heirs in the context of succession crisis, there was an inescapably political aura about *The Rape of the Lock*, which first appeared in its five-canto form a few months before Anne's death. Yet the aura was almost impossible to pin down. Pope could even reinforce it while at the same time celebrating his impunity by issuing a spoof pamphlet, *A Key to the Lock; or, A Treatise proving, beyond all Contradiction, the Dangerous Tendency of... The Rape of the Lock* (1715), in which he pseudonymously accused himself of seditious libel and recommended that both author and printer-publisher be brought (in the usual formula) to 'condign Punishment'. The trick here was to raise a political objection to *The Rape of the Lock* that made little sense in its specifics (that the poem was a hostile allegory of recent treaties with the Dutch Republic) but could fruitfully be applied in other ways.[160]

More explicitly political is *Windsor Forest* (1713), which at its opening poses Defoe's 'what if the queen should die' question with a delicacy that Defoe himself could never approach. In the idealized pastoral opening of *Windsor Forest*, 'Peace and Plenty tell, a STUART reigns'. But Pope subtly darkens the vision with intimations of this reigning Stuart's impending death: the 'Reaper' tempted by Windsor's harvest two lines earlier; the 'Shades' shunned by Windsor's trees before that.[161] In the 'Norman Yoke' passage that follows about William I, and by implication William III, the same landscape is transformed by political conditions, 'To savage Beasts and savage Laws a Prey, | And Kings more furious sand severe than they'. In this phase of the poem, the manuscript version that circulated in 1712 contained an imperative couplet that Pope withdrew from the printed text: 'Oh may no more a foreign Master's Rage | With wrongs yet Legal, curse a future

---

[160] *The Prose Works of Alexander Pope, Volume 1: The Earlier Works, 1711–1720* (Oxford: Basil Blackwell, 1936), 202. For the Jacobite reading thereby opened up, see Howard Erskine-Hill, *Poetry of Opposition and Revolution: Dryden to Wordsworth* (Oxford: Clarendon Press, 1996), 71–89.

[161] *Twickenham Edition of Pope*, 1: 152 (*Windsor Forest*, lines 42, 40, 22). With 'Thin Trees arise that shun each others Shades', there is also an ominous echo of the devastated English navy in *Annus Mirabilis*, which like 'thin scattering trees admit the light, | And shun each other's shadows as they grow' (*Poems of Dryden*, 1: 161, st. 126).

Age!' Yet even without this couplet—which Pope did not feel secure enough to restore in print until 1736, and then only as a footnote—the mischievous analogy between William of Normandy and William of Orange, as fellow usurper-tyrants, survives strongly enough.[162] Perhaps the implied comparison was just about deniable; perhaps it was tolerable so long as it did not stray, as in the manuscript distich, into a call for remedial action. Either way, these were brilliant manoeuvres at that exquisite moment of danger that Dryden had encountered with *Heroic Stanzas* and *The Hind and the Panther*: the moment of impending regime change that required poets to consider meaning in light of alternative outcomes as well as present conditions—to future-proof their text, in effect. Three years later, with George I on the throne, a Jacobite journalist lamented that 'What might lawfully be printed in Queen Anne's Reign is become Treason now'.[163] The change is nowhere more dramatically seen than in the career of Pope's friend and ally Bolingbroke: in 1711 the Secretary of State who energetically managed the press-control system; in 1731 the seditious libeller whose wily prose precipitated the *Craftsman* trial.

Alongside Pope's finesse in navigating the margins of seditious libel, Defoe inevitably comes across as somewhat clumsy: perhaps even the dogged pillory-peeper *The Dunciad* takes him to be. Yet if we look forward to *Robinson Crusoe* and Defoe's fiction more broadly, it becomes clear that he did indeed learn something from his seditious libel entanglements under Queen Anne, and something of enduring importance. There's a long tradition in rise-of-the-novel criticism in which scholars attribute the brilliant ventriloquism of Defoe's novels of 1719–24 to his experience of constructing authorial personae as a political pamphleteer in the previous reign. Yet we might put the relationship in different terms. It was not ventriloquism that Defoe learned and carried into the novel genre, or not only that. It was also political encoding, or the enrichment of literary texts with layers of

---

[162] See Pat Rogers, *Pope and the Destiny of the Stuarts: History, Politics, and Mythology in the Age of Queen Anne* (Oxford: Oxford University Press, 2005), 94–5. As Joseph Hone notes, Pope exploits the currency of the two-conquerors analogy in the Tory-Jacobite literary underground ('Pope and the Politics of Panegyric', *Review of English Studies* 66 (2015), 106–23, esp. 109–11).

[163] *Robin's Last Shift*, 31 March 1716, qtd by Hyland, 'Liberty and Libel', 888.

meaning that were sufficiently shrouded to be deniable but evident enough to be retrieved. He beautifully illustrates Mark Goldie's claim that in the decades following the licensing lapse, the perpetuation of post-publication restraints could be 'creative for the literary imagination...because the need to evade censors and magistrates encouraged authors towards inventive modes of expression, in order to convey criticism while avoiding retribution'. Such methods, Goldie adds, could also energize the practice of reading and 'enlarge the boundaries of commentary, not least because audiences enjoy decoding hidden meaning'.[164] The rhetorical advantages of encoding were such, indeed, that the technique could even outlast the practical need. *A Journal of the Plague Year* (1722), an astonishing feat of proto-realism focused literally on the 1660s, also uses metaphors of contagion and panic to address more immediate issues by implication: the predicament of Dissenters following the Whig schism of 1717–20; the financial crisis and scandal of the South Sea Bubble.[165]

The most compelling instance is *Robinson Crusoe*, which demands to be read as much more than a novel of literal shipwreck and survival, however vivid or concrete its surface narrative. As Defoe acknowledged when his cloak of anonymity was stripped away by a rival author, the novel is also an 'Allegorick History' poised somewhere between fact and fiction, and reflects the trials of a writer who has endured 'a Life of Wonders in continu'd Storms...been in Slavery worse than *Turkish*...Shipwreck'd often, tho' more by Land than by Sea'.[166] One thinks here of Defoe's imprisonment and ruin following *The Shortest Way*, and the plaintive letters he addressed at the time to Harley: 'The Gulph is too Large for me to Get ashore again', he writes in one.[167] The analogy reaches beyond mere shipwreck metaphors,

---

[164] *CP*, 4: xvi.

[165] See David Womersley, 'Confessional Politics in Defoe's *Journal of the Plague Year*', in David Womersley with Paddy Bullard and Abigail Williams (eds), *Cultures of Whiggism* (Newark: University of Delaware Press, 2005), 237–56; Pat Rogers, '"This Calamitous Year": *A Journal of the Plague Year* and the South Sea Bubble', in his *Eighteenth-Century Encounters* (Totowa: Barnes & Noble, 1985), 151–67.

[166] Daniel Defoe, *Robinson Crusoe*, ed. Thomas Keymer with James Kelly (Oxford: Oxford University Press, 2007), 266–7 (Appendix 1, Preface to *Serious Reflections*, 1720); hereafter *RC*.

[167] *Letters of Defoe*, 16 (May–June 1704?).

however. More broadly, Defoe's retrospective account of *Robinson Crusoe* as figurative autobiography turns the castaway experience into a great emblem of incarceration. In a passage from *Serious Reflections* that was to be adopted by Albert Camus as an epigraph to *La Peste* (1947), he writes enigmatically of 'a State of forc'd Confinement, which in my real History is represented by a confin'd Retreat in an Island'. The entire novel thus expresses 'one kind of Imprisonment by another' (*RC*, p. 267).

It would be misguided, of course, to attempt systematic correlation between *Robinson Crusoe*'s plot and its author's life. Occasionally, the hard outlines of Bunyanesque allegory come into view, as when Crusoe writes of arriving at '*the Island of Despair*' (*RC*, p. 60). But for the most part the connections are to do with general psychological or spiritual states, and with broad patterns of oscillation between good and bad fortune. That said, Defoe's talk of the island as symbolic confinement inevitably suggests his past as a political prisoner, and the link is reinforced by the cry Crusoe teaches his parrot—'*Poor Robin Crusoe... Where have you been? How came you here?*' (p. 121)— with its echo of Defoe's public lament when punished for *The Shortest Way*: 'Alas, *Poor De Foe!* what hast thou been doing, and for what hast thou suffer'd?'[168] More generally, Camus intuited something important when using Defoe's words from *Serious Reflections* to invite a political reading of his own novel, an allegory of oppression in which plague connotes Nazi occupation. For Defoe's imprisonment after *The Shortest Way* was not only a matter of personal misfortune; it was also, in his own eyes, the symptom of a larger, communal persecution, resurgent after 1702 but severest under the restored Stuart monarchy of 1660–88, which is almost exactly the span of Crusoe's island ordeal. This was a period of 'Trampling on *Laws*, Oppressing of *Subjects*, Invading *Property*, Persecuting for *Conscience*, and Suspending the *Laws*', as Defoe characterized it in 1712, and it culminated after 1685 with 'the Popish and Tyrannical Government of King *James* II'.[169]

---

[168] *Political Writings of Defoe*, 3: 201 (*A New Test of the Church of England's Honesty*, 1704).

[169] Defoe, *Present State of the Parties*, 4.

The celebrated passage in which Crusoe refers to his island exile as 'my Reign, or my Captivity, which you please' (*RC*, p. 117) usefully indicates the equal and opposite political echoes sounded by his situation and language. Chronological correspondence is important here, and the pointed simultaneity between Crusoe's isolation and the reign at home of the restored Stuarts suggests a related thematic correspondence, linking Crusoe's captivity and reign with England's imprisonment, as it might be seen, in the Restoration years. Crusoe is shipwrecked and stranded on 30 September 1659, in the last full year of the Commonwealth; the day and month are also important, in keeping with Defoe's emphasis in *Serious Reflections* on the providential significance of dates. The day of shipwreck heralds three key moments, for Defoe, in the extended national crisis surrounding James II's reign: James's marriage to Mary of Modena on 30 September 1673, an event inseparable in the public mind from his conversion to Catholicism; the execution at Taunton of several prominent Monmouth rebels, including Defoe's schoolfellows Benjamin Hewling and William Jenkyn, on 30 September 1685; William of Orange's Declaration of 30 September 1688, announcing his intention to intervene. The date of Crusoe's return to England is no less significant. He reaches his homeland on 11 June 1687, two years to the day after Monmouth landed at Lyme to raise his ill-fated rebellion. Yet this is also a more auspicious time, when an increasingly concerted and formidable opposition to James II was already acting (in Defoe's words elsewhere) 'to restore the Liberties of the People, which the Arbitrary Proceedings of that King had ruin'd and subverted'.[170] As Michael Seidel puts it in his pioneering account of the pattern, 'Crusoe endures an exile that parallels what Defoe saw as a condition of the home island's regressive turn toward more and more oppressive home rule... and he returns just as his land is about to regain a legitimate status, or return to its senses'.[171]

Several indications point up the relationship between Crusoe's afflictions on one hand and Stuart oppression on the other. It may be speculative to associate the summer storms on Crusoe's island with

---

[170] *Satire, Fantasy and Writings on the Supernatural by Defoe*, 2: 45 (*Jure Divino*, 1706).
[171] Michael Seidel, 'Crusoe in Exile', *PMLA*, 96 (1981), 363–74 (366).

the rain-drenched rout at Sedgemoor, as Tom Paulin does in his bravura account of *Robinson Crusoe* as a novel of survivor's guilt, or to hear the jeering of Judge Jeffreys at the Bloody Assizes in the 'cruel bloody entertainment' of the cannibals on the shore.[172] But it's hard not to think of Defoe's friends and fellow rebels, and his own mysterious escape after Sedgemoor, when considering the incongruous imagery of judicial sentencing, death by hanging, and sudden reprieve that haunts the novel. On this issue, a direct political hint comes when Crusoe compares his landing on the island to reprieve from the gallows, and quotes a rare line of verse: '*For sudden Joys, like Griefs, confound at first*' (*RC*, p. 41). Early readers would have recognized the source as a controversial broadside of 1672 by Robert Wild, a Dissenting minister and satirist, entitled *Dr. Wild's Humble Thanks for His Majesties Gracious Declaration for Liberty of Conscience*.[173] Wild's poem voices the mingled hopes and fears of Dissenters on the vexed issue of religious toleration, and by citing it Defoe connects Crusoe's island ordeal with the Puritan condition of jeopardy and alienation under Stuart rule. By highlighting the 'sudden joys' provoked by this promise of religious rights, he also sounds an ironic note, given the well-founded suspicion that later emerged that Stuart policies on toleration were a ploy to strengthen a hostile Catholic interest. As Defoe robustly put it years later (glancing at the fate of Huguenots in Catholic France), 'I told the *Dissenters*, I had rather the Church of *England* should pull our Cloaths off by Fines and Forfeitures, than the Papists should fall both upon the *Church*, and the *Dissenters*, and pull our Skins off by Fire and Fagot'.[174] Crusoe's perils, like those of his co-religionists, are only beginning at this point.

Defoe's political frankness in nonfictional works of this period makes clear that by the time of *Robinson Crusoe* there was no longer much need for protective encoding when writing about the Stuart past. At least, there was no such need when writing in Whiggish terms. Jacobite reminiscence was another matter, and only months after

[172] *RC*, 142; see Tom Paulin, *Crusoe's Secret: The Aesthetics of Dissent* (London: Faber, 2005), 80–104.

[173] Robert Wild, *A Letter from Dr. Robert Wild ... with His Poetica Licentia* (1709), 13.

[174] Daniel Defoe, *An Appeal to Honour and Justice* (1715), 52; Defoe refers specifically here to James II's Declarations of 1687–8.

*Robinson Crusoe* a young journeyman printer named John Matthews was executed for handling *Vox Populi, Vox Dei* (1719), a muddled but compelling blend of divine-right and popular sovereignty arguments that called for Stuart restoration.[175] Yet personal or professional safety was never the sole motive for political innuendo. It was also a technique of emphasis, in which the interpretative exertions required of readers served to enlist them as co-creators of meaning: complicit in this meaning at the imaginative level, and possessing it with a fullness arising from their own participation. 'This Work is chiefly recommended to those who know how to Read it', Defoe teasingly writes about *Moll Flanders*,[176] and the same goes for *Robinson Crusoe*. Approached with the kind of knowingness in which readers of the day had become expert, *Robinson Crusoe* not only marks Defoe's escape from his past life as a seditious libeller, but also offers an account of that life and the historical conditions that shaped it. Moreover, it employs the guileful techniques of seditious libel to encode and communicate the account. In this sense, the pamphleteer Pope publicly derided and the novelist he privately admired were but two sides of the same authorial coin.

---

[175] For this episode, see Paula McDowell, *The Women of Grub Street: Press, Politics, and Gender in the London Literary Marketplace, 1678–1730* (Oxford: Clarendon Press, 1998), 74–82; also Paul Chapman, 'Matthews, John (1701?–1719), Printer', *ODNB*.

[176] Daniel Defoe, *Moll Flanders*, ed. G. A. Starr and Linda Bree (Oxford: Oxford University Press, 2011), 2.

# 3
# 1730–1780
# The Trade of Libelling: Fielding, Johnson

'The true Castalian stream is a shower of eggs, and a pillory the poet's Parnassus.' Thus a bookseller named Puff in Samuel Foote's farce *The Patron* (1764), a prolific dealer in seditious libel who brags that he 'would not give two-pence for an author that is afraid of his ears'.[1] With its play on classical tropes of poetic inspiration, Foote's line gives an elegant twist to a standard routine in eighteenth-century satire about the commodification of literature in modern Grubstreet. Poetry now is a matter of urban hustle, not pastoral retreat, brazenly commercial in its motives, politically transgressive in its methods. Foote specialized in the comedy of book-trade cynicism, where literature and politics are market-driven and the oxygen of publicity is all. In *The Author* (1757), disaffection has long been a lucrative posture for old Vamp, a sometime publisher of Jacobite polemic who cheerfully boasts that 'in the Year Fifteen, when I was in the treasonable Way, I never squeak'd; I never gave up but one Author in my Life, and he was dying of a Consumption, so it never came to a Tryal'. Vamp also has form as a proto-pornographer, and one side of his face is earless ('Crop'd close!—bare as a Board!', he exclaims) 'for nothing in the World but an innocent Book of Bawdy'.[2] In *The Devil upon Two Sticks*,

---

[1] Samuel Foote, *The Patron* (1764), 18, 17.
[2] Samuel Foote, *The Author* (1757), 10. Norma Clarke proposes that Vamp is 'recognizably a portrait of Ralph Griffiths', citing Griffiths's legal troubles with seditious and obscene libel in the 1740s (*Brothers of the Quill: Oliver Goldsmith in Grub*

first performed in 1768, a connoisseur of libels named Dr Squib views prosecution and conviction as the acme of success in a publishing career. Newgate is a rite of passage to be embraced, Squib tells a lowly but ambitious apprentice, and 'there has many a printer been raised to the pillory from as slender beginnings'.[3]

This breezy, shameless character-type recurs in better-known novels and plays over the next few years. The fictional publisher of Smollett's *Humphry Clinker* (1771) assures its fictional author that 'if you should be sentenced to the pillory, your fortune is made'.[4] In Sheridan's *The Critic* (1779), a bumptious playwright describes a marketing technique he calls 'the PUFF COLLUSIVE... much used by bold booksellers and enterprising poets', in which a publisher first brings out a poem, then an attack on the poem, 'and then establishes it by threatening himself with the pillory'.[5] All these figures are descendants of the mercenary publisher Bookweight in Fielding's early play *The Author's Farce* (1730), who hires a scholar to supply his title pages with '*Latin* Sedition Motto's', turns down a libel against the ministry because he has two in press already, and rejects a defence of the ministry (by the same author) because, he says, 'they don't sell so well'.[6] Here is a satirical vision in which works of literature and especially political literature—partisan pamphlets, poems on affairs of state, topical application dramas—become mere stock in trade,

---

*Street* (Cambridge, MA: Harvard University Press, 2016), 185; for the works at issue, see below, pp. 175–6). Griffiths may indeed be in play, but Foote's character does not refer, as Clarke says, 'to having been "in the treasonable way" in 1745'; he's an old hand who has been making hay since the Hanoverian accession. Perhaps this is a composite caricature merging Griffiths (*c*.1720–1803) with a veteran of the Curll era: the obvious candidate is Richard Francklin, who co-published amatory titles with Curll in the 1710s, was jailed for the *Craftsman* in the 1730s, and was now among Foote's own publishers.

[3] Samuel Foote, *The Devil upon Two Sticks* (1778), 34; this is the posthumous first edition.

[4] Tobias Smollett, *The Expedition of Humphry Clinker*, ed. Thomas R. Preston (Athens: University of Georgia Press, 1990), 5.

[5] *The Dramatic Works of Richard Brinsley Sheridan*, ed. Cecil Price, 2 vols (Oxford: Clarendon Press, 1973), 2: 516.

[6] Henry Fielding, *Plays*, ed. Thomas Lockwood, 3 vols (Oxford: Clarendon Press, 2004–11), 1: 326, 327 (*The Author's Farce*, II.v, in the revised 1734 version).

devoid of meaning or value beyond their capacity to sell, and pushing the envelope of tolerable utterance simply as a promotional gambit.

Nor, as Fielding makes clear in his later journalism, was this vision entirely a fiction. It arose from real-life cases in which seditious libel became a commercial practice, and legal retribution a badge of honour, a unique selling point. In a spoof history of bookselling arts in the *Covent-Garden Journal*, Fielding celebrates the popular appetite for 'Blasphemy, Treason, Bawdry and Scandal', and outlines the business models and marketing practices developed by canny publishers to profit from it. The technique of choice

> was for the Merchant himself to mount in the most public Part of the Town into a wooden Machine called the Pillory, where he stood for the Space of an Hour proclaiming his Goods to all that past that Way. This was practised with much Success by the late Mr. Curl, Mr. Mist and others, who never failed of selling several large Bales of Goods in this Manner.[7]

The joke was an old one in Fielding's repertoire, first tested in his Walpole-era periodical the *Champion*, which lists laws invented 'for the Benefit and Advantage of Booksellers, whose Copies never fail to sell well, when they have been advertized in the Pillory'.[8] Now he develops the point by giving the pillory a profession-specific name: 'the PUBLISHING-STOOL'. With a sly comment on the hierarchies of power at work in the libelling trade, he adds that booksellers fearful of being bedaubed by eggs or filth could delegate the stunt to mere subordinates; they could employ 'their Understrappers, that is to say their Writers for such Purposes'.[9]

At what point did prosecution for seditious libel, or even an hour in the pillory, become a good career move for book-trade professionals? The idea was certainly not new in Fielding's day. As early as the 1640s, John Taylor claimed to have been advised by the republican

---

[7] Henry Fielding, *The Covent-Garden Journal and A Plan of the Universal Register-Office*, ed. Bertrand A. Goldgar (Oxford: Clarendon Press, 1988), 282 (No. 51, 27 June 1752).

[8] Henry Fielding, *Contributions to The Champion and Related Writings*, ed. W. B. Coley (Oxford: Clarendon Press, 2003), 40 (4 December 1739).

[9] Fielding, *Covent-Garden Journal*, 283 (No. 51, 27 June 1752).

poet George Wither that he should 'Snarle at the State, and let your Satyre's pen | Write against Government'; Taylor would then be tried and punished as Wither had been, and 'Then shall you Thrive, and be as you would be; | Your Books would sell, your selfe get Coyn and Fame, | And then (like mine) Renown'd shall be your Name'.[10] Given the undoubted hazards of his era, even reckless, much-arrested Wither (whose life Denham once claimed to have saved to avoid himself becoming the worst living poet) was probably joking.[11] Courting the pillory was still prohibitively dangerous for many more decades, though by the early eighteenth century authors who emerged unscathed were turning the experience to advantage. It was in this spirit that Ned Ward exploited his 1706 pillorying for *Hudibras Redivivus* by commissioning a new frontispiece portrait of himself as political martyr. In the motto appended to an earlier portrait, Ward is merely a humble imitator of Samuel Butler; now he becomes a fearless scourge of power, 'an Honest FACE, | Arm'd against ENVY and DISGRACE; | Who lives Respected still in SPITE | Of THOSE that punish them y$^t$ WRITE'. Thereafter, the same motto appeared in newspaper advertisements for reprints of comparatively innocuous works like *The London Spy*.[12] Even in his nonpartisan social satires, Ward positioned himself for the rest of his career as the embodiment of transgression and defiance.

That said, Ward prudently waited for Queen Anne's death before striking this artful marketing pose, when the offence given by *Hudibras Redivivus* was water under the bridge. By the time of George I, moreover, state-inflicted mutilation for seditious libel was becoming a distant memory; it was easier to brand oneself as a pillory-defying satirist when there was no longer much danger of getting branded. Yet there remained the real hazard of being maimed or even killed by an

---

[10] John Taylor, *Aquamusæ: or, Cacafogo, Cacadæmon, Captain George Wither Wrung in the Withers* (Oxford, 1645), 8.

[11] In John Aubrey's account, Denham laughs the king into clemency by urging 'that whilest George Withers lived, he should not be the worst Poet in England' (*Brief Lives*, ed. Kate Bennett (Oxford: Clarendon Press, 2015), 352).

[12] See, for the engraving by William Sherwin, the 3rd edition (1715) of *Hudibras Redivivus*, and, for a representative ad, *Evening Post*, 25–28 April 1719 (announcing Ward's five-volume *Works*).

inflamed, partisan, or simply an unruly crowd. Only towards the middle of the eighteenth century did the risk of serious injury or death in the pillory recede for book-trade professionals, and it persisted for other categories of offenders—other deviants from officially sanctioned truth or nature like perjurers and especially sodomites—until the early nineteenth.

Eighteenth-century engravings tend to filter out crowd violence, and in a print study by Samuel Wale, the death of the thief-taker James Egan (pilloried at Smithfield in 1756) is indicated only by tasteful details: the buckling of Egan's knees and a single scar on his forehead; a grave look worn by one spectator; the remonstration of another with a third who stoops for a rock (Figure 3.1).[13] There are horrifying newspaper accounts, however, of lynch-mob violence, especially involving the most easily scapegoated categories of sexual offender. It was one such case, when a coachman named William Smith was stoned to death while being pilloried for attempted sodomy, that occasioned Edmund Burke's landmark speech of 1780 urging Parliament 'to abolish the punishment of the pillory since it was liable to such violent perversion, as to be rendered not the instrument of reproach and shame, but of death and murder'. In practice, abolition was still decades away, though when it came the decisive arguments were those pioneered by Burke: in particular, that it violated justice and law for a non-capital offence to be made capital in effect by negligent officers or enraged spectators, and that the punishment thus inflicted was a 'death of torment' more cruel than official methods of execution.[14] At this point, however, Burke was still a controversial, even suspect, figure for his stance on the American war, and some accused him of exploiting Smith's death to weaken

---

[13] For Egan's case (his perjuries had caused several innocent men to be hanged), see Frank McLynn, *Crime and Punishment in Eighteenth-Century England* (Oxford: Oxford University Press, 1991), 31.

[14] *The Writings and Speeches of Edmund Burke, Volume 3: Party, Parliament, and the American War, 1774–1780*, ed. Warren M. Elofson, John A. Woods, and William B. Todd (Oxford: Clarendon Press, 1996), 585 ('Speech on Pillory', 11 April 1780). On this case and the larger trajectory, see Greg T. Smith, 'The Decline of Public Physical Punishment in London, 1760–1840', in Carolyn Strange (ed.), *Qualities of Mercy: Justice, Punishment, and Discretion* (Vancouver: UBC Press, 1996), 21–51.

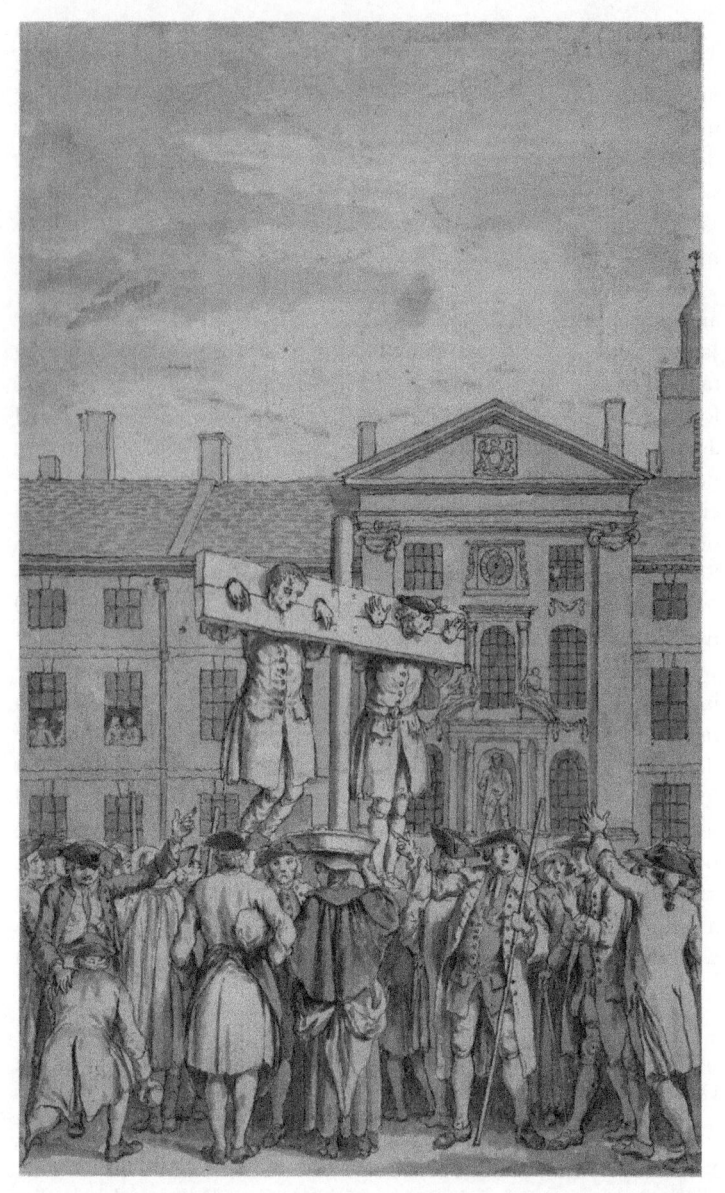

**Figure 3.1** Samuel Wale, *Egan and Salmon, the Thief-Takers, Pilloried at Smithfield* (1756), pen and grey and brown ink drawing with grey wash on paper, © the Trustees of the British Museum. All rights reserved. Egan died in the pillory when a projectile crushed his skull; Salmon died of his injuries days later.

state sanctions against seditious writing. In the liberal present, thundered the *Morning Post*, 'the *pillory* is become the only restraint on republicanism and treason; no wonder therefore that the patriots of the present day, with Mr. Burke at their head, should embrace the earliest opportunity to attempt a *reform* in such ignominious punishments.'[15] Authors, printers, and publishers should still be made to live in the pillory's shadow, in fear and expressive constraint.

Yet this was wishful thinking from the *Morning Post*, and in the later part of the century—until the French Revolution raised the stakes—it was far from clear that the pillory really could restrain republicanism or treason, or even just plain-vanilla sedition. After the violent episodes from Queen Anne's reign evoked in Pope's *Dunciad*, book-trade pillorying was more often than not a counter-productive affair, and by the time of Burke's speech it was generations since any author, publisher, or printer had suffered serious harm from a hostile crowd. Pillories became theatres of authorial defiance, not public shame, and were typified not by mob retribution against the libeller but by popular resistance to the state. As late as 1759, Adam Smith articulated the traditional theory of pillorying as public stigmatization, indeed as more dreadful in this respect than capital punishment. But for all the eloquence of Smith's account (written to serve a broader argument about sentiment and sympathy), he was out of date on several counts. 'The judge who orders a criminal to be set in the pillory, dishonours him more than if he had condemned him to the scaffold', Smith contends, going on to assert a binary opposition between execution and exhibition:

> A brave man is not rendered contemptible by being brought to the scaffold; he is, by being set in the pillory. His behaviour in the one situation may gain him universal esteem and admiration. No behaviour in the other can render him agreeable. The sympathy of the spectators supports him in the one case, and saves him from that shame, that consciousness that his misery is felt by himself only, which is of all sentiments the most unsupportable. There is no sympathy in the other;

---

[15] *Morning Post*, 14 April 1780, in Rictor Norton (ed.), *Homosexuality in Eighteenth-Century England: A Sourcebook*, 23 February 2007/25 November 2014, <https://rictornorton.co.uk/eighteen/1780burk.htm>.

or, if there is any, it is not with his pain, which is a trifle, but with his
consciousness of the want of sympathy with which this pain is attended.

With this reference to 'trifling' pain, Smith is at his most resolutely
theoretical, and discounts the real-world possibility of lynching. He
also discounts the possibility of moral support from the crowd, for the
spectatorial sympathy he imagines is weak and paradoxical, extending
only to the criminal's condition of being *not* sympathized with. Such as
it is, our sympathy

is with his shame, not with his sorrow. Those who pity him, blush and
hang down their heads for him. He droops in the same manner, and
feels himself irrecoverably degraded by the punishment, though not by
the crime. The man, on the contrary, who dies with resolution, as he is
naturally regarded with the erect aspect of esteem and approbation, so
he wears himself the same undaunted countenance; and, if the crime
does not deprive him of the respect of others, the punishment never
will. He has no suspicion that his situation is the object of contempt or
derision to any body, and he can, with propriety, assume the air, not
only of perfect serenity, but of triumph and exultation.[16]

Yet things were no longer reliably working like this—as Smith, who
cites the pillory as a philosophical instance, not a topical question, no
doubt understood. We now know that Defoe's triumph of 1703 was
partly a matter of Victorian mythologizing, and more mixed on the
ground than was later assumed. Other book-trade pilloryings during
Queen Anne's reign had been little less harsh in effect than the
disasters suffered by libellers of the Exclusion Crisis (see pp. 96–100).
But the picture alters markedly with the Hanoverian accession,
which need not surprise us if Samuel Johnson was right to say that
'the present family on the throne came to the crown against the will
of nine tenths of the people'.[17] In the early years of George I's reign,
some of these nine-tenths turned out in force to support Jacobite
libellers, greatly eroding the force of a government crackdown on
seditious speech and writing (one historian describes 'an unprecedented

---

[16] Adam Smith, *The Theory of Moral Sentiments*, ed. D. D. Raphael and
A. L. Macfie (Oxford: Clarendon Press, 1976), 60–1 (I.iii.2.9–10).

[17] *Boswell's Life of Johnson*, ed. G. B. Hill, rev. L. F. Powell, 2nd edn, 6 vols
(Oxford: Clarendon Press, 1964), 5: 271.

campaign of official suppression' against the opposition press) that followed the 1715 rising.[18] When Isaac Dalton was pilloried in 1716 for printing his anti-Hanoverian weekly *The Shift Shifted*, a newspaper reported that 'he was so far from being pelted that a Gathering of Money was made for him, and the Standers by gave him repeated Huzza's'. Two years later Edward Bisse, a West Country rector pilloried for persistent Jacobite sermonizing in Bristol and elsewhere, was insulted by a single Hanoverian loyalist, on whom the crowd promptly turned.[19] Perhaps Foote's Vamp had little to fear from spectators during the 'treasonable' phase of his career.

## Defeating the pillory: Mist, Curll, Shebbeare, Wilkes

Admittedly, the picture is not clear-cut throughout an extended period in which, as historians have long argued, we must think not of a single London mob but of plural mobs, riotously different in partisan or sectarian persuasion.[20] For the gung-ho bookseller in Charles Johnstone's *Chrysal* (1760–5), the danger of the pillory 'is only a mere bug-bear, while the mob is on my side'. But there was often a rival mob to worry about.[21] Just how contested the pillory was as a space, with different factions vying to give it different meanings, is illustrated by one of Fielding's reference-points in the *Covent-Garden Journal*: the Jacobite journalist and printer Nathaniel Mist, whose *Weekly Journal* involved him in at least fourteen brushes with the law, and in official eyes did 'more mischief than any other Libel being wrote ad captum of the common People'.[22] The fullest account we

[18] P. B. J. Hyland, 'Liberty and Libel: Government and the Press during the Succession Crisis in Britain, 1712–1716', *English Historical Review*, 101 (1986), 863–88 (884).

[19] *Norwich Gazette*, 29 December 1716–5 January 1717, qtd by Nicholas Rogers, *Crowds, Culture, and Politics in Georgian Britain* (Oxford: Clarendon Press, 1998), 57; Paul Monod, *Jacobitism and the English People, 1688–1788* (Cambridge: Cambridge University Press, 1989), 149–50.

[20] See Tim Harris, *London Crowds in the Reign of Charles II*; Rogers, *Crowds, Culture, and Politics*.

[21] Charles Johnstone, *Chrysal; or, The Adventures of a Guinea*, 4 vols (1760–5), 4: 135.

[22] TNA, SP 35/13, fo. 56 (Charles Delafaye's memorandum on Mist's *Weekly Journal* with 'A Method proposed for Suppressing News Papers of this Nature',

have of Mist's eventual pillorying in 1721 reports a pitched battle 'near the State-Machine' in which a Tory mob defeated rival Whigs, while their hero 'stood *calm and undisturb'd* all the Time, in the View of several thousand People, who upon his being taken down, expressed their Satisfaction by universal and loud Huzza's'.[23]

Yet things did not go entirely Mist's way. Moves to prosecute his protectors for rioting and cursing the king were defeated by the *ignoramus* verdict of a stubborn jury, but several of his journeymen were then ambushed and beaten up by Whig heavies, the motive being 'that Mr. Mist, when in the Pillory, was not used as they wished'.[24] Thereafter, Mist and his authors toned down their *ad captum vulgi* approach, and often used a style of indirection 'so guarded', one senior lawyer noted, 'that an information cannot be brought on any part of it'. It was a shift of emphasis that seems elegantly acknowledged when *Mist's Weekly Journal* was renamed as *Fog's* in 1728.[25] Yet reasons were found to arrest Mist again on several occasions following the pillory episode, despite an obvious awareness in official circles that this was merely to score further own goals. As a former Lord Chancellor put it in 1722, 'there never was a Mist or any other person taken up or tryed but double $y^e$ number of papers were sold upon it, beside $y^e$ Irritating the people from $y^e$ false notion of Persecution'.[26]

More careful pillory-management was involved when the other publisher named by Fielding, the irrepressible Edmund Curll, was convicted in 1728 after a complex set of legal actions involving both obscene and seditious libel. Curll controlled his punishment more securely than Mist by focusing attention on the seditious work (a politically awkward memoir that was originally sponsored, Curll claimed, by Queen Anne herself) and using it to garner support from

---

1 November 1718); see also Paul Chapman, 'Mist, Nathaniel (*d.* 1737)', *ODNB*. *Ad captum vulgi*: within the capacity of the crowd.

[23] *Daily Journal*, 24 February 1721, qtd by Pat Rogers, 'Nathaniel Mist, Daniel Defoe, and the Perils of Publishing', *Library*, 10.3 (2009), 298–313 (303).

[24] *Daily Journal*, 25 February 1721, qtd by Rogers, 'Nathaniel Mist, Daniel Defoe', 303.

[25] Jeremy Black, *The English Press in the Eighteenth Century* (London: Croom Helm, 1987), 115, quoting Earl Cowper to his wife, 28 May 1721.

[26] TNA, SP 35/30, fo. 134 (9 March 1722).

a broad constituency. Reportedly, the crowd abused the one spectator who tried to hurl an egg, and otherwise cheered Curll on:

> for being an artful, cunning (though wicked) fellow he had contrived to have printed papers dispersed all about Charing-Cross, telling the people, he stood there for vindicating the memory of queen Anne: which had such an effect on the mob, that it would have been dangerous to have spoken against him: and when he was taken down out of the pillory, the mob carried him off, as it were in triumph, to a neighbouring tavern.[27]

The handbill in question, which survives in a single known copy, is a masterpiece of prevarication in which Curll casts himself as no threat to the present regime, merely a faithful servant to the late queen's wishes. He tiptoes quietly past the obscene libels, *A Treatise of the Use of Flogging* and *Venus in the Cloister*, though elsewhere he presents these works as morally wholesome warnings against Popish corruption—an argument that was accepted in court (though not necessarily believed) by a sympathetic judge.[28]

Lower down the social scale, where the crime was one of orality, not print, there are several recorded cases in which attempts to punish displays of disaffection backfired. When in 1716 two Southwark women were pilloried for singing Jacobite laments, a spontaneous whip-round among spectators raised £4 on their behalf (several months' wages for a servant); when the previous year a man was pilloried for speaking seditious words against George I, Tory spectators stormed the scaffold and released him amid cries of 'High Church and Sacheverell forever'.[29] Instead of imposing public shame or eliciting mob violence, J. M. Beattie comments, 'the judge had simply provided the anti-Hanoverian crowd with an opportunity for an

---

[27] Paul Baines and Pat Rogers, *Edmund Curll, Bookseller* (Oxford: Clarendon Press, 2007), 168.

[28] Baines and Rogers, *Edmund Curll*, 167. The broadside, headed 'To the Spectators', is reproduced in *The John Johnson Collection: Catalogue of an Exhibition* (Oxford: Bodleian Library, 1971), 26.

[29] Hyland, 'Liberty and Libel', 886; Nicholas Rogers, 'Popular Protest in Early Hanoverian London', *Past and Present*, 79.1 (1978), 70–100 (71); for other cases, see David Cressy, *Dangerous Talk: Scandalous, Seditious, and Treasonable Speech in Pre-Modern England* (Oxford: Oxford University Press, 2010), 238–43.

effective demonstration of its opposition to the new regime'.[30] These minor festivals of pro-Stuart mutiny were too frequent and widespread for comfort, which may be why ministers determined to secure an exemplary book-trade punishment took the extraordinary step, in 1719, of using treason legislation, not the common law of seditious libel, against John Matthews, a 19-year-old printer of *Vox Populi, Vox Dei*. Conveniently, Matthews could then be executed by hanging, not fêted in the pillory, with high-profile felons alongside him— 'Constable the Highwayman, and Moor the pretended Blind-man, with young Matthews the Printer'—as a way to dilute or inhibit political protest.[31] This brutal expedient was never repeated (though at least one attempt was made in the following decade),[32] and Matthews became the last book-trade professional to be executed in England, at least *ex officio*. Yet his fate speaks volumes about ministerial anxieties concerning libellers and their capacity to become popular heroes in the early Hanoverian era. The indications are, indeed, that by this time the political offenders at greatest risk of mob violence were not those who sowed sedition but those who informed against it. When John Middleton was pilloried in 1723 for making false allegations of treason, twenty constables, with 104 assistants to back them up, failed to control an enormous crowd who pelted Middleton with mud until he choked to death.[33]

---

[30] J. M. Beattie, *Crime and the Courts in England, 1660–1800* (Oxford: Clarendon Press, 1986), 466.

[31] *Daily Post*, 6 November 1719 (Moor was an ingenious shoplifter). On the underground network behind *Vox Populi, Vox Dei*, see Paula McDowell, *The Women of Grub Street: Press, Politics, and Gender in the London Literary Marketplace, 1678–1730* (Oxford: Clarendon Press, 1998), 74–82. At Tyburn, Matthews made no attempt at grandstanding, and remained 'grave and composed' (*Weekly Packet*, 7–14 November 1719). No doubt he wanted to ensure that the one concession made to him—remission of quartering—would be honoured.

[32] In 1728 the Exeter printer Edward Farley was charged with treason for reprinting the notorious 'Persian Letter' (a transparent allegory of Hanoverian usurpation and Whig corruption) from *Mist's Weekly Journal*. But a year later Farley died in prison, 'loaded with irons', while ministers were still considering how to proceed (Black, *English Press*, 96).

[33] Robert Shoemaker, *The London Mob: Violence and Disorder in Eighteenth-Century England* (London: Hambledon, 2004), 94–6.

Ministers and their officials are not always the quickest learners, and the authorities were to persevere with the publishing stool for many further decades. More broadly, there even seems to have been a mid-century uptick in London pillorying rates (Robert Shoemaker describes 'a temporary surge to more than ten per year in the 1750s and 1760s'), though at the same time use became concentrated on a smaller range of offences, with fraud and perjury to the fore.[34] As a sanction against seditious libel, there is no better instance of the pillory's increasing counter-productiveness than the triumph of the novelist and pamphleteer John Shebbeare just months before Smith published his timeworn view of the pillory as certain abjection. A rancorous, last-ditch Jacobite, Shebbeare had already been arrested for *The Marriage Act* (1754), a sentimental novel interspersed with tirades against the venality of ruling Whigs. From 1756 his ever more incendiary series of *Letters to the People of England* was closely monitored by the attorney general, though officials dissuaded Prime Minister Newcastle from ordering proceedings against the fourth *Letter* for the now familiar reason that 'it would from the Poison that is gone forth amongst the People end in an Acquittal, as it will be hardly possible to get a Jury whose prepositions [*sic*] will not lead them to that way of thinking'.[35] Shebbeare was intent on provoking a showdown, however, and cranked up the rhetoric in each new instalment. In the *Sixth Letter* he forced the government's hand with, among other flourishes of audacious innuendo, a motto from Revelation that pointed unmistakably to the heraldic white horse of the House of Hanover: 'And I looked, and behold a pale Horse: and his Name that sat on him was Death, and Hell followed with him.'[36]

The ensuing prosecution succeeded, thanks to deft legal footwork from Lord Chief Justice Mansfield, whose ruling that satires on deceased kings (William III, George I) could still be actionable prompted

---

[34] Shoemaker, *London Mob*, 88; forgery became a capital offence in 1729, and so drops from the list.

[35] William Sharp to Newcastle, 20 August 1756, qtd by M. John Cardwell, *Arts and Arms: Literature, Politics and Patriotism during the Seven Years War* (Manchester: Manchester University Press, 2004), 129.

[36] John Shebbeare, *A Sixth Letter to the People of England, on the Progress of National Ruin* (1757), title page, adapting Revelation 6: 8; see Cardwell, *Arts and Arms*, 242.

Horace Walpole's comment that this was to make history a libel.[37] For Mansfield, the *Sixth Letter* 'approached the nearest to high treason without actually committing it, of any paper he ever read'.[38] Yet the punishment conspicuously failed, not least because of the connivance of the under-sheriff of Middlesex, Arthur Beardmore, in subverting it on Shebbeare's behalf, though he did so out of Wilkite principle, not Tory sympathy.[39] As with Curll, broadsides were distributed by supporters 'inviting the friends of the liberty of the press and of Old England... to see the British champion', and Shebbeare showed up at Charing Cross in a handsome coach, not the usual prisoner's cart.[40] Instead of having the pillory's upper board closed down on his wrists and neck, he was allowed to stand behind the structure and look between the unclosed boards—so enabling Beardmore, when prosecuted for contempt of court, to swear, with all the guile of a libeller himself, that in performing his duties he 'saw Shebbeare's head *through* the pillory'.[41] For the duration of his non-punishment, Shebbeare was shielded from the weather by his footman's umbrella (a fashionable novelty at the time) and occasionally lounged forward to rest at ease on the lower board.

'The whole intent | Of that Parade was Fame, not Punishment', Charles Churchill fumed in his satire *The Author* (1763). To the judge who later sentenced Beardmore, it was intolerable that a brazen libeller had been allowed 'to stand *in Triumph*, erect upon the Pillory, with a Servant holding an Umbrella over his Head, instead of standing with his Head *in* the Pillory, by way of Disgrace and *Ludibrium* (which is the Intent of this kind of Punishment)'.[42] The anonymous author of *Memoirs of the Pillory* (1759) made scathing contrasts between the lenity of the Hanoverian regime that Shebbeare reviled and the

[37] Horace Walpole, *Memoirs of King George II*, ed. John Brooke, 3 vols (New Haven: Yale University Press, 1985), 3: 39–40.

[38] John Almon, *Biographical, Literary, and Political Anecdotes, of Several of the Most Eminent Persons of the Present Age*, 3 vols (1797), 1: 374.

[39] Norman S. Poser, *Lord Mansfield: Justice in the Age of Reason* (Montreal: McGill-Queen's University Press, 2013), 268–9.

[40] Walpole, *Memoirs*, 3: 40.

[41] Almon, *Biographical, Literary, and Political Anecdotes*, 1: 375.

[42] *The Poetical Works of Charles Churchill*, ed. Douglas Grant (Oxford: Clarendon Press, 1956), 255; *Reports of Cases Adjudged in the Bar of King's Bench, Since the Death of Lord Raymond*, 2nd edn, 2 vols (1771), 2: 797. *Ludibrium*: mockery, derision.

brutality of the Stuart dynasty he wished to restore. 'O Doctor! do not your Ears tingle?', this pamphleteer asks after a graphic account of Prynne's mutilation, and then concludes with a scornful echo of Pope on Defoe: 'This was not like a Criminal suffering the just Sentence of the Law. With a Countenance unmortified and unabashed, you dispensed your Smiles, your Nods, and Compliments, through the Aperture that ought to have received your Head...*you gloried in your Shame.*'[43]

None of this is to say that the pillory had no residual power to intimidate. Authors and their publishers still feared it and took steps to avoid it. But the risks associated with failure were now diminished—or at any rate the physical risks, for mid-century judges responded to the declining terror of the pillory by ramping up the accompanying fines and prison terms, which could be ruinous. Even flamboyant, well-connected John Wilkes was circumspect when excoriating the Bute and Grenville ministries in his radical Whig *North Briton* of 1762–3, and would put his leading articles through two-stage revision by other hands before committing them to print. Churchill would edit for style and then consult the seasoned bookseller William Johnston (or later an Inner Temple lawyer named Charles Sayer), who would estimate whether the writing was libellous, 'for fear I have got too near the pillory', as Wilkes put it.[44] Thanks to these precautions, government lawyers failed to find reliably actionable text until the reckless 45th number of the *North Briton*, at which point technical wrangling over parliamentary privilege, a duelling injury, and then a timely trip to France saved Wilkes from trial in person. His only pillorying came in conservative satire, notably Plate II of William Hogarth's *The Times* (1762–3), which shows Wilkes alongside the other sensation of the season, the Cock-Lane Ghost, there to exemplify meretricious celebrity as well as conspiracy and defamation. In this scene, Hogarth's few

---

[43] *Memoirs of the Pillory: Being a Consolatory Epistle to Dr. Shebbeare*, 2nd edn (1759), 21, 49–50, playing on *Dunciad Variorum*, ii.139 ('un-abash'd Defoe'), and Philippians 3: 19 ('whose glory is in their shame').

[44] *The Correspondence of John Wilkes and Charles Churchill*, ed. Edward H. Weatherly (New York: Columbia University Press, 1954), 3; see Arthur H. Cash, *John Wilkes: The Scandalous Father of Civil Liberty* (New Haven: Yale University Press, 2006), 72 and n.

spectators have lost interest in the pillory behind them, except for a boy who urinates copiously on Wilkes's stockings. The detail jokily mirrors the focal point of the composition, the irrigating fountains pumped by Prime Minister Bute from a gracious, bountiful statue of George III (see Figure 3.2).[45] Then there was Smollett's pugnacious pro-Bute organ *The Briton*, which gloatingly represents Lord Goth (Wilkes's protector and alleged instigator Lord Temple) as urging Aniseed (Wilkes) and Brawn (Churchill) to cross the rhetorical line into outright treason: 'Had ye but courage to incur the smart of pains and penalties—how should I rejoice to see my Aniseed exalted to the pillory! to behold our parson Brawn shorn of his ears!'[46]

Yet humiliation was easier to inflict in print than in real life, and when an offender was finally pilloried in person for the *North Briton*—a peripheral figure named John Williams, who restored the offending 45th number to a 1765 reprint of the journal—the sanction failed yet again. This time the flowers were real, a fact that possibly explains, by way of conflation, the Victorian myth about Defoe. Throughout his sixty minutes of fame, Williams was cheered by a 10,000-strong crowd, who gave him a nosegay of laurel and myrtle, emblematic of victory, and raised a collection of 200 guineas, more than double his crushing fine of £100. Much of the money no doubt came from Wilkes's allies in the opposition elite, who are shown in a broadside entitled *The Pillory Triumphant; or, No. 45 for Ever* as mingling in New Palace Yard to congratulate Williams (Figure 3.3). Even more alarmingly for the ministry, the event culminated in a symbolic execution for Bute, represented as usual in Whig satire by a jackboot and Scotch bonnet. This may have been the unspecified book-trade pillorying remembered years later by the Prussian visitor Johann Wilhelm von Archenholz, who travelled extensively in England after the Seven Years War: 'The pillory, which was crowned with garlands of flowers, was surrounded by persons of the first rank, who

---

[45] On the complex, ambivalent politics of Plate II, unfinished by Hogarth and posthumously published, see Ronald Paulson, *Hogarth: Art and Politics, 1750–1764* (Cambridge: Lutterworth Press, 1993), 389–94.

[46] Tobias Smollett, *Poems, Plays, and The Briton*, ed. Byron Gassman (Athens: University of Georgia Press, 1993), 316 (4 September 1762).

**Figure 3.2** William Hogarth, *The Times*, Plate 2 (1762–3), etching and engraving on paper, by courtesy of the Lewis Walpole Library, Yale University. Fruit trees are watered from a statue of George III, while a boy urinates on John Wilkes, whom Hogarth imagines in the pillory alongside Fanny Lynes, the supposed Cock Lane Ghost.

**Figure 3.3** Jefferyes Hamett O'Neale (?), *The Pillory Triumphant; or, No. 45 for Ever* (1765), broadside etching, by courtesy of the Lewis Walpole Library, Yale University. John Williams, pilloried before Westminster Hall for reprinting *North Briton* 45, is fêted by well-wishers; a counter-demonstration ridicules the Earl of Bute, former Tory prime minister and a primary target of Wilkes's paper.

discoursed familiarly with this lucky criminal; to whom ... the pillory seemed a triumphal car.'[47]

What makes these repeated miscalculations so surprising is that ministers and their officials had long recognized, in private deliberations at least, that in a world where public opinion increasingly mattered, prosecuting and punishing dissident writers was a risky business. Persecution could not only make authors into heroes

---

[47] Johann Wilhelm von Archenholz, *A Picture of England*, 2 vols (1789), 1: 64–5. For a modern account of the event, see Cash, *John Wilkes*, 178–9.

or martyrs, but could also lend their works the allure of the forbidden—which was not to say writing should not be policed, but that it had to be policed with circumspection. Numerous efforts to suppress the manuscript newsletter of John Dyer, a Tory journalist, had failed during the 1690s, and with each new indictment, Godolphin complained, 'the consequence of it has been that his letters have been more sought after than they were before' (this from a starting-point of 500 copies, if an early estimate by L'Estrange is to be believed). The attempt to silence a writer by authority 'is a remedy that instead of curing the disease does most commonly make it worse', Godolphin saw, and in Dyer's case it was complicated legally by the fact of scribal publication.[48] Print entailed the same problems on a larger scale. Charles Delafaye, the official charged with press management for much of the Walpole era, was a bureaucrat of a new and impressive kind: urbane, energetic, efficient, with formidable reach. But even Delafaye sometimes despaired of the task before him. 'We can not govern authors and printers', he admitted in 1732 after botched attempts to prosecute the too crafty *Craftsman*—the first an outright failure, the second an embarrassing pyrrhic victory—increased that paper's circulation.[49]

A preference for quiet extra-legal intimidation—arrests, interrogations, and warnings without the fuss, expense, and uncertainty of prosecution—is evident when the failed Jacobite rebellion of 1745–6 gave rise to a minor spate of romances and other sympathetic fictions about the rising. In 1746, the young Ralph Griffiths was arrested for his swashbuckling *Ascanius, or The Young Adventurer* (a virtuoso of the forbidden, Griffiths had his next brush with the law on publishing John Cleland's pornographic *Memoirs of a Woman of Pleasure*). In 1749, Eliza Haywood was arrested for *A Letter from H[enry] G[orin]g Esq., One of the Gentlemen of the Bed-Chamber to the Young Chevalier*. But no prosecution

---

[48] *The Marlborough–Godolphin Correspondence*, ed. Henry L. Snyder, 3 vols (Oxford: Clarendon Press, 1975), 1: 125 (8 October 1702); for L'Estrange on Dyer in 1688, and for the legal status of manuscript, see Love, *Scribal Publication*, 11–12, 74–5, 184–91; also (on manuscript after 1714) Stephen Karian, *Jonathan Swift in Print and Manuscript* (Cambridge: Cambridge University Press, 2010), 72–99.

[49] Black, *English Press*, 115, quoting Delafaye to Earl Waldegrave, 31 March 1732.

ensued in either instance.[50] Unwillingness to prosecute in literary cases was intensified by the nagging related problem of jury independence, even after 'special juries' legislation was passed in 1730 to fix the issue.[51] In 1713 Secretary of State Bolingbroke held back from proceeding against Defoe's *Review* because 'I must confess I have been very much discourag'd by the success of some late Tryalls of Libellers'; in 1756 Lord Chancellor Hardwicke deplored what he frankly called 'the Impossibility of getting Juries to convict' for seditious libel.[52] Quite apart from juries, even the most hard-nosed of establishment judges may sometimes have had mixed feelings, among them John Willes, Lord Chief Justice of the Common Pleas from 1737. Though now gamekeeper in chief, Willes had been very much a poacher in his youth, and reportedly came close to personal disaster. 'Queen Anne's ministry had caught him scribbling libels', reported Lord Carteret, Willes's patron: 'I had even an interest with men in power—I saved him from the pillory.'[53]

We should not overstate the recalcitrant jury problem, and writers of the period sometimes note the countervailing phenomenon of jury deference. Even when sympathetic to a libel, or entertained by it, jurors might still fall into line. As one observer wrote in 1740, 'I have known many an honest Englishman laugh, and extremely fond to read a paper, who, if he had been upon the Jury that was to try the author, would have voted for his losing his ears'.[54] That said, there is no question that powerful trends—from Habermas's emergent 'public

---

[50] Kathryn R. King, *A Political Biography of Eliza Haywood* (London: Pickering & Chatto, 2012), 181–6; see also L. M. Knapp, 'Ralph Griffiths, Author and Publisher, 1746–1750', *The Library* 4th ser. 20.1 (1939–40), 197–213; Catherine Ingrassia, 'Additional Information about Eliza Haywood's 1749 Arrest for Seditious Libel', *Notes & Queries*, 44 (1997), 202–4.

[51] See James Oldham, *Trial by Jury: The Seventh Amendment and Anglo-American Special Juries* (New York: NYU Press, 2006), 25–44, 127–52.

[52] Hyland, 'Liberty and Libel', 869, quoting a Bolingbroke memorandum of 20 April 1713; Black, *English Press*, 117, quoting Hardwicke to Newcastle, 29 August 1756.

[53] Walpole, *Memoirs*, 1: 111; see David Lemmings, 'Willes, Sir John (1685–1761)', *ODNB*.

[54] *An Historical View of the Principles, Characters, Persons, &c. of the Political Writers in Great Britain* (1740), 25, qtd by Black, *English Press*, 117.

sphere' to the giddy pace of book-trade expansion—were conspiring to make press control more difficult by the year. It was left to opposition satirists to exult in both the marketability of seditious libel and the relative impunity of its producers. 'Can Statutes keep the *British* press in awe, | While that sells best, that's most against the Law?' asked James Bramston in a verse satire of 1733; Bramston also voiced admiration for Curll as one who 'has... a public spirit shewn, | And pleas'd our ears regardless of his own'.[55] Richard Savage—who began his career by writing lightly encoded Jacobite poems which circulated in manuscript and twice got him arrested—created a cynical alter ego with the inspired name of Iscariot Hackney in his satirical pamphlet *An Author To Be Lett* (1729). A consummate denizen of Grubstreet, Iscariot exults that 'one of my Books had the Honour of being presented for a Libel, by the Grand-Jury, and another was made a Burnt-Offering by the Hands of the Common Hangman'.[56] *An Author To Be Lett* was later republished with a *Grubstreet Journal* item in the same vein, celebrating the ineffectiveness of the pillory for any purpose except career advancement: 'The Pillory has had a Hymn composed in its honour, by a very eminent Writer; and amongst Printers it is so universally esteemed, that he, who has had the honour to mount that Rostrum, is always looked upon amongst them, as a Graduate in their profession.'[57] For precisely the reason

---

[55] James Bramston, *The Man of Taste* (1733), 8. In the Cambridge University Library copy, an early reader comments creatively that 'Curl a book seller famous for publishing Libells and Baudy books... suffered the Pillory with Loss of Ears.'

[56] Richard Savage, *An Author To Be Lett* (1729), 4. For the five Jacobite poems and their consequences, see Clarence Tracy, *The Artificial Bastard: A Biography of Richard Savage* (Toronto: University of Toronto Press, 1953), 29–33. Savage was a cat with nine lives: released from his first arrest (1715) after informing on a printer, he was saved after his second (1717) by a general amnesty covering acts of sedition associated with the 1715 rising. The poems survive only because a government investigator, Robert Girling, documented Savage's offences with the rigour of a textual scholar. His transcriptions provide copy text for *The Poetical Works of Richard Savage*, ed. Clarence Tracy (Cambridge: Cambridge University Press, 1962), 15–26.

[57] *A Collection of Pieces in Verse and Prose... Publish'd on Occasion of The Dunciad* (1732), 35 (*Grubstreet Journal* 59, 18 February 1731). On Defoe's *Hymn to the Pillory*, see above, pp. 144–5.

offered here—that the pillory was now promotional as much as punitive—these graduates were a dwindling band.

## Performance and print under Walpole

So what was the hapless would-be censor to do, as the primary weapon in his arsenal was increasingly turned against him? As noted above, extra-legal intimidation was one answer, a time-honoured practice that was privately articulated as policy in the 1750s when Hardwicke advised Newcastle to favour underhand methods over public prosecution: 'in some glaring instances it may be prudent to take up the persons, though you don't intend to proceed to trial', his lordship silkily wrote.[58] Legal historians, with their touching view of law as binding on governments in practice, often neglect the extent to which harassment had long been the norm when formal processes failed to get the job done. In this respect, histories of press control that focus on jurisprudential debate and statutory change look slightly to one side of the phenomenon itself.[59] For the same reason, the fairly short list of authors convicted of seditious libel between Defoe and Shebbeare should not be taken to indicate growing book-trade impunity or freedom of the press. In matters of political censorship between the licensing lapse of 1695 and the *North Briton* affair of the 1760s, the list of authors arrested, interrogated, warned, and released, often leaving large sureties for future good behaviour, is more telling: it also includes Nicholas Amhurst (1737), Abel Boyer (1714), Mary

[58] Hardwicke to Newcastle, 29 August 1756, qtd by Black, *English Press*, 117.

[59] See, for example, Hamburger's groundbreaking 'The Development of the Law of Seditious Libel and the Control of the Press', *Stanford Law Review*, 37 (1985), 661–765, which valuably emphasizes the flexibility and ingenuity required by officials in framing viable prosecution charges, and rebukes earlier historians for failing 'to notice that, in response to ever changing legal and political circumstances, the Crown relied at different times on different laws to restrain the press, and . . . turned from one law to another only when the law that had been its most effective instrument of control became for some reason unusable' (664). Though alert to this pragmatism, however, Hamburger neglects the extent to which governments responded not only by using imaginative proxy charges but also by bending the law or working outside it. Rule of law was certainly a central pillar of Whig ideology; how far it governed Whig practice is something else.

Barber (1734, as a proxy for Swift), Charles Churchill (1763), John Dyer (1703), Charles Gildon (1707), William Guthrie (1743), Eliza Haywood (1749), Bevil Higgons (1696), John Kelly (1737), Delarivier Manley (1709), Matthew Prior (1715), Abel Roper (1711, 1714), Richard Savage (1715, 1717), and Paul Whitehead (1739, as a proxy for Pope). This before one starts on the publishers and printers, who in a notable shift from the priorities of Scroggs in the 1680s, or Harley under Queen Anne, became the targets of choice on Delafaye's watch.[60] Even stolid, respectable Samuel Richardson had a brush with the authorities as printer and possible co-author of crypto-Jacobite material after the Atterbury treason trial of 1723; even the future Great Cham became a fugitive for a 1739 pamphlet of his composition, if Johnson's first major biographer is to be believed.[61] In the heyday of Grubstreet, only debt landed more authors in jail than seditious libel.

Subsidy, not suppression, was another answer, or the two could operate in tandem. Bribery was famously the *modus operandi* of Prime Minister Walpole (who in the 1730s may have been spending £20,000 annually on client writers) and his like-minded successor Henry Pelham, dubbed by Horace Walpole 'the purchaser of opponents'.[62] There is ample evidence, however, of control by co-option throughout the extended period. Like Defoe in 1703, Shebbeare in 1758 survived the pillory in good shape physically, but like Defoe he was broken financially by imprisonment, which in his case lasted three years, plus

---

[60] On occasion, Delafaye would even refuse information about authors, whom he viewed as hired hands libelling to order: 'printers and publishers ... got scoundrels not worth a Groat that lived in Garretts to write at so much a sheet', he wrote in 1723, so government 'would now fall upon printers and publishers as the more effectual way to put a stop to Libelling' (TNA, SP 43/66, qtd by T. C. Duncan Eaves and Ben D. Kimpel, *Samuel Richardson: A Biography* (Oxford: Clarendon Press, 1971), 23).

[61] Eaves and Kimpel, *Samuel Richardson*, 19–35; for Johnson, see below, pp. 215–16.

[62] Laurence Hanson, *Government and the Press, 1695–1763* (Oxford: Clarendon Press, 1967), 109; for further details, see Tone Sundt Urstad, *Sir Robert Walpole's Poets: The Use of Literature as Pro-Government Propaganda, 1721–1742* (Newark: University of Delaware Press, 1999), 56–97. For 'purchaser of opponents', see Horace Walpole, *Memoirs*, 3: 39.

direct financial penalties. Recruitment followed ruin in both cases: Defoe as writer and agent for Harley, who engineered payment of his fines with Godolphin's help; Shebbeare as a royal pensioner who thereafter (the *ODNB* laconically reports) 'distinguished himself as a loyal and energetic supporter of George III and his ministers in pamphlets and newspaper articles'—so lending weight to Smollett's claim that his noisy Jacobitism was never much more than a market-friendly pose.[63] Money talked, or rather money silenced; patronage did the trick where punishment failed. Shebbeare was often compared at this juncture with Johnson ('*She*-bear' to his '*He*-bear', one wag scoffed), who also accepted a pension from George III and thereafter found, Johnson famously admitted, 'the pleasure of cursing the House of Hanover...amply overbalanced by three hundred pounds a year'.[64] As Wilkes jeered in the Commons, 'the two famous doctors, Shebbeare and Johnson, are in this reign the state hirelings called pensioners...the known pensioned advocates of despotism'.[65] The difference is that whereas Johnson's reputation survived his elevation to the civil list (nominally the pension recognized his scholarship, and he was not expected to produce copy for the ministry), in Shebbeare's case payment was a beautifully effective stroke of press control, buying him off and discrediting his pen in a single move.

Shebbeare's reputation never recovered, and it was the pension more than the pillory that brought the shame. For Horace Walpole, he was a mere opportunist who 'had long declared that he would write himself into a place or the pillory'; he probably inspired Johnstone's cynical bookseller in *Chrysal*, who produces seditious libel as a method of blackmail or extortion: 'A *pension*, or a *pillory* is the word.' The formula stuck like glue to Shebbeare, who was still being ridiculed the same way a decade later. He was always already corrupt, William

---

[63] M. John Cardwell, 'Shebbeare, John (1709–1788)', *ODNB*; see also James R. Foster, 'Smollett's Pamphleteering Foe Shebbeare', *PMLA*, 57.4 (1942), 1053–1100.

[64] *Boswell's Life of Johnson*, 4: 113 n. 2; 1: 429; see also Nicholas Hudson, *A Political Biography of Samuel Johnson* (London: Pickering & Chatto, 2015), 100–1.

[65] *Boswell's Life of Johnson*, 3: 79 n., quoting Wilkes's speech of 16 April 1777. Wilkes alludes to Johnson's now embarrassing gloss on 'Pension' in the 1755 *Dictionary*: 'In England it is generally understood to mean pay given to a state hireling for treason to his country.'

Mason alleged: 'The same abusive, base, abandon'd thing, | When pilloried, or pension'd by a king'.[66]

Intimidation, then, or a more or less blatant system of payoffs and bribes—though Walpole and the Pelhams also used secret service funds to bury their dealings with authors, especially when a prominent opposition critic was involved.[67] Or, third, the nostalgic censor could look back to the golden age before 1695, for even in the second quarter of the eighteenth century the idea, indeed the practice, of licensing was by no means dead. This was especially the case during Walpole's tumultuous last years in office, and it may be in response to setbacks like the obstacle-ridden *Craftsman* prosecutions and the counter-productive pillorying of Curll that pre-publication controls returned to the political agenda. The process begins in the later 1720s, when little could be done about print satires like *Gulliver's Travels* or *The Dunciad* beyond providing indirect reminders—taken to heart by Swift, Pope, and their booksellers—that even the best-connected authors must watch their step.[68] But dramatic satire was a different matter, potentially more disruptive as a public spectacle, yet more controllable given that stage-specific legal restrictions, including theatre patents and vagrancy laws, were still available for use.[69] In 1728 Gay's *Beggar's Opera*, with its witty focus on ministerial sleaze, was a model of political insinuation that blurred identities and distributed blame in such a way as to inhibit prosecution. Gay was insistent about his theme, but more reticent or mixed in the messages he gave out

---

[66] Walpole, *Memoirs*, 3: 39; Johnstone, *Chrysal*, 4: 135; William Mason, *An Epistle to Dr Shebbeare* (1777), 9.

[67] This was the mechanism used to silence Johnson's earlier associate William Guthrie (from 1746, £200 per annum) and Fielding's sometime partner James Ralph (from 1753, £300 per annum): see Black, *English Press*, 103–4.

[68] For *The Dunciad*, see above, pp. 117–19; on *Gulliver's Travels*, see Paul Langford, 'Swift and Walpole', in Claude Rawson (ed.), *Politics and Literature in the Age of Swift: English and Irish Perspectives* (Cambridge: Cambridge University Press, 2010), 52–78; James McLaverty, 'The Revision of the First Edition of *Gulliver's Travels*: Book-Trade Context, Interleaving, Two Cancels, and a Failure to Catch', *Papers of the Bibliographical Society of America*, 106 (2012), 5–35.

[69] See Judith Milhous, 'Theatre Companies and Regulation', in Joseph Donohue (ed.), *The Cambridge History of British Theatre, Volume 2: 1660–1895* (Cambridge: Cambridge University Press, 2004), 108–25.

concerning its proper application. It was then for like-minded journalists to feign outrage about the play as 'the most venomous *allegorical Libel* against the G——t that hath appeared for many Years past', so lodging it in the public mind as just such a thing.[70]

At first Walpole responded to *The Beggar's Opera* with quick-witted theatricality of his own. At the opening night, he reportedly defused Lockit's pointed song about bribery (II.x), with the eyes of the audience fixed on his box, by calling for an encore: a display of teflon-coated insouciance that he would resume in another mode when satirized by Fielding in *Jonathan Wild*.[71] But when a full-scale and more strident encore was threatened in Gay's sequel *Polly* (1729), Walpole instead became proactive, and had his Lord Chamberlain prohibit performance 'without any reasons assigned', as Gay complained in tones of bewildered innocence.[72] At this point styles of censorship diverge by medium, for Walpole had no corresponding powers to prevent publication, which then took place with new twists of the knife from Gay, who was, he insists with poker face, 'as firmly attach'd to the present happy establishment as any of those who have the greatest places or pensions'. Sales predictably soared.[73] Nor could Walpole prevent the sophisticated ridicule of opposition journalists, who lined up with ironic endorsements of the stage ban. The *Craftsman* proposed an 'Index Expurgatorius' to be managed by the ridiculous impresario and laureate-in-waiting Colley Cibber, which would remove political content from all plays. *Fog's* solemnly catalogued

---

[70] Bertrand A. Goldgar, *Walpole and the Wits: The Relation of Politics to Literature, 1722–1742* (Lincoln: University of Nebraska Press, 1976), 69, quoting the *Craftsman* for 17 February 1728.

[71] For a newly discovered witness to Walpole's display of chutzpah, see Ilias Chrissochoidis and Richard Virr, 'An Annotated Wordbook of *The Beggar's Opera* (1728)', *Notes & Queries*, 60.1 (2013), 111–13: 'He, observing the manner the audience applied the last line to him, parried the thrust by encoring it with his single voice & thus not only blunted the practical shaft, but gained a general huzza from the audience' (112). On Walpole and *Jonathan Wild*, see below, pp. 197–8.

[72] John Gay, *The Beggar's Opera and Polly*, ed. Hal Gladfelder (Oxford: Oxford University Press, 2013), 75.

[73] Gay, *Beggar's Opera and Polly*, 75–6.

*Polly*'s most innocuous lines and alleged their seditious meaning—an old trick of Pope's from *A Key to the Lock*.[74]

Satirical farce was not the only dramatic genre to cause trouble. A similar episode occurred with *The Fall of Mortimer* (1731), a historical drama reviving the topical application methods of the *Duke of Guise* era, this time with obvious reference to Prime Minister Walpole. The authorities responded by suppressing *The Fall of Mortimer* as 'a false, infamous, scandalous, seditious, and treasonable libel',[75] and the Little Haymarket was forced to close until the following year. As the rhetorical overkill suggests (the adjectival pile-up was routine, but 'treasonable' raised the stakes), tragedies of this kind could arouse anxieties about public order that satire rarely involved, not least when the play ended by urging, as here, that in cases of ministerial corruption 'A Hempen Collar's always to be had'.[76] Rubbing salt in the wound was the afterpiece with which *The Fall of Mortimer* was often paired, Fielding's *The Welsh Opera*, which sounded genial comic echoes of the mainpiece's corruption theme: now Walpole is re-imagined as Robin the Butler, who profits from his office by stealing the spoons. Like *Polly*, however, *The Fall of Mortimer* survived and thrived in print, with four editions in quick succession, and four more when the play was revived as an anti-Bute drama in 1763 (Wilkes supplied a sly dedication to Bute, and sent him a presentation copy with gilt-edged leaves). In as clear an instance of Sheridan's 'puff collusive' as one could hope to find, a bogus denunciation appeared under the title *Remarks on an Historical Play, Called, The Fall of Mortimer, Shewing Wherein the Said Play May Be Term'd a Libel against the Present Administration*. Like the well-known 'attack' on Richardson's *Pamela* ten years later in *Pamela Censured* (which helpfully selects and reprints the novel's steamiest scenes), this pamphlet distils *The Fall of Mortimer* to its seditious essence, emphasizing the theme of corruption and especially the red line

---

[74] Goldgar, *Walpole and the Wits*, 83; for *A Key to the Lock*, see above, p. 149.

[75] Vincent J. Liesenfeld, *The Licensing Act of 1737* (Madison: University of Wisconsin Press, 1984), 18, citing the presentment of the Middlesex Grand Jury, 7 July 1731. On the authorship of *The Fall of Mortimer*, apparently adapted by either William Mullart or William Hatchett from an earlier application tragedy of 1691, see Thomas Lockwood's discussion in Fielding, *Plays*, 2: 9, 21–2.

[76] *The Fall of Mortimer* (1731), 64.

crossed in the plot with Mortimer's hanging. Luckily for the playwright, this hanging was a matter of historical fact, 'else would such a sentence on a *Prime Minister* [have] been downright Treason even on the Stage'. It was borderline incitement even so: 'If *Prime Ministers* are treated thus on the Stage, to what Extremes will not *People* go in private!'[77]

Theatre historians have documented the untenability of the restraints, hastily improvised and dubiously lawful, used against *Polly* and *The Fall of Mortimer*.[78] Expedients like this were clearly inadequate in the face of a broader and more concerted theatrical campaign against Walpole that gathered pace in the mid 1730s, involving a range of genres from irregular farce and ballad opera (including Fielding's virtuoso contributions) to topical application tragedies like William Havard's excruciating but sensational *King Charles the First*, with its executed ministers and king.[79] The result was the consolidation and extension of existing measures in the Stage Licensing Act of 1737, which required pre-performance approval of all new plays or new parts of old, and expressly included paratextual materials, which were often—since the time of Behn's arrest for a 1682 epilogue or Shadwell's denunciation of Dryden for a 1690 prologue—more pointed than the plays they surrounded. Contrary to whatever narrative of progressive liberalization we might construct, theatre was now more closely regulated and controlled than at the height of the Exclusion Crisis turmoil half a century earlier.

About print the Act says nothing, though it was widely feared to be a stalking-horse for the reintroduction of press licensing. Even before its passage, the opposition peer Lord Chesterfield predicted this outcome in a monitory speech, thanks, he suggested, to an unholy alliance of Grubstreet opportunism and ministerial paranoia. Plays

[77] *Remarks on an Historical Play, Called, The Fall of Mortimer*, 2nd edn (1731), 22, 10.

[78] See Matthew J. Kinservik, *Disciplining Satire: The Censorship of Satiric Comedy on the Eighteenth-Century London Stage* (Lewisburg: Bucknell University Press, 2002), 55–94.

[79] See Liesenfeld, *Licensing Act*, 60–155; also David Thomas, 'The 1737 Licensing Act and Its Impact', in Julia Swindells and David Francis Taylor (ed.), *The Oxford Handbook of the Georgian Theatre, 1737–1832* (Oxford: Oxford University Press, 2014), 91–106.

would be written in order to be banned, and then published 'with the Refusal in capital Letters on the Title Page', so generating more profit than performance could ever have done. Next, Parliament would be asked to prohibit publication as well as performance; legislation would then snowball to include the new genres into which seditious libel would overflow, for instance satires written 'by Way of Novels, secret Histories, Dialogues, or under some such Title'. Then would come a bill putting 'the Press under a general Licence, and then we may bid adieu to the Liberties of *Great Britain*'—all of which, Chesterfield implied, was the intention all along.[80]

He was right about the opening phase. The first play banned from performance under the Licensing Act, in 1739, was *Gustavus Vasa, The Deliverer of His Country* ('As it was to have been Acted'), which gave a vaguely Jacobite inflection to the liberation rhetoric of its hero, a sixteenth-century Swede, and featured the assassination of a royal favourite. It's hard to believe in its author, Henry Brooke, as a committed incendiary, but Brooke was certainly a good observer of market trends who was later to become (with *The Fool of Quality*, 1765–70) a fashionable sentimental novelist of the Sterne era. Publication was supported by 929 subscribers, among whom Chesterfield donated ten guineas and Swift bought ten copies; Brooke addressed them in a high-toned dedication complaining that he had been 'condemn'd and punish'd in my Works without being accus'd of any Crime'.[81] Then there was James Thomson's turgid Patriot drama *Edward and Eleonora* ('As it was to have been Acted'), banned just before its opening night and published in trade and subscription editions with an authorized dedication to the Princess of Wales, royal figurehead of the Patriot opposition, and a half-title advertisement highlighting the prohibition in Gothic type (connoting Saxon liberty).[82] According

---

[80] Liesenfeld, *Licensing Act*, 146, quoting the version of Chesterfield's speech given in the *London Magazine* for April 1737.

[81] Henry Brooke, *Gustavus Vasa: The Deliverer of His Country* (1739), p. v; on the subscriber list, see D. D. Eddy and J. D. Fleeman, 'A Preliminary Handlist of Books to Which Dr. Samuel Johnson Subscribed', *Studies in Bibliography*, 46 (1993), 187–220 (194).

[82] The wording of this notice ('The Representation of this Tragedy, on the Stage, was prohibited in the Year One Thousand Seven Hundred and Thirty-Nine') may also allude to the non-appearance of Pope's widely expected follow-up

to a later rumour, Thomson added provocative last touches after completing the play 'in order to induce the Licenser to prohibit its representation'.[83]

Most blatant of all was *The Levee* (1741) by John Kelly, a serial seditious libeller who, when arrested for going too far in *Fog's Weekly Journal* in 1737, talked his way out of custody by claiming to be merely mercenary, not political, 'being by reiterated misfortunes reduced to write for his Daily bread'.[84] This much-used excuse was probably true, and like Brooke, Kelly followed where the market led, hitting the jackpot soon afterwards with *Pamela's Conduct in High Life* (1741), an opportunist continuation of Richardson's bestseller. Between these landmarks, *The Levee* was an amusing but scarcely inflammatory send-up of the notorious 'levee' rituals at which Walpole received clients and distributed favours, 'Offer'd to, and accepted for Representation by the Master of the Old-House in *Drury-Lane*, but by the INSPECTOR of FARCES denied a Licence'.[85] As Matthew Kinservik notes, 'Inspector of Farces' (for Lord Chamberlain) was a deftly insulting touch, 'an effective way of diminishing the dignity of the censorial enterprise'.[86]

The next stage predicted by Chesterfield is less clear, and some historians have dismissed the scare about impending press licensing as an opposition ploy. Perhaps the real lesson of Chesterfield's speech was that in the long run the game was up for pre-publication censorship, hampered as it increasingly was by market forces: by the public appetite for dissident writing, and by the energy and ingenuity of the writers who supplied it. Ban sedition in one genre and it pops up in

---

to *One Thousand Seven Hundred and Thirty-Eight* (see above, pp. 118–19), so indicating a larger context of formal censorship and informal constraint.

[83] James Sambrook, *James Thomson, 1700–1748: A Life* (Oxford: Clarendon Press, 1991), 196, quoting the *Gentleman's and London Magazine* (Dublin) for June 1762.

[84] TNA, SP 36/41/2, fo. 133 ('The humble Petition of John Kelly'); for Kelly's career, see Thomas Keymer and Peter Sabor, *Pamela in the Marketplace: Literary Controversy and Print Culture in Eighteenth-Century Britain and Ireland* (Cambridge: Cambridge University Press, 2005), 66–82.

[85] John Kelly, *The Levee: A Farce* (1741), title page.

[86] Matthew J. Kinservik, 'The Dialectics of Print and Performance after 1737', in Swindells and Taylor (ed.), *Oxford Handbook of Georgian Theatre*, 123–39 (134).

another; prohibit it from the stage and it becomes a bigger phenomenon on the page. Yet the threat that press licensing might at least be attempted again cannot be dismissed, if only because officials so clearly felt the existing system to be failing. Before Delafaye's retirement in 1734, legal actions had been frequent enough for one witness to allege that, even in the tense last years of Queen Anne's reign, 'there were not so many Prosecutions against Libellers and Pamphleteers, as have been since [Walpole's] *meek Administration*, neither were any Attempts made to invade the *Liberty of the Press*'.[87] Even so, prosecution of journals such as the *True Briton* (1723), *Mist's* (1729), the *Craftsman* (1729, 1731), and the *Universal Spy* (1732) achieved little deterrent effect, though these actions probably encouraged enhanced use by journalists, in more or less rudimentary ways, of codes and disguise. Shortly after the Stage Licensing Act passed, what Michael Harris calls 'a sudden and comprehensive series of actions' was again launched against opposition papers, and it may be significant that these actions focused especially on journalism *about* censorship, notably an ironic *Craftsman* leader (2 July 1737) that urged the suppression of Shakespeare for his many blatant attacks on the Walpole ministry.[88] The *Craftsman*'s editor (Nicholas Amhurst, pseudonym 'Caleb D'Anvers') spent ten days in custody, but as usual in these years it was the printer, Henry Haines, who took the rap. Arrested at gunpoint while setting type, Haines was convicted by a special jury and jailed for two years: 'Poor *Haines*'s ears in pain for *Caleb*'s wit', a satirist wrote.[89] Paradoxically, it was in connection with the *Craftsman* that the

[87] *The Doctrine of Innuendo's Discuss'd, or the Liberty of the Press Maintain'd* (1731), 16.

[88] Michael Harris, *London Newspapers in the Age of Walpole: A Study of the Origins of the Modern English Press* (Rutherford: Fairleigh Dickinson University Press, 1987), 147, 125. The Shakespeare joke was less outlandish than it might seem. Four years earlier the Treasury Solicitor, Nicholas Paxton, sent Delafaye a *Craftsman* paper (13 January 1733) 'in which is a quotation from Shakespeare which I think libelous as it is introduced and applied'. Delafaye did not proceed. The passage at issue was John of Gaunt's 'sceptered isle' speech in *Richard II* (II.i.40–66), which, a fictional *Craftsman* reader suggests, 'deserves a Place in your Paper, at this Juncture' (TNA, SP 36/29/1 fo. 11).

[89] Harris, *London Newspapers in the Age of Walpole*, 141–5; Thomas Newcomb, *A Supplement to One Thousand Seven Hundred Thirty-Eight: Not Written by Mr. Pope* (1738), 7.

expression 'Trade of libelling' seems to have first been used in print, though for most of those concerned it was a sincere vocation.[90]

This episode threw the *Craftsman* into disarray, but new and in some ways fiercer journals took up the baton, notably *Common Sense* and in due course Fielding's *Champion*. Whether operating through indictment or intimidation, the limits of state power were no less exposed than before. Stung by Chesterfield's speech and the broader outcry that followed, Hardwicke used the Lords' proceedings against Paul Whitehead's *Manners* to deny that press licensing was being contemplated, despite the provocations all around. As a crony of the Lord Chancellor reported, he 'made an excellent speech to explain the true meaning of the liberty of the press, which he said he found was not at all generally understood, that it was not a liberty to defame and libel, but that it was opposed to previous restraints put upon the press, as had been formerly done by licencers and other methods'.[91] For Jeremy Black, the speech is evidence that no new licensing plans were afoot. But this was at best an evasive denial, interspersed with menacing asides of the kind in which Hardwicke specialized. 'If the liberty of the press consists in defamation, it were much better we were without such liberty', his lordship opined. As for 'the freedom which some gentlemen think themselves entitled to in censuring the conduct of their superiors', this, Hardwicke learnedly revealed, 'is a freedom unknown to our constitution, and subversive of our known statutes'.[92] It's a remarkable fact that these alarming words were spoken during a parliamentary debate about a work of poetry—though alongside Whitehead's satire, Hardwicke also had the journalism of the *Craftsman* and its immediate successors in his sights.

Numerous satirists played on the threat as generally perceived, including Pope, whose jeremiad against the age in *One Thousand Seven Hundred and Thirty-Eight*—'Yet may this Verse (if such a Verse remain) | Show there was one who held it in disdain'—parenthetically raises the

---

[90] *The Grand Accuser the Greatest of All Criminals* (1735), 77; this pamphlet was a character assassination, ministerially sponsored, of Viscount Bolingbroke.

[91] Black, *English Press*, 115–16, quoting Francis Hare to Francis Naylor, 17 February 1739.

[92] George Harris, *The Life of Lord Chancellor Hardwicke*, 3 vols (1847), 1: 430, 431.

fear of retrospective censorship.[93] Then there was Johnson's ironic suggestion, in his *Compleat Vindication of the Licensers of the Stage* (1739), that expurgations and imprimaturs were poor half-measures, and that schools should be forbidden to teach reading 'without a license from the Lord Chamberlain'.[94] Nor were these references to impending press censorship confined to opposition satire. A widespread sense that the campaign against Walpole was now crossing the line into sedition so often, and so flagrantly, that mere *ad hoc* prosecution would no longer do is detectable in neutral and also pro-ministerial sources. 'Certainly the manner in which [Walpole] is abused, exceeds all bounds and is an abuse of the liberty of the press which ought not to be suffered, for many of those writings very much savour of sedition', wrote the Dutch foreign minister in 1739.[95] The following year the pro-Walpole *Daily Gazetteer* blamed the Stage Licensing Act squarely on Fielding's plays, adding that the reckless journalism that Fielding and his collaborator James Ralph were now producing would precipitate press licensing. The *Champion* 'has out-stripped all the *Vehicles* of *Sedition* in the Service of the *Opposition*'; in it, Fielding 'is endeavouring by frequent Provocations to draw the same on the Press'.[96]

Launched in 1739, the *Champion* certainly intensified rumours among political insiders that new legislation was imminent. As a recently discovered letter about Fielding from a well-informed (if somewhat excitable) observer puts it:

> those y$^t$ know no other way of persuading but by Gibbets, axes &c will try no other. & this brings into my mind a Bill, I have great reason to fear is preparing about the *Licentiousness* (as they call it) of the press.

---

[93] *The Twickenham Edition of the Works of Alexander Pope*, ed. John Butt et al., 11 vols (London: Methuen, 1938–68), 4: 309 (*Epilogue to the Satires*, i.171–2).

[94] Samuel Johnson, *Political Writings*, ed. Donald J. Greene (New Haven: Yale University Press, 1977), 73.

[95] Jeremy Black, *Walpole in Power* (Stroud: Sutton, 2001), 111, quoting an intercepted letter (14 April 1739) from François Fagel to his envoy in London.

[96] Martin C. Battestin with Ruthe R. Battestin, *Henry Fielding: A Life* (London: Routledge, 1989), 286, quoting the *Daily Gazetteer* for 17 October and 9 October 1740.

There is not one of the Courtiers but I hear talk of such a Bill. The champion's way of writing, they say, makes it necessary.[97]

In fact the *Champion* had two ways of writing, and the interplay between them was part of its force: high-octane polemic from Ralph, couched in the severe idiom of classical republicanism; urbane ridicule from Fielding, with frequent focus on censorship as a metonym for the broader iniquities of Whig oligarchy. In early papers, Fielding taunts the ministry with exaggerated, gratuitous gestures of concealment—he must now apply himself to politics, 'when.......... when............. when..................... at this Time'—as though nothing substantive at all might now be said. Printers were panic-buying extra stocks of dashes 'to keep the first and last Letter of proper Names and other Words asunder, as

*R———t, M———r*'; authors like himself were even now omitting the initial letter, 'for, I do not know many Parts of my Body, for which I have a greater Respect than my Ears'.[98] Later papers report Job Vinegar's travels among the venal race of the PTFGHSIAMSKI, with virtuoso use of what Fielding elsewhere calls 'emvowelled' words, gutted of inside characters in the *Craftsman* tradition.[99] Here the natives elevate corruption into a matter of ritualized worship: 'The PTRTS talk of LBRTY, but do thou, O HUM-CLUM give us MNEY.' They celebrate the constitutional merits of 'STLTO-FRTOCY, a Word very difficult to translate' (but 'Stulto-Fartocracy' is a reasonable guess).[100]

Alongside Ralph's more open invectives, passages like this were indeed provocations, not least in Fielding's elaborate games with innocuous terms ('DRNKNG, GMNG, SMKNG, WNCHNG...in CVNT

---

[97] John Upton to James Harris, 3 December 1740, qtd by Frederick G. Ribble, 'New Light on Henry Fielding from the Malmesbury Papers', *Modern Philology*, 103 (2005), 51–94 (57).

[98] Fielding, *Contributions to The Champion*, 176 (14 February 1740), 40 (4 December 1739), 177 (14 February 1740).

[99] See Henry Fielding, *The Jacobite's Journal and Related Writings*, ed. W. B. Coley (Oxford: Clarendon Press, 1975), 96 (No. 1, 5 December 1747): 'As for all the Words which I *embowel* or rather *emvowel*, I will never so mangle them, but they shall be as well known as if they retained every Vowel in them.'

[100] Fielding, *Contributions to The Champion*, 239 (20 March 1740), 391 (28 June 1740).

GRDN'), as though the Licensing Act had created a world in which all discourse collapses into mere mumble.[101] As so often in Fielding, the leading note is comic relish more than satirical rage, but his vision of a gagged society is no less insistent for that. Official propagandists come in for special ridicule. Notable among them is the apostate figure of Ralph Courteville ('RALPH FREEMAN, alias, COURT, EVIL'), principal author of the *Daily Gazetteer*, who, Fielding reports, started his career in opposition 'and, with the Help of a *Spelling-Master*, wrote many *seditious* Libels against our *present most excellent Administration*'. On being arrested and interrogated, however, Courteville had been 'frightened out of all the little Wits he ever had, and became an Advocate for the *Minister*, in order to save his own dear and precious Carcase'.[102] Elsewhere Fielding affects to internalize the hardline opinions now promulgated by the *Gazetteer*, denouncing opposition writers 'who have wickedly and foolishly opposed the Measures of a Minister, and ... stood up in Defence of a certain seditious Word, called *Liberty*'.[103]

In the event, new press legislation did not materialize, though that may only be because circumstances overtook it when Walpole was finally toppled in February 1742. Fielding marked the moment in a revision to *Joseph Andrews* later that spring, but at the same time suggested that the culture of self-enrichment associated with Walpole was still in place. Rescued by Parson Adams from a potential rapist, Fanny initially fears her deliverer, and suspects that Adams 'had used her as some very honest Men have used their Country; and had rescued her out of the hands of one Rifler, in order to rifle her himself'.[104] There had been a change of personnel, not political culture.

---

[101] Fielding, *Contributions to The Champion*, 446 (4 September 1740). Fielding's play on the interchangeable U/V of early modern typography is a mischievous further touch.

[102] Fielding, *Contributions to The Champion*, 480, 481 (16 October 1740). Courteville may once have been a *Craftsman* writer, and indeed a contributor (the editor claimed) of 'such venomous Libels against the *great Man* ... that even I was ashamed to print them' (*Craftsman*, 29 October 1737, qtd in *Contributions to The Champion*, 481 n.; see also Harris, *London Newspapers in the Age of Walpole*, 109–11).

[103] Fielding, *Contributions to The Champion*, 184 (16 February 1740).

[104] Henry Fielding, *Joseph Andrews*, ed. Martin C. Battestin (Oxford: Clarendon Press, 1967), 140 (II.x).

## Fielding and Walpole: the art of thriving

So much then for the censor's dilemma; what about that of the libeller? Fielding and Johnson both gave up the practice on Walpole's fall, indeed somewhat before it—though in Fielding's case there are still pointed anti-ministerial sallies in *Shamela*, a work speed-written from a debtors' jail in March 1741. Sooner or later, both became establishment figures and pro-government writers, albeit with complications: Fielding for the Pelhams under George II, Johnson for the ministries of Grafton and North under George III.[105] For all that, much can be learned from the differing methods employed by each as the literary campaign against Walpole reached its crescendo. The lessons they learned had a marked impact on their mature writings in the post-Walpole era, in which creative techniques of indirection outlive the political constraints that first inspired them.

It was once standard to interpret as anti-ministerial all Fielding's satire before *Pasquin* and *The Historical Register for the Year 1736*, the incendiary farces that helped provoke the Stage Licensing Act, and the *Champion*, with its vision of a kleptocracy maintained in power by patronage and bribes, electoral chicanery, and stringent press control. There are certainly offensive touches in several of Fielding's early plays, and relevant external evidence, albeit of a murky kind, exists in the apparent suppression of *The Grub-Street Opera*, which was rehearsed but withdrawn from performance in 1731, allegedly 'by a certain Influence which has been very *prevailing* of late Years'.[106] Yet on inspection many other Fielding comedies resist this rubric, or satirize politics in scattershot, non-partisan style; his sheer

---

[105] For these trajectories, see Hudson, *Political Biography of Johnson*, esp. 119–50; J. A. Downie, *A Political Biography of Henry Fielding* (London: Pickering & Chatto, 2009), esp. 147–72.

[106] Fielding, *Plays*, 2: 33 (*The Welsh Opera*, Preface). Fielding did not write this preface and disavowed the whole edition as 'incorrect and spurious' (2: 25). The author was possibly Elizabeth Rayner, publisher of the unauthorized *Welsh Opera* on behalf of her husband William Rayner, a prolific dealer in seditious libel who was shortly to suffer two years' imprisonment for a *Craftsman*-related pamphlet (see Harris, *London Newspapers in the Age of Walpole*, 90–8; McDowell, *Women of Grub Street*, 110–11).

inconsistency is now established.[107] If Fielding was not always writing against Walpole, however, he was always thinking about him, as both critic and connoisseur of that '*Art of thriving*' for which Walpole stood in his mind: the craftily self-serving *modus operandi* of a Jonathan Wild, a Shamela, or a Blifil, which was also, he writes in a 1743 essay, 'the very Essence of that excellent Art, called *The Art of Politics*'.[108] What makes this pattern so interesting is the typically self-implicating tenor of Fielding's writing, and the way in which, while satirizing mercenary, manipulative conduct, he fashioned his own theatrical career as a performance in just this vein. Like his immediate precursor Gay, Fielding oscillated in the 1730s between seeking ministerial patronage and writing anti-ministerial satire; there's a sense in which his entire output during the Walpole era demands to be seen as an extended exercise in extortion, albeit one performed with surpassing wit and charm.

A case in point is Fielding's five-act comedy *The Modern Husband* (1732), which he went so far as to dedicate to Walpole, without much obvious irony, but with an almost menacing emphasis on Walpole's need to recruit the best pens in order to repair his tarnished reputation. On the face of it, Fielding downplays the force of the opposition campaign: the 'little Artifices' of Walpole's enemies, their 'little Malice and Envy'. But at the same time he makes this campaign, with glorious failure of tact, the central topic of his dedication. And then calumnies, however false, can all too easily become entrenched, which makes it essential that Walpole enlist, and reward, the most skilful rhetoricians in his defence: 'Protect, therefore, Sir, an Art from which You may promise Your self such notable Advantages.' The comedy that follows is clearly not an anti-Walpole satire. But it flaunts its undeveloped potential as such a thing, not least in the 'levee' scene (perhaps the

---

[107] For the critical history, see Thomas Keymer, 'Fielding's Theatrical Career', in Claude Rawson (ed.), *The Cambridge Companion to Henry Fielding* (Cambridge: Cambridge University Press, 2007), 17–37; the view of Fielding the playwright as always already oppositional was killed off by Robert D. Hume, *Henry Fielding and the London Theatre, 1728–1737* (Oxford: Clarendon Press, 1987).

[108] Henry Fielding, *Miscellanies, Volume One*, ed. Henry Knight Miller (Oxford: Clarendon Press, 1972), 154–5 ('An Essay of the Knowledge of the Characters of Men').

inspiration for Kelly's banned play) in which corrupt Lord Richly distributes patronage to his minions. Elsewhere *The Modern Husband* is full of latently political asides about hypocrisy and corruption: about a modern world where virtue is 'nothing more than a Sound, and Reputation is its Echo', and where cuckoldry is 'almost the only Title of Honour that can't be bought'.[109] Look what I might go on to write, Fielding seems to be saying, unless you pay up; see how damaging theatre will become if its rising star moves into outright opposition. Walpole did not respond, or responded with too little, and the eventual consequence was *The Historical Register* (1737), with its running analogies between the illusions of theatre, the deceptions of politics, and the extraction of money from the public as the motive of those holding power in either field. As Fielding's dramatist Medley explains while rehearsing his play, there is 'a strict Resemblance between the States Political and Theatrical, there is a Ministry in the latter as well as the former...and tho' the Publick damn both, yet while they both receive their Pay, they laugh at the Publick behind the Scenes'.[110]

In some ways *The Historical Register* can now look innocuous, even quite genial, with its satire falling on politicians as a class as often as on ministers specifically. When one of Medley's actors cries 'Hang foreign Affairs, let us apply ourselves to Money' ('be sure to snatch hastily at the Money', Medley directs him), he plays the role of a politician in general, not specifically a Walpole Whig. When Hen the auctioneer invites bids for Lot 1 ('A most curious Remnant of Political Honesty'), the joke targets ministerial clients, but balance is restored with reference to the opposition in Lot 2: 'A most delicate Piece of Patriotism...ten Pounds for this Piece of Patriotism?' Even the speech that outraged pro-Walpole journalists—Medley's announcement that 'when my Politicks come to a Farce, they very naturally lead me to the Play-House, where...there are some Politicians too, where there is Lying, Flattering, Dissembling, Promising, Deceiving, and Undermining'—is not necessarily partisan. Only in the closing act, when Medley insists that while vice and folly are eternal, 'what

---

[109] Fielding, *Plays*, 2: 211, 222, 257 (*The Modern Husband*, Dedication, I.iv, IV.i).
[110] Fielding, *Plays*, 3: 432 (*The Historical Register*, II.i).

I intend to ridicule in the following Scene, is the whole and sole Production and Invention of some People now living', do we unambiguously enter the realm of anti-Walpole satire. Here is the familiar opposition argument that the fish rots first from the head, or that all corruptions in modern society trickle down from a corrupt administration.[111]

Clearly enough, the words on the page (which, given Fielding's improvisatory habits and creative opportunism, may not on any given night have been the words on the stage) were only part of the problem posed by *The Historical Register*. The threat lay first in Fielding's presentation of the play as a topical farce that could be endlessly, damagingly renewed each year, and second in elements of unscripted performance that moved his satire across the boundary into personal lampoon. As one alarmed witness reports, here was 'Foundation visibly laid for annual Misrepresentation and personal Abuse (for a Person like S$^r$· Rob$^t$· Walpole, and actually dress'd in his very Peruke and Coat was exhibited on the Stage)'.[112] Even rehearsal—the hall-of-mirrors phenomenon of a rehearsal play in actual rehearsal—could be part of the act. The same source reports Fielding startling those present by attending rehearsals of another comedy 'in a compleat Suit of *Black Velvet*', a gesture that sartorially evoked Dryden, his great precursor in the teasing arts of politically encoded theatre.[113]

*The Historical Register*, in other words, was not actionable in terms of its text, but elements of performance may have made it so, and the threat of future intensification was plainly there. Fielding then added a more pointed afterpiece, *Eurydice Hiss'd*, with a wittily damaging double application in which Pillage, a cynical, desperate, self-absorbed playwright, stands for both Fielding himself on the failure of his recent comedy *Eurydice* and Walpole on the failure of the Excise Bill. The profiteering manipulator of a stage-play world,

---

[111] Fielding, *Plays*, 3: 419 (I.i), 427 (II.i), 416 (I.i), 435 (III.i).

[112] H. Diack Johnstone, 'Four Lost Plays Recovered: *The Contrast* and Other Dramatic Works of John Hoadly (1711–1776)', *Review of English Studies*, 57 (2006), 487–506 (493), quoting John Hoadly's manuscript preface of *c*.1772–6 to his play *The Contrast*.

[113] Johnstone, 'Four Lost Plays Recovered', 491.

Pillage knows, and acts on the knowledge, that 'all Government is but a *Farce*, and perhaps a damn'd one too'.[114] His role opens up a dizzying series of jokes about the theatricality of politics and the politics of theatre. Hisses are rife in both houses, the playhouse and the Commons or Lords; a theatre manager clings to support by aping a prime minister ('his Levée is compos'd of Actors soliciting for Parts, Printers for Copies, Boxkeepers, Scenemen, Fidlers and Candle-Snuffers'); both debase literature by making it the province of 'Court Laureats' and 'Scribblers, who for Hire | Would write away their Country's Liberties' (Colley Cibber, comedian and panegyrist, is the implied target). As Wolsey sees before his fall under Henry VIII, power itself is a demeaning charade, and finally futile: ''Tis all a Cheat, | Some Men play little Farces, and some great.'[115]

There's no record on this occasion of Walpole calling for an encore. But in another indication of the obstacles posed to censorship by the absence of a politically unified elite, one witness attending a double bill of *The Historical Register* and *Eurydice Hiss'd* reported the show-stealing presence of Frederick, Prince of Wales, sponsor of the Patriot opposition: 'The whole was a Satire on Sir Robert Walpole, and I observed that when any strong passages fell, the Prince, who was there, clapped, especially when in favour of liberty.'[116] However objectionable Fielding made himself to the ministry, nobody was going to arrest the latest darling of Leicester House.

Traditionally, Walpole's Stage Licensing Act has been viewed as a disaster for Fielding, at least until he was able to reinvent himself as a novelist with *Joseph Andrews*, almost five years after the sudden stop put to his theatre career. But it may have been no such thing. Creatively, the spirit of Walpole continued to energize Fielding's

---

[114] This was the interpretation of the ministerially funded *Daily Gazetteer* (7 May 1737), alluding to Pillage's speech about Wolsey as 'Author of a Farce, | Perhaps a damn'd one too' (*Plays*, 3: 449). For Fielding's double-edged riposte to the *Gazetteer* in the opposition journal *Common Sense* (21 May 1737), see *Contributions to The Champion*, 1–6 (esp. 4–5).

[115] Fielding, *Plays*, 3: 449, 455–6, 449.

[116] Hume, *Henry Fielding and the London Theatre*, 238, quoting the Earl of Egmont's diary for 18 April 1737.

satire, with its distinctive mixed tone of condemnation and relish—a tone perhaps acquired from Machiavelli, whose writing Fielding admired.[117] In *Shamela*, the heroine's self-interested 'Vartue' represents the prostitution of all values in Walpole's England, including the corruption of 'Pollitricks'. She herself is 'that young Politician', and the author who created her has an outlook so 'agreeable to the Age' that his next project should be a life of Walpole, '*his Honour* himself'.[118] Yet there's also a winning exuberance to Shamela through all her mercenary dealings: a shameless but irresistible brio, with none of the anger vented by Pope or Swift when handling similar themes.

Much the same is true of *Jonathan Wild*, which Fielding may have begun as early as 1737 or as late as 1742, and then published with seeming belatedness in 1743. Here Walpole is reimagined as a ruthless crime boss, yet also as charismatic, engagingly wily, with little trace of the earnest rhetoric of Patriot virtue usually associated with the Wild/Walpole analogy (a long-term staple of opposition journalism) in other hands.[119] Moreover, although sometimes Fielding targets Walpole with amusing directness—Walpole's elegant mistress Maria Skerritt becomes Wild's slutty Molly Straddle—elsewhere he lifts clear of the moment to satirize party politics and power relations in a more abstract mode. These are the passages that give *Jonathan Wild* its enduring resonance: the forthright speech, for example, in which Wild explains the party system as a grand exercise in distraction by the ruling class, a maze of decoys foisted on the people 'that while they are listening to your Jargon, you may with the greater Ease and

[117] See Thomas Keymer, 'Fielding's Machiavellian Moment', in Claude Rawson (ed.), *Henry Fielding (1707–1754), Novelist, Playwright, Journalist* (Newark: University of Delaware Press, 2008), 58–91.

[118] Henry Fielding, *The Journal of a Voyage to Lisbon, Shamela, and Occasional Writings*, ed. Martin C. Battestin with Sheridan W. Baker and Hugh Amory (Oxford: Clarendon Press, 2008), 172, 190, 147, 153.

[119] See, for example, the 23 June 1739 number of *Common Sense*, against which an information was filed by Attorney General Sir Dudley Ryder 'for printing & publishing a Libel on the House of Commons & the Ministry comparing them to Jonathan Wild & his Gang' (TNA, KB 15/54, fo. 15). For an overview of the Wild–Walpole analogy and its complications in Fielding's hands, see Downie, *Political Biography of Fielding*, 137–43.

Safety, pick their Pockets'.[120] Passages like this are hard to map on to Walpole specifically, while the favourite allegations of Fielding's farces or the anti-Walpole campaign more broadly—in particular the allegation of bribery—are oddly muted. Whatever its original conception, *Jonathan Wild* was only residually, and rather intermittently, a work of pointed opposition satire; finally, the gangster/minister analogy took Fielding in a new, more universalizing, direction.

We shall never know for certain why *Jonathan Wild* took so long to appear, which was not until Walpole's fall had removed its capacity to do political damage, or why from a strictly topical standpoint it pulls its satirical punches. But the weight of evidence, some of it relatively new, suggests that in the end Fielding's debt to Walpole was a matter of hard cash as much as creative inspiration. Unable to have Fielding arrested, instead the Great Man negotiated—in much the style, very likely, of his attempts to contain Pope and Swift over informal suppers and private meetings in the era of *Gulliver's Travels* and the first version of *The Dunciad*.[121] When *Jonathan Wild* at last appeared as a volume of Fielding's 1743 *Miscellanies*, published by subscription, Walpole was incongruously there on the list as the foremost subscriber: ten copies in de luxe royal paper format, costing twenty guineas; ten copies of a satire likening him to a double-dealing underworld kingpin. Perhaps this was a cool reprise, in print, of his performance of amused invulnerability when he rose to applaud *The Beggar's Opera*. But it may have been part of a deal to which Fielding uneasily alludes several times in 1740 or thereabouts: a dream-vision in the *Champion* about taking a bribe from Walpole; another *Champion* paper about being paid to stop a book; more frankly, his admission in the preface to a now forgotten poem that he had 'been obliged with Money to silence my Productions, professedly and by Way of Bargain given me for that Purpose'. He had also been paid, he confesses, to ridicule people he honoured.[122]

---

[120] Henry Fielding, *Miscellanies, Volume Three*, ed. Bertrand A. Goldgar and Hugh Amory (Oxford: Clarendon Press, 1997), 69 (II.vi).

[121] For the surviving evidence, see Howard Erskine-Hill, 'Pope and the Poetry of Opposition', in Pat Rogers (ed.), *The Cambridge Companion to Alexander Pope* (Cambridge: Cambridge University Press, 2007), 134–49 (137–9).

[122] Fielding, *Miscellanies, Volume One*, 248 (*Of True Greatness*, January 1741); see also *Contributions to The Champion*, 62–9 (13 December 1739), 473–5 (4 October 1740).

Later comes an oddly self-righteous *Jacobite's Journal* paper comparing authors to advocates in law: one profession is no less entitled than the other to take payment for mounting prosecutions or defences, and 'I do not think a Writer, whose only Livelihood is his Pen, to deserve a very flagitious Character, if, when one Set of Men deny him Encouragement, he seeks it from another, at their Expence'.[123]

The smoking-gun evidence emerged some years ago in the shape of a breathless letter sent by one Fielding intimate to another just days before publication of *The Opposition: A Vision* (1741)—an anonymous satire, but acknowledged by Fielding—in which he abruptly switched sides. 'Our Friend F–l–g is actually reconciled to $y^e$ great Man', Thomas Harris tells his brother James in December 1741, '& as He says upon very advantageous Terms.'[124] We know no more about these terms or their impact, if any, on either the text or the timing of *Jonathan Wild*. But there's now little doubt that Walpole was handling Fielding with both stick and carrot—or that Fielding had engineered a situation in which Walpole, unable to prosecute, was forced to pay. A few weeks after the date of this letter, *Joseph Andrews* appeared, with its gleeful sideswipe about 'certain Mysteries or Secrets in all Trades from the highest to the lowest, from that of *Prime-Ministring*, to this of *Authoring*'.[125] Again Fielding's analogy is between Walpole and himself, united by professions that are at root commercial: masterly accomplices in the art of thriving.

In the post-Walpole era (even, with *The Opposition*, in its dying days) Fielding went on to become a highly effective pro-government writer, most stridently so in his journal the *True Patriot* (1745–6) during the Jacobite rebellion. Yet the arts of subterfuge he learned in opposition, specifically those of ironic or allegorical suggestion, stayed with him for the remainder of his career, and continued to enrich his art. *Tom Jones* has little in common with the Jacobite fictions for which Griffiths and Haywood were arrested after the rising, but it makes virtuoso use of glancing parallels, notably between the novel's hero and the

---

[123] Fielding, *Jacobite's Journal*, 215 (No. 17, 26 March 1748).

[124] Frederick G. Ribble, 'Fielding's Rapprochement with Walpole in Late 1741', *Philological Quarterly*, 80.1 (2001), 71–81 (74–5), quoting Thomas Harris's letter of 5 December 1741.

[125] Fielding, *Joseph Andrews*, 89.

wandering Pretender. In so doing it approaches Jacobitism with a subtlety, even a degree of imaginative sympathy, that transcends the polemical binaries of the *True Patriot*.[126] In all its official postures, Fielding's novel is of course an unimpeachably Whig document. The hero is a Hanoverian loyalist for whom 'the Cause of King *George* is the Cause of Liberty', and his zeal is reaffirmed by a wise old hermit who remembers the traumatic depredations of James II. The heroine is tyrannized by a Jacobite father who acts out his retrograde politics in domestic life. Even the narrator strikes Whiggish poses, eschewing the role of a '*jure divino* Tyrant' and existing only to serve his readers' welfare, by mutual consent, like a good Lockean.[127] Yet all these moves are balanced by counter-moves. Not only the hero but also the novel's worst villains are diehard Whigs, from murderous Ensign Northerton to devious Blifil, while the Man of the Hill is counterbalanced, structurally and thematically, by a band of gypsies who model absolute monarchy in utopian style. For all his contract-theory professions, the narrator turns authoritarian when it suits him, not least when stepping bossily in after the gypsy interlude 'to prevent our History from being applied to the Use of the most pernicious Doctrine, which Priestcraft had ever the Wickedness or the Impudence to preach'.[128] Squire Western, an endearing more than alarming figure, is fully reconciled with Sophia and Tom in the novel's irenic ending. The sinister loose thread is scheming Blifil, who ends *Tom Jones* preparing to enter Parliament via a rotten borough—so that Whig corruption, not Jacobite reaction, remains the ongoing threat.

Complications of this kind persist to the last, not least in Fielding's final word about the Great Man, an aside in his posthumously published *Journal of a Voyage to Lisbon* that incongruously praises Walpole as 'one of the best of men and of ministers'. The compliment, however, is peculiarly unstable. Fielding goes on to contextualize it in all the wrong ways, talking first about Walpole's funding of the navy—notoriously a focus of corruption allegations, not least in Fielding's

[126] On this pattern, see John Allen Stevenson, *The Real History of Tom Jones* (Basingstoke: Palgrave Macmillan, 2005), 17–46.

[127] Henry Fielding, *Tom Jones*, ed. Martin C. Battestin and Fredson Bowers (Oxford: Clarendon Press, 1975), 440 (VIII.ix); 77 (II.i).

[128] Fielding, *Tom Jones*, 673; XII.xiii.

own *Vernoniad* (1741)—and then launching into a denunciation, very much in his old *Champion* idiom, of 'the supporters of tyranny, the invaders of the just liberties and properties of mankind, the plunderers of the industrious'.[129] The explicit praise is undeniable, but so is the implicit blame. Both sit on the page in juxtaposition, equally available as interpretative options, neither confirmed nor denied. This is the abiding hallmark of Fielding's rhetoric as a satirist, never better defined than in William Empson's classic essay on 'double irony' in *Tom Jones*, where thesis and antithesis are both put in question, without any compensating offer of a middle way.[130] If Fielding's career as a libeller taught him anything, it was to leave his audience to make up their minds from functionally indeterminate textual evidence. As he warns the reader of *Tom Jones*, 'tho' we will always lend thee proper Assistance in difficult Places... thou art highly mistaken if thou dost imagine that we intended, when we began this great Work, to leave thy Sagacity nothing to do'.[131] Political interpretation is for the reader to undertake, certainly with cues and prompts, but with an emphasis on the exercise of independent judgment that itself has political meaning.

## Lives of the opposition poets

Like Fielding, Johnson moved in later career from opposition libel to pro-government polemic, though like Fielding again (indeed more so) he typically resisted party lines. In 1756 he could articulate the official rationale for the Seven Years War, though not without first declaring, in a sentence more memorable than everything to follow, that from the standpoint of indigenous peoples 'the American dispute between the French and us is... only the quarrel of two robbers for the spoils of a passenger'.[132] In *Taxation No Tyranny* (1775), written for Lord North's administration during the American revolution, he proved to be such

---

[129] Fielding, *Journal of a Voyage to Lisbon, Shamela, and Occasional Writings*, 618, 619.
[130] William Empson, '*Tom Jones*', *Kenyon Review* 20 (1958), 217–49, reprinted in his *Using Biography* (Cambridge, MA: Harvard University Press, 1984), 131–57.
[131] Fielding, *Tom Jones*, 614 (XI.ix).
[132] Johnson, *Political Writings*, 188 ('Observations on the Present State of Affairs').

a loose cannon that the pamphlet was toned down by the officials who commissioned it.[133] Johnsonian conservatism was never predictable, even when, like Fielding in the *Voyage to Lisbon*, but in more direct and extended style, he took the opportunity of his last major work, the *Lives of the Poets*, to reassess the literary campaign against Walpole, and by implication his own role in it.

Before coming to Pope, Thomson, and other anti-Walpole poets in the 1781 volumes, Johnson first encounters the theme of censorship when composing his seventeenth-century lives (1779), notably Milton's. He may also have given special attention to the topic—which he presents as a problem, a conundrum resisting easy solution—because it was prominently in the air again as he wrote. Radical encroachments of the early 1770s—notably the newspaper polemics of 'Junius' (an incendiary so expert in subterfuge that his identity remains uncertain) and Wilkes's defeat of the ban on parliamentary reporting—were still fresh in the public memory. In combination, the failed seditious libel trials of two Junius printers in 1770, the powerful new 'liberty of the press' rhetoric that Junius turned on these events, and the unyielding insistence of Lord Chief Justice Mansfield that only judges could determine the criminality of a text (juries being limited to the fact of publication) aroused lingering fears that new measures would be devised to deal with the declining efficacy of prosecution.[134] More immediately, the turbulent political climate near the end of the American war (events of 1780 include the Gordon Riots and the foundation of the Society for Constitutional Information, one of several activist reform associations) resulted in increased calls for tighter press control. It was even suggested a few years later, by Hardwicke's son Philip Yorke, that American independence could be attributed directly to a lax censorship regime: 'The publication of the debates and opposition speeches have lost America.'[135]

---

[133] See Hudson, *Political Biography of Johnson*, 169–75.

[134] See Poser, *Lord Mansfield*, 256–9, and, for the broad development of 'liberty of the press' concepts after 1760, Trevor Ross, *Writing in Public: Literature and the Liberty of the Press in Eighteenth-Century Britain* (Baltimore: Johns Hopkins University Press, 2018).

[135] Yorke to Sir Robert Murray Keith, 16 December 1784, qtd by Black, *English Press*, 98. On Junius, Wilkes, and the possibility of new censorship legislation, see

Freestanding republications of Milton's *Areopagitica* are a good way to pinpoint tense junctures in the negotiation of press freedom. In 1738, shortly after the Stage Licensing Act, a new edition was published by Andrew Millar in response to post-1737 rumours of impending press legislation, accompanied by a preface in which Thomson extolled 'the Liberty of the Press'; without this liberty, Thomson added, 'our Souls themselves are imprisoned in a dark Dungeon'.[136] Another new *Areopagitica* edition came out in 1780, provoked not only by a resurgent risk of pre-publication censorship legislation but also by the following remarkable paragraph in Johnson's 'Life of Milton':

> He published about the same time his *Areopagitica, a Speech of Mr.* John Milton *for the liberty of unlicensed Printing*. The danger of such unbounded liberty, and the danger of bounding it, have produced a problem in the science of Government, which human understanding seems hitherto unable to solve. If nothing may be published but what civil authority shall have previously approved, power must always be the standard of truth; if every dreamer of innovations may propagate his projects, there can be no settlement; if every murmurer at government may diffuse discontent, there can be no peace; and if every sceptick in theology may teach his follies, there can be no religion. The remedy against these evils is to punish the authors; for it is yet allowed that every society may punish, though not prevent, the publication of opinions, which that society shall think pernicious; but this punishment, though it may crush the author, promotes the book; and it seems not more reasonable to leave the right of printing unrestrained, because writers may be afterwards censured, than it would be to sleep with doors unbolted, because by our laws we can hang a thief.[137]

What should we make of this perplexing passage? One early reader found it very simple. The *London Magazine* reviewer took Johnson to be promoting an ongoing ministerial agenda to tighten censorship.

---

Donald Thomas, *A Long Time Burning: The History of Literary Censorship in England* (New York: Praeger, 1969), 92–112.

[136] Sambrook, *James Thomson*, 173. *Areopagitica* was reprinted again in the year of Fox's Libel Act (1792); shortly beforehand, Milton's title was echoed in *Areopagitica: An Essay on the Liberty of the Press* (1791), an anonymous pamphlet dedicated to Fox (Thomas, *Long Time Burning*, 108).

[137] Johnson, *Lives of the Poets*, 1: 252.

He 'pays his court to the prejudices of the times', the review claims, and lends his voice to government ambitions 'to abridge the liberty of the press'.[138] But Johnson's argument is harder than that to pin down, as though even when discussing censorship in the abstract, Johnson draws on the techniques of censorship-evasion, in which no unambiguous position is securely attributable to a text. Or he writes in the sceptical mode attributed to him by the modern critic Fred Parker, 'in which thinking is a process without conclusion, an unresolved dialectic': an essayistic mode in Montaigne's sense, exhibiting not assertive dogmatism but 'a mind perpetually in movement, a mind that never reposes on the stability of truth'.[139]

Things start simply enough with a statement of biographical fact. But then they get very slippery, and it remains unclear for the rest of the passage whether Johnson is speaking in his own voice, or attempting in something like free indirect style to summarize Milton's argument, or using a dual voice that reports Milton's basic case while glossing it with Johnsonian commentary. Even if we select the simplest of these options, the writing seems wilfully unstable. With 'The danger of such unbounded liberty', Johnson looks set to unleash a characteristic defence of authority and subordination. But then he springs a surprise, with studied stylistic and political balance ('The danger of such unbounded liberty, and the danger of bounding it'), then a shift into dispassionate, almost donnish, abstraction, with more than a hint of his signature 'vanity' theme: 'a problem...which human understanding seems hitherto unable to solve.' The sentence that follows enacts the irresolution by offering alternative perspectives without choosing between them. Only one of the four propositions that Johnson outlines, the first, addresses the danger of licensing, while the remaining three stress the danger of licence. But it's the first proposition—couched almost in the idiom of Junius, if not indeed Foucault—that packs the rhetorical punch: 'power must always be the standard of truth.' Then follows an extended tricolon ('if every dreamer...if every murmurer...if every sceptick') that could have

---

[138] *London Magazine*, 50 (1781), 594, quoted in *Lives of the Poets*, 1: 384.

[139] Fred Parker, *Scepticism and Literature: An Essay on Pope, Hume, Sterne, and Johnson* (Oxford: Oxford University Press, 2003), 238.

been written to order for W. K. Wimsatt, reiterating essentially a single anxiety about the destabilization of church and state.[140]

So where might we find resolution or synthesis? At first sight, Johnson's long closing sentence seems to offer such a thing. 'The remedy... is to punish the authors' (an interesting specification at this late date, when in practice it was nearly always a publisher or printer in the dock): in other words, to allow printing without prior licensing, but to prosecute those who abuse this freedom, as *Areopagitica* proposes. However, Johnson then comes up with the now familiar objection that to prosecute a work is in practice to puff it, whatever personal damage the author might suffer.[141] The analogy that follows, between a society that allows unlicensed printing and a householder who invites unimpeded burglary, solves nothing at all. It indicates what by now, at least in literary circles, was a rather unusual nostalgia for seventeenth-century licensing, and implies a mindset very different from that of the *Dictionary* decades earlier, where Johnson disparagingly defines 'licenser' as 'a tool of power'. Yet his conclusion also holds back from explicitly confirming this indication in favour of licensing, which remains at the level of analogical suggestion, and does nothing to cut through the problem just posed: that the only sanction against a dangerous book is a sanction now known to enhance the danger. Which is where Johnson drops the topic and resumes his narrative of Milton's career. It's hard not to feel that the radical Whig churchman Francis Blackburne had a better grasp of Johnson's procedure than the *London Magazine*, and his analysis anticipates later accounts of Johnson's writing as pendulum-like oscillation.[142] This was, Blackburne says in a book-length refutation of the 'Life of Milton' (with *Areopagitica* republished as a long appendix), 'a curious see-saw of the arguments pro and con'. At the end of

---

[140] On Johnsonian parallelism and antithesis, see W. K. Wimsatt, *The Prose Style of Samuel Johnson* (New Haven: Yale University Press, 1941), 15–49.

[141] See, for example, 'crush of overwhelming evil' in *Lives of the Poets*, 4: 72, or 'heavy crush of disaster' in *A Journey to the Western Islands of Scotland*, ed. Mary Lascelles (New Haven: Yale University Press, 1971), 92.

[142] See Freya Johnston and Lynda Mugglestone (eds), *Samuel Johnson: The Arc of the Pendulum* (Oxford: Oxford University Press, 2012), esp. 1–10.

his discussion, Johnson 'sneaks away from the question, and leaves it as he found it'.[143]

The question crops up elsewhere, albeit in passing. It crops up especially in the 'Life of Thomson', where Johnson now distances himself from his own literary stance of the 1730s. 'At this time', he writes, 'a long course of opposition to Sir Robert Walpole had filled the nation with clamours for liberty, of which no man felt the want, and with care for liberty, which was not in danger.'[144] This was just the objection to opposition hyperbole that Johnson had placed in Walpole's mouth when composing parliamentary debates for the *Gentleman's Magazine* (largely from his own invention, and presented, in an officially tolerated dodge, under metathetic names). There 'Sir Retrob Walelop' protests of his critics that 'even in their own opinion they are complaining of grievances which they do not suffer'.[145] But now he makes the point in his own person, and with heavier emphasis. Explicitly the target is Thomson's *Liberty* of 1734 ('a very long poem, in five parts', Johnson wearily calls it), but the implicit effect is also to disavow his own best-known contribution to the campaign, his imitation of Juvenal under the title *London* (1738). There Walpole's England is a place of 'Sense, Freedom, Piety, refin'd away', a place of 'slavish Tenets', and a place in which censorship—the 'licens'd Stage' of recent legislation—'lull[s] to servitude a thoughtless Age'.[146]

In the 'Life of Thomson', Johnson treats the 1737 Act as mere background, without the analysis or evaluation he bestows on censorship when writing about Milton. But the Stage Licensing Act provides

---

[143] Francis Blackburne, *Remarks on Johnson's Life of Milton, To Which Are Added, Milton's Tractate of Education and Areopagitica* (1780), 59, 67. Earlier, Blackburne comments on Johnson's 'see-saw meditations, the shifty wiles of a man between two fires, who neither dares fight nor run away' (p. vi).

[144] Johnson, *Lives of the Poets*, 4: 99.

[145] Samuel Johnson, *Debates in Parliament*, ed. Thomas Kaminski, Benjamin Beard Hoover, and O M Brack, Jr, 3 vols numbered 11–13 (New Haven: Yale University Press, 2012), 12: 579 (debate of 13 February 1741, published February–April 1743).

[146] *The Poems of Samuel Johnson*, ed. David Nichol Smith and Edward L. McAdam, 2nd edn (Oxford: Clarendon Press, 1974), 60–81 (*London*, lines 105, 55, 59, 60); 'a licens'd Stage' is Johnson's 1748 revision from the original, more emphatic, 'our silenc'd Stage'.

him with two telling examples of prohibition that promotes, in cases where banned plays reappeared as bestselling playtexts. He forgets how well *Edward and Eleonora* did as a subscription edition (it sold a phenomenal 4,500 copies and reportedly brought Thomson £1,000),[147] but notes the success of *Gustavus Vasa*, to which he was himself a subscriber. More remarkable than these memories of theatrical sedition remediated as print is Johnson's serene observation that 'it is hard to discover why either play should have been obstructed'.[148] This may be true of Thomson's largely anodyne tearjerker, but Brooke's play was a different matter, freighted with Jacobite innuendo. Brooke goes beyond the usual attacks on ministerial corruption by choosing as his hero a popularly supported challenger to an illegitimate dynasty, and his play also stages the corrupt minister's assassination. In this respect, *Gustavus Vasa* has something in common with Johnson's own writing of the era—writing that underpinned Blackburne's sense of his commentary on *Areopagitica* as not only evasive but also hypocritical. In ironic tones, Blackburne looks back on the 1730s as a golden age of uncensored writing unlike the regulated present: a time 'when many an honest Jacobite propagated his discontents without the least apprehension for his ears'. Blackburne slyly alleges that the younger Johnson, for all his pensioned loyalty now, was part of the process. He was a murmurer at government himself: 'Perhaps times and seasons might be noted... when the good Doctor himself stole some trifles into the world through the press, which did not much favour the legal settlement of the crown, or tend to abate the discontents of the people.'[149]

## Johnsonian sedition: *London, Marmor Norfolciense*

What did Blackburne mean? The plural is intriguing—*some* trifles—for reaching beyond the most obvious candidate for Jacobite

---

[147] Sambrook, *James Thomson*, 196; Johnson, *Lives of the Poets*, 4: 370 n.

[148] Johnson, *Lives of the Poets*, 4: 100.

[149] Blackburne, *Remarks on Johnson's Life of Milton*, 65, 64. Wilkes made the point more strongly in Parliament: both Shebbeare and Johnson had 'repeatedly and publicly' represented Hanoverian rule as usurpation, and in their writings had treated 'the late king [George II], and king William, with the utmost virulence and scurrility' (see above, p. 180).

innuendo in Johnson's output, *Marmor Norfolciense* ('The Norfolk Marble', 1739). This clandestine satire had been Exhibit A for anyone keen to attack the mature Johnson's political sincerity ever since a 1775 piracy outed him as author amidst a barrage of sarcasm. How foolish to imagine, the editor of this reprint commented, that 'such bitter Reflections, keen Sarcasms, and personal Invectives against the *illustrious* HOUSE OF HANOVER' could possibly come from the pen of Johnson, now a grateful pillar of the Hanoverian establishment![150] But Blackburne clearly looks beyond *Marmor Norfolciense* alone, and by emphasizing stealth of publication he registers the clandestine aura of other works in which Johnson uses anonymity, not as a token or conventional gesture, but as a practical safeguard against retribution. The most telling case is his verse satire *London*, published in May 1738, with timing engineered to coincide with Pope's *One Thousand Seven Hundred and Thirty Eight* (the first dialogue) for enhanced political impact.[151]

Simply the choice of Juvenal's third satire as the base-text for *London* was provocative in view of highly politicized earlier renderings, notably by Oldham during the Exclusion Crisis and Dryden after the Glorious Revolution (see above, p. 83). But Johnson goes beyond these precursors in weaponizing his Latin source. Where Oldham and Dryden more or less faithfully report all aspects of Juvenal's catch-all satire on urban corruption, Johnson discards parts irrelevant to his purpose—an excursus on sexual depravity, for example—to focus on venality and ministerial peculation in a world he describes, with fierce economy, as 'devote to Vice and Gain' (line 37). At 263 lines, *London* is barely more than half the length of Dryden's translation (503 lines), partly because of Dryden's occasional additions, partly Johnson's stylistic compression, but mainly because some passages simply drop out. What remains, updated and applied

---

[150] Francis Webb (ed.), *Marmor Norfolciense . . . With Notes, and a Dedication to Samuel Johnson, LL.D.* (1775), pp. iii–iv. Here was the classic fate of the political apostate: compare Dryden's embarrassment by malicious revivals of *Heroic Stanzas* (pp. 51–4) and Southey's predicament with belated piracies of *Wat Tyler* (pp. 58–60).

[151] See Harry M. Solomon, *The Rise of Robert Dodsley: Creating the New Age of Print* (Carbondale: Southern Illinois University Press, 1996), 69.

with an explicitness not open to Dryden in the 1690s, is a fierce emphasis on corrupting money and—the poem's presiding term—gold: 'your Thirst of Pow'r and Gold' (line 62); 'Slaves to Gold' (line 178); 'the golden Pile' of *London*'s venal protagonist (line 208); his 'shining Train, and golden Coach' (line 235). 'Turn from the glitt'ring Bribe thy scornful Eye, | Nor sell for Gold, what Gold could never buy', warns Thales, the poem's spokesman (lines 87–8). As Christopher Ricks once brilliantly observed, this language contaminates the poem's whole landscape, even its memory, with the aura of cash: the Thames becomes a 'silver Flood' (line 22); ancient Wessex is 'ALFRED'*s* golden Reign' (line 248).[152] Moreover, when 'Greenwich smiles upon the silver Flood'—in a poem 'Where Looks are Merchandise, and Smiles are sold' (line 179)—it would not have struck readers as irrelevant that a colossal statue of George II had recently been erected on the riverbank at Greenwich.[153] In the greed-is-good London of the poem, even the monarch approves the river of cash, the corrupting current, and prepares to trade his smiles for currency.

Further intensifying this vision of ubiquitous civic corruption is Johnson's insistence that the creative arts, even truth itself, are now contaminated by the lure of wealth. While his own honest muse is (in the poem's most famously emphatic line) 'BY POVERTY DEPREST' (line 177), a client 'Laureat Tribe' flatters power in 'servile Verse' (line 198), while bribery does similar work in Parliament itself: 'Here let those reign, whom Pensions can incite | To vote a Patriot black, a Courtier white' (lines 51–2). In another glance at Walpole's sleazily pecuniary methods of press control, the poem looks fondly back to pre-conquest England for its absence of paid spies and '*Special Juries*' (line 252). No less striking is Johnson's almost Orwellian sense that the most dangerous effect of Walpole's cultural interference is not the servile panegyric he funds but the anaesthetizing—indeed emasculating—blandness of the drama being performed after 1737: 'With warbling Eunuchs fill a licens'd Stage, | And lull to Servitude a thoughtless Age' (lines 59–60). Here censorship becomes social mind

---

[152] Christopher Ricks, *The Force of Poetry* (Oxford: Clarendon Press, 1984), 81.

[153] Clive Aslet, *The Story of Greenwich* (Cambridge, MA: Harvard University Press, 1999), 147. Johnson lived in Greenwich for some months in 1737; Rysbrack's statue dates from 1735.

control, significant not only for killing off theatre as a political forum but also for the mind-numbing trivia it fosters instead.

Yet as well as being a satire about (among its larger targets) censorship, *London* was also, potentially at least, a satire subject to censorship. The poem's self-consciousness about the processes that constrain or jeopardize it—the role of censorship as at once explicit theme and limiting condition—makes *London* a peculiarly illuminating case study in the poetics of seditious libel. So too does the survival of a manuscript draft (Figure 3.4) which enables us to measure Johnson's sense, or that of his printer or publisher, of where the notoriously indistinct line between admissible and seditious utterance now lay. The draft is incomplete, representing about 30 per cent of the published text. But enough survives to indicate that the manipulative kleptocrat at the centre of the poem, given the cratylic name Orgilio in the published version, was originally 'Sejano', by this time so familiar a sobriquet for Walpole that Johnson might as well have named the Great Man outright.[154] A few years earlier, the highly publicized *Craftsman* trials had turned on the presentism of history in opposition usage, and as one pro-government writer complained, 'the Character of *Sejanus*, *Wolsey*, or any other of the wickedest Ministers' were now taken by readers to mean Walpole 'upon the least Wink'.[155] In *The Vanity of Human Wishes*, published after Walpole's fall and indeed his death, Johnson could use the Wolsey parallel with impunity, and he does so at length. But in 1738, 'Sejano' would have looked like courting prosecution.

No less revealing is the draft version of the distich about client poets—'The Laureat Tribe in servile Verse relate, | How Virtue wars with persecuting Fate'—which picks, albeit without gutted names or historical surrogates, a far more powerful collective target, and attacks them in more trenchant terms. In the manuscript, the emphasis falls on client peers: '[W]ith servile Grief dependent Nobles sigh | [A]nd

---

[154] The draft, now in the Hyde Collection at Harvard, is reproduced in *The Poems of Samuel Johnson*, ed. Nichol Smith and McAdam, 412–14; for 'Sejano', see line 208.

[155] *The Grand Accuser the Greatest of All Criminals* (1735), 30, qtd by Urstad, *Sir Robert Walpole's Poets*, 210. Urstad gives further examples on pp. 209–13; see also Lund, *Ridicule, Religion*, 198–9.

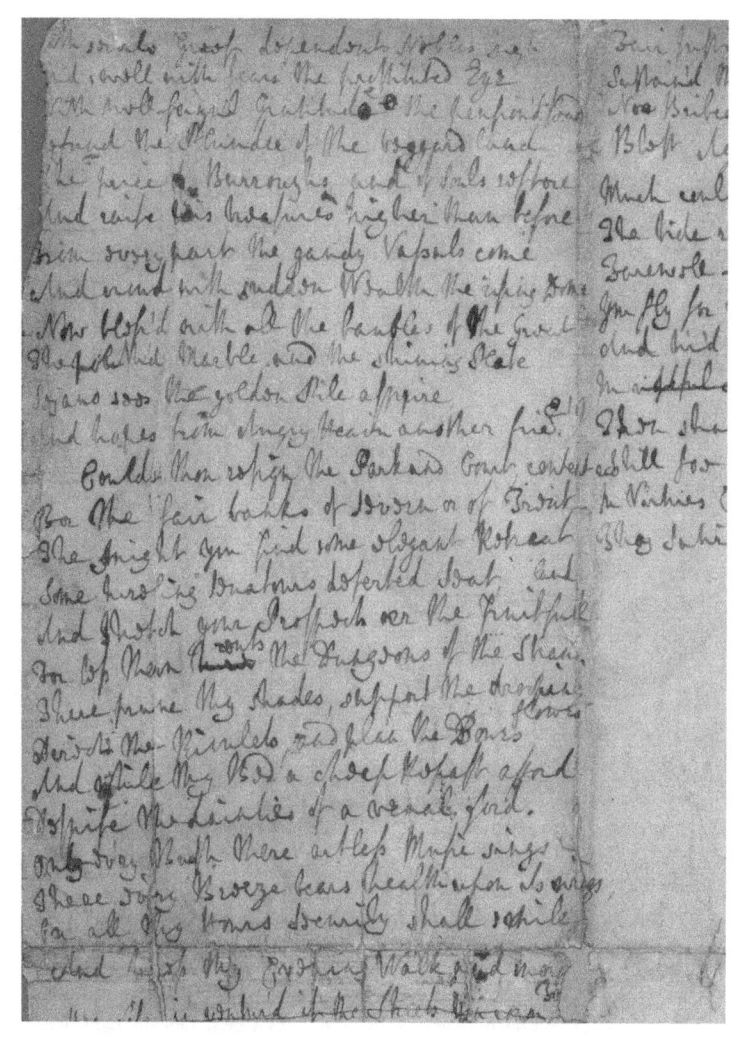

**Figure 3.4** Samuel Johnson, detail from *London* (1738), autograph manuscript, MS Hyde 50 (33), Houghton Library, Harvard University, by permission. The detail shows an early version of lines 198–223, starting with an unpublished couplet on the 'servile Grief' and 'prostituted Eye' of 'dependent Nobles'.

swell with tears the prostituted Eye' (lines 198–9). Even the first published edition went too far at this juncture in the poem, since 'servile Verse' (in the second and subsequent editions) was a retreat from the original and more abusive print reading, 'venal Verse'. We cannot know whether these and other changes arose from Johnson's independent second thoughts or from the caution of his publisher or printer (respectively Robert Dodsley and Edward Cave), to whom he made a pre-publication offer 'of altering any stroke of satire which you may dislike'.[156] Either way, the textual variants speak volumes about the expressive constraints operating on poets and poems at this delicate juncture, no less powerfully for being internalized. The variant readings give a rare insight into processes of accommodation with censorship that were no doubt widely practised in the period as satires made their transition from script into print.

At the same time, some of *London*'s more easily deniable but potentially more incendiary hints survive in the published version, or may even have been intensified. In the penultimate verse paragraph, Johnson deplores rates of execution so high that the hangman risks running out of hemp for the gallows; then he notes the need for ropes 'To rig another Convoy for the K—g' (line 247). The dashed noun (spelled fully out in the draft) is as gratuitous as any elision in Fielding's *Champion*, and in practice disguises nothing. It serves instead to flaunt the poem's proximity to underground or clandestine satire, as though something more alarming is being suggested than a rather familiar opposition complaint about royal transfers of wealth from Britain to Hanover. Some commentators have detected an implication that what George II really deserves is hemp for a noose—which, if so, would be to enter the treasonable territory of imagining the king's death.[157] But Johnson prudently leaves the reader to join the dots, and

---

[156] *The Letters of Samuel Johnson*, ed. Bruce Redford, 5 vols (Oxford: Clarendon Press, 1992), 1: 14 (to Edward Cave, April 1738). It may be significant that Cave (a wily operator who was in longstanding conflict with ministers over parliamentary reporting) declined to act as publisher and eventually subcontracted the printing (A. D. Barker, 'The Printing and Publishing of Johnson's *Marmor Norfolciense* (1739) and *London* (1738 and 1739)', *Library*, 6th series, 3 (1981), 287–304).

[157] Christine Gerrard, *The Patriot Opposition to Walpole: Politics, Poetry, and National Myth, 1725–1742* (Oxford: Oxford University Press, 1994), 237; Erskine-Hill, *Poetry of Opposition and Revolution: Dryden to Wordsworth* (Oxford: Clarendon Press,

drops his hint in a way that would comfortably be covered by Fazakerley's *Craftsman* defence: that seditious meaning is not drawn out of a work but read into it, in which case it belongs to a prosecutor's illicit imagination, not a defendant's innocent text.

In the event, *London* elicited no action, and it was *Manners*, with *One Thousand Seven Hundred and Thirty Eight* behind it, that led to Dodsley's arrest and humiliation, not in the pillory but at the Bar of the House of Lords, where he was forced to grovel on his knees (an exquisite penalty for a publisher of his social ambitions). At a time of more strident provocations, Johnson's revisions did just enough to keep official attention focused elsewhere—though there is a sinister edge to Pope's reported prediction that the author of *London* would 'soon be *déterré*', a hunting term for unearthing prey that has gone to ground.[158] The most daring satires from Johnson's pen come somewhat later, and were handled by printers and publishers with greater tolerance for risk than Cave or Dodsley, among them John Brett, a former Mist employee, who was shortly to be arrested and interrogated for *Common Sense*.[159] They were published within two weeks of one another in May 1739, soon after the new stage licensing provisions had been first implemented in the case of *Gustavus Vasa*. Both satires are written in the voice of slow-witted Whig loyalists, and as such they adopt a mode of Scriblerian irony that was not Johnson's strength. But both are also lifted by moments of zany exuberance that recall Swift, and both have something of Swift's instability, or the unsettling, irreducible double irony that Empson found in Fielding. Secure positions are hard to pin down; implied endorsements are undercut.

There's no question that *A Compleat Vindication of the Licensers of the Stage*, Johnson's swift response to the *Gustavus Vasa* prohibition, is an oppositional text, though if we listen to passages out of context, they can be hard to distinguish, for all their immediate function as parody of the pro-Walpole press, from Johnson's own later voice in his

1996), 122–3. On constructive treason and imagining the king's death, see below, pp. 245–6.

[158] *Boswell's Life of Johnson*, 2: 85.

[159] J. D. Fleeman with James McLaverty, *A Bibliography of the Works of Samuel Johnson* (Oxford: Clarendon Press, 2000), 38–43. For Brett, see Harris, *London Newspapers in the Age of Walpole*, 38–9; Johnson, *Political Writings*, 20.

Tory pomp. When the persona in which he voices the pamphlet (a ministerially hired pen) praises 'that system of subordination and dependence to which we are indebted for the present tranquillity of the nation', or again 'that decent submission to our superiors, and that proper awe of authority which we are taught in courts', the wordy formality and complacent tone are at best weak irony markers. Instead we come oddly close in sentiment and diction to authentically Johnsonian utterances recorded in Boswell's *Life*, or to his pro-government pamphlets of the 1770s.[160] It's as though Johnson's vindicator, at one level a risible hireling and stooge, also expresses an authentic part of Johnson himself, a part that would later predominate.

But Johnson also gives his vindicator moments of sheer mania, or that dizzying mix of rational tone and moral oblivion that marks Swift's Modest Proposer. There's the dismay he voices about the way 'seditious poets' have not only formed confederacies, but worse than this, 'confederacies which owe their rise to virtue'. And there's his dim-witted befuddlement on finding in opposition drama 'infamous passages, in which venality and dependence are represented as mean in themselves, and productive of remorse and infelicity'.[161] Beyond these comic flourishes, the most telling parts of the *Compleat Vindication* are those in which the vindicator resumes *London*'s 'warbling Eunuchs' theme to urge extension of the Stage Licensing Act into a more comprehensive mechanism for dumbing down the public discourse and securing hegemony for the Whig elite. Here Johnson ironically adopts and exaggerates the arguments of the day for press as well as theatre licensing. Not just new but old plays should be examined for proleptic sedition and placed on an '*Index Expurgatorius*'; no journalism should be permitted except the ministerially sponsored *Gazetteer*; offending sections of poems and plays should be replaced with connecting passages by Cibber, since 'the Poet Laureat may easily supply these vacuities by inserting some of his own verses in praise of wealth, luxury, and venality'. Finally, why not go to root causes and ban the 'pernicious arts' of literacy itself, which threaten the peace of mind of

---

[160] Johnson, *Political Writings*, 60, 68. On this theme in Johnson, see Nicholas Hudson, *Samuel Johnson and the Making of Modern England* (Cambridge: Cambridge University Press, 2003), 18–32.

[161] Johnson, *Political Writings*, 65, 67.

the public and 'the interruption of ministerial measures'? In a brilliant pirouette on Fazakerley's notion that the reader, not the author, makes the libel, the vindicator proposes new legislation to suppress schools, and that it should 'be made felony to teach to read, without a license from the Lord Chamberlain'.[162] In the tradition of satire about speech, print, and power that runs from *Gulliver's Travels* to *Nineteen Eighty-Four* and beyond, Johnson's *Compleat Vindication* deserves a place.

We end with a clever *reductio ad absurdum* of both recent and possibly impending licensing laws: an ironic theory of seditious libel and how to pre-empt it that sits alongside Johnson's guarded practice of the mode in *London* and, more decisively, *Marmor Norfolciense*. Sir John Hawkins is the only authority, though a formidable one, for the story that Johnson was in hiding when the *Compleat Vindication* was published because he feared arrest for *Marmor Norfolciense*, an elaborate mock prophecy that develops the mode of Swift's *Windsor Prophecy* (1711) and was published two weeks before the *Vindication*. In it, an ancient inscription on a recently disinterred stone predicts usurpation and tyranny at the time of unearthing. To this Johnson adds the Scriblerian device of a pedantic, and loyally Hanoverian, commentator who struggles to explicate the significance of the text while recoiling with dawning horror from its topical implications. As Hawkins writes:

> A publication so inflammatory as this, could hardly escape the notice of any government, under which the legal idea of a libel might be supposed to exist. The principles it contained were such as the Jacobites of the time openly avowed; and warrants were issued and messengers employed to apprehend the author, who, though he had forborne to subscribe his name to the pamphlet, the vigilance of those in pursuit of him had discovered. To elude the search after him, he ... took an obscure lodging in a house in Lambeth-marsh, and lay there concealed till the scent after him was grown cold.[163]

One thinks again of Pope's term '*déterré*', with Johnson gone to ground like a hunted fox. We can neither verify nor falsify this account, though the balance of probabilities is with Hawkins, who (unlike

---

[162] Johnson, *Political Writings*, 69, 71, 73.
[163] Sir John Hawkins, *The Life of Samuel Johnson, LL.D.*, ed. O M Brack, Jr (Athens: University of Georgia Press, 2009), 46.

Boswell, Piozzi, and other early biographers) knew Johnson at the time, and would not have invented an episode he thought disgraceful. Perhaps more important is the literary question: is this a text that raises new stakes; does it cross a line at which Johnson had previously stopped when writing or revising *London*?

On one hand, the verses at the centre of *Marmor Norfolciense* are encoded as *London* is not: their complaint about oppression by standing armies is literally just a complaint about 'scarlet reptiles', which 'glutton on the industrious peasants spoil, | Rob without fear, and fatten without toil'. On the other hand, the addition of an editorial persona makes the application inescapable, though Johnson complicates the process by having his commentator make obtuse guesses (a recent plague of ladybirds in Kent?) while also musing self-consciously on the vagaries of interpretation. 'Let us endeavour to keep the just mean', he resolves, 'between searching ambitiously for far-fetched interpretations, and admitting such low meaning, and obvious sense, as is inconsistent with those great and extensive views which it is reasonable to ascribe' to the inscription's ancient author.[164] Eventually, as in the *Compleat Vindication*, political decoding becomes not only the pamphlet's method but also its self-conscious subject, as the commentator recoils from his apprehension of seditious meaning, despairs of his ability to find safer interpretation, and leaves his 'loose and unconnected hints entirely to the candour of the reader'. Yet again, the reader is made complicit in the construction of forbidden meaning. Instead Johnson's commentator proposes establishing a thirty-strong committee of exegetes who would interpret the inscription as their first assignment, and then join a long-term government payroll 'in examining pamphlets, songs, and journals, and drawing up informations, indictments, and instructions for special juries'. They might even enter the ministry in some capacity (attorney general, solicitor general?) and 'will excell above all, as licensers for the stage'.[165] In a single move, Johnson contrives a Scriblerian comedy of fatuous antiquarian scholarship and embeds within the pamphlet a defence of itself as politically indecipherable. Or, to the extent that the

---

[164] Johnson, *Political Writings*, 25, 33.
[165] Johnson, *Political Writings*, 42, 46, 47.

commentator deplores the political meanings he senses, Johnson presents the pamphlet as explicitly rejecting, not promoting, its own apparent potential as a dissident text. Finally, Johnson's interest is again in the hermeneutics of censorship as an object of attention in its own right, not merely an immediate means to expressive ends.

Yet it's also true that *Marmor Norfolciense* breaks new ground (beyond the scattered hints of *London*) by focusing attention on kings rather than ministers: on the House of Hanover as opposed to the Whig ministry. If anything makes it a work to go into hiding for, this is it. Hawkins singles out the closing vision of the verse prophecy, in which a horse drains the blood of a supine lion, and the horrified commentary of Johnson's antiquary, who observes that 'a horse is born in the arms of H——'. But, he adds, 'my zeal for the present happy establishment will not suffer me to pursue a train of thought that leads to such shocking conclusions. The idea is detestable, and such as...can enter into the mind of none but a virulent Republican, or bloody Jacobite.'[166] Here, for once, the frequently indistinct line between tolerable opposition and seditious utterance is clear and consistent, and it was precisely this move from critique of ministerial policy to critique of the Hanoverian succession that made it impossible for Shebbeare's *Sixth Letter* to be ignored at a later point in the same reign. Only two years before *Marmor Norfolciense*, when reviving *Fog's Weekly Journal* in 1737, the mistake of John Kelly after satirizing Walpole in his first five numbers was to mock the queen in the sixth; it was this move that got him arrested, and the same shift of target from ministry to royalty was the downfall of other journalists at the time, including, in 1743, Johnson's predecessor as parliamentary reporter for the *Gentleman's Magazine*, William Guthrie (for seditious essays in *Common Sense* and *Old England*).[167] From the government's point of view, the desire to suppress strictly partisan writing—Patriot as opposed to Jacobite polemic—may have been no less strong. But it was at the point where anti-ministerial satire tipped into anti-Hanoverian invective that sufficient pretext existed to act,

---

[166] Johnson, *Political Writings*, p. 42.
[167] Harris, *London Newspapers in the Age of Walpole*, 130–1, 141; within three years, Guthrie was on the government payroll.

accompanied by the greatest likelihood of legal success. If Johnson did indeed take to Lambeth Marsh for a while, he was probably wise to do so.

In a hostile compilation of 1782 called *The Deformities of Samuel Johnson* (in ironic reference to the new fashion for 'Beauties of' publications), James Thomson Callender attacked Johnson's *Dictionary* for its politically tendentious flourishes. 'For his definitions of Excise, Gazetteer, Pension, and Pensioner', Callender writes, 'he would, in Queen Anne's reign, have had a very fair chance of mounting the pillory'.[168] The image is incongruous, but it has occurred to others too. Fifty years later, Thomas Carlyle (perhaps tuning into Johnson's sense of Richard Savage as his reckless alter ego) imagined Johnson's early career in Grubstreet as having no other aim 'than to clutch what Provender ... he could get, always if possible keeping *quite* clear of the Gallows and Pillory'.[169]

The most striking version of this unexpected vision comes from Eyre Crowe, who, seven years after painting Defoe in the pillory at Temple Bar, chose as a subject Johnson's much-mythologized performance of contrition in Uttoxeter market for the childhood sin of refusing to work on his father's bookstall.[170] In *Dr Johnson Doing Penance in the Market Place of Uttoxeter* (1869; see Figure 3.5), Johnson is, like Defoe, the object of curious spectatorship: a spectatorship that takes place without derision, even from the urchins on the market cross, but without any celebratory edge. At the height of his career, the Great Cham stands bedraggled in the rain, exhibiting shame, seeking atonement. Perhaps Crowe also knew from Boswell how vigorously Johnson maintained traditional views of the pillory as inherently a place of abjection, insisting as he did that even Shebbeare had been enduringly disgraced by his hour there.[171] In the painting, the pillory contributes

---

[168] James Thomson Callender (?), *The Deformities of Samuel Johnson* (1782), 3. A *Beauties of Johnson* had appeared in 1781; on this vogue more broadly, see Daniel Cook, 'Authors Unformed: Reading "*Beauties*" in the *Eighteenth Century*', *Philological Quarterly* 89 (2010), 283–309.

[169] *The Works of Thomas Carlyle*, ed. Henry Duff Traill, 30 vols (Cambridge: Cambridge University Press, 2010), 28: 109.

[170] For this episode, see *Boswell's Life of Johnson*, 4: 373 and n.

[171] 'He could not mouth and strut as he used to do, after having been there' (*Boswell's Life of Johnson*, 3: 315).

**Figure 3.5** Eyre Crowe, *Dr Johnson Doing Penance in the Market Place of Uttoxeter* (1869), oil on canvas, by permission of Dr. Johnson's House Trust Ltd. Crowe depicts a poignant episode in Boswell's *Life of Johnson*; the pillory is his own embellishment.

to an iconography of defeat (the rain, the smoke, the dead game), and Johnson seems almost to acknowledge its presence in the frame—perhaps even *his* rightful presence in *its* frame—as he stands in the characteristic posture of the pilloried miscreant: the hangdog, 'drooping' posture described by Adam Smith.[172] Years earlier, Crowe had used the pillory to crystallize the Victorian view of Defoe: divisive, mendacious, yet oddly transcendent. By resuming his pillory theme in this later painting, he proposes that Defoe, the flagrant seditious libeller, and Johnson, the penitent conservative moralist, had a great deal more in common than we tend to assume.

[172] See above, p. 164, and compare Figure 1.4 on p. 68.

# 4
# 1780–1820
# Southey's New Star Chamber: Literature, Revolution, and Romantic-Era Libel

In a magazine piece of 1901 on 'Delaware's Blue Laws', Theodore Dreiser reported a surprising tour of Wilmington, Dover, and Georgetown. 'In each of these three places are to be seen a pillory and a whipping post, such as were common in England during the eighteenth century, and flourished in the colonies up to the beginning of the present union', Dreiser writes. He saw one such pillory in action in the prison yard at New Castle (Figure 4.1), and pondered not only the physical brutality of retribution in Delaware, and its unmistakably racial aspect, but also the degrading consequences for all concerned: punished, punisher, spectator. A crowd of two hundred gaped, winced, and laughed as the malefactors were exhibited and chastised, though no lasting bodily injury was sustained. The response was unreflecting, however: 'Of the mental scars, stretching red across the sensibilities and finer feelings, the spectators took no thought. Of the influence which the contemplation of such a spectacle must have upon their own minds—not a thought.'[1] That said, most of the Delawareans to whom Dreiser spoke agreed that spectacular punishment of this kind was now an embarrassing anachronism, though it was the

---

[1] *Theodore Dreiser's Uncollected Magazine Articles, 1897–1902*, ed. Yoshinobu Hakutani (Newark: University of Delaware Press, 2003), 256–63 (257); first published in *Ainslee's Magazine* for February 1901.

*Poetics of the Pillory: English Literature and Seditious Libel, 1660–1820.* Thomas Keymer, Oxford University Press (2019). © Thomas Keymer.
DOI: 10.1093/oso/9780198744498.001.0001

**Figure 4.1** Samuel M. Fox, *Delaware Pillory and Whipping Post* (c.1889), photographic print (albumen), by permission of the Library of Congress Prints and Photographs Division. Dreiser is right that structures combining pillories and whipping posts existed in England (an example survives in Coleshill, Warks), but they seem to have been more widespread in the mid Atlantic states, as here in the prison yard at New Castle, Del.

pillory and not the whip that was most widely seen as having to go (a preference doubtless connected with the toxic legacy of slavery). Four years later, a leading newspaper could report that 'Standing in the pillory as a punishment for crime went out of existence in Delaware tonight when at 10 o'clock Gov. Lea signed a bill abolishing the crude instrument of disgrace and torture'.[2] And that was that for the pillory in the Anglo-American world, at least as an official sanction. Remarkably, whipping continued to be practised in Delaware into the early 1950s, and was formally abolished in 1972.[3]

Photography was not quite available in June 1830, when the last Londoner to be pilloried, a 'wilful and corrupt' perjurer named Peter James Bossy, underwent his sentence, and the pillory was at last abolished by statute in 1837.[4] It survived a little longer in British North America, and a malefactor named John MacKenzie was pilloried in Charlottetown in 1876, seven years after newly confederated Canada abolished the punishment, though two years before Prince Edward Island fell into line (Figure 4.2). Defoe's wooden angel died hard. But all these episodes were in the big scheme of things anomalies or aftershocks, exotic throwbacks to a disciplinary regime that may have prevailed in the seventeenth or eighteenth centuries—Dreiser called pillorying 'this relic of an older order of civilization' (p. 261)— but could no longer flourish in the nineteenth.

It was not just that the idea of the penitentiary, which emphasized private guilt and moral correction, not public shame and ostracization, held increasing sway.[5] To liberal and moderate conservative opinion, it was now inescapable that the pillory was unjust as well as ineffectual, for reasons best articulated in an influential essay of

---

[2] *Chicago Daily Tribune*, 21 March 1905.

[3] Matthew Pat, 'Corporal Punishment', in Wilbur R. Miller (ed.), *The Social History of Crime and Punishment in America: An Encyclopedia*, 5 vols (Los Angeles: Sage, 2012), 1: 333–6 (335).

[4] Antony E. Simpson, 'Spectacular Punishment and the Orchestration of Hate: The Pillory and Popular Morality in Eighteenth-Century England', in Robert J. Kelly and Jess Maghan (eds), *Hate Crime: The Global Politics of Polarization* (Carbondale: Southern Illinois University Press, 1998), 177–220 (191, 213).

[5] For the contribution of novels to this cultural shift, see John Bender, *Imagining the Penitentiary: Fiction and the Architecture of Mind in Eighteenth-Century England* (Chicago: University of Chicago Press, 1987), esp. 139–98 on Fielding.

**Figure 4.2** Robert Harris, *The Charlottetown Pillory* (*c.*1876), ink wash and pencil on paper, gift of the Robert Harris Trust, 1965, by permission of the Confederation Centre Art Gallery, CAG H-123.

1814 by the young reformer Thomas Noon Talfourd (who later, as blasphemy displaced sedition in the sights of Victorian censors, played a key role defending publishers in the 1840s).[6] Officially inflicted mutilation was now unheard of, so the residual essence of the punishment was simply disgrace, executed via the shaming mechanism of mob derision. Yet the crowd was too fickle or unruly, Talfourd argued, to inflict the penalty directed by the court in reliable or proportionate ways. Spectators could intensify the penalty to the

[6] See Joss Marsh, *Word Crimes: Blasphemy, Culture, and Literature in Nineteenth-Century England* (Chicago: University of Chicago Press, 1998), 94–8, 104–7.

point of death, or they could undo the penalty by celebrating the crime. When sentencing a malefactor to the pillory, Talfourd insists, a judge constitutes the mob in effect as a court of appeal: a court that was factious and disorderly in character, arbitrary and violent in conduct. When hostile, 'the people act the part of unauthorized executioners, and become familiar with the most brutal of pleasures—the delight in pain, the horrible laugh of demoniac exultation at the sufferings of a fellow being'. When sympathetic, they assume the power 'to rejudge the criminal, to annul the sentence, and to frustrate every end of public justice by turning a judicial punishment into an antijudicial victory'. Either way, as Talfourd sums it up elsewhere, the subversion of due legal process leaves 'justice perpetually insulted in the execution of its own sentences'.[7]

Talfourd later claimed to have influenced the Pillory Abolition Act of 1816, which marked the end of pillorying for seditious and other categories of libel, indeed for all offences except perjury and subornation (at last addressed by legislation in 1837).[8] His arguments were less original than he liked to think—the broad strokes are already present in Burke's extemporized speech of 1780 (see above, pp. 161–3)—but they certainly informed debate among journalists and politicians. As the bill worked its way through Parliament, Leigh Hunt's *Examiner* reported one sponsor of the bill (James Maitland, Earl of Lauderdale, a radical peer) objecting that in some cases the pillory 'was no punishment at all, and the law was defeated', while in others 'it exceeded all jurisdiction of law, and actually inflicted death, where the law did not inflict death'.[9] Sodomites were slain, libellers were cheered, the result being a travesty of justice either way.

---

[7] Thomas Noon Talfourd, 'Brief Observations on the Punishment of the Pillory', *The Pamphleteer* 4, No. 8 (1814), 534–49 (547, 544); 'Modern Periodical Literature', *New Monthly Magazine* 14 (September 1820), 303–10 (307).

[8] 'As the subject had not been investigated before, and the abolition followed so speedily, it may reasonably be presumed that this essay had no small share in terminating an infliction in which the people were, at once, judges and executioners' (Talfourd, 'Modern Periodical Literature', 307). For the Pillory Abolition Act and Talfourd's role, see Smith, 'The Decline of Public Physical Punishment in London, 1760–1840', in Carolyn Strange (ed.), *Qualities of Mercy: Justice, Punishment, and Discretion* (Vancouver: UBC Press, 1996), 21–51 (32–41).

[9] *The Examiner*, No. 393 (9 July 1815), 438.

Lauderdale illustrated his point with the example of Shebbeare, whose celebrated stunt of 1758 was now a distant memory (newly embellished with each retelling, including, this time, glasses of wine passed up to the scaffold from the crowd). Yet by this late stage in the pillory's history, unruly mobs had frustrated the punishment of political offenders on many occasions, and as organized acts of resistance, not spontaneous celebration. Perhaps Lauderdale preferred not to talk about the revolution panic of the 1790s, when he notoriously affected Jacobin chic and lived out the role of 'Citizen Maitland'. But he might have pointed to relevant instances from that era, foremost among them the attorney John Frost, an ally of Pitt in the parliamentary reform movement of the 1780s, but by 1793 a radical republican who was sentenced to prison and the pillory for speaking seditious words. Two attempts were made to complete Frost's sentence at the end of his prison term, but on both occasions handbills were rushed out to alert potential supporters, a defensive gambit pioneered by the publisher Curll in the 1720s: 'THIS DAY at TWELVE o'CLOCK, JOHN FROST is to STAND on the PILLORY at CHARING CROSS, for Supporting the RIGHTS of the PEOPLE!!!'[10] The handbills inspired officials with such anxiety about street protest that the pillorying was first suspended and then remitted—officially because Frost's health was too poor, though he then miraculously lived until 1842.[11]

By this time the pillory was rarely used in London except for extreme cases, though some provincial circuit judges still followed the old ways.[12] In 1791, Attorney General Sir Archibald Macdonald assured Parliament

[10] Both handbills survive in the British Library; this is the wording of the first, distributed 5 December 1793. For Curll, see above, pp. 166–7.

[11] John Barrell, *The Spirit of Despotism: Invasions of Privacy in the 1790s* (Oxford: Oxford University Press, 2010), 31–2; see also 75–86. The unexpected beneficiary of this episode, if only for a while, was a man 'convicted of an unnatural crime' and undergoing sentence in the Charing Cross pillory as the handbills circulated: 'The populace remained very quiet at first, as they thought it was Mr. Frost, but on discovering their mistake, they evinced a contrary disposition, the effects of which the peace officers prevented' (*Morning Post*, 15 November 1793).

[12] In his survey of surviving assizes records from 1793–4, Clive Emsley locates two provincial pilloryings for seditious libel (John Hooton of Lancaster; John Jackson of Brampton, Derbys) and four for seditious words (Emsley, 'An Aspect of Pitt's "Terror": Prosecutions for Sedition during the 1790s', *Social History* 6 (1981), 155–84, Appendix B, 179–81).

that of seventy book-trade prosecutions since 1760, involving fifty convictions and twelve 'rather severe sentences', only seven offenders had been sentenced to the pillory (the most recent being John Luxford, printer of the *Morning Herald*).[13] Seditious-libel pillorying was now more frequent in Ireland than England, but in 1793 it held so few terrors for the Dublin Paineite Richard Dry that he underwent the ritual voluntarily when given the option of trading remission for a lengthened prison term.[14] A few years later, when the journalist Peter Finnerty was pilloried for an article in his United Irishmen organ *The Press*, a sympathetic crowd turned out to cheer him, and one high-profile supporter held an umbrella aloft over Finnerty's head in a gesture probably intended to evoke Shebbeare. In the wake of this pyrrhic victory by Dublin Castle, Serjeant-at-Law Edmond Stanley urged the Irish House of Commons that 'the best mode of preventing these abominable publications...would be to indict the penalty of whipping, instead of pillory, for seditious publications; for the pillory at present, when inflicted for this offence, was a triumph'.[15]

Overshadowing passage of the Pillory Abolition Act were yet more recent instances on both sides of the Irish Sea. Foremost among them was the unstated but momentous example of Daniel Isaac Eaton, the radical bookseller whose punishment for publishing Tom Paine's *The Age of Reason, Part the Third* (1811) became, more than a century after Defoe, the culminating instance of counter-productive pillorying in book-trade cases. On this occasion Eaton's charge was blasphemous libel, for as Kevin Gilmartin notes, blasphemy charges where the real offence was political were a routine feature of Romantic-era press control.[16] But just

---

[13] *Parliamentary Register*, 29 (1791), 475. For Macdonald, this was evidence that 'the Law Officers of the Crown, for many years, had not, generally considered, been persecutors of the Press'.

[14] *The Sun*, 28 October 1793. On the intensification of seditious libel prosecutions in 1790s Dublin, see James Kelly, 'Regulating Print: The State and the Control of Print in Eighteenth-Century Ireland', *Eighteenth-Century Ireland* 23 (2008), 142–74, esp. 169 ff.

[15] Jonathan Jeffrey Wright, 'An Anglo-Irish Radical in the Late Georgian Metropolis: Peter Finnerty and the Politics of Contempt', *Journal of British Studies* 53 (2014), 660–84 (664–5); *Evening Mail*, 26–28 February 1798.

[16] Kevin Gilmartin, *Print Politics: The Press and Radical Opposition in Early Nineteenth-Century England* (Cambridge: Cambridge University Press, 1994), 115.

getting Eaton to the pillory by whatever means must have felt like a triumph to prosecutors. They had been trying to land him there since the 1790s, when Eaton and his counsel fended off several seditious libel actions thanks to sympathetic juries and the greater discretion conferred on juries by Fox's Libel Act of 1792.[17] A further government crackdown came in 1808–11, a period that saw the largest number of actions since the Paineite scare of 1792–3.[18] Over the next few years, the brazenness of libellers—the explicitness of revolutionaries for whom it no longer seemed necessary to shroud seditious content in irony or ambiguity—aroused frequent outrage in the Tory press. Spencean and related forms of democratic radicalism posed a new and distinctive threat to the established order, but conservatives often viewed it through a long lens, and compared modern libellers explicitly or implicitly with offenders from other ages. In one fairly genial example (a verse satire on Sir Francis Burdett and his circle, framed as a burlesque of Dryden), William Cobbett receives special attention as an alarming blend of Milton's Satan and Pope's Defoe, scandalously defiant of the law: 'C–bb–tt, exalted high, | Amid that unwash'd train, | Roar'd lies and libels out amain; | Yet still he 'scapes the pillory, | And sells the sland'rous strain.'[19] In this context, Eaton's conviction by a special jury was a much-needed victory for the presiding judge, Lord Chief Justice Ellenborough, the period's most unyielding advocate of the pillory—and hence, as Shelley saw him, a latter-day heretic-burner who cherished 'antiquated precedents gathered from times of priestly and tyrannical dominion'.[20]

---

[17] See Michael T. Davis, '"Good for the Public Example": Daniel Isaac Eaton, Prosecution, Punishment and Recognition, 1793–1812', in Michael T. Davis (ed.), *Radicalism and Revolution in Britain, 1775–1848: Essays in Honour of Malcolm I. Thomis* (Basingstoke: Macmillan, 2000), 110–32. For Fox's Libel Act, see below, pp. 248–9.

[18] Philip Harling, 'The Law of Libel and the Limits of Repression, 1790–1832', *Historical Journal* 44 (2001), 107–34 (125; also 109 for the underlying statistics).

[19] Horace Twiss, *Posthumous Parodies and Other Pieces* (1814), 14 ('Sir Francis's Feast, or the Jacobin Journalists ... Being a Paraphrase of *Alexander's Feast*').

[20] *The Prose Works of Percy Bysshe Shelley, Volume 1*, ed. E. B. Murray (Oxford: Clarendon Press, 1993), 63 (*A Letter to Lord Ellenborough, Occasioned by the Sentence Which He Passed on Mr. D. I. Eaton*).

Eaton's punishment did not turn out as intended, however. Henry Crabb Robinson was at the Old Bailey to see it. He describes in his diary a mob that 'was not numerous, but decidedly friendly' to Eaton; they cheered their support for the 'round, grinning face' put there to elicit their derision. 'As I expected, his punishment of shame was his glory', Crabb Robinson comments: 'The whole affair was an additional proof of the folly of the Ministers, who ought to have known that such an exhibition would be a triumph to the cause they meant to render infamous.'[21] In the published account of Cobbett, Crabb Robinson's modest crowd swells to between 12,000 and 20,000 spectators, and Cobbett contrasts their behaviour with the brutal scapegoating of sodomites and swindlers who had recently endured the pillory on the same spot. In particular, he remembers a group of 'wretches guilty of *unnatural offences*'—surely the Vere Street coterie, pilloried in 1810—whose features 'were almost instantly rendered indistinguishable by the peltings in mud, blood, addled eggs, guts, garbage, dead dogs and cats, and every species of filth, while the air was filled with hootings and execrations' (Cobbett expresses no disapproval of this, incidentally).[22] By contrast, Eaton was applauded 'after the manner of the Theatre; that is to say, by *clapping of the hands*, and by cries of *bravo, bravo!*' The cheers were periodically renewed as the scaffold rotated every so often by 90 degrees, a standard refinement of late-stage pillory-construction, designed to intensify the malefactor's objectification, but here enhancing his celebrity. Cobbett adds that when Eaton's hour of glory was over, one protester placed a cockerel on the scaffold, recalling the single most inflammatory publication of Eaton's career, a mock-Aesopian fable of 1793 in which a tyrannical gamecock—connoting not only Louis XVI but also George III—is beheaded as a criminal despot.[23] As with Finnerty's umbrella in Ireland a few years earlier,

---

[21] *Diary, Reminiscences, and Correspondence of Henry Crabb Robinson*, ed. Thomas Sadler, 2 vols (Boston: Houghton, Mifflin & Co., 1870), 1: 248 (26 May 1812).

[22] *Cobbett's Political Register* 21 (January–June 1812), 750 (13 June 1812). On Vere Street, see Peter Bartlett, 'Sodomites in the Pillory in Eighteenth-Century London', *Social & Legal Studies* 6 (1997), 553–72 (559–60).

[23] *Cobbett's Political Register* 21 (January–June 1812), 748, 748–9 (13 June 1812).

there were spectators who fully grasped the pillory's potential as a forum of symbolic theatre: as a space in which the official message of guilt and shame might be subverted or vividly replaced.

It should not be forgotten that prosecution and conviction, which also involved heavy trial costs and eighteen months in Newgate, left Eaton ruined, and probably hastened his death in 1814. But the pillorying itself, traditionally the spearhead of retribution and deterrence, was a disastrous own goal by the authorities. Worse still occurred in Dublin in 1811, when the nationalist magazine editor Walter Cox was pilloried for an allegory entitled 'The Painter Cut: A Vision', which enthusiastically prophesied a Napoleonic invasion that would free Ireland from union with Britain. Not only did the crowd fail to pelt Cox for publishing the offending text; instead they pelted the police in Capel Street as Cox was returned to prison. From there, Cox orchestrated gloating accounts of his trial and exhibition, illustrated by an engraving of himself lounging at ease on the scaffold amidst the accolades of the crowd: 'not less than twenty thousand persons', the magazine claimed (see Figure 4.3).[24] In 1814, fears of similar disorder in London prevented the execution of sentence on the war hero and radical parliamentarian Thomas, Lord Cochrane, convicted of conspiracy to defraud, but singled out for the pillory by Ellenborough, some thought, for his political role in the Burdett circle. 'It was soon perceived that it would by no means be prudent, or even safe, to put Lord Cochrane in the pillory', observed a contemporary.[25] The perception was intensified when Burdett threatened to join Cochrane there in solidarity, so that the last politically motivated pillorying in England was a non-event, defeated before it could begin by an invincible combination of elite string-pulling and threatened popular riot. Perhaps the surprising thing is that the end took so long to arrive. The forces now constraining the

---

[24] 'Exhibition of Walter Cox', *Irish Magazine* (April 1811), 145; see C. J. Woods, 'Cox, Walter', *Dictionary of Irish Biography*.

[25] Hewson Clarke, *The History of the War, from the Commencement of the French Revolution to the Present Time*, 3 vols (1816), 3: 20. For this episode, see Timothy Jenks, *Naval Engagements: Patriotism, Cultural Politics, and the Royal Navy, 1793–1815* (Oxford: Oxford University Press, 2006), 249–90.

**Figure 4.3** 'Mr. Walter Cox, on the Pillory', *Irish Magazine* (April 1811), by permission of The Board of Trinity College Dublin. Cox is shown outside the Royal Exchange (now City Hall), Dublin, 'cheered by a numerous and respectable assemblage of his fellow Citizens'.

authorities—opposition within the social and political establishment; public opinion and its growing power—had been observable since the Star-Chamber pilloryings of the 1630s, but only now did the penny finally drop.

## Allegories, parodies, polemics: Walter Cox, William Hone, and others

A common feature of the offending texts in all these Romantic-era cases is that they were more or less void of protective ambiguity, requiring little interpretative work by readers to disclose their seditious drift. Consider 'The Painter Cut: A Vision', authored not by Cox himself but by Thomas Finn of Carlow, later a Tory opponent of Daniel O'Connell, and a man remembered after his death as 'a well-known public writer and clever man, not remarkable, however, for very strong political principles'.[26] Finn's mobility notwithstanding, during his time as an *Irish Magazine* author (under the incongruous pseudonym 'Orellana') he was, or chose to pose as, a firebrand republican.[27] A year later, he contributed trenchant material deploring the slaughter of Carlow rebels during the 1798 rising, but 'The Painter Cut: A Vision' was easily his biggest splash. In it, the painter in question is not an artist or labourer but a painter in the nautical sense of 'a rope attached to the bow of a (usually small) boat for tying it to a ship, quay, etc.': in this case, a tie securing a small, subordinate vessel to a large, dominant mother-ship. Hence the metaphorical sense of 'to cut (also slip) the painter', first recorded in 1699, as 'to effect a separation, sever a connection; to free oneself of something; to break free': an idiom that obviously lends itself to political use (one *OED* illustration is a late-Victorian passage about decolonization).[28] No prizes, then, for guessing the identity of the tethered vessels. Looking back after thirty-five years on 'the celebrated and very clever paper called "The Painter Cut"' as the finest hour of the *Irish Magazine*, the historian Thomas Mooney called Finn's vision 'a paper ably, but mysteriously worded, in which Ireland was presented to the mind as

---

[26] Maurice Lenihan, 'Portrait of Turlough O'Callaghan', *Notes & Queries*, 4th series, 6 (15 October 1870), 324.

[27] A man at the cutting edge of early modern genocide, Francisco de Orellana (1511–46) was a gold-hunting conquistador who fought his way through the Amazon basin and helped Pizarro conquer Peru.

[28] 'To "cut the painter" ... *i.e.*, to throw off the sovereignty of the old country' (*OED*, s.v. Painter, 1.b, 2).

a small boat attached, by cords, to a ship, (England,) which might be easily, and ought to be, cut away'.[29]

In truth there was little mystery about the basic allegory. Finn's text begins with the narrator 'recapitulating the unparrallelled sufferings that Ireland has borne for so many ages'; he later specifies 'a slavery already borne for six hundred years', which dates the suffering closely enough to the first Anglo-Norman incursions.[30] What follows is an allegory in which exploitative union with Britain is severed by means of French intervention, but this is an emphatically self-glossing allegory, and ends with an unmistakable appeal to United Irishmen or their heirs: '*The Painter is Cut* and \*\*\*\*\*\*\* *is free*' (295). At the close of this speech, it scarcely makes a difference that the word 'Ireland' is conventionally disguised by seven asterisks, exactly corresponding in number to the obliterated letters. The blank is as obvious as Susannah's celebrated instruction to full-bladdered Tristram Shandy, as she pulls up the sash, 'to \*\*\*\* \*\*\* \*\* \*\*\* \*\*\*\*\*\*'.[31] Rather than shroud a meaning made inescapable by its context, the magazine's gesture of concealment merely highlights a climate of oppression in which subterfuge becomes prudent. The typographical gesture validates the vision.

So light was the allegorical encoding that at trial Cox's counsel made only token attempts to deny the seditious import alleged by prosecutors. Instead he acknowledged that 'allegory may be a libel' (citing the 'Persian Letter' from *Mist's Weekly Journal*, a Jacobite *cause célèbre* of the Walpole era), and concentrated instead on the evidence implicating Cox as publisher, which he claimed was flawed.[32] Yet for all its provocative transparency of meaning, 'The Painter Cut' looks like the height of obscurity alongside the main objects of political

---

[29] Thomas Mooney, *The History of Ireland, From Its First Settlement to the Present Time* (Boston, 1845), 1114.

[30] Thomas Finn, 'The Painter Cut: A Vision', in *The Irish Magazine, or Monthly Asylum for Neglected Biography* (July 1810), 293–5 (293, 295).

[31] Laurence Sterne, *Tristram Shandy*, ed. Melvyn New and Joan New (Gainesville: University Presses of Florida, 1978), 449 (V.xvii).

[32] 'Second Trial of Mr. Walter Cox', *Irish Magazine* (April 1811), 152. For the Persian Letter (24 August 1728), see Jeremy Black, 'An Underrated Journalist: Nathaniel Mist and the Opposition Press during the Whig Ascendancy', *British Journal for Eighteenth-Century Studies* 10 (1987), 27–41.

censorship over the ensuing decade, when governments faced an explosion of cheap (or, worse, free) print from the radical press, notably during the postwar climate of unrest and repression that followed Napoleon's defeat, mass demobilization, and a series of failed harvests.[33] The period to 1821 saw the last great wave of seditious libel prosecutions, when cases were mounted with varying degrees of success against radical authors and their publishers, with notable peaks in the aftermath of the Spa Fields riots (twenty-three King's Bench actions in 1817) and then the Peterloo massacre and Cato Street conspiracy (forty-three King's Bench actions in 1820; thirty-two in 1821).[34] There was no need for prosecutors to excavate subtexts or resolve ambiguities, however. Delicate interpretative questions were rarely at issue in the official indictments and informations, and the common feature in most if not all these trials was the brazen, outspoken quality of the offending text.

The targets were radicals such as T. J. Wooler—a printer and journalist with so little regard for verbal caution that he would set his polemics directly in type without first writing them out—who was tried twice in 1817 for his satirical weekly *The Black Dwarf*.[35] Then there was Sir Francis Burdett for an 1820 commentary on the Peterloo massacre that excoriated the authorities responsible as 'bloody Neroes' and called for urgent redress;[36] John Thelwall for no less inflammatory comments on Burdett's behalf in an 1821 number of *The Champion* (one among several equally trenchant editorials about

---

[33] On the last of these factors, see Gillen D'Arcy Wood, *Tambora: The Eruption That Changed the World* (Princeton: Princeton University Press, 2014).

[34] Harling, 'Law of Libel', 109. These King's Bench figures take in most metropolitan indictments and informations, but there were also many actions against provincial vendors (for an earlier phase of which see Clive Emsley, 'Aspect of Pitt's "Terror"', Appendices A and B, 176–84).

[35] See James Epstein, *Radical Expression: Political Language, Ritual, and Symbol in England, 1790–1850* (New York: Oxford University Press, 1994), 36 and 29–69 *passim*. Procedural errors voided the first trial, and Wooler was acquitted in the second (but convicted and imprisoned in 1820 on a different charge).

[36] Marc Baer, 'Burdett, Sir Francis (1770–1844)', *ODNB*.

Peterloo and Cato Street, so probably a specimen charge);[37] John Hunt for denouncing the House of Commons, a few weeks before Thelwall's offending paper, as an institution 'composed of venal boroughmongers, grasping placemen, greedy adventurers, and aspiring title-hunters... a body in short containing a far greater proportion of public criminals than public guardians'.[38] There was little in the way of strategic indirection in any of this journalism, though only Burdett and Hunt were duly convicted.

A more modest spike in actions occurred at the end of the decade, but again with patchy success. During the 'Captain Swing' disturbances of 1830–1, Cobbett was prosecuted for a *Political Register* article entitled 'Rural War', which defended a spate of machine-breaking and rick-burning by farm labourers and implicitly incited further action. Rural arsonists and Luddites were to be applauded for their achievements in slowing the introduction of threshing machines and the erosion of labouring-class incomes; 'it is unquestionable that their acts have produced good, and great good too.'[39] Cobbett had previously been fined and imprisoned for seditious libel during the Perceval ministry's crackdown of 1810, and it's a measure of changing conditions that he now hit new peaks of rhetorical recklessness, yet got away with it even so. The case against him was meticulously prepared with reference to further works including *Rural Rides*: 'perhaps the only canonical text of Romantic period literature', James Grande writes, 'that lies marked up in the Treasury Solicitor's archives as evidence of sedition'.[40] But Cobbett remained defiant throughout the trial, and provocatively ended his defence by 'bequeath[ing] my revenge', in case of conviction and death in jail, 'to the labourers of England'.[41] All these circumstances notwithstanding, the prosecution ended in failure, with the jury deadlocked.

---

[37] Michael Scrivener, *Seditious Allegories: John Thelwall and Jacobin Writing* (University Park: Pennsylvania Statue University Press, 2001), 201. The case was dropped 'thanks to a technicality' (p. 202).

[38] Harling, 'Law of Libel', 124 (quoting the *Examiner*, 21 February 1821).

[39] James Grande, *William Cobbett, the Press and Rural England: Radicalism and the Fourth Estate, 1792–1835* (Basingstoke: Palgrave Macmillan, 2014), 186, quoting *Cobbett's Political Register*, 11 December 1830; see also, for the earlier case, p. 61.

[40] Grande, *Cobbett, the Press and Rural England*, 191.

[41] *A Full and Accurate Report of the Trial of William Cobbett, Esq.* (1831), 32.

Each of these polemics, no question, was a powerful text, but none could be called complex or subtle. The trials they provoked turned mostly on raw questions of political sympathy or allegiance, with prosecution and defence appealing to jurors to forbid or approve explicit meanings, not ponder and decode veiled implications. There were few if any cases in these postwar years that we might think of as 'literary' in character, and little of the hermeneutic ducking and diving that marked prominent eighteenth-century episodes such as the 1731 *Craftsman* trial (see above, pp. 115–16) or Nathaniel Mist's in 1728. The fascinating exception was the case of the satirist William Hone when prosecuted for blasphemous libel in a series of liturgical parodies (*The Late John Wilkes's Catechism*, *The Sinecurist's Creed*, and *The Political Litany*) which he used to attack ministerial corruption in 1817. Conducting his own defence in rambling but locally brilliant style, Hone developed a strategic taxonomy of parodic types that anticipates modern theories of parody, distinguishing in particular between parodies mocking a base text and those appropriating a base text to mock a target beyond it. 'There were two kinds of parodies,' Hone told the court: 'one in which a man might convey ludicrous or ridiculous ideas relative to some other subject; the other, where it was meant to ridicule the thing parodied.'[42] His own exercises were of the former, outward-facing type, and ridiculed not the liturgy but the government—so that in effect Hone was audaciously confessing to sedition, of which he was not charged, in order to refute the official, though proxy, charge of blasphemy. By his own logic, he could be guilty of one transgression or the other but not both—and blasphemy was the offence alleged. Hone's defence turned on an elaborate array of precedents from Martin Luther to Walter Scott ('this poetical placeman') in which scriptural sources were parodied for ulterior ends, and from these examples he intended to write a history and theory of parody as a

---

[42] *The Three Trials of William Hone, for Publishing Three Parodies* (1818), First Trial, 18. Cf. Linda Hutcheon's account of parody's potential for, in relation to the parodied source, 'a range of pragmatic "ethos" (ruling intended effects), from the reverential to the playful to the scornful'; the 'reverential' type retains a capacity for satirical aggression, but directs the aggression outwards to a target in the world (*A Theory of Parody: The Teachings of Twentieth-Century Art Forms* (Urbana: University of Illinois Press, 2000), 26).

genre: an ambition he never realized, though notes survive.[43] Hone was also steeped in seditious libel case-law from Star Chamber through Defoe to Wilkes, and he partly modelled his defence on published accounts of Lilburne's treason trial (in 1649, under the Rump Parliament) for Leveller pamphleteering and related offences.[44]

Despite facing a special jury constructed with, he alleged, 'all the picking and packing of the Crown-office' (Third Trial, p. 15), Hone won his first trial, for the catechism, amidst embarrassing eruptions of courtroom laughter and applause. At this point, Ellenborough brought himself in to preside personally over the remaining trials, for the creed and the litany. But the damage was done, and Hone simply replayed his catechism defence 'that an article may be humourously parodied, in order to excite ridicule, without either the humour or the ridicule being directed towards the article parodied' (Second Trial, p. 29). He won again on both occasions, so, it was said, hastening the decline and death of Ellenborough—already shaken by the abolition of pillorying as a tool of censorship the previous year—who offered his resignation as Lord Chief Justice following the third trial, but then limped on in office for a few more months.[45] Other prosecutions were dropped in the wake of Hone's acquittal, which, Harling suggests, 'put parodies beyond the reach of prosecution' and left the government 'with no viable legal means of controlling satire'.[46] The outcome certainly created an enduring disinclination

---

[43] Hone, *Three Trials*, Third Trial, 31. On the 'History of Parody' project and its origins in Hone's defence, see Marsh, *Word Crimes*, 39–41; also David Francis Taylor, 'The Practice of Parody', in Paddy Bullard (ed.), *The Oxford Handbook of Eighteenth-Century Satire* (Oxford: Oxford University Press, 2019). Notably, Hone's examples included a 1741 number of the *Champion* ridiculing Walpole as 'Pharoah of N-rf-lk', written by Fielding's co-author and successor James Ralph in an antiministerial style pioneered by Fielding himself (First Trial, 24; for an earlier example, see Fielding's parody of the litany ('FROM THE PRIME MINISTER GOOD LORD DELIVER US'), *Contributions to The Champion*, 313 (10 May 1740).

[44] See Marcus Wood, *Radical Satire and Print Culture, 1790–1822* (Oxford: Clarendon Press, 1994), 123–31; also, on Hone and Defoe (whom Hone thought 'a man after my own heart'), 117.

[45] Michael Lobban, 'Law, Edward, first Baron Ellenborough (1750–1818)', *ODNB*.

[46] Harling, 'Law of Libel', 132. Of 26 libel charges filed in King's Bench in 1817, only two (8%) ended with sentences. The success rate improved to about

to act in cases likely to involve literary interpretation, with its tendency to render conviction uncertain and to guarantee excruciating attention, in the public courtroom and published reports, to the applicability or otherwise of encoded sedition. Shortly before Hone's trial, the Home Secretary, Viscount Sidmouth, was advised by Crown lawyers that even Spencean polemics were now 'drawn up with so much dexterity— authors had so profited by former lessons of experience, that greater difficulties to conviction presented themselves than at any former time'.[47] In this context, to target writing of any additional complexity was a fool's errand.

Other practical impediments accumulated in the wake of pillory abolition. Home Office resources remained scant while cheap print continued to explode in quantity, and though the sporadic, unpredictable nature of official actions against seditious libel may in some respects have enhanced the effect of exemplary intimidation, more and more offenders were left unpunished, indeed unpursued. There was certainly no attention to spare for tricky cases of literary indirection, even if officials still had the appetite to bestow it. As time went on, even blunt prose for the masses went unchecked. Over the five-year period from 1824 to 1828 inclusive, no seditious libel actions were filed in King's Bench at all. Impunity could still not be counted on, but it was now unmistakable, in Harling's words, 'that the odds favoured the gambler and not the house'.[48]

So, increasingly, did the rules. Shortly before the setback inflicted on the authorities by Hone, the Wooler trials were no less disastrous for the attention they focused on the special-jury system and its abuse, which led to rapid reform of the City juror list (Hone benefited, for all his protestations about his juries). New legislation followed in 1825 to inhibit jury-packing.[49] Another longstanding weapon in the arsenal of

---

50% in 1819–20, thanks to a new focus on easier targets, notably small-scale vendors (125–6), but 'by the early 1820s [the authorities] had all but abandoned libel prosecutions' (p. 110).

[47] Harling, 'Law of Libel', quoting Sidmouth's speech on Habeas Corpus suspension, *Hansard*, 24 February 1817.

[48] Harling, 'Law of Libel', 122.

[49] Epstein, *Radical Expression*, 55–71; James Oldham, *Trial by Jury: The Seventh Amendment and Anglo-American Special Juries* (New York: NYU Press, 2006), 166–71.

ministers, the *ex officio* information (which, without necessarily leading to prosecution, imposed imprisonment without trial, or alternatively crushing sureties and an ongoing threat of arrest), was weakened by legislation in 1820.[50] In 1819 the Blasphemous and Seditious Libels Act removed the conceptual vagueness that ministers had exploited for generations by defining seditious libel as work 'tending to bring into hatred or contempt the person of his majesty, his heirs or successors, or the regent, or the government and constitution of the United Kingdom': still a capacious definition, but a constraint nonetheless on prosecutors' room for manoeuvre. Radicals could no longer protest, as Burdett had protested just two years earlier, that in its strategic indistinctness the doctrine of libel 'was a thousand times worse than the plan adopted by the tyrant *Caligula*, who posted up his laws, but in places so high, and in letters so small, that though it was impossible to read them, it was death to commit an infraction upon their provisions'.[51] The crime was now clear, and in a way that would have curtailed numerous actions that had been taken since the 1695 lapse of pre-publication censorship. Moreover, as government and constitution came to be recognized, notably in the Reform Bill debates of 1830–2, as flexible entities open to change, bringing these moving targets incontrovertibly into hatred or contempt proved harder to do, or at least harder to prove. At the same time, seditious discourse became less of an imperative for radicals like Wooler, who is said to have commented, when the Reform Bill finally passed in 1832: 'these damned Whigs have taken all the sedition out of my hands'.[52] The ensuing years were scarcely a serene new age of political consensus. But while blasphemy, and increasingly obscenity, came to flourish as prosecution charges through the nineteenth century, seditious libel markedly declined.[53]

---

[50] Harling, 'Law of Libel', 113.

[51] William Hone, *Trial by Jury and Liberty of the Press: The Proceedings at the Public Meeting, December 29, 1817* (1818), 12; for context see Gilmartin, *Print Politics*, 115–21.

[52] James Epstein, 'Wooler, Thomas Jonathan (1786?–1853)', *ODNB*.

[53] From 1821 to 1834, Donald Thomas counts 27 convictions for seditious libel, mainly concentrated in 1821–2, alongside 72 for blasphemous libel (*A Long Time Burning: The History of Literary Censorship in England* (New York: Praeger, 1969), 176). On

In his classic study of the waning of literary censorship and the rise of assumptions supporting freedom of the press, Donald Thomas points to 'a new belief in political tolerance' within the establishment before 1832 that looks forward to the values of John Stuart Mill.[54] The fact that, in its cumulative effect, so much new legislation now worked to inhibit seditious libel prosecution would seem to support that view; so would recorded opinions from parliamentarians of different stripes. As William Bulwer, the novelist's brother, warned Parliament in 1830 with reference to Cobbett (and with Hone in the background), 'prosecutions made proselytes' and were liable to fail; 'it was by the press, and not by the pillory or the prison, that a libeller could be reduced to his natural insignificance.'[55] Trial by what is contrary, as Milton said long ago.

There were countervailing legislative measures, however, and countervailing points of view. In the opinion of Thomas Love Peacock, literature was now constrained by an invisible but irresistible combination of patronage and hegemony, and a dawning age of ideological conformism left little or no need for legal actions. Liberty of expression was apparently ample but actually spurious, and 'though there is no censorship of the press there is an influence widely diffused and mighty in its operation that is almost equivalent to it'.[56] With this emphasis on 'influence' (pensions, sinecures), Peacock probably had in mind the political apostasy of Wordsworth, Southey, and Coleridge, three recurrent targets of his satirical fiction. But sticks remained important, alongside the carrots, in the regulation of print. In practice, the restrictions on prosecution implied by the Blasphemous and Seditious Libels Act were accompanied by severe compensating measures on the punishment side, including, potentially, transportation for fourteen years. Here was an act of 'wholesome Terror', opined the long-serving Prime Minister Lord Liverpool, that would put 'some

---

Victorian blasphemy, see Marsh, *Word Crimes*, 78 ff.; also, for the Obscene Publications Act (1857) and its consequences, 207–15.

[54] Thomas, *Long Time Burning*, 177.

[55] Grande, *Cobbett, the Press and Rural England*, 186, quoting *Hansard*, 23 December 1830.

[56] Thomas Love Peacock, *Nightmare Abbey*, ed. Nicholas A. Joukovsky (Cambridge: Cambridge University Press, 2016), 118 ('An Essay on Fashionable Literature').

check upon the great Licentiousness of the Press as it has existed for some Years'.[57] This statute, moreover, was just one of a number of repressive measures (the notorious 'Six Acts' of 1819) that aimed to limit seditious words and deeds in the wake of Peterloo, among which it was eclipsed as a constraint on print by the Publications Act. Like Bolingbroke's Stamp Act targeting Grubstreet a century earlier, the 1819 Publications Act deployed a range of fiscal mechanisms, including a fourpenny newspaper stamp, to devastate the twopenny radical press; Cobbett's *Political Register* lost 80 per cent of its circulation, and was one of few such organs to survive.[58] There was little need to prosecute seditious libellers when the most dangerous media forms they inhabited could instead be taxed out of existence by revenue laws.

And so, in the very period when seditious libel swims belatedly into clear definition as a legal concept, it also recedes from view as a practical charge, though it was not formally abolished by Parliament until 2009.[59] At that point, the novelist Will Self observed that 'in amongst the fast-growing leylandii of political correctness, with their multiple fronds of legislation blocking out the light of day, there stands that hoary old oak seditious libel'. This may have been a crime against extended metaphor, but Self's wording then rather deftly connects seditious libel doctrine with Stuart and even Papal regimes of press control (perhaps with an eye on the seminal Star Chamber case *De libellis famosis*, 1605). He also catches the doctrine's double

---

[57] Simon Devereaux, 'Transportation, Penal Practices, and the English State, 1770–1830', in Strange (ed.), *Qualities of Mercy*, 52–76 (p. 63, quoting Liverpool to Lord Grenville, 27 November 1819). In Edinburgh, fourteen years' transportation had been used as early as 1793 against five Scots radicals including Thomas Muir, a lawyer convicted of seditious practices including promotion, circulation, and public recitation of *Rights of Man*.

[58] Harling, 'Law of Libel', 131. Even the window tax, at its costliest between 1808 and 1823 and disproportionately affecting the poor, may be seen as a backdoor censorship measure. As Dickens put it when calling for abolition, 'They cannot read without light' (to Charles Knight, 8 February 1850; see William St Clair, *The Reading Nation in the Romantic Period* (Cambridge: Cambridge University Press, 2004), 310).

[59] See Index on Censorship/English PEN, *A Briefing on the Abolition of Seditious Libel and Criminal Libel*, <https://www.englishpen.org/wp-content/uploads/2015/09/seditious_libel_july09.pdf>.

face, at once subtly mercurial and an instrument of blunt force. Seditious libel 'has always been a shape-shifting law, capable of being employed as a cudgel against satirists, incendiarists, malcontents and revolutionaries alike. A mature democracy, with a tradition of open government and freedom of speech, has no need of such ancient Star Chamber inquisitions.'[60]

## The 'King Chaunticlere' trial: arbitrary innuendo and necessary sense

It's true, of course, that back in the 1790s some writers were still using time-honoured techniques of functional ambiguity to pre-empt prosecution (which, after *Rights of Man*, might come not only from the Crown Office but also from the Association for the Preservation of Liberty and Property against Republicans and Levellers, a hyperactive vigilante group).[61] We may contrast the direct polemics about Peterloo that brought Thelwall his 1821 libel charge with his indirect gamecock fable of 1793 as published by Eaton in *Politics for the People, or Hog's Wash*, a democratic periodical named in mocking allusion to Burke's *Reflections on the Revolution in France*, with its much-derided talk of a 'swinish multitude'.[62] Neither prosecution succeeded, but they failed for very different reasons. Read alongside the texts that provoked them, these trials clarify the extent to which practices and thresholds changed in the intervening years.

---

[60] Quoted by Index on Censorship, 'UK Government Abolishes Seditious Libel and Criminal Defamation', 13 July 2009, <http://humanrightshouse.org/Articles/11311.html>.

[61] See Mark Philp, *Reforming Ideas in Britain: Politics and Language in the Shadow of the French Revolution, 1789–1815* (Cambridge: Cambridge University Press, 2013), 40–70.

[62] For the implications of Eaton's title (which he varied from time to time), see Marilyn Butler's headnote to the fable in her anthology *Burke, Paine, Godwin, and the Revolution Controversy* (Cambridge: Cambridge University Press, 1984), 185. For convenience I refer to the fable as Thelwall's, though as John Barrell and Jon Mee point out, it was originally an oral performance, and Thelwall's widow described Eaton, in remediating the fable for print, as 'dressing it up in certainly very strong terms, which Thelwall would never have used' (Cecil Thelwall, *The Life of John Thelwall*, 2 vols (1837), 1: 110; Barrell and Mee (eds), *Trials for Treason and Sedition, 1792–1794*, 8 vols (London: Pickering & Chatto, 2006–7), 1: 350).

In the earlier case, technically though not of course ideologically, Thelwall is as close to Roger L'Estrange in his dissident years, for whom beast fable could circumvent Williamite censorship 'by a Train of Mystery and Circumlocution',[63] as to his own forthright journalistic self of the Peterloo era. Nor was the use of encoded fable—a pervasive, self-conscious feature of *Hog's Wash*—simply a matter of self-protection, for as Marilyn Butler observes of the journal, 'the intention was from the outset to challenge Burke's assumptions about the stupidity and non-intellectuality of the masses'.[64] *Hog's Wash* was always accessible in style, but it also made demands of its popular audience; it sought to stimulate the interpretative faculties of readers, and make them co-create and possess, through the work of decoding, the topical messages it promoted. Again, the underlying assumption is continuous with the classic theory of fable voiced in the 1690s by L'Estrange, for whom 'Nothing makes a Deeper Impression upon the Minds of Men, or comes more Lively to their Understanding, then Those Instructive Notices that are Convey'd...under the Cover of some Allegory or Riddle'; it was for this reason that 'the Wisdom of the Ancients has been still Wrapt up in *Veils* and *Figures*'.[65] Perhaps these words underlie the crisper formulation of Blake—who names Aesop among his models—in his celebrated letter of 1799 defending the poetics of indirection: 'The wisest of the Ancients consider'd what is not too Explicit as the fittest for Instruction, because it rouzes the faculties to act.'[66] In this respect, there was something inherently antiauthoritarian about Aesopian fable; it conferred authority, instead, on the reader's own judgment.

This theory notwithstanding, 'King Chaunticlere; or, The Fate of Tyranny' (in the eighth number of *Hog's Wash*, 16 November 1793) leaves little to interpretative chance. The paper begins with an emphatic political steer, and repeatedly associates the gamecock at the centre of the tale with the paraphernalia of absolute monarchy. Chaunticlere is a figure already long associated with strutting

---

[63] L'Estrange, *Fables, of Aesop*, sig. A2; see above, pp. 84–5.
[64] Butler (ed.), *Burke, Paine, Godwin*, 185.
[65] L'Estrange, *Fables, of Aesop*, sigs A2–A2$^v$.
[66] *The Letters of Willliam Blake*, ed. Geoffrey Keynes, 3rd edn (Oxford: Clarendon Press, 1980), 8 (to Dr Trusler, 23 August 1799).

kingship, and in *Hog's Wash* he becomes 'a very fine majestic kind of animal', 'a haughty, sanguinary tyrant', 'fond of foreign wars and... inordinate taxation'.[67] His appearance bespeaks ceremonial royalty: 'his ermine spotted breast, the fine gold trappings about his neck and shoulders, the flowing robe of plumage tucked up at his rump, and, above all, that fine ornamented thing upon his head there—his crown... I believe you call it' (p. 187). Yet when Chaunticlere is caught and decapitated—'if guillotines had been in fashion, I should have certainly guillotined him', says Thelwall, unless this was an Eaton embellishment (p. 187)—the preening monarch turns out to be much the same as his subjects. He is 'no better than a common tame scratch-dunghill pullet', and for culinary purposes worse, 'for he was tough, and oily, and rank with the pollutions of his luxurious vices' (p. 188). Throughout the fable, its applicability to the world of 'men and women' as well as 'cocks and hens'—both of which, the message is, should rid themselves of tyrants—is unmistakable (p. 187). Yet even so, complications arise from the surplus of possible meanings put into play by Thelwall. Also framing the narrative are physiological questions about the voluntariness or otherwise of muscular spasms following decapitation, which suggest an invitation to read the fable (in which Chaunticlere struts and flaps after death, headless chicken-style) as exploring the distinction between considered action and conditioned reflex. Beyond this, John Barrell persuasively reads 'King Chaunticlere' as an autobiographical sketch about the author's own experience of overcoming habitually ingrained attitudes through the exertion of intellect and will; the tale becomes 'an account of how Thelwall himself, a "complete Church-and-King man" in later adolescence, became a more or less overt republican in the early 1790s'.[68]

Even if one reads the fable as purely an allegory of despotism and regicide, there remains the basic question of identification. Is

[67] John Thelwall, 'King Chaunticlere; or, The Fate of Tyranny', in Butler (ed.), *Burke, Paine, Godwin*, 187. For pre-existing connotations, see Samantha J. Rayner, *Images of Kingship in Chaucer and His Ricardian Contemporaries* (Woodbridge: Boydell & Brewer, 2008), 151–9.

[68] John Barrell, *Imagining the King's Death: Figurative Treason, Fantasies of Regicide, 1793–1796* (Oxford: Oxford University Press, 2000), 107.

Chauntidere a generalized king, a king in theory, or is he the particular king who now occupies the throne? Here was a longstanding crux in the history of seditious writing, most famously at issue when excerpts from Algernon Sidney's *Discourses Concerning Government* were used against him at trial in 1683, with Sidney protesting in vain that prosecutors had maliciously construed theoretical passages about kingship, or historical passages about ancient kings (Tarquin, Nero, Domitian), as simply denoting Charles II. Interpreted thus, insisted Solicitor General Heneage Finch in the notorious language of the medieval Treason Act, these passages were 'sufficient to prove his Compassing the Death of the King'.[69] And then if Chauntidere is indeed a real-life, modern-day king, in the same way that Sidney's Nero was Charles II, then which one exactly? Louis XVI, the recently guillotined French king, or George III, his now uneasy counterpart in Windsor Castle? This was blurring of a kind deftly pioneered by L'Estrange's *Fables* a few years after Sidney's execution, when the usurping hawk of 'The Kite, Hawk, and Pigeons' implicitly incriminates William III ('an Enemy-Prince'), but with just enough suggestion of Cromwell and the civil wars ('our Broils of Famous Memory') to embed a more acceptable alternative meaning.[70] An incidental benefit of the subterfuge is the analogy thereby implied: between William and Cromwell as counterfeit liberators bent on absolute power; between George and Louis as *ancien-régime* tyrants ripe for deposition. While making the allusion deniable, the doubling of identities intensifies the satire.

There are several reasons why Eaton's trial for publishing 'King Chauntidere' and related material in *Hog's Wash* has been central to the debate about revolution-era press control launched by Barrell's monumental study *Imagining the King's Death* (2000). First there is Eaton's sheer prominence among the ninety-three state trials for seditious libel, constructive treason, and related offences mounted in London, Dublin, and Edinburgh between 1792 and 1798 (probably a

---

[69] Alan Roper, 'Innuendo in the Restoration', *JEGP*, 100.1 (2001), 22–39 (28), citing *The Arraignment, Tryal & Condemnation of Algernon Sidney, Esq; for High-Treason* (1684), 53. For the implications and ongoing currency of this 1351 formulation (25 Edw. 3 St. 5 c. 2), see Barrell, *Imagining the King's Death*, 29–36.

[70] *Fables, of Aesop*, 21; see above, p. 77.

larger number than in the entire 1760–91 period since George III's accession, though short of the high points associated with Jacobite rebellion in the mid 1710s and 1740s).[71] In 1792, special alarm was generated by the second, more radical part of Paine's *Rights of Man* and its broad dissemination in cheap reprints for artisan readers: alarm satirized by Eaton in an ironic pamphlet, *The Pernicious Effects of the Art of Printing upon Society, Exposed* (1794), which urges the government to destroy all printing presses and type foundries, and then 'issue a proclamation against reading, and burn all private libraries'.[72] Actions against authors and publishers peaked in 1793–4, and it was only with the notorious 'Gagging' Acts of 1795 (the Seditious Meetings Act, the Treasonable and Seditious Practices Act), which imposed unprecedented new constraints on radical associations and their public activities, that book-trade prosecutions returned to normal levels.[73] This was, as Eaton's defence counsel put it with heavy sarcasm, 'peculiarly and emphatically an age of sedition': an age in which 'the press teems with libels calculated to vilify every thing that is great and good, libels designed to subvert the foundation of all government, to dissolve the bonds of society, and to introduce confusion and anarchy'.[74]

Paine himself was tried only *in absentia*—a wise precaution, as with Wilkes a generation beforehand—and the nearest he came to the pillory was in graphic satire (Figure 4.4). That said, the American

[71] Kenneth R. Johnston, *Unusual Suspects: Pitt's Reign of Alarm and the Lost Generation of the 1790s* (Oxford: Oxford University Press, 2013), Appendix 1, 329–30. In 1795 the Attorney General Sir John Scott (later Lord Eldon) is said to have observed that 'there had been more prosecutions for libel within the last two years than there had been for twenty years before' (Davis, '"Good for the Public Example"', 112).

[72] Daniel Isaac Eaton, *The Pernicious Effects of the Art of Printing upon Society, Exposed* (1794), 15.

[73] For an excellent overview, see Jon Mee, 'Treason, Seditious Libel, and Literature in the Romantic Period' (2016), *Oxford Handbooks Online*; also Mee's fuller account of these years in *Print, Publicity, and Popular Radicalism in the 1790s: The Laurel of Liberty* (Cambridge: Cambridge University Press, 2016), esp. 19–109 and, on Thelwall, 168–87.

[74] *The Trial of Daniel Isaac Eaton, for Publishing a Supposed Libel, Intituled Politics for the People; or, Hog's Wash* (1794; photofacsimile reprint in vol. 1 of Barrell and Mee (eds), *Trials for Treason and Sedition*), 31.

*Revolution and Romantic-Era Libel* 247

**Figure 4.4** James Gillray, *Tom Paine's Nightly Pest* (1792), hand-coloured etching on paper, by courtesy of the Lewis Walpole Library, Yale University. Anticipating Paine's December trial, Gillray imagines the absent Paine as haunted by nightmares of justice and retribution, including a gibbet, instruments of whipping, and the pillory.

envoy Gouverneur Morris may not have been joking when he called Paine 'cock sure of bringing about a revolution in Great Britain but I think it quite as likely that he will be promoted to the pillory'.[75] Book-trade professionals handling *Rights of Man* or related works became prime targets. Smaller fry than Paine himself could be

---

[75] W. A. Speck, *A Political Biography of Thomas Paine* (London: Pickering & Chatto, 2013), 123, quoting Gouverneur Morris to Robert Morris, 15 February 1792. As the long-postponed trial approached, the author of a verse epistle to Paine's counsel, the celebrity lawyer and future Lord Chancellor Thomas Erskine, gloated that 'Your Client's sure of *Pillory* Promotion' (*The World*, 28 November 1792).

brought to trial with less fear of popular protest or celebrity grandstanding, and in these years attention focused especially on publishers and distributors of *Rights of Man, Part the Second* and the *de facto* third part, Paine's *Letter Addressed to the Addressers of the Late Proclamation*. Eaton was arrested on at least six occasions (twice for selling Paine) and prosecuted on four, though it was not until 1796 that the authorities at last secured his libel conviction for publishing Charles Pigott's *Political Dictionary* and another work. After that, Eaton decamped to Federalist America, only to fall foul there of the Alien and Sedition Acts of 1798.[76]

A second reason for Eaton's prominence today is the unusual richness of the trial records surviving from his 'Chaunticlere' prosecution and similar cases of the period, a characteristic bound up with the awkwardly timed passage in 1792 of Fox's Libel Act: awkward, that is, for the administration, for whom it complicated the task of securing convictions, though Pitt himself supported this landmark measure. Fox's Act overturned a common-law tradition associated especially with Lord Chief Justice Mansfield a generation earlier (Romanticists, following Junius and other radicals of the period, sometimes speak of a 'Mansfield doctrine'), though in fact the tradition was much older. Its *locus classicus* was a seventeenth-century ruling by Mansfield's precursor Sir William Scroggs, made during the licensing lapse of the Exclusion Crisis. Scroggs limited the discretion of juries to mere questions of fact (whether the defendant had written, printed, or published a work) as opposed to the underlying interpretative question (did the work indeed constitute sedition)? And although his ruling was sometimes challenged in practice, judges strenuously reinforced it throughout the eighteenth century.[77] This is what Defoe meant when he protested in 1704 about seditious libel juries 'being accounted only Judges of Evidence, Judges of Fact, and not of the

---

[76] For these lesser-known episodes in Eaton's career, see Michael T. Davis, ' "I Can Bear Punishment": Daniel Isaac Eaton, Radical Culture and the Rule of Law, 1793–1812', in Louis A. Knafla (ed.), *Crime, Punishment and Reform in Europe* (Westport: Praeger, 2003), 89–106.

[77] For Mansfield in the 1770s and 1780s, see Mee, 'Treason, Seditious Libel'; for Scroggs and his Defoe-era successor Sir John Holt, see above, pp. 122–3.

Nature of it';[78] now, after Fox, the 'Nature' of a text was in jurors' hands too, or in the wording of the Act, 'the whole matter'.

The Act also restated the authority of judges to direct jury deliberations, which in practice could offset any liberalizing effect, but the consequence in either case was to open up libel proceedings to new uncertainties and disputes. Courtrooms became abstruse seminars in more or less fanciful hermeneutics; trials became great theatres of adversarial interpretation, in which, as Eaton's prosecutor reminded the jury when proposing his own reading of the fable, 'whether the meaning be fair or not, it is your province to determine'.[79] Trial reports grew in length to accommodate all this patient decoding, with the ebb and flow of competing interpretations; they were often then gleefully published by acquitted libellers, not least because prosecution speeches, though vigorously contested in court, then served the useful function of spelling out, in the unimpeachable form of official records, the seditious implications embedded in the offending text. In Dublin, Walter Cox's attorney Leonard MacNally was one of many defence lawyers to revel in these consequences. Where once 'the question of libel or no libel was to be decided on the Bench, and not in the Jury-box', juries were now decisively empowered by 'the immortal Fox'. Further, the alleged libel, 'which otherwise would have slept for ever on the bookseller's shelf, will be multiplied... a thousand times, by the reports of this day's trial, which every barrister, and every student, or other gentleman, has a right not only to take notes of, but to publish'.[80]

In the case of 'King Chaunticlere', Eaton even published, ahead of his 1794 trial, the indictment against him, illustrated with a headpiece featuring his resplendent gamecock (later a defiant personal symbol when Eaton renamed his shop 'The Cock and Swine'). The indictment reprinted the fable with parenthetical glosses alleging seditious meaning; *innuendo* was the technical legal term for this kind of gloss, meaning roughly the opposite of the word in its modern sense, not the

---

[78] *Political and Economic Writings of Daniel Defoe*, ed. W. R. Owens and P. N. Furbank, 8 vols (London: Pickering & Chatto, 2000), 8: 153.

[79] *Trial of Eaton*, 12.

[80] 'Second Trial of Walter Cox', *Irish Magazine* (April 1811), 151.

implicit hint or coded message in a text but the explicit decoding of an interpreter.[81] So where the fable talks of Chaunticlere as 'a haughty old tyrant' and 'restless despot', the indictment helpfully adds '[meaning our said LORD THE KING]'.[82] This was the traditional style of parenthetical innuendo that Sidney had disputed in his 1683 treason indictment, where, in quotations from his writings, 'Whatsoever is said of the expulsion of *Tarquin*, the insurrection against *Nero*, the slaughter of *Caligula* or *Domitian* ... is all applyed by *innuendo* unto the King'.[83] The difference is that, whereas Sidney could only make unavailing protests in his dying speech, Eaton was able to redirect the hostile commentary of his accusers into a highly effective form of republican satire. In his reprint of the indictment and, later, his edition of the trial, the innuendos not only spelled out and publicized the incendiary identification for anyone dim enough to have missed it. They also seemed to confirm as state-sanctioned fact a resemblance between doomed gamecock and threatened king that could only be implied elsewhere, enshrining it in a legal document in the public domain, immune to prosecution like nothing else. Clodhopping officialdom was again being outwitted, its measures neatly turned against itself.[84]

A third reason for Barrell's focus on the 'King Chaunticlere' trial is the rhetorical and forensic brilliance of the exegetes involved, prosecutor William Fielding versus defence counsel John Gurney, and the emergence from their duel of the so-called 'Gurney defence', an audacious but also unanswerable rebuttal of prosecution charges that was frequently deployed in later trials. It's Gurney who is the hero of Barrell's account, whereas Fielding—by a beautiful quirk of history, Henry Fielding's son—comes over as a reactionary

---

[81] In the words of Eaton's prosecutor, 'necessary innuendos, as they are called in law, that is, when a part is said to be offensive, it is necessary, in point of law, that that very expression should be so pointed out, and should be said to be so far criminal, as that it means so and so' (*Trial of Eaton*, 12); see also above, p. 121 n.98.

[82] *The King against Daniel Isaac Eaton, Copy of the Indictment* (1793), 3.

[83] *Colonel Sidney's Speech, Delivered to the Sheriff on the Scaffold December 7th 1683* (1683), 5.

[84] Barrell suggests that Eaton took his lead in this gesture from Paine's *Letter Addressed to the Addressers*, which mockingly quotes the indictment targeted against Part 2 of *Rights of Man*, including the cumbersome innuendos (*Imagining the King's Death*, 110).

sentimentalist in the mode of Burke's *Reflections*, wounded to tears by Thelwall's regicidal imaginings. Yet Fielding Jr was smart enough to anticipate not only Gurney's defence but also Barrell's own analysis of the counter-productive nature of prosecutions, which (to recall Johnson's words when discussing *Areopagitica*) served only to promote the prosecuted text. As he wearily acknowledged of the court proceedings, 'whenever a libel is prosecuted, it draws it into a second course of agitation, and... the very observations made upon the libel in a Court of Justice, become, as it were, a promulgation of the libel itself'.[85] Fielding also had melancholy premonitions of the indeterminacy-based defence that would be deployed against his prosecution, and worked as rigorously as possible to argue for semantic stability and closure. There was what he called an 'unavoidable meaning to be affixed' to Thelwall's fable (p. 23), and this unavoidable meaning centred on the regal language associated with Chauncticlere, and on the evident contemporaneity of the guillotine allusion. The fable articulated 'not only an indifference to the character of the King, but a perfect detestation of such character, and suggest[ed] that the means of getting rid of such a character must be by a stroke similar to that which has taken place in a neighbouring unhappy country' (p. 24).

A fair cop, one might think. But Fielding's logocentrism was no match for his adversary's deconstructive wiles. In one proto-postmodern moment, Gurney re-reads Fielding's dour assertions of inherent meaning as instead mere effusions of readerly desire. He acknowledged that in law 'the sole purpose of an innuendo, is to fix the true meaning', or again 'the natural, the plain, the obvious, the necessary sense'. But in this case the prosecution had transformed innuendo into 'an arbitrary thing at the pleasure of the drawer of an indictment'. Here was an exercise of free-floating readerliness in which Fielding, or the officials with whom he worked, had given 'unbridled and unbounded licence to an imagination the most wanton and the most heated' (p. 36). In so doing, they resembled the fanciful, extravagant author of the *Arabian Nights*. They were not discovering but making libels, and their attempt to extract sedition from the fable

[85] *Trial of Eaton*, 21.

resembled the efforts of Swift's projectors to extract sunbeams from cucumbers. That may have generated a courtroom laugh, but in fact it was a missed trick on Gurney's part, given Swift's sterner and more richly applicable satire, in the same third voyage of *Gulliver's Travels*, on tendentious interpretation in treason prosecutions.[86]

Then Gurney historicizes, comparing Pitt's censorship regime with the Stuart era, when 'there was then the same cry of sedition... when all the time the sedition was the sedition of the ministers against the people' (p, 48). The difference is that even Stuart censors stopped short of prosecuting authors of political theory (Gurney tiptoes quietly past Algernon Sidney at this point). 'I believe neither the records of the Star chamber', he asserts, 'nor the annals of Jeffreys will furnish an indictment in which a general reflection upon the nature and tendency of tyranny, or the desert of tyrants, has been deemed a libel upon the king of Great Britain' (p. 43).[87] Here was Gurney's most devastating point, which was not only that Chaunticlere stood innocently for kingship in the abstract or at most for absolutism in France, but also that if any sedition could be located at all, it lay not in Thelwall's original fable but instead in the prosecution gloss, with the shocking connection it proposed between despotic gamecock and praiseworthy king.

Gurney was less original in this poker-faced move than Barrell suggests, and a conspicuous precedent exists in Nicholas Fazakerley's *Craftsman* defence of 1731, which blamed prosecutors for assuming resemblances between text and world that neither he nor respectable jurors would ever have dreamed of. How could anyone imagine this tale about corruption to have anything to do with incorruptible Walpole, or with his upstanding colleagues? Fazakerley had asked.[88] Indeed, the defence gambit of locating culpability with the prosecutor

---

[86] See Jonathan Swift, *Gulliver's Travels*, ed. David Womersley (Cambridge: Cambridge University Press, 2012), 280–3 (III.vi), concerning 'a Set of Artists very dextrous in finding out the mysterious Meanings of Words, Syllables and Letters'. Swift has most immediately in mind the reliance of prosecutors on decoded correspondence following the Atterbury plot of 1721–2.

[87] On this point, made much of by Erskine when defending Paine's *Rights of Man* as comparable to Milton or Locke, see Mee, *Print, Publicity*, 85–6.

[88] 'I hope you have a better opinion of his majesty's present ministers of state', Fazakerley warned jurors with poker face, 'than to think that the expressions are

who unpacked a seditious meaning, not the author who first implied it, may already have been routine by Fazakerley's time. As one pro-government jurist testily wrote a year beforehand, 'it has often been urged in Defence of Libellers, that he who applies a Libel makes it'; this notion 'has given Birth to much Wit, but is quite wide of Law'.[89]

That said, Gurney took the argument he inherited significantly further, and to brilliant effect. The real libeller now was the indictment writer, for 'why is it to be supposed that this game cock, which is described as an haughty and sanguinary tyrant, nursed from his infancy in blood and slaughter, must necessarily mean the present mild and merciful king of Great Britain?' (p. 38). Only a seditious mind would connect two such dissimilar things; seditious meaning, insofar as it existed at all, was not a property of the text itself but an interpretative construct that exposed nothing so much as the reader's own dark dreams. It followed that jurors would become complicit in sedition by endorsing the gloss; their duty as grateful, loyal subjects was to reject the scandalous analogy proposed by prosecutors, acquit the defendant, and so vindicate the reputation of George III. All of which sounds audaciously tongue in cheek—but it was enough for a sympathetic jury to work with, and succeeded not only in Eaton's case but in several later trials where the same defence was rehearsed.[90] Gurney's defence also gave added barb to the trial report, which, reprinted by Eaton himself, with all the prosecution innuendos carefully preserved, could be made to look like officialdom's own libel on its sovereign. On this issue, *Hog's Wash* had already printed verses in which a litigious man sues Aesop for a fable about an ass, and in the process makes a fool of himself by explaining how closely and fully the cap fits. 'All Circumstances so agree | And all the Neighbours say 'tis Me', the man declares in a rather obvious instance of unforced error.[91] Here was a context in which prosecutors were damned if they proceeded, damned if they didn't.

---

applicable to them' (T. B. Howell, *A Complete Collection of State Trials*, 21 vols (1816), 17: 652); see also above, pp. 115–16.

[89] *State Law; or, The Doctrine of Libels, Discussed and Examined*, 2nd edn (1730?), 75.

[90] See Barrell, *Imagining the King's Death*, 114.

[91] 'What Makes a Libel?', *Politics for the People* 5 (26 October 1793), title page; see Mee, *Print, Publicity*, 41–2.

## Trumpets of sedition?

What, then, can we say were the consequences of all this for 'high' literature in the 1790s? For all our ongoing attention to the politics of Romanticism, and to the radical sympathies of its early protagonists, it becomes hard to demonstrate that deep or intricate protective encoding was now required of poets or novelists, or that a Romantic lyric could imperil its author as a 'poem on affairs of state' might have done a century earlier. Theatre continued to be policed in advance under the provisions of 1737, and playwrights still used strategies of indirection recalling topical-application tragedies of the 1730s; even well-connected Sheridan adopted the method in *Pizarro* (1799), a play inviting interpretation, as David Francis Taylor demonstrates, as 'a considered intervention in Britain's occupation of colonial Ireland'.[92] But in other genres, while there are certainly striking instances of internalized constraint—not regulatory or punitive censorship but the invisible, socially constituted check on expression that Pierre Bourdieu terms structural or constitutive censorship—there is at best limited evidence that major creative writers of the 1790s were subject to official attention of the kinds turned on Marvell under Charles II, Dryden under William III, or Pope, Swift, and Gay in the Walpole era.[93] We may find *Lyrical Ballads*, with its emphasis on folk community and demotic language, to be as radically democratic in implication as *Rights of Man*, but it was the latter work that preoccupied officials in the revolutionary decade, especially as mediated to artisan readers in affordable mass reprints. When the attorney general warned a minor Paineite author 'to publish your reply to Mr. Burke in an octavo form, so as to confine it probably to that class of readers who may

---

[92] David Francis Taylor, *Theatres of Opposition: Empire, Revolution, and Richard Brinsley Sheridan* (Oxford: Oxford University Press, 2012), 120.

[93] See Pierre Bourdieu's 1982 essay 'Censorship and the Imposition of Form', reprinted in his *Language and Symbolic Power*, ed. John B. Thompson, trans. Gino Raymond and Matthew Adamson (Cambridge, MA: Harvard University Press, 1991), 137–59. On the implications of this concept for Enlightenment France, see Sophia Rosenfeld, 'Writing the History of Censorship in the Age of Enlightenment', in Daniel Gordon (ed.), *Postmodernism and the Enlightenment: New Perspectives in Eighteenth-Century French Intellectual History* (London: Routledge, 2001), 117–45.

consider it coolly', and threatened prosecution if it appeared 'cheaply for dissemination among the populace', it was not textual content that mattered but material format and price.[94] Books addressed to the 'cool' class of readers, even when politically explicit, could go about their business with a kind of *permission tacite*. In this respect we might compare the panic-stricken 1790s with the nervous early years of the Restoration period, when Stuart authorities were too busy with rabble-rousing Fifth Monarchist pamphlets—'*Two-Hundred-Thousand* Seditious Copies...Printed, since the blessed Return of his Sacred Majesty', L'Estrange estimated—to devote much anxiety to *Paradise Lost*, which was licensed despite official awareness of its republican hints.[95] If seditious writing was defined above all by its socially disruptive potential, whatever threat might be posed by the literary was far outweighed by the threat of democratic polemic and mass reproduction.

Consider the 'Jacobin' or 'Godwinian' novel and its chief exponents. Novelists and their publishers were certainly vigilant throughout the decade, and we know that in the obscure though fascinating case of George Cumberland's *The Captive of the Castle of Sennaar, An African Tale* (1798), a novel was withdrawn from sale when a senior lawyer among the author's friends found a digression about tyranny and kleptocracy 'dangerous, under Mr Pitts maladministration, to publish'. The lawyer was former Lord Advocate Henry Erskine (brother of Thomas, the future Lord Chancellor who had defended Paine)—but Erskine was no more expert in such matters than the veteran seditious libeller John Horne Tooke, another friend of Cumberland, who saw no obstacle to immediate publication. No trouble ensued when the novel finally appeared, with the offending passage

---

[94] St Clair, *Reading Nation*, 309, quoting Sir John Scott (later Lord Eldon) to Thomas Cooper on his *Reply to Mr. Burke's Invective* (1792). Cooper later wrote that he had 'no right to complain' about this warning and observed in the ministry's defence that 'the republican sentiments of Dr. Price, Dr. Priestley, and Mr. Godwin were allowed without molestation'; the *Rights of Man* prosecutions were specifically for cheap editions, and 'a defensive measure on the part of the government, certainly excusable, probably justifiable' (*The Institutes of Justinian* (Philadelphia, 1812), 630).

[95] Roger L'Estrange, *Truth and Loyalty Vindicated* (1662), sig. A2ᵛ; on *Paradise Lost*, see above, p. 30.

intact, in 1810, at the height of the Perceval crackdown.[96] This was at most a case of temporary self-censorship by a dilettante author, and though it suggests a climate of anxiety, it provides no evidence at all of official scrutiny of fiction. Radical artisan societies, not fashionable circulating libraries, were the real worry.

Better-known novelists had a keen sense of themselves as political martyrs or potential martyrs, but again with limited external evidence to back up their own perceptions, at least as regards their fiction. In *Anna St Ives* (1792), a work described by Gary Kelly as 'the most completely Jacobinical' novel of the period, Thomas Holcroft implemented his sense of the genre's potential as a vehicle for radical, even revolutionary, social analysis and opinion.[97] But what landed Holcroft in the dock for treason in 1794 was not this massive, earnest, moralizing text (which weighed in, like Richardson's *Clarissa*, at seven volumes) but his role in bringing together the most formidable radical associations of the era, the London Corresponding Society and the Society for Constitutional Information, for a proposed convention that sounded to officials alarmingly like a revolutionary *Assemblée nationale*.

William Godwin argued the cause of Holcroft and his fellow defendants in his *Cursory Strictures on the Charge Delivered by Lord Chief Justice Eyre* (1794), a pamphlet that brilliantly exposed the incoherence and absurdity of treason as a relevant charge. But Godwin's great novel of the same year, *Caleb Williams*, about the trickle-down effects in private life of political despotism, turned out to be of less interest to the Home Office than he liked to think. In its primary title (*Things as They Are*), the novel announced a radically disenchanted social analysis, while the plot, by focusing on surveillance, pursuit, and incarceration, pervasively implies a public context of repression. Even so, there is a whiff of showboating about Godwin's second-edition headnote on the climate prevailing at the time of first publication, when 'Terror was the order of the day; and it was feared that even the humble novelist

---

[96] George Cumberland, *The Captive of the Castle of Sennaar, An African Tale*, ed. G. E. Bentley (Montreal: McGill-Queen's University Press, 1991), pp. xliii–xlviii; the novel sold 226 copies and garnered one review.

[97] Gary Kelly, *The English Jacobin Novel, 1780–1805* (Oxford: Clarendon Press, 1976), 119.

might be shown to be constructively a traitor'.[98] Scholars often quote these words today, though without remembering E. P. Thompson's wise warning, long ago, about 'the characteristic vice of the English Jacobins—self-dramatization'.[99] Feared by whom, it seems fair to ask, and on what grounds? At the very least, Godwin was looking somewhat aside from where the priorities of hard-pressed censors really lay. A year earlier, the ministry had been untroubled by his *Enquiry Concerning Political Justice* as not worth prosecuting at a time when so much cheap print, from *Rights of Man* to *Politics for the People*, cried out for official attention. For Pitt, the *Enquiry* was too expensive for artisans to purchase ('a three guinea book could never do much harm among those who had not three shillings to spare'), and also too arduous to read: the work of a verbose, pointy-headed theoretician.[100] There's no evidence that *Caleb Williams* was even on his radar.

Nor for that matter should Godwin's paratextual talk of 'Terror' (a term much favoured by 1790s activists who saw Pitt as 'the English Robespierre') be accepted without question. The repression is undeniable, and startling by modern standards. But it's easy to point to more intense levels of censorship, both formal and informal, during earlier political crises, though we never allege a Townshend reign of terror in 1715–16, or a Pelham reign of terror in 1745–6, periods of Jacobite insurrection that saw larger numbers of sedition prosecutions, including specifically book-trade prosecutions, than across the entire 1790s.[101] As one historian robustly writes of the much-touted analogy

---

[98] William Godwin, *Caleb Williams*, ed. Pamela Clemit (Oxford: Oxford University Press, 2009), 312 (headnote dated 29 October 1795).

[99] E. P. Thompson, *The Making of the English Working Class*, revised edn (Harmondsworth: Penguin, 1968), 173.

[100] Peter H. Marshall, *William Godwin* (New Haven: Yale University Press, 1984), 122, quoting Godwin's own information about cabinet discussion of the *Enquiry* in May 1793.

[101] Clive Emsley, 'Repression, "Terror" and the Rule of Law in England During the Decade of the French Revolution', *English Historical Review* 100 (1985), 801–25 (822); Emsley draws here on research by Nicholas Rogers and Paul Monod on the Jacobite scares. See also Steve Poole, 'Pitt's Terror Reconsidered: Jacobinism and the Law in Two South-Western Counties, 1791–1803', *Southern History* 17 (1995), 65–87, which argues that Emsley's count misses much informal harassment by provincial magistrates.

with France, 'given the contrast between what happened to opponents of the Montagnard Republic and what happened to English radicals and critics of Pitt, the parallel is ludicrous'.[102] If the case is to be made for any novel of the 1790s as seriously constrained by anxiety about prosecution, it would probably centre on *Nature and Art* (1796), which Elizabeth Inchbald kept in manuscript for two years after a friend at court, the queen's attorney general George Hardinge, warned her against satirizing George III in the character of Lord Rinforth. In the published version (where Rinforth becomes Lord Bendham), Inchbald softened the effect, having already joked to Godwin about revising the text with 'Newgate before my Eyes'. Yet the novel remains politically explicit in other respects, with no adverse consequences for author or publisher.[103]

As for poetry, Kenneth R. Johnston has argued that what he calls Pitt's 'Reign of Alarm' (a tactical retreat from 'Reign of Terror') created in the literary world a lost generation of 'persons who were *not* tried for treason or sedition in 1790s Britain', but who nevertheless were penalized, damaged, or cowed in other ways. We should extend this category to include poets such as Wordsworth and Coleridge, Johnston proposes, creatively stifled by an atmosphere he likens to McCarthyism and the Red Scare, and we should recognize as a consequence 'the loss of a "republican voice"' in British culture that might otherwise have endured after Paine.[104] It's certainly true that in the famous 'Spy Nozy' affair of 1797, Wordsworth and Coleridge were subject to the attentions of a government agent sent from London to Somerset to monitor their activities.[105] But all the evidence is that the spy in question (an intellectually underpowered official named James Walsh) was there because locals mistook the

---

[102] Emsley, 'Repression, "Terror" and the Rule of Law', 802. For allegations against Pitt as 'the English Robespierre', and his 'system of TERROR... infinitely more pernicious in its tendency than France ever knew', see Emsley, 'Aspect of Pitt's "Terror"', 155.

[103] See Amy Garnai, *Revolutionary Imaginings in the 1790s: Charlotte Smith, Mary Robinson, Elizabeth Inchbald* (Basingstoke: Palgrave Macmillan, 2009), 122–46 (esp. 138, quoting Inchbald's undated letter to Godwin).

[104] Johnston, *Unusual Suspects*, pp. xv, xvii.

[105] 'Spy Nozy' is from Coleridge's joke in *Biographia Literaria* about the spy overhearing, and misunderstanding, a conversation about Spinoza.

Wordsworth circle for French scouts prospecting for an invasion site, not because he wanted to overhear *The Borderers* being read aloud. When Walsh discovered that this was 'no French affair, but a mischiefous gang of disaffected Englishmen',[106] the Home Office lost interest. It's at best ambitious to attribute to the episode, and the pressures it typifies, the large consequences for literary history that Johnston alleges, amidst heavy reliance on the argument from absence. These consequences include the forestalling of an enduringly radical 'literary triumvirate' that might otherwise have formed among Wordsworth, Coleridge, and Thelwall, who were instead 'driven apart by collateral damage from the reign of Alarm'. Then there is the forestalling, again, of a resolutely political verse tradition that might have been founded by Wordsworth's poem on his own life, non-publication of which in 1805 Johnston implausibly attributes to a passage in Book 10 reflecting on Pitt—so that *The Prelude* and with it *The Recluse*, 'these delayed and incomplete masterworks', also become 'casualties of Pitt's Reign of Alarm'.[107]

In fact, before this sequence of *The Prelude* was written, Coleridge had been willing and able to publish a far more violent attack on Pitt in his war eclogue 'Fire, Famine, and Slaughter', which plays relentlessly on eighteenth-century conventions of concealment—'Four letters form his name'—to indicate a supervising evil in the poem that could only be deciphered one way. Coleridge's poem foretells, and implicitly recommends, sanguinary vengeance against Pitt ('They shall seize him and his brood— | They shall tear him limb from limb!'), and speaks volumes about what could now be published without eliciting prosecution or even, so far as can be determined, any official interest at all.[108] In sentiment, 'Fire, Famine, and Slaughter' suggests

---

[106] Johnston, *Unusual Suspects*, 233, quoting Walsh's report in TNA, HO 42/41; for a more measured account, see Nicholas Roe, *Wordsworth and Coleridge: The Radical Years* (Oxford: Clarendon Press, 1988), 234–62.

[107] Johnston, *Unusual Suspects*, 240, 251.

[108] *The Complete Poetical Works of Samuel Taylor Coleridge*, ed. E. H. Coleridge, 2 vols (Oxford: Clarendon Press, 1912), 1: 237–40 (lines 71–2). The poem was published pseudonymously in the *Morning Post* for 8 January 1798; 'Four letters form his name' is the newspaper reading, revised as 'Letters four do form his name' when (remarkably) the now Tory Coleridge included the poem 'with an Apologetic Preface' in his 1828 edition of *Sibylline Leaves*.

a degree of extremism beyond that of many prosecuted radicals of the 1790s. It lends credence to the scandalized remark, decades later, of no less an authority than Thelwall himself that Coleridge was 'a down right zealous leveller & indeed in one of the worst senses of the word he was a Jacobin, a man of blood'.[109] Yet when Coleridge spoke, even before publishing 'Fire, Famine, and Slaughter', of having 'snapped my squeaking baby-trumpet of sedition',[110] his point was not just that the trumpet was a juvenile toy, but also that it was somehow mouse-like: a thin, slight, high-pitched thing that no one could really hear. Or, if people could hear it, they were listening for poetic effect, not political instruction. For Barrell, it's symptomatic of a growing separation between imaginative literature and practical politics that in 1803 the staunchly Tory Scott could recite 'Fire, Famine, and Slaughter' from memory with admiration at a dinner party: 'Opposite in politics, Scott and the Coleridge of 1798 are at one in the belief that the products of the imagination transcend the most violent political differences.'[111]

More nuanced versions exist of Johnston's basic case about the relationship between government repression and Romantic verse, notably John Bugg's fine study of what he calls a 'poetics of gagging': a mode typified by 'an array of stutters, elisions, truncated utterances, and paranoid whispers', exemplified after the 1795 Gagging Acts in numerous literary 'performances of stifled expression' that range from Coleridge's 'This Lime-Tree Bower My Prison' to Wollstonecraft's *The Wrongs of Woman*.[112] Yet the features Bugg identifies are easier to explain as creative response to, or imaginative displacement of, the atmosphere of surveillance and repression he describes, than as functional political encoding driven by immediate threats of regulatory or punitive censorship of the kinds experienced by dissident poets under

[109] Marginalia in Thelwall's copy of *Biographia Literaria*, quoted by Roe, *Wordsworth and Coleridge*, 5.

[110] *Collected Letters of Samuel Taylor Coleridge*, ed. Earl Leslie Griggs, 6 vols (Oxford: Clarendon Press, 1956–71), 1: 240; having snapped the trumpet, he 'hung up its fragments in the chamber of Penitences' (to Charles Lloyd, Senior, 15 October 1796).

[111] Barrell, *Imagining the King's Death*, 651.

[112] John Bugg, *Five Long Winters: The Trials of British Romanticism* (Stanford: Stanford University Press, 2014), 6, 20.

Charles II, William III, or Walpole. Coleridge was not encoding an oppositional argument with his trope of the bower as a prison, even though, as Bugg eloquently shows, there's a looming political valence to the trope, coloured as it is by public context as well as the more usually cited biographical circumstances and themes of imaginative transcendence. Something similar applies, a generation later, to the much-debated case of Keats's 'To Autumn', which, as Nicholas Roe and others have argued, brings conspiracy fears, enclosure protests, and the recent Peterloo massacre within its penumbra of connotation.[113] But the poem does so more as an act of imaginative amplification than as strategic indirection of verse that was driven by politics above all, or otherwise at risk of Home Office action. 'To Autumn' has elements in common with the functional ambiguity of earlier writing, though it was ambiguity of a kind that had come to outlive the practical constraints that first inspired it. Greater political frankness was now well within the scope and expressive licence of poets, but that was not the creative priority of the poems in question. These were not texts calibrating their position on the brink of seditious discourse, and there was no risk of their springing up armed men.

## Censorship, copyright, and *Wat Tyler*

Yet there remains the intriguing case of Robert Southey, Coleridge's partner in utopian Pantisocracy in his revolutionary early years, who rose, like Dryden before him, to become a Tory poet laureate with skeletons in the cupboard. If only for this reason, Southey nicely completes an arc that looks back to the seventeenth century with *Heroic Stanzas*, the republican sin of Dryden's youth that haunted his royalist maturity. In their roles as successively poachers and gamekeepers—or, if one accepts Johnson's jaundiced view of view of the laureateship, as exponents of 'servile' or 'venal' verse (see above, pp. 210–12)—both poets bear witness to a print culture suffused by censorship, albeit with differences of form and intensity. Yet there are also more specific reasons that make Southey a key test case for

---

[113] Nicholas Roe, *John Keats and the Culture of Dissent* (Oxford: Oxford University Press, 1998), 153–65.

seditious libel doctrine in the Romantic period, and for its viability, above all, as a mechanism for controlling the literary imagination. First, there's the unusual self-consciousness about literature and censorship that characterizes Southey's writing throughout his career. Even before his laureateship began in 1813, he voiced some of the period's most uncompromising statements about freedom of expression, and in a letter written days after the Perceval assassination felt certain 'that nothing but an immediate suspension of the liberty of debate & the liberty of the press can preserve us'. Personally, he would 'have every Jacobine Journalist confined, so that it should not be possible for them to continue their treasonable vocation'.[114] Yet Southey's early opinions about this treasonable vocation were purely celebratory, and during the heyday of *Rights of Man* he practised it with gusto himself. In a whimsical ballad composed in 1792, he imagines authorship as quite literally the essence of Paineite sedition, leading not to the poet's traditional laurel crown but instead to the libeller's wooden collar: 'Lo the Author—sedition distils from his pen | "Your monarchs pull down & set up rights of men" | No wreath of bright bay here his temples surrounds | But the pillory encircles who goes beyond bounds.'[115]

The historical irony of the stanza is compelling. Yet this is not the only place in which the future laureate imagines his poetic vocation as courting persecution, not preferment. Later in 1792 we find Southey reading and imitating Juvenal, fully aware of Johnson's *London* as a precedent for topical deployment of Juvenal's third satire, but selecting a different source, the eighth, presumably for its critique of social hierarchy. He's no less aware of the new wave of libel prosecutions now being targeted at figures like the Paineite publisher James Ridgway, which he equates (albeit with more vehemence than accuracy) with Stuart, even Tudor, censorship regimes. Since Southey has 'no wish to fall under the inquisitorial jurisdiction of our new Star chamber—to lose my hand nose & ears like Lilburne or the Englishman whom Elizabeth punishd for writing against her intended

---

[114] *The Collected Letters of Robert Southey*, ed. Tim Fulford, Ian Packer, and Lynda Pratt, *Romantic Circles* (2009–), <https://dev.rc.umd.edu/editions/southey_letters> (Letter 2096, to John Rickman, 18 May 1812).

[115] *Collected Letters of Southey*, Letter 21 (to Thomas Phillipps Lamb, 5 August 1792).

marriage with Anjou—or to run away like Ridgeway—my poor imitation must lie in my desk'.[116] What happened to this imitation next is unknown, and no further trace of it now survives, with one possible exception. A distich by Southey found its way into an imitation of the same satire undertaken by Wordsworth and his friend Francis Wrangham in 1795, and Wordsworth apparently thought it the best in the poem. By this stage in the history of punitive censorship, the lines at issue are hardly likely to have cost anyone their hands or ears. But they turn Juvenal's focus on the mismatch between rank and virtue into a question about the inherent majesty of the king, and then about the nobility of dukes, that steps beyond the usual limits of anti-court satire: 'Heavens! who sees majesty in George's face | Or looks at Norfolk and can dream of Grace?'[117]

Then there is Southey's explicit interest in creating a merger of low and high by publishing his own very literary verse in *Politics for the People*, the incendiary popular journal of Daniel Isaac Eaton: a crucial move, at least in the conception, at a time when it was not so much the message as the medium—and with it, crucially, the social class of readers—that generated official retribution. Decades later, Southey flatly denied ever meeting Eaton, and called it 'not possible that I should have forgotten so notorious a person'.[118] But in 1794 he talked of wanting to publish his poem about Muir and the transported Scots martyrs in Eaton's paper ('this high season ingredient goes to the Salmagundi for swine'). He hoped that other accomplished poets would do likewise, 'so that we may raise the reputation of the HogWash'.[119] This declaration may have been no more than private epistolary bravado, and in the end 'To the Exiled Patriots' appeared

---

[116] *Collected Letters of Southey*, Letter 34 (to Grosvenor Charles Bedford, 6 December 1792). Lilburne escaped mutilation in the pillory, and no author's hand had been severed since the notorious case of Stubbe in 1579. For Ridgway, see Ralph A. Manogue, 'The Plight of James Ridgway, London Bookseller and Publisher, and the Newgate Radicals, 1792–1797', *Wordsworth Circle*, 27 (1996), 158–66.

[117] See Stuart Gillespie's discussion, quoting this couplet, in his *English Translation and Classical Reception: Towards a New Literary History* (Chichester: Wiley-Blackwell, 2011), 127.

[118] *Collected Letters of Southey*, Letter 2951 (to Charles Watkin Williams Wynn, 22 March 1817).

[119] *Collected Letters of Southey*, Letter 85 (to Robert Lovell, 5–6 April 1794).

in the less controversial, and certainly less conspicuous, context of Coleridge's provincially published *A Moral and Political Lecture* (1795). But it has been suggested that two other poems published by Eaton in *Politics for the People* under the initials 'W.T.', which the youthful Southey 'sometimes used to identify himself as a descendant of Wat Tyler', may have been Southey's work.[120] If so, he was removing himself from the protected arena of polite letters and entering an avowedly democratic, mass-oriented vehicle that by now was a known target for prosecution.

Wat Tyler, leader of the 1381 Peasants' Revolt under Richard II, was of course the subject of Southey's most enduringly notorious work, a three-act tragedy composed during or immediately after the 1794 treason trials, and with obvious relevance to them, though it then remained in manuscript for many years. When the text was eventually published without authority in 1817 (as *Wat Tyler: A Dramatic Poem*), one protagonist in this murky imbroglio even claimed that it was to Eaton that Southey had originally offered his manuscript, in the hope that 'if not published as a separate pamphlet, it might be published in a periodical work then publishing weekly by the aforesaid Daniel Isaac Eaton'—which again can only mean *Politics for the People*.[121] This claim, though made under oath, may not have been true. But we know beyond question that, however literary the blank verse of *Wat Tyler*, the young Southey did not have a high-end publisher in view. In January 1795, he visited Newgate to negotiate the sale with Ridgway and another bookseller named Henry Symonds, also then imprisoned for seditious libel. At first the only obstacle to publication appeared to be the shortness of the manuscript, so that, Southey told a correspondent, 'I am to send them *more sedition* to make a 2 Shilling pamphlet'.[122] Then, when no such pamphlet appeared, Southey concluded (he later averred) 'that upon farther reflection they thought the thing unfit for publication, & my own after thought concluded so

---

[120] Michael T. Davis, "'That Odious Class of Men Called Democrats": Daniel Isaac Eaton and the Romantics, 1794–1795', *History*, 84 (1999), 74–92 (83).

[121] 'Wintherbotham Affidavit', in Robert Southey, *Later Poetical Works, 1811–1838*, ed. Tim Fulford, Lynda Pratt et al., 4 vols (London: Pickering & Chatto, 2012), 3: 514.

[122] *Collected Letters of Southey*, Letter 123 (to Edith Fricker, *c.*12 January 1795).

actively in this judgment, that I made no application to know why the printing was delayed, nor ever inquired for the manuscript, thinking in fact no more of it than of a college or school exercise'.[123]

Rich ironies surround the belated publication of *Wat Tyler* in 1817, an event of enduring significance in the history of copyright as well as censorship: phenomena closely connected since the origins of the Stationers' Company in the sixteenth century, but intertwining in Southey's case with special, and delicious, complexity.[124] Piracy of the drama to some extent replayed Dryden's experience in the 1680s, when the Cromwell elegy was maliciously republished during his Stuart laureateship, or again Johnson's during his heyday as a conservative moralist in 1775, when the seditious 'Norfolk Marble' pamphlet embarrassingly reappeared in print (see above, pp. 51–4 and 208).[125] Southey had undertaken the same kind of political journey between writing his drama in 1794 and seeing it published in 1817. But if he turned—to recall Johnson's sly apology for Dryden's shift of allegiance from Cromwell to Charles—he turned *without* the nation, which in both years was in, or was perceived by the authorities to be in, an alarming state of revolutionary ferment. Southey was attacked for his apostasy by radicals and reformists alike, most memorably William Hazlitt, who skilfully lampooned him as consistent in the fact, if not the content, of his political extremism: an 'Ultra-jacobin' who was now an 'Ultra-royalist'; a 'frantic demagogue' who was now a 'servile court-tool'; a writer who once 'did not stop short of general anarchy' but now 'goes the whole length of despotism'. As Hazlitt gleefully summed up (with a glance at Milton's rebel angels in Book II of *Paradise Lost*), there was 'no other person in whom "fierce extremes" meet with such mutual self-complacency'.[126]

---

[123] *Collected Letters of Southey*, Letter 2972 (to William Peachy, 9 April 1817).

[124] See St Clair's landmark account of the episode and its consequences in *Reading Nation*, 316–38. See also below, n. 152.

[125] Coleridge was a more recent victim of the same phenomenon, when 'Fire, Famine, and Slaughter' was republished after 1813 in several newspapers, including, in 1822, the *Black Dwarf* (Casie LeGette, *Remaking Romanticism: The Radical Politics of the Excerpt* (Basingstoke: Palgrave Macmillan, 2017), 85–7).

[126] *Selected Writings of William Hazlitt*, ed. Duncan Wu, 9 vols (London: Pickering & Chatto, 1998), 4: 158, 157 (from the *Examiner*, 9 March 1817).

We may look to caricature of the period for visual correlatives to Hazlitt's insight. In James Gillray's graphic satire *New Morality*, published with the *Anti-Jacobin Review and Magazine* for August 1798, Southey appears as an ass-eared incendiary who helps Coleridge disgorge from the Cornucopia of Ignorance a flood of radical publications including works by Mary Wollstonecraft and Horne Tooke (Figure 4.5). In a beautifully ludicrous touch, their own contributions to the cause, intellectually abstruse and formally self-regarding, are labelled 'Southeys Saphics' and 'Colridge Dactylics'.[127] Two decades later, in the anonymous print *A Poet Mounted on the Court-Pegasus* (1817), it's no longer sedition that gushes from the spigot but 'Adulation', 'Sycophancy', 'Apostacy'. Southey has become a dandified, sybaritic laureate who toasts the king with one hand and with the other discards *Wat Tyler*, unaware that the devil, or perhaps a printer's devil, lurks behind to snatch the manuscript away (Figure 4.6).

The ironies run still further. There's no record of Dryden or Johnson ever responding to the piracies of *Heroic Stanzas* and *Marmor Norfolciense*, and in both cases these works were already, however obscurely, in the public domain. Southey by contrast was vocal in protest, as the prominence of the *Wat Tyler* piracy required him to be. On first hearing news of it, he denounced his own play as 'a piece of sedition...peppered like a Turkeys gizzard', and was joined in this by a mischievous opposition MP, William Smith, who called in parliament for the author, poet laureate or no, to be charged with sedition.[128] *Wat Tyler*, insisted Smith, was 'the most seditious book that was ever written; its author did not stop short of exhorting to general anarchy'; why had the authorities not sought out this author for arrest and prosecution?[129] Southey then developed a more measured argument involving a distinction between the work inherently, as historical drama, and the work as a publishing event in the present moment. *Wat Tyler* was not in itself 'a

[127] On these details and their implications, see Nicholas Roe, *The Politics of Nature: William Wordsworth and Some Contemporaries*, 2nd edn (Basingstoke: Palgrave Macmillan, 2002), 73–8.

[128] *Collected Letters of Southey*, Letter 2917 (to John Rickman, *c*.14 February 1817).

[129] Lionel Madden (ed.), *Robert Southey: The Critical Heritage* (London: RKP, 1972), 237, quoting *Hansard*, 14 March 1817.

**Figure 4.5** James Gillray, detail from *New Morality* (1798), hand-coloured etching on paper, by courtesy of Princeton University Library. Gillray's design ridicules English supporters of the French Revolution, among them Southey and Coleridge, shown feeding asinine print from the Cornucopia of Ignorance.

seditious performance; for it places in the mouths of the personages who are introduced nothing more than a correct statement of their real principles'. These were just characters talking among themselves while the dramatist was nowhere to be seen, indifferent, paring his fingernails. On the other hand, it was also 'a mischievous publication' as things now stood at the febrile political juncture of

**Figure 4.6** Charles Williams, *A Poet Mounted on the Court-Pegasus* (1817), hand-coloured etching on paper, by permission of the Library of Congress. Southey wears a laurel wreath and toasts the king from his laureate's butt of sack, surrounded by his encomia to royalty; the lurking demon holds a wreath of nettles and a copy of *Wat Tyler*.

1817, 'the errors which it contains being especially dangerous at this time'.[130] On the other side of the argument from Southey's attempt to separate author and text was Hazlitt's insistence on the continuity and pervasiveness of expressive selfhood, made with poker-faced reference to Wordsworth's doctrine that 'The Child is Father of the Man'.[131] In this light, the Tory laureate who now deplored *Wat Tyler* could not be dissevered from the revolutionary firebrand who once composed it.

There was more. When Southey shifted ground and attempted to have *Wat Tyler* suppressed not for seditious libel but for infringement of literary property, Lord Chancellor Eldon refused his injunction with reference to a common-law tradition, grounded in a case involving Joseph Priestley in 1791, that 'there can be no property in what is publicly injurious'.[132] In other words, seditious libel fell outside copyright protection as derived from the 1710 Statute of Anne. The result was that a work recommended for suppression by its own author, and a work the senior lawyer in government thought publicly injurious, was projected into bestseller status by a flood of uncontrolled reprints, some costing as little as twopence. The first piracy was withdrawn by its publisher William Sherwood in deference to Eldon's opinion, which must have given Southey a moment's hope. But the Sherwood edition was then itself pirated in a race to the bottom by rival low-cost publishers, including alarmingly named ventures like, some years later, 'Lee's Library for Labourers'; new piracies continued to appear for a further twenty years. Also in on the act was William Hone, who issued an early reprint of *Wat Tyler* with a preface highlighting other suspect items in Southey's back catalogue (an encomium to the seventeenth-century regicide Henry Marten, for example), with

---

[130] Robert Southey, *A Letter to William Smith, Esq. M.P.* (1817), 6.

[131] See *Selected Writings of Hazlitt*, 4: 157: 'According to this theory of personal continuity, the author of the Dramatic Poem, to be here noticed, is the father of Parliamentary Reform' (the title of an illiberal recent article by Southey). Hazlitt repeats his point in *The Spirit of the Age*, where Southey 'is ever in extremes, and ever in the wrong!' (*Selected Writings of Hazlitt*, 7: 215). For Hazlitt's mischievous allusion to Wordsworth's 'The Rainbow', see Kim Wheatley, *Romantic Feuds: Transcending the 'Age of Personality'* (Farnham: Ashgate, 2013), 26–30.

[132] See the editors' introduction to *Wat Tyler* in Robert Southey, *Later Poetical Works*, esp. 3: 443.

sideswipes along the way at Southey's fellow-travelling 'Jacobin poets' of the 1790s, Coleridge and Wordsworth.[133] The result was, St Clair calculates, that *Wat Tyler* single-handedly outsold, for years afterwards, the entire loyalist, in-copyright oeuvre of the mature Southey.[134]

In recent scholarship, Eldon has been applauded for the rigour of his principles in making such an obviously counter-productive legal judgment, or (for those who credit him with less foresight) derided for unwittingly unleashing a torrent of bargain-basement sedition.[135] This was the objection at the time of Wordsworth, who followed the same political trajectory as Southey and was now a self-confessed 'Alarmist' about revolution, when he wrote of 'a general outcry among sensible people...against the remissness of Government in permitting the free circulation of injurious writings'.[136] Nor was it just a matter of permitting, since Eldon's ruling was now actively generating the piracy of unprotected sedition. What has not been much considered is the possibility that Eldon made his ruling more knowingly, and as a matter of long-term strategy. It's certainly true that in the history of censorship one occasionally has an exhilarating sense that judges could practise the law with a degree of integrity, or even uphold it in the face of adverse consequences for government interests. But one should not get carried away with this rosy vision, and Eldon was nothing if not the hard-nosed type, with an impressive record, reaching back to the 1790s, in the arts of political repression. Over and above the sheer pleasure to be had in making a puffed-up laureate squirm for his youthful posturing, Eldon may have been playing a

---

[133] 'Preface to Hone's Edition of Robert Southey's *Wat Tyler*', ed. Kyle Grimes, *The William Hone BioText*, <http://honearchive.org/etexts/wat-tyler/wat-tyler-preface-dw.html>; Marsh reports that this edition sold perhaps 60,000 copies (*Word Crimes*, 100). For 'Lee's Library for Labourers' and other cheap editions, see the editors' introduction to *Wat Tyler* in Southey, *Later Poetical Works*, 3: 448–9.

[134] St Clair, *Reading Nation*, 317–18.

[135] Scholars have tended to follow the lead of Paul M. Zall, who sees Eldon as torn between reactionary instinct and rigorous principle when making a decision with 'ramifications which were to prove embarrassing to the Chancellor, but he held to it doggedly' ('Lord Eldon's Censorship', *PMLA*, 68 (1953), 436–43 ([438]).

[136] *The Letters of William and Dorothy Wordsworth, Volume 3: The Middle Years, Part 2, 1812–1820*, ed. Ernest de Selincourt, revised Mary Moorman and A. G. Hill, 2nd edn (Oxford: Clarendon Press, 1970), 375 (to Daniel Stuart, 7 April 1817).

longer game with his insistence on withholding copyright protection from *Wat Tyler*, which in effect ensured that no profit, indeed no livelihood, could henceforward be made by writing or publishing seditious works. A quarter of a century earlier, when warning Thomas Cooper to answer Burke's *Reflections* in octavo format, Eldon had sought to control radical print by making it too expensive to be worth reading. Now he was making it too cheap to be worth writing.

Authors and publishers might still, of course, be motivated by ideology or selfless principle in the books they chose to produce. But the *Wat Tyler* precedent meant that the trade of libelling—seditious writing and publishing as a business strategy—was at an end. Over the next few years, a probably co-ordinated series of rulings by Eldon and other judges, denying publishers' injunctions against piracies of radical or heterodox books, confirmed a strange new effect of 'seditious commons': an absence of copyright protection that came to influence both creative and commercial decisions and behaviour. St Clair has documented the consequences for poetry by Byron and Shelley after 1817, as *Don Juan*, *Cain*, and *Queen Mab* joined the canon of copyright-free literary works from which authors and official publishers could make little or nothing, while piracies came to circulate in large numbers among the urban and rural poor. The ubiquity of these heterodox poems is a classic case, in St Clair's account, in which 'the law had brought about the very effect it was designed to prevent' by ensuring the spread of transgressive literature.[137] Yet even Byron was dismayed and deterred by losing control over, and revenues from, his own literary property, and after his death in 1824, two years after Shelley's, no new generation of poetic rebels arose to fill their shoes. Instead, the supply of 'injurious' literature available to be pirated dried up. Eldon's *Wat Tyler* ruling may have required a degree of patience for its consequences to be seen, but Eldon himself lived until 1838, by which time it was clearly working its supply-side magic. As at least one contemporary understood, the ruling had established a powerful, albeit disguised, new form of censorship—censorship without censors—that could work to police ideological conformity within authors' own minds: 'Men who have much at stake will avoid all

---

[137] St Clair, *Reading Nation*, 325, and see 317–38 *passim*.

questionable positions, and endeavour to write, not what they believe to be true, but what will fall in with the prejudices of those who may have to judge them: and English literature will be subject to an indirect censorship of the press.'[138]

## The most seditious book that was ever written

One further question remains to be asked amidst all this attentiveness to the legal consequences of the *Wat Tyler* case and to the controversy that followed publication in 1817, with the rhetorical virtuosity of the leading antagonists: Southey and Coleridge on one side; Hazlitt and Smith on the other. What exactly was at stake in the text itself? What made it, in Smith's gleeful hyperbole, 'the most seditious book that was ever written'? Partly we might attribute the furore to a factor already mentioned: the fun to be had from taunting a preening, noisily reactionary poet laureate, and alongside it the chance to re-examine, and question again, his violent swing from (loosely speaking) left to right. But we should not neglect the particular, distinctive content of Southey's drama, and the specific anxieties it induced amidst the social unrest of 1817, as seeming to revive, and catapult into the present, not just 1790s radicalism in general, but the most extreme revolutionary positions of the era. What made *Wat Tyler* so unusually alarming at the time of publication—and what had made it too hot to handle in the first place to its prospective publishers, Ridgway and Symonds? These were men, after all, who had been willing enough to publish *Rights of Man*, Pigott's *Treachery No Crime*, and Cobbett's *The Soldier's Friend*, alongside several other provocative works, courting prosecution on each occasion.[139]

Part of the answer is suggested by the renewed interest in topical application tragedy that took hold in the 1790s: the genre, more even than Fielding's anti-ministerial farces, that had precipitated stage

---

[138] Nassau William Senior, 'Cases of Walcot v. Walker; Southey v. Sherwood; Murray v. Benbow; and Lawrence v. Smith', *Quarterly Review* (April 1822), 123–38 (137); Senior was perceived at the time as writing on behalf of John Murray, Byron's publisher.

[139] For their joint activities in the 1790s, see Manogue, 'Plight of Ridgway'; also Mee, *Print, Publicity*, 87, 138–9 and *passim*.

licensing in 1737. Mischievously, radical publishers were now reviving banned plays from the Patriot campaign against Walpole that looked to history for usable tales of insurrection or usurpation. Brooke's *Gustavus Vasa* and Havard's *King Charles the First* (the first featuring an assassinated minister, the second an executed minister and king) were among the tragedies disinterred and republished in 1793–4, and revivals of this kind may have inspired Southey to attempt the genre himself. Yet in the process Southey also broke new ground, not least in his choice of a protagonist from below, whose centrality to the action suggested not dynastic rivalry or elite republicanism, as in earlier tragedies, but the alarming spectre of revolution erupting from the labouring class, and developing from practical grievance into political principle.

If we look back to the 1730s, there is indeed a play about the Peasants' Revolt, Sir Robert Henley's *Wat Tyler and Jack Straw; or The Mob Reformers* (1730), and possibly also a second in 1733, *Wat Tyler, or The State Menders* (though this instance does not survive, and may have been a reprint of Henley with variant title).[140] In the run-up to the Excise Crisis of 1733, amidst nationwide anger about new powers of search and confiscation given to revenue officers, a medieval rebellion sparked by poll-tax collection might seem an obvious subject for presentist treatment on the stage. But though *The Mob Reformers* is certainly a topical play, with wilfully anachronistic jokes about the Mississippi and South Sea Bubbles in the opening scene, it's emphatically not an oppositional play. Henley's Tyler is a ludicrous buffoon and his comrade Jack Straw a drunken lecher; the real heroes are Sir William Walworth, the steadfast Lord Mayor who slays Tyler to restore order and safeguard the throne, and Walworth's romantic-interest son (a historical embellishment by Henley). This is loyalist or at most reformist drama, a call for harmonious co-operation between the interests of merchants and grandees, city and court, with no sympathy at all for plebeian insurrection. The original performance advertisements leave no doubt about the message, at a time when the ministry was still trading on fears of Jacobite insurrection: 'Being the

---

[140] William J. Burling, *A Checklist of New Plays and Entertainments on the London Stage, 1700–1737* (Madison, NJ: Fairleigh Dickinson University Press, 1992), 194.

Representation of that Celebrated and Heroick Action of Sir William Walworth, a Lord Mayor of London, perform'd in the Reign of King Richard the Second; shewing how he stab'd the Insolent Rebel, Wat Tyler, at the Head of his Rout, in Smithfield, for which Reason the Dagger, which he so loyally employ'd, was added to the City's Arms, and remains there still, as a Memorial of the King's Gratitude and the Lord Mayor's Loyalty.'[141]

Staged at Bartholomew Fair before an audience of apprentices and artisans, the 1730 *Wat Tyler* was a play or 'droll' of a special kind: a moralizing opportunity, in the potentially riotous milieu of an urban fair, to remind Londoners of their historical role as a bastion against violent incursions into the seat of government.[142] The play also typifies the hostile or dismissive style in which the Peasants' Revolt was routinely treated between the civil war era and the revolution years in which Southey turned to the subject: witness, in the earlier period, royalist works like *The Just Reward of Rebels*, a 1642 chapbook, and John Cleveland's *The Idol of the Clownes; or, Insurrection of Wat the Tyler* (1654), a thinly disguised attack on Cromwell. Even Algernon Sidney disparages Tyler as an unworthy usurper in his *Discourses Concerning Government*, which groups him, as a mere 'rascal', with illegitimate pretenders such as Perkin Warbeck. And in the Walpole era opposition journalists, despite their fondness for historical hints and shadows, avoided him in favour of more comfortably patrician models of resistance to absolute power.[143]

Elsewhere Tyler crops up from time to time (with Jack Straw and the Lollard preacher John Ball) at moments of threatened or actual popular unrest, but almost always to be excoriated or ridiculed as a

---

[141] Arthur H. Scouten (ed.), *The London Stage, 1660–1800, Part 3: 1729–1747*, 2 vols (Carbondale: Southern Illinois University Press, 1961), 1: 74.

[142] See Anne Wohlcke's reading of the play in *The 'Perpetual Fair': Gender, Disorder and Urban Amusement in Eighteenth-Century London* (Manchester: Manchester University Press, 2014), 182–4.

[143] Algernon Sidney, *Discourses Concerning Government*, ed. Thomas G. West (Indianapolis: Liberty Fund, 1996), 237–8; Fielding's guarded references in the *Champion* (p. 219, 4 March 1740; p. 523, 15 November 1740) are typical of the Walpole era. For Tyler's reputation across the extended period, see Alastair Dunn, *The Peasants' Revolt: England's Failed Revolution of 1381* (Stroud: Tempus, 2004), 187–94.

proxy for some modern scapegoat. During the 'Wilkes and Liberty' disturbances of the early 1770s, one publication represented him as a spitting image of Lord Mayor William Beckford (father of the author of *Vathek*), the point being that Beckford's Wilkite radicalism betrayed the office once held by loyal Walworth; Wilkes appears on the same page as a squinting Jack Cade, leader of a popular revolt under Henry VI.[144] Only after the French Revolution does Tyler prominently enter an oppositional pantheon of heroes, and only then in the alarming context of *Rights of Man*, Thelwall's *The Tribune*, and other radical publications. Paine vindicates Tyler as 'an intrepid disinterested man' unfairly maligned by modern party writers: 'That his memory should be traduced by court sycophants, and all those who live on the spoil of a public, is not to be wondered at. He was, however, the means of checking the rage and injustice of taxation in his time, and the nation owed much to his valour.'[145] The Jacobin embrace of Tyler, however, only generated a loyalist backlash in which his actions foretold the present turmoil, or inaugurated a subversive agenda 'enforced by every popular incendiary, from Wat Tyler to Tom Pain'.[146]

In this context, Southey could scarcely have picked a more provocative subject. He then enhanced the provocation by means of persistent anachronism: anachronism so studied and conspicuous that it obviously discredits his later claim that the play merely 'places in the mouths of the personages who are introduced nothing more than a correct statement of their real principles'.[147] Inescapably, the principles of Southey's Tyler are those of modern Jacobinism, not medieval Lollardy. He may be speaking in cod medievalese when he

[144] Joseph Cradock, *The Life of John Wilkes, Esq; in the Manner of Plutarch* (1773), frontispiece; a copy of the plate is in the British Museum Department of Prints and Drawings (No. 1868,0808.13221).

[145] Thomas Paine, *Rights of Man, Common Sense, and Other Political Writings*, ed. Mark Philp (Oxford: Oxford University Press, 1995), 284 n. See also Thelwall's defence of Tyler as one 'who, though an ignorant man (one of the swinish multitude!) had an honourable mind that disdained every subterfuge of art' (*The Politics of English Jacobinism: Writings of John Thelwall*, ed. Gregory Claeys (University Park: Pennsylvania State University Press, 2010), 322).

[146] John Gifford, *A Plain Address to the Common Sense of the People of England* (1792), 7–8.

[147] Southey, *Letter to Smith*, 6.

reminds his followers of 'their long withholden rights', but this is the language, more fundamentally, of the revolutionary *Déclaration des droits de l'Homme*.[148] So it is again when Southey's John Ball urges the rebels to 'Boldly demand your long-forgotten rights, | Your sacred, your inalienable freedom' (ii.48–9), and instructs them that 'Equality is the sacred right of man, | Inalienable, tho' by force withheld' (iii.114–15). 'Inalienable' is especially good in these instances, a word first recorded in 1647, but one that only really catches on during the decade of the American revolution. All this is a far cry from the insurgent lexicon of the historical Ball: a trenchant enough language of protest insurrection, but uncoloured by Southey's insistent patina of Enlightenment radicalism.[149] Indeed, at the point in the drama where Southey most unambiguously commits the move of imagining the king's death, he does so in the name of political principle. It's specifically as spokesman for 'the sovereign people' that Tyler threatens the king at the culmination of Act II: 'The hour of retribution is at hand, | And tyrants tremble—mark me, King of England' (iii.204, 244–5).

The third and perhaps most provocative feature of *Wat Tyler* is the way the drama becomes, in Southey's hands, not simply a work that commits seditious libel but a work that makes seditious libel its subject. In the 'great age of sedition' to which Eaton's defence counsel sarcastically alluded in 1794, and more specifically in the immediate period of the treason trials later that year, it's a work self-consciously about seditious speech or writing, the silencing of seditious speech or writing, and finally the inadequacy of seditious discourse. It becomes a kind of meta-seditious libel, shaped with implicit reference to 'constructive treason' prosecution as a tool of political coercion in the present. In this sense, the title *Wat Tyler* is something of a misnomer, the real focus of interest as the drama develops being the itinerant

---

[148] Southey, *Later Poetical Works*, 3: 483 (*Wat Tyler*, ii.48–9); further references are given parenthetically in the text.

[149] See *OED*, s.v. 'Inalienable', 'Inalienably', 'Inalienability'. The first three political occurrences to be recorded are from 1777, 1774, and 1776 respectively. For the reported words of the historical Ball (and the question of their authenticity), see Steven Justice, *Writing and Rebellion: England in 1381* (Berkeley: University of California Press, 1994), esp. 14–23, 102–11.

preacher John Ball, whose levelling speeches dominate Southey's second and third acts, and whose condemnation and execution for treason end the work.

In giving this prominence, and eloquence, to Ball, it seems fair to say that it was not Paine so much as Burke who set Southey thinking. In an unusually playful passage in his *Appeal from the New to the Old Whigs* (1791), Burke uses the historical Ball to mock, by implication, Dr Richard Price, the Dissenting preacher whose 1789 *Discourse on the Love of Our Country* (which celebrated the unfolding French Revolution as a liberation resembling the Glorious Revolution in England) was an early blast in the revolution controversy. Price had already been a primary target of Burke's *Reflections*; now Burke satirically recasts him as 'the Abbé John Ball', 'the enlightened Dr. Ball', a 'great teacher of the rights of man' whose doctrines might almost have flowed 'from the new arsenal of Hackney' (now the epicentre of radical Dissent).[150] Knowingly stripped by Burke of his Lollard identity, Ball comes to look instead like a modern revolutionary: 'that reverend patriarch of sedition, and prototype of our modern preachers, was of opinion with the national assembly, that all the evils which have fallen upon men had been caused by an ignorance of their "having been born and continued equal as to their rights."'[151] This is among the drollest passages anywhere in Burke, but Southey seems to have taken it in real earnest, and put Ball as a Price-like figure at the heart of his drama—though Price died three years before *Wat Tyler*, and if Southey also had in mind a minister actually convicted of seditious preaching in the 1790s, there is only one candidate. That is the Baptist minister William Winterbotham, who was with Ridgway in Newgate when Southey tried to negotiate publication, and then became the conduit (albeit, it now seems, unwittingly) for eventual publication two decades later.[152]

---

[150] *The Writings and Speeches of Edmund Burke, Volume 4: Party, Parliament, and the Dividing of the Whigs, 1780–1794*, ed. P. J. Marshall, Donald C. Bryant, and William B. Todd (Oxford: Clarendon Press, 2015), 450, 451, 452, 453.

[151] *Writings and Speeches of Burke, Volume 4*, 450; the quoted phrase is from the *Déclaration des droits de l'Homme*.

[152] Winterbotham's 1793 conviction for two sermons preached in Plymouth has been called 'a celebrated instance of overreaction by the authorities through

The seditious discourse theme is inaugurated in Southey's opening act when Tyler's daughter repeats Ball's doctrine 'that all mankind are brethren' (i.122): a doctrine Tyler then indulgently calls 'Rank sedition— | High treason, every syllable, my child!' (i.124–5). But it's with Ball's release from prison in Act II that the focus on seditious utterance becomes central, notably in the longest speech of the play, Ball's stirring address to the assembled rebels as ardent revolutionary patriots, 'Englishmen met in arms to advocate | The cause of freedom!' (ii.55–6). The problem is that for all his eloquence, Ball never allows himself to become quite stirring enough. With his pious entreaties that the rebels temper their impulse for revenge against tyranny with Christian love or mercy, he fatally weakens their insurgency in its elemental drive. The third act of the drama, in which Tyler is stabbed, the rebellion defeated, and Ball led away to execution for treason, is at one level a critique of the brutality of modern censorship, laced with thinly disguised allusions to the 1794 treason trials, with their contrived charges and special juries. Ball speaks of justice at this point as merely an instrument of power, exercised via 'The vain and empty insult of a trial' (iii.203). Or as the Lord Chief Justice Eyre of the day, cynical Sir John Tresilian, happily muses, 'there's nothing like | A fair free open trial, where the king | Can chuse his jury and appoint his judges' (iii.163–5).

On this point Southey's drama follows very much the trajectory of Godwin's celebrated pamphlet about the treason trials, *Cursory*

---

nervousness in the wake of the French Revolution' (Susan J. Mills, 'Winterbotham, William' (1763–1829), *ODNB*). For his role in the publication of *Wat Tyler*, see the editorial matter in Southey, *Later Poetical Works*, 3: 445–8 and 513–15. The Baptist essayist John Foster reported in 1843 that Winterbotham was not directly responsible, but had shown the *Wat Tyler* manuscript to two friends in Worcester who then transcribed it without his knowledge; one of the two then 'managed the concern for its publication' (3: 446). This story now seems confirmed by marginalia by the Unitarian minister James Kennedy Esdaile (d. 1832) in a copy of Southey's *Letter to William Smith* held in the Fisher Library, Toronto (3rd edn, p. 5, shelfmark D-10 00608). Where Southey complains that 'some skulking scoundrel' had surreptitiously obtained the text and engineered publication, Esdaile comments: 'It was, I believe, Mr. Benjamin Stokes, of the firm of Evans & Stokes, grocers, in the City of Worcester, and living in Turkey [St.], parish of St. Clement's, into whose hands a copy of Southey's "Wat Tyler" fell, and who had it printed and published.'

*Strictures*, though by setting his action in the actual century from which the treason statute derives, he dramatizes a complaint that Godwin at the same juncture could only assert: that Enlightenment civility was now hurtling back into medieval barbarism. Both works culminate in the same startling '*coup de théâtre*', as Marilyn Butler calls it in Godwin's case, achieved via unsparing quotation from the 1351 treason statute, with its detailed specifications of the punishment involved: hanging 'but not until you are dead'; castration and disembowelment while still alive; decapitation and dismemberment; display of the butchered parts.[153] Southey's Tresilian does little more than versify the words that Godwin gives to his real-life Lord Chief Justice of the 1790s, ending with the same hypocritical kiss-off to the convicted traitor:

> you shall be hanged by the neck,
> But not till you are dead—your bowels opened—
> Your heart torn out and burnt before your face—
> Your traitorous head be sever'd from your body—
> Your body quartered, and exposed upon
> The city gates—a terrible example—
> And the Lord God have mercy on your soul!'
> (iii.255–60)

Again, however, there's a telling difference. Where Godwin, naturally enough, minimizes the offences of the 1794 defendants, Southey reverses the pattern to insist that his play's main spokesman for revolution has not in fact been treasonous enough. As Ball himself is made to acknowledge—'that old seditious heretic', one loyalist calls him (iii.152); 'that old seditious priest' (iii.160), says another—his speech, though seditious in its critique of Ricardian tyranny, has been fatally hamstrung all along by his Christian ethics. He's undone by his preference for peace and love, and thus unsatisfactory political compromise, over the sanguinary alternative of no-holds-barred insurrection. Faced with the option 'boldly to proceed thro' blood and slaughter, | Till we should all be equal and all happy', Ball acknowledges, 'I chose the milder way:—perhaps I erred' (iii.120–2). Only too late does he realize that 'The seemly voice of pity has

---

[153] See Marilyn Butler's headnote to *Cursory Strictures* in her *Burke, Paine, Godwin*, 170, and the final paragraph of the pamphlet, 178.

deceiv'd me, | And all this mighty movement ends in ruin!' (iii.134–5). He has failed to break the eggs required by the omelette. It's impossible to escape the Jacobin conclusion here, a conclusion nowhere spelled out with such disquieting clarity in other radical works of the period, even the forthright polemics for which Paine, Eaton, and their allies were prosecuted at the time. Only uncompromising revolutionary violence will establish the rights of man; seditious speech that countenances restraint is in fact a betrayal of the cause.

It was not, then, mere personal malice that made Southey's opponents call, in 1817, for the now Tory poet laureate's prosecution. *Wat Tyler* went beyond the latest incarnations of revolutionary extremism, said Smith in Parliament ('The Spencean plan could not be compared with it'), and compounded the effect by enlisting the imagination and the passions: 'Why, then, had not [the authorities] ... discovered the author of that seditious publication, and visited him with the penalties of the law?'[154] There was much more to come in the way of tongue-in-cheek torment. 'The publication teems with this political blasphemy from beginning to end', exulted Wooler's *Black Dwarf*, which (following Smith) pretended to want to implicate Southey in an alleged Spencean plot the previous winter to overthrow the government, and assassinate the king, under cover of the Spa Fields riot. Southey was 'guilty of throwing opinions like fire-brands among the people'. Were it not for his ministerial friends, 'there is no question, but the poet laureate ere this had been in custody'—in custody, though not of course in the pillory, abolished as a sanction against seditious libel the previous year.[155]

In practice, Southey's only punishment was his merely metaphorical pillorying from critics like these, and there was never the slightest chance that he would be brought to trial like Wooler, Thelwall, or Hunt in the same years. Yet he had written something more disruptive than all these other libellers of the Liverpool era, the callowness of *Wat Tyler* notwithstanding—or even in part because of that callowness, if one were to view the thin characterization of the drama's protagonists, and their status as simple mouthpieces, as heralding a Brechtian logic

[154] Madden (ed), *Robert Southey: The Critical Heritage*, 237.
[155] Madden (ed.), *Robert Southey: The Critical Heritage*, 239.

of political didacticism. Not only was Southey's verse drama more genuinely Jacobin in content than most works of the 1790s that have conventionally been given that label (works by Godwin, Holcroft, or Wollstonecraft, say), and unsettling enough, on publication, for contemporaries to find in it the full-blooded Spenceanism of the 1810s. *Wat Tyler* also gave its revolutionary prescriptions—encoded, however lightly, as literary drama—an imaginative, creative life that was increasingly rare in the seditious journalism of the 1810s, not least because the traditional arts of ambiguity and disguise were no longer needed in practice. The forces of censorship were on the retreat, albeit in slow and erratic ways, and with them the discipline that had activated so many extraordinary feats of literary indirection over the previous century and a half. Yet precisely for this reason *Wat Tyler* now seemed to possess unusual power by virtue of its capacity, above all, to involve readers as active interpreters of topical messages left implicit in the text, and so make them complicit in the creation of seditious meaning. To rephrase Godwin on *Caleb Williams*, the reader of *Wat Tyler* becomes constructively a traitor.

# Conclusion: England in 1820

Generations after Joseph Browne was pilloried for his ironic compliments to named statesmen in *The Country Parson's Honest Advice* (1706), published at a time when identities were normally veiled by dashes or historical surrogates, Shelley could confidently write, in *The Mask of Anarchy*, of meeting 'Murder on the way— | He had a mask like Castlereagh'.[1] Browne's poem hints at nothing worse in its protagonists than personal or political double-dealing, but *The Mask of Anarchy* explicitly casts the Foreign Secretary and Leader of the Commons as a borderline cannibal, a figure tossing human hearts to his pack of bloodhounds. Castlereagh is only the first of a grim procession. Fraud is Lord Chancellor Eldon, who dashes out the brains of children playing at his feet; Hypocrisy is Home Secretary Sidmouth, an agent of darkness disguised in the garb of piety, shedding crocodile tears for the Peterloo dead. From these opening *ad hominem* strokes, *The Mask of Anarchy* moves unmistakably on to the king himself (Anarchy's 'white horse, splashed with blood' (line 30), makes exactly the allusion to the Hanoverian coat of arms that was Johnson's riskiest move in *Marmor Norfolciense* (1739), and the same point had landed Shebbeare in the pillory in 1758). *The Mask of Anarchy* then develops a universalized call for radical political change. Where *The Country Parson's Honest Advice* makes no allusion at all to the Jacobite restoration for which Browne yearned, Shelley openly imagines revolutionary upheaval, driven by a rising of the masses (albeit a non-violent rising) 'like

---

[1] *The Poems of Shelley, Volume Three: 1819–1820*, ed. Jack Donovan, Cian Duffy, Kelvin Everest, and Michael Rossington (Harlow: Longman, 2011), 37 (*The Mask of Anarchy*, lines 5–6).

*Poetics of the Pillory: English Literature and Seditious Libel, 1660–1820*. Thomas Keymer, Oxford University Press (2019). © Thomas Keymer.
DOI: 10.1093/oso/9780198744498.001.0001

Lions after slumber | In unvanquishable number' (lines 151–2). In the celebrated incantation of *The Mask of Anarchy*, the people were many; their rulers were few.

Poets and their publishers, of course, were not quite out of the woods when Shelley composed this incendiary poem in 1819, and several qualifications must be made. We know that in other poems composed shortly before *The Mask of Anarchy*, Shelley struggled with the boundaries of permissible expression, and muted his text at key moments; a little later, *Swellfoot the Tyrant* (1820) was suppressed in its anonymous pamphlet form as a 'seditious and disloyal libel', and *Hellas* (1822) posed difficulties for its publisher Charles Ollier, who cancelled several lines from the verse and the notes.[2] As for *The Mask of Anarchy* specifically, its intended publisher, Leigh Hunt, clearly baulked at printing the poem when Shelley sent it to him (through, with nice insouciance, the regular post) for the *Examiner* in September 1819. Hunt then waited until 1832, as the Reform Bill was transforming the political landscape, before publishing *The Mask of Anarchy* as a freestanding pamphlet, and accompanied the text with a circumspect preface emphasizing the 'kind-heartedness of the spirit that walked in this flaming robe of verse'.[3] At that point, Hunt still withheld the names of ministerial targets who remained alive (Eldon, Sidmouth), though there could be no doubting the referent in either case, and Mary Shelley followed suit in 1839 when including *The Mask of Anarchy* in *The Poetical Works of Percy Bysshe Shelley*, with Sidmouth ('\* \* \*') still living and Eldon ('Lord E——') just recently dead. Token gestures of concealment were still in order, and though public prosecutions for seditious libel were now very rare indeed, conservative prosecutorial societies had been making dogged attempts to fill the void. It was not so long since Byron's *Vision of Judgment* (1822), a gleeful parody of

[2] See Michael J. Neth, 'A Committee of One: Shelley's Preemptive Self-Censorships in the Draft Manuscripts of *Laon and Cythna* and Legal Censorship of the Press', in Michael Edson (ed.), *Publishing, Editing, and Reception: Essays in Honor of Donald H. Reiman* (Newark: University of Delaware Press, 2015), 215–43; Michael Rossington, 'Tragedy: *The Cenci* and *Swellfoot the Tyrant*', in Michael O'Neill and Anthony Howe with Madeleine Callaghan (eds), *The Oxford Handbook of Percy Bysshe Shelley* (Oxford: Oxford University Press, 2013), 299–308 (300).

[3] *Poems of Shelley, Volume Three*, 731.

Southey's verse obituary on George III, had embroiled its publisher (Leigh Hunt's brother John) in a prosecution for 'calumniating the late King' and disturbing the peace, instigated by the Constitutional Association for Opposing the Progress of Disloyal and Seditious Principles.[4] When the case finally came to court in 1824, Hunt was found guilty and fined £100—a moderate punishment by the standards of the previous century, but one best avoided even so.

*The Mask of Anarchy* and *The Vision of Judgment* still belong, then, in a world of discernible legal inhibition for oppositional verse. Yet what these envelope-pushing poems most crucially indicate is not so much the survival or endurance of literary censorship as a gradual but decisive shift in the borderlines of what could be uttered: a shift that was now giving poets greater expressive licence than earlier generations had enjoyed, and publishers greater latitude in committing it to print. At the close of the Hanoverian era, hostility to rulers, and to the established order more broadly, could be made overt and strident to a degree unthinkable at the start. Beyond that, political transformation, whether in the form of dynastic change or plebeian revolution, could be envisioned or urged with increasingly minimal use of the arts of disguise. As Marsh, Barrell, and others have argued from various perspectives, a more or less transcendent category of the imaginative or literary—'Literature, with a capital L'—was gaining ever more widespread recognition in the cultural landscape, a process already observable when Shelley wrote *The Mask of Anarchy*, and far advanced by the time the poem entered his published canon.[5] The process brought with it, if not absolute immunity, a degree of security that Dryden under William III, or Pope under Walpole, could scarcely have dreamed of. Censorship for the poet, as never before, was becoming a matter of Bourdieu's constitutive censorship or, as

---

[4] See Marsh, *Word Crimes*, 104. Marsh calls the *Vision of Judgment* prosecution 'the first criminal trial for publishing a poem', presumably meaning the first in the nineteenth century. Earlier criminal trials included those of Joseph Browne, convicted and pilloried in 1706 for *The Country Parson's Honest Advice*, and Stephen College, convicted and executed in 1681 for (among other treasonable offences) *A Ra-Ree Show*.

[5] Marsh, *Word Crimes*, 104; see also Barrell, *Imagining the King's Death*, 644–56; Mee, 'Treason, Seditious Libel'.

Sophia Rosenfeld puts it, 'censorship without censors';[6] the inward poet, not the proscribing licenser or the prosecuting lawyer, was now the primary constraint on politically inflected literary discourse.

Perhaps the most fearless poem of the Peterloo aftermath was Shelley's trenchant, and formally innovative, sonnet 'England in 1819', which he wrote between one and three months after *The Mask of Anarchy*. The poem opens by invoking the debility of George III as emblem of a desperate national condition, and then hurtles through a catalogue of social ills before pivoting (as James Chandler describes the manifest effect of the closing couplet) towards 'the possibility of a millenarian illumination that will mark its general rebirth'.[7] On this occasion, Shelley's flaming robe of verse was evidently too hot for Hunt to handle: 'I do not expect you to publish it, but you may show it to whom you please', Shelley told him.[8] But Mary Shelley included 'England in 1819' in the *Poetical Works* of 1839 without the slightest gesture of defensive revision, and indeed, since the title was her own, with special emphasis laid on its political charge. If anything seems to have disconcerted her or her publisher or printer about the poem's Lear-like evocation of George III—'An old, mad, blind, despised and dying King' in the manuscript notebook; 'An old, mad, blind, despised, and dying king' in the published text—it was Shelley's cavalier way with the Oxford comma.[9]

Her first thought for a title had been 'England in 1820', the year of George III's death. But whatever the specific historical referent, as Chandler suggests, Mary Shelley seems to have been interested in

---

[6] See Sophia Rosenfeld, 'Writing the History of Censorship in the Age of Enlightenment', in Daniel Gordon (ed.), *Postmodernism and the Enlightenment: New Perspectives in Eighteenth-Century French Intellectual History* (London: Routledge, 2001), 117–45 (124–8).

[7] James Chandler, *England in 1819: The Politics of Literary Culture and the Case of Romantic Historicism* (Chicago: University of Chicago Press, 1998), 27.

[8] See the headnote in *Poems of Shelley, Volume Three*, 189, quoting Shelley's letter to Hunt of 23 December 1819.

[9] I'm grateful to Michael Rossington for pointing out to me how characteristically liberal, though also inconsistent, Mary Shelley is with comma pointing as a copyist and editor; he also suggests that the now decapitalized 'king' might be read as a defensive, universalizing move that deflects attention from George III specifically.

pointing up an affinity with oppositional poems of earlier generations, reaching from Anna Laetitia Barbauld's controversial *Eighteen Hundred and Eleven* (1812) all the way back to Pope's verse fragment *One Thousand Seven Hundred and Forty*, which finally reached print in 1797.[10] Even as she quietly evoked Pope, however, she could also celebrate a freedom unknown to Pope, who throughout the early decades of the Hanoverian era practised satirical indirection with astonishing virtuosity, but eventually reached a state of impasse. In his last years, after a complicated episode of proxy retribution for his *One Thousand Seven Hundred and Thirty Eight*, he had been forced to conclude that 'Ridicule was become as unsafe as it was ineffectual' (see above, pp. 118–19).

Expressively, the gain over the intervening century was of course immense. Yet one may also detect an accompanying sense of loss: loss of the rhetorical power that flowed from conscious strategies of indirection or disguise; loss, with it, of the capacity of encoded literature to enlist the imaginative collaboration of readers required to listen for telling ambiguities or subtextual implications, and then to interpret accordingly. It's a notable fact that in 1821, when Thelwall, John Hunt, and other political journalists stood trial for their explicit oppositional polemics about Peterloo, Hone turned instead to Defoe as his source and inspiration for *The Right Divine of Kings to Govern Wrong!*, a satire closely based on Defoe's *Jure Divino* of 1706. Hone could not quite bring himself to celebrate Defoe as a verse technician, and in this respect he no doubt thought more of Pope's *Dunciad*, which supplies his satire's title and primary epigraph. Defoe, however, was 'the ablest politician of his day, an energetic writer, and, better than all, an honest man'. Moreover, in an era of resurgent priestcraft and Tory authoritarianism, the literary strategies that Defoe turned on church and state during the reign of Queen Anne could surpass the radical writing of the present for 'energetic thoughts, forcible touches, and happy illustrations'. If readers of the present day were in need of quotable phrasing and rhetorical power, Hone suggested, or a fund of 'occasional illustration and emphatic expression', there could be no

---

[10] Chandler, *England in 1819*, 114–21 and n. 68.

better source than *Jure Divino* to reinforce their opinions and render them eloquent.[11]

Writing in the same year, Byron turned his mind to eighteenth-century satire for instances of oppositional literature that he found more compelling, imaginatively and rhetorically, than anything achieved by political journalists of the present:

> I have lately been reading Fielding over again.—They talk of Radicalism—Jacobinism &c. in England (I am told) but they should turn over the pages of "Jonathan Wild the Great".—The inequality of conditions and the littleness of the great—were never set forth in stronger terms—and his contempt for Conquerors and the like is such that had he lived *now* he would have been denounced in the "Courier" as the grand Mouth-piece and Factionary of the revolutionists.[12]

A critique of high-political corruption and predatory social relations that could only address its targets through clever indirection, *Jonathan Wild* gained an amplitude surpassing the work of modern radical writers, for all the expressive freedoms they now enjoyed. Constrained in its character as an attack on Walpole, and forced into commensurate feats of functional ambiguity, it could become something larger and richer for posterity, much as *Gulliver's Travels*, with the same proximate contemporary target, could become for Orwell the most powerful critique of 'what would now be called totalitarianism': a work so far transcendent of its time and place that it encompassed political conditions unknown to its author.[13] In effect, for Byron, *Jonathan Wild* was as much a satire on Prime Minister Liverpool as on his predecessor Walpole; more important, it was a satire on elite

---

[11] William Hone, *The Right Divine of Kings to Govern Wrong!*, Preface, <http://honearchive.org/etexts/right-divine/right-divine-front.html>; for commentary, see Kyle Grimes, 'Daniel Defoe, William Hone, and *The Right Divine of Kings to Govern Wrong!* A New Electronic Edition', *Digital Defoe* 4 (2012), 31–40.

[12] *Byron's Letters and Journals, Volume 9: 'In the wind's eye', 1821–1822*, ed. Leslie A. Marchand (London: John Murray, 1979), 50. The *Courier* was a conservative, pro-government newspaper to which Coleridge contributed, among other pieces, letters defending Southey over *Wat Tyler*.

[13] See George Orwell, 'Politics vs. Literature: An Examination of *Gulliver's Travels*', in his *Collected Essays, Journalism and Letters*, ed. Sonia Orwell and Ian Angus, 4 vols (New York: Harcourt, Brace & World, 1970), 4: 205–23 (213).

predation and social injustice in any time and place. 'And yet', Byron continues, 'I never recollect to have heard this turn of Fielding's mind noticed though it is obvious in every page.'[14] Here is a tribute that would probably have surprised the Fielding of 1743, and one that would certainly have dismayed his son, the prosecutor of Daniel Isaac Eaton, in the 1790s. But it stands as a fitting comment on the creative stimulus, as much as the constraining power, of literary censorship, and on the rich achievements of the many poets, satirists, and others who, over the previous century and a half, danced on the brink of seditious libel.

---

[14] *Byron's Letters and Journals, Volume 9*, 50–1.

# Select Bibliography

Allsopp, Niall, 'A Surreptitious State of Marvell's *Miscellaneous Poems* (1681)?', *Notes & Queries*, 62.2 (2015), 268–70.

Astbury, Raymond, 'The Renewal of the Licensing Act in 1693 and Its Expiry in 1695', *The Library* 33 (1978), 296–322.

Backscheider, Paula R., *Daniel Defoe: His Life* (Baltimore: Johns Hopkins University Press, 1989).

Baines, Paul, 'Crime and Punishment', in *The Cambridge Companion to Alexander Pope*, ed. Pat Rogers (Cambridge: Cambridge University Press, 2007).

Baines, Paul, *The House of Forgery in Eighteenth-Century Britain* (Aldershot: Ashgate, 1999).

Baines, Paul, and Pat Rogers, *Edmund Curll, Bookseller* (Oxford: Oxford University Press, 2007).

Baird, John D., 'Literary Politics and Political Satire: Paul Whitehead and Alexander Pope', *Lumen*, 35 (2016), 19–36.

Balme, Christopher B., *The Theatrical Public Sphere* (Cambridge: Cambridge University Press, 2014).

Barker, A. D., 'The Printing and Publishing of Johnson's *Marmor Norfolciense* (1739) and *London* (1738 and 1739)', *Library*, 6th series, 3 (1981), 287–304.

Barrell, John, *Imagining the King's Death: Figurative Treason, Fantasies of Regicide, 1793–1796* (Oxford: Oxford University Press, 2000).

Barrell, John, *The Spirit of Despotism: Invasions of Privacy in the 1790s* (Oxford: Oxford University Press, 2010).

Bartlett, Peter, 'Sodomites in the Pillory in Eighteenth-Century London', *Social & Legal Studies*, 6 (1997), 553–72.

Battestin, Martin C., with Ruthe R. Battestin, *Henry Fielding: A Life* (London: Routledge, 1989).

Beattie, J. M., *Crime and the Courts in England, 1660–1800* (Oxford: Clarendon Press, 1986).

Bender, John, *Imagining the Penitentiary: Fiction and the Architecture of Mind in Eighteenth-Century England* (Chicago: University of Chicago Press, 1987).

Bird, Wendell, *Press and Speech under Assault: The Early Supreme Court Justices, the Sedition Act of 1798, and the Campaign against Dissent* (New York: Oxford University Press, 2016).

Black, Jeremy, 'An Underrated Journalist: Nathaniel Mist and the Opposition Press during the Whig Ascendancy', *British Journal for Eighteenth-Century Studies*, 10 (1987), 27–41.

Black, Jeremy, *The English Press in the Eighteenth Century* (London: Croom Helm, 1987).

Black, Jeremy, *Walpole in Power* (Stroud: Sutton, 2001).

Bourdieu, Pierre, 'Censorship and the Imposition of Form', in his *Language and Symbolic Power*, ed. John B. Thompson, trans. Gino Raymond and Matthew Adamson (Cambridge, MA: Harvard University Press, 1991), 137–59.

Bricker, Andrew, 'Libel and Satire: The Problem with Naming', *ELH*, 81.3 (2014), 889–921.

Bugg, John, *Five Long Winters: The Trials of British Romanticism* (Stanford: Stanford University Press, 2014).

Burling, William J., *A Checklist of New Plays and Entertainments on the London Stage, 1700–1737* (Madison, NJ: Fairleigh Dickinson University Press, 1992).

Bywaters, David, *Dryden in Revolutionary England* (Berkeley and Los Angeles: University of California Press, 1991).

Cardwell, M. John, *Arts and Arms: Literature, Politics and Patriotism during the Seven Years War* (Manchester: Manchester University Press, 2004).

Carnell, Rachel, *A Political Biography of Delarivier Manley* (London: Pickering & Chatto, 2008).

Cash, Arthur H., *John Wilkes: The Scandalous Father of Civil Liberty* (New Haven: Yale University Press, 2006).

Chandler, James, *England in 1819: The Politics of Literary Culture and the Case of Romantic Historicism* (Chicago: University of Chicago Press, 1998).

Chapman, Paul Michael, *Jacobite Political Argument in England, 1714–1766* (London: Jacobite Studies Trust, 2013).

Chrissochoidis, Ilias, and Richard Virr, 'An Annotated Wordbook of *The Beggar's Opera* (1728)', *Notes & Queries*, 60.1 (2013), 111–13.

Clarke, Norma, *Brothers of the Quill: Oliver Goldsmith in Grub Street* (Cambridge, MA: Harvard University Press, 2016).

Clegg, Cyndia Susan, *Press Censorship in Caroline England* (Cambridge: Cambridge University Press, 2008).

Clegg, Cyndia Susan, *Press Censorship in Elizabethan England* (Cambridge: Cambridge University Press, 1997).

Clegg, Cyndia Susan, *Press Censorship in Jacobean England* (Cambridge: Cambridge University Press, 2001).

Connell, Philip, *Secular Chains: Poetry and the Politics of Religion from Milton to Pope* (Oxford: Oxford University Press, 2016).

Cook, Daniel, 'Authors Unformed: Reading "*Beauties*" in the *Eighteenth Century*', *Philological Quarterly* 89 (2010), 283–309.

Coster, Stephanie, 'Robert Boulter and the Publication of Andrew Marvell's *Miscellaneous Poems*', *RES*, 69 (2018), 259–76.

Cowan, Brian, 'Making Publics and Making Novels', in *The Oxford Handbook of the Eighteenth-Century Novel*, ed. J. A. Downie (Oxford: Oxford University Press, 2016), 55–70.

Cranfield, Geoffrey Alan, *The Press and Society: From Caxton to Northcliffe* (London: Longman, 1978).

Cressy, David, *Dangerous Talk: Scandalous, Seditious, and Treasonable Speech in Pre-Modern England* (Oxford: Oxford University Press, 2010).

Crist, Timothy, 'Government Control of the Press after the Expiration of the Printing Act in 1679', *Publishing History*, 5 (1979), 49–77.

Crosby, Mark, 'The Voice of Flattery *vs* Sober Truth: William Godwin, Thomas Erskine and the 1792 Trial of Thomas Paine for Sedition', *RES*, 62 (2011), 90–112.

Darnton, Robert, *Censors at Work: How States Shaped Literature* (New York: Norton, 2014).

Darnton, Robert, *The Corpus of Clandestine Literature in France, 1769–1789* (New York: Norton, 1995).

Darnton, Robert, *The Forbidden Best-Sellers of Pre-Revolutionary France* (New York: Norton, 1995).

Darnton, Robert, '"What is the History of Books?" Revisited', *Modern Intellectual History*, 4.3 (2007), 495–508.

Davis, Michael T., '"Good for the Public Example": Daniel Isaac Eaton, Prosecution, Punishment and Recognition, 1793–1812', in *Radicalism and Revolution in Britain, 1775–1848: Essays in Honour of Malcolm I. Thomis*, ed. Michael T. Davis (Basingstoke: Macmillan, 2000), 110–32.

Davis, Michael T., '"I Can Bear Punishment": Daniel Isaac Eaton, Radical Culture and the Rule of Law, 1793–1812', in *Crime, Punishment and Reform in Europe*, ed. Louis A. Knafla (Westport: Praeger, 2003), 89–106.

Davis, Michael T., '"That Odious Class of Men Called Democrats": Daniel Isaac Eaton and the Romantics, 1794–1795', *History*, 84 (1999), 74–92.

Deazley, Ronan, *On the Origin of the Right to Copy: Charting the Movement of Copyright Law in Eighteenth-Century Britain (1695–1775)* (London: Bloomsbury, 2014).

Devereaux, Simon, 'Transportation, Penal Practices, and the English State, 1770–1830', in *Qualities of Mercy: Justice, Punishment, and Discretion*, ed. Carolyn Strange (Vancouver: UBC Press, 1996), 52–76.

Dobranski, Stephen B., *Milton, Authorship, and the Book Trade* (Cambridge: Cambridge University Press, 1999).

Dottin, Paul, *The Life and Strange and Surprising Adventures of Daniel Defoe* (New York: Macaulay, 1929).

Downie, J. A., *A Political Biography of Henry Fielding* (London: Pickering & Chatto, 2009).

Downie, J. A., *Robert Harley and the Press: Propaganda and Public Opinion in the Age of Swift and Defoe* (Cambridge: Cambridge University Press, 1979).

Dunn, Alastair, *The Peasants' Revolt: England's Failed Revolution of 1381* (Stroud: Tempus, 2004).

Dzelzainis, Martin, '1649', in *The Oxford History of Popular Print Culture, Volume 1: Cheap Print in Britain and Ireland to 1660*, ed. Joad Raymond (Oxford: Oxford University Press, 2011), 609–18.

Dzelzainis, Martin, 'Andrew Marvell and the Restoration Literary Underground: Printing the Painter Poems', *The Seventeenth Century*, 22.2 (2007), 395–410.

Dzelzainis, Martin, 'L'Estrange, Marvell and the *Directions to a Painter*: The Evidence of Bodleian Library, MS Gough London 14', in *Roger L'Estrange and the Making of Restoration Culture*, ed. Anne Dunan-Page and Beth Lynch (Aldershot: Ashgate, 2008), 53–66.

Eaves, T. C. Duncan, and Ben D. Kimpel, *Samuel Richardson: A Biography* (Oxford: Clarendon Press, 1971).

Eddy, D. D., and J. D. Fleeman, 'A Preliminary Handlist of Books to Which Dr. Samuel Johnson Subscribed', *Studies in Bibliography*, 46 (1993), 187–220.

Empson, William, '*Tom Jones*', *Kenyon Review*, 20 (1958), 217–49.

Emsley, Clive, 'An Aspect of Pitt's "Terror": Prosecutions for Sedition during the 1790s', *Social History*, 6 (1981), 155–84.

Emsley, Clive, 'Repression, "Terror" and the Rule of Law in England During the Decade of the French Revolution', *English Historical Review*, 100 (1985), 801–25.

Epstein, James, *Radical Expression: Political Language, Ritual, and Symbol in England, 1790–1850* (New York: Oxford University Press, 1994).

Erskine-Hill, Howard, 'Alexander Pope: The Political Poet in His Time', *Eighteenth-Century Studies*, 15.2 (1981–2), 123–48.

Erskine-Hill, Howard, *Poetry of Opposition and Revolution: Dryden to Wordsworth* (Oxford: Clarendon Press, 1996).

Erskine-Hill, Howard, 'Under Which Caesar? Pope in the Journal of Mrs. Charles Caesar, 1724–1741', *RES*, 33 (1982), 436–44.

Ezell, Margaret J. M., *The Oxford English Literary History, Volume 5: 1645–1714: The Later Seventeenth Century* (Oxford: Oxford University Press, 2017).

Feather, John, *A History of British Publishing* (London: Routledge, 1988).

Feather, John, 'The English Book Trade and the Law, 1695–1799', *Publishing History*, 12 (1982), 51–75.

Felski, Rita, *The Limits of Critique* (Chicago: University of Chicago Press, 2015).

Firth, Sir Charles, 'The Political Significance of *Gulliver's Travels*', *Proceedings of the British Academy*, 9 (1919–20), 237–59.

Fleeman, J. D., and James McLaverty, *A Bibliography of the Works of Samuel Johnson* (Oxford: Clarendon Press, 2000).

Foster, James R., 'Smollett's Pamphleteering Foe Shebbeare', *PMLA*, 57.4 (1942), 1053–100.

Foxon, David, *Pope and the Early Eighteenth-Century Book Trade*, revised and ed. James McLaverty (Oxford: Clarendon Press, 1991).

Franklin, Michael J., *Orientalist Jones: Sir William Jones, Poet, Lawyer, and Linguist, 1746–1794* (Oxford: Oxford University Press, 2011).

Furbank, P. N., and W. R. Owens, *A Political Biography of Daniel Defoe* (London: Pickering & Chatto, 2006).

Garnai, Amy, *Revolutionary Imaginings in the 1790s: Charlotte Smith, Mary Robinson, Elizabeth Inchbald* (Basingstoke: Palgrave Macmillan, 2009).

Gearin-Tosh, Michael, 'Marvell's "Upon the Death of Lord Hastings"', *Essays and Studies*, 34 (1981), 105–22.

Geary, Christopher, and Thomas Keymer, 'Seditious Libel in Eighteenth-Century Dublin: *Polyphemus's Farewel* (1714)', *Eighteenth-Century Ireland/Iris an dá chultúr*, 31 (2016), 170–7.

Gerrard, Christine, *The Patriot Opposition to Walpole: Politics, Poetry, and National Myth, 1725–1742* (Oxford: Oxford University Press, 1994).

Gillespie, Stuart, *English Translation and Classical Reception: Towards a New Literary History* (Chichester: Wiley-Blackwell, 2011).

Gilmartin, Kevin, *Print Politics: The Press and Radical Opposition in Early Nineteenth-Century England* (Cambridge: Cambridge University Press, 1994).

Goldgar, Bertrand A., *Walpole and the Wits: The Relation of Politics to Literature, 1722–1742* (Lincoln: University of Nebraska Press, 1976).

Goldie, Mark, 'Roger L'Estrange's *Observator* and the Exorcism of the Plot', in *Roger L'Estrange and the Making of Restoration Culture*, ed. Anne Dunan-Page and Beth Lynch (Aldershot: Ashgate, 2008), 73.

Grande, James, *William Cobbett, the Press and Rural England: Radicalism and the Fourth Estate, 1792–1835* (Basingstoke: Palgrave Macmillan, 2014).

Green, Thomas A., *Verdict According to Conscience: Perspectives on the English Criminal Trial Jury, 1200–1800* (Chicago: University of Chicago Press, 1985).

Greene, Jody, 'Public Secrets: Sodomy and the Pillory in the Eighteenth Century and Beyond', *The Eighteenth Century: Theory and Interpretation*, 44 (2003), 203–32.

Greene, Jody, *The Trouble with Ownership: Literary Property and Authorial Liability in England, 1660–1730* (Philadelphia: University of Pennsylvania Press, 2005).

Grimes, Kyle, 'Daniel Defoe, William Hone, and *The Right Divine of Kings to Govern Wrong!* A New Electronic Edition', *Digital Defoe*, 4 (2012), 31–40.

Guerinot, J. V., *Pamphlet Attacks on Alexander Pope, 1711–1744: A Descriptive Bibliography* (New York: New York University Press, 1969).

Habermas, Jürgen, *The Structural Transformation of the Public Sphere*, tr. Thomas Burger with Frederick Lawrence (Cambridge: Polity Press, 1989).

Hamburger, Philip, 'The Development of the Law of Seditious Libel and the Control of the Press', *Stanford Law Review*, 37 (1985), 661–765.

Hammond, Paul, 'The Autograph Manuscript of Dryden's *Heroique Stanza's* and Its Implications for Editors', *Publications of the Bibliographical Society of America*, 76 (1982), 457–70.

Hammond, Paul, *The Making of Restoration Poetry* (Woodbridge: D. S. Brewer, 2006).

Hanson, Laurence, *Government and the Press, 1695–1763* (Oxford: Clarendon Press, 1967).

Harling, Philip, 'The Law of Libel and the Limits of Repression, 1790–1832', *Historical Journal*, 44 (2001), 107–34.

Harris, Michael, *London Newspapers in the Age of Walpole: A Study of the Origins of the Modern English Press* (Rutherford: Fairleigh Dickinson University Press, 1987).

Harris, Tim, *London Crowds in the Reign of Charles II: Propaganda and Politics from the Restoration until the Exclusion Crisis* (Cambridge: Cambridge University Press, 1990).

Hart, W. H., '"Nero the Second": A Jacobite Ballad', *Notes & Queries*, 4th series 6 (15 October 1870), 322.

Hay, Douglas, Peter Linebaugh, John G. Rule, E. P. Thompson, and Cal Winslow, *Albion's Fatal Tree: Crime and Society in Eighteenth-Century England* (London: Allen Lane, 1975).

Hayward, Ian, *The Revolution in Popular Literature: Print, Politics and the People, 1790–1860* (Cambridge: Cambridge University Press, 2004).

Higgins, Ian, 'Censorship, Libel and Self-Censorship', in *Jonathan Swift and the Eighteenth-Century Book*, ed. Paddy Bullard and James McLaverty (Cambridge: Cambridge University Press, 2013), 179–98.

Hill, Christopher, 'Censorship and English Literature', in *The Collected Essays of Christopher Hill, Volume 1: Writing and Revolution in 17th-Century England* (Amherst: University of Massachusetts Press, 1985), 32–72.

Hinds, Peter. *'The Horrid Popish Plot': Roger L'Estrange and the Circulation of Political Discourse in Late Seventeenth-Century London* (Oxford: Oxford University Press, 2010).

Holberton, Edward, *Poetry and the Cromwellian Protectorate: Culture, Politics, and Institutions* (Oxford: Oxford University Press, 2008).

Hone, Joseph, 'A New Portrait of Defoe in the Pillory', *Notes & Queries*, 63 (2016), 70–1.

Hone, Joseph, 'Pope's Lost Epic: *Alcander, Prince of Rhodes* and the Politics of Exile', *Philological Quarterly*, 94 (2015), 245–66.

Hone, Joseph, 'Pope and the Politics of Panegyric', *RES*, 66 (2015), 106–23.

Horsley, Lee Sonsteng, 'The Trial of John Tutchin, Author of the *Observator*', *Yearbook of English Studies*, 3 (1973), 124–40.

Hudson, Nicholas, *A Political Biography of Samuel Johnson* (London: Pickering & Chatto, 2015).

Hudson, Nicholas, *Samuel Johnson and the Making of Modern England* (Cambridge: Cambridge University Press, 2003).

Hume, Robert D., *Henry Fielding and the London Theatre, 1728–1737* (Oxford: Clarendon Press, 1987).

Hunter, J. Paul, 'From Typology to Type: Agents of Change in Eighteenth-Century English Texts', in *Cultural Artifacts and the Production of Meaning: The Page, the Image, and the Body*, ed. Margaret J. M. Ezell and Katherine O'Brien O'Keeffe (Ann Arbor: University of Michigan Press, 1994), 41–69.

Hutcheon, Linda, *Irony's Edge: The Theory and Politics of Irony* (London: Routledge, 2004).

Hutcheon, Linda, *A Theory of Parody: The Teachings of Twentieth-Century Art Forms* (Urbana: University of Illinois Press, 2000).

Hyland, P. B. J., 'Liberty and Libel: Government and the Press during the Succession Crisis in Britain, 1712–1716', *English Historical Review*, 101 (1986), 863–88.

Ingrassia, Catherine, 'Additional Information about Eliza Haywood's 1749 Arrest for Seditious Libel', *Notes & Queries* n.s. 44 (1997), 202–4.

Jenkinson, Matthew, *Culture and Politics at the Court of Charles II, 1660–1685* (Woodbridge: Boydell, 2010).

Jenks, Timothy, *Naval Engagements: Patriotism, Cultural Politics, and the Royal Navy, 1793–1815* (Oxford: Oxford University Press, 2006).

Johnston, Kenneth R., *Unusual Suspects: Pitt's Reign of Alarm and the Lost Generation of the 1790s* (Oxford: Oxford University Press, 2013).

Johnston, Freya, and Lynda Mugglestone (eds), *Samuel Johnson: The Arc of the Pendulum* (Oxford: Oxford University Press, 2012).

Johnstone, H. Diack, 'Four Lost Plays Recovered: *The Contrast* and Other Dramatic Works of John Hoadly (1711–1776)', *RES*, 57 (2006), 487–506.

Justice, Steven, *Writing and Rebellion: England in 1381* (Berkeley: University of California Press, 1994).

Karian, Stephen, *Jonathan Swift in Print and Manuscript* (Cambridge: Cambridge University Press, 2010).

Keeble, N. H., *The Restoration: England in the 1660s* (Oxford: Blackwell, 2002).

Kelly, Gary, *The English Jacobin Novel, 1780–1805* (Oxford: Clarendon Press, 1976).

Kelly, James, 'Regulating Print: The State and the Control of Print in Eighteenth-Century Ireland', *Eighteenth-Century Ireland*, 23 (2008), 142–74.

Kewes, Paulina, 'Acts of Remembrance, Acts of Oblivion: Rhetoric, Law, and National Memory in Early Restoration England', in *Ritual, Routine, and Regime: Repetition in Early Modern British and European Cultures*, ed. Lorna Clymer (Toronto: University of Toronto Press, 2006), 103–31.

Kewes, Paulina, 'Dryden and the Staging of Popular Politics', in *John Dryden: Tercentenary Essays*, ed. Paul Hammond and David Hopkins (Oxford: Clarendon Press, 2000), 57–91.

Keymer, Thomas, 'Circulation', in *The Oxford Handbook of English Prose, 1640–1714*, ed. Nicholas McDowell and Henry Power (Oxford: Oxford University Press, forthcoming).

Keymer, Thomas, 'Defoe's Ears: *The Dunciad*, the Pillory, and Seditious Libel', *The Eighteenth-Century Novel*, 6–7 (2009), 159–96.

Keymer, Thomas, 'Fictions, Libels and Unions in the Long Eighteenth Century', in *Literature and Union: Scottish Texts, British Contexts*, ed. Gerard Carruthers and Colin Kidd (Oxford: Oxford University Press, 2018), 97–122.

Keymer, Thomas, 'Fielding's Machiavellian Moment', in *Henry Fielding (1707–1754), Novelist, Playwright, Journalist: A Double Anniversary Tribute*, ed. Claude Rawson (Newark: University of Delaware Press, 2008), 58–91.

Keymer, Thomas, 'Fielding's Theatrical Career', in *The Cambridge Companion to Henry Fielding*, ed. Claude Rawson (Cambridge: Cambridge University Press, 2007), 17–37.

Keymer, Thomas, 'Obscenity and the Erotics of Fiction', in *The Cambridge History of the English Novel*, ed. Robert L. Caserio and Clement C. Hawes (Cambridge: Cambridge University Press, 2012), 131–46.

Keymer, Thomas, 'The Practice and Poetics of Curlism: Print, Obscenity, and the *Merryland* Pamphlets in the Career of Edmund Curll', in *Bookish Histories: Books, Literature, and Commercial Modernity, 1700–1900*, ed. Ina Ferris and Paul Keen (New York: Palgrave Macmillan, 2009), 232–56.

Keymer, Thomas, and Peter Sabor, *Pamela in the Marketplace: Literary Controversy and Print Culture in Eighteenth-Century Britain and Ireland* (Cambridge: Cambridge University Press, 2005).

King, Kathryn R., *A Political Biography of Eliza Haywood* (London: Pickering & Chatto, 2012).

Kinservik, Matthew J., *Disciplining Satire: The Censorship of Satiric Comedy on the Eighteenth-Century London Stage* (Lewisburg: Bucknell University Press, 2002).

Kinservik, Matthew J., 'The Dialectics of Print and Performance after 1737', in *The Oxford Handbook of the Georgian Theatre, 1737–1832*, ed. Julia Swindells and David Francis Taylor (Oxford: Oxford University Press, 2014), 123–39.

Kitchin, George, *Sir Roger L'Estrange: A Contribution to the History of the Press in the Seventeenth Century* (London: Kegan Paul, 1913).

Knapp, L. M., 'Ralph Griffiths, Author and Publisher, 1746–1750', *The Library*, 4th ser. 20.1 (1939–40), 197–213.

Knight, Charles A., *A Political Biography of Richard Steele* (London: Pickering & Chatto, 2015).

Knights, Mark, *Representation and Misrepresentation in Later Stuart Britain: Partisanship and Political Culture* (Oxford: Oxford University Press, 2005).

Knoppers, Laura Lunger, *Constructing Cromwell: Ceremony, Portrait, and Print, 1645–1661* (Cambridge: Cambridge University Press, 2000).

Knoppers, Laura Lunger, '"England's Case": Contexts of the 1671 Poems', in *The Oxford Handbook of Milton*, ed. Nicholas McDowell and Nigel Smith (Oxford: Oxford University Press, 2009), 571–88.

Kroll, Richard, '"Tales of Love and Gallantry": The Politics of *Oroonoko*', *Huntington Library Quarterly*, 67.4 (2005), 573–605.

Kropf, C. R., 'Libel and Satire in the Eighteenth Century', *Eighteenth-Century Studies*, 8.2 (1974–5), 153–68.

Langford, Paul, 'Swift and Walpole', in *Politics and Literature in the Age of Swift: English and Irish Perspectives*, ed. Claude Rawson (Cambridge: Cambridge University Press, 2010), 52–78.

LeGette, Casie, *Remaking Romanticism: The Radical Politics of the Excerpt* (Basingstoke: Palgrave Macmillan, 2017).

Leonard, John, 'Self-Contradicting Puns in *Paradise Lost*', in *A Companion to Milton*, ed. Thomas N. Corns (Oxford: Blackwell, 2001), 393–410.

Lewalski, Barbara K., *The Life of John Milton: A Critical Biography* (Oxford: Blackwell, 2000).

Liesenfeld, Vincent J., *The Licensing Act of 1737* (Madison: University of Wisconsin Press, 1984).

Love, Harold, *English Clandestine Satire, 1660–1702* (Oxford: Oxford University Press, 2004).

Love, Harold, *Scribal Publication in Seventeenth-Century England* (Oxford: Clarendon Press, 1993).

Lund, Roger D., '"An Alembick of Innuendos": Satire, Libel, and *The Craftsman*', *Philological Quarterly*, 95.2 (2016), 243–68.

Lund, Roger D., *Ridicule, Religion and the Politics of Wit in Augustan England* (Farnham: Ashgate, 2012).

McDowell, Nicholas, *Poetry and Allegiance in the English Civil Wars: Marvell and the Cause of Wit* (Oxford: Oxford University Press, 2008).

McDowell, Paula, *The Invention of the Oral: Print Commerce and Fugitive Voices in Eighteenth-Century Britain* (Chicago: University of Chicago Press, 2016).

McDowell, Paula, *The Women of Grub Street: Press, Politics, and Gender in the London Literary Marketplace, 1678–1730* (Oxford: Clarendon Press, 1998).

McElligott, Jason, *Royalism, Print and Censorship in Revolutionary England* (Woodbridge: Boydell, 2007).

McGann, Jerome J., *The Textual Condition* (Princeton: Princeton University Press, 1991).

McGirr, Elaine M., *Heroic Mode and Political Crisis, 1660–1745* (Newark: University of Delaware Press, 2009).

Mack, Maynard, *Alexander Pope: A Life* (New Haven: Yale University Press, 1985).

McKenzie, D. F., *Making Meaning: 'Printers of the Mind' and Other Essays*, ed. Peter D. MacDonald and Michael F. Suarez (Amherst: University of Massachusetts Press, 2002).

McKenzie, D. F., 'Printing and Publishing 1557–1700: Constraints on the London Book Trades', in *The Cambridge History of the Book in Britain, Volume 4: 1557–1695*, ed. John Barnard and D. F. McKenzie with Maureen Bell (Cambridge: Cambridge University Press, 2002), 553–67.

McKenzie, D. F., and Maureen Bell, *A Chronology and Calendar of Documents Relating to the London Book Trade, 1641–1700*, 3 vols (Oxford: Oxford University Press, 2005).

McKeon, Michael, *The Secret History of Domesticity: Public, Private, and the Division of Knowledge* (Baltimore: Johns Hopkins University Press, 2005).

McLaverty, James, *Pope, Print, and Meaning* (Oxford: Oxford University Press, 2001).

McLaverty, James, 'The Revision of the First Edition of *Gulliver's Travels*: Book-Trade Context, Interleaving, Two Cancels, and a Failure to Catch', *Papers of the Bibliographical Society of America*, 106 (2012), 5–35.

McLynn, Frank, *Charles Edward Stuart* (Oxford: Oxford University Press, 1991).

McLynn, Frank, *Crime and Punishment in Eighteenth-Century England* (Oxford: Oxford University Press, 1991).

McRae, Andrew, *Literature, Satire and the Early Stuart State* (Cambridge: Cambridge University Press, 2004).

McWilliams, John, ' "A Storm of Lamentations Writ": *Lachrymae Musarum* and Royalist Culture after the Civil War', *Yearbook of English Studies*, 33 (2003), 273–89.

Malcolm, Noel, *Aspects of Hobbes* (Oxford: Oxford University Press, 2002).

Maltzahn, Nicholas von, *An Andrew Marvell Chronology* (Basingstoke: Palgrave Macmillan, 2005).

Maltzahn, Nicholas von, 'L'Estrange's Milton', in *Roger L'Estrange and the Making of Restoration Culture*, ed. Anne Dunan-Page and Beth Lynch (Aldershot: Ashgate, 2008), 27–54.

Maltzahn, Nicholas von, 'Marvell's Ghost', in *Marvell and Liberty*, ed. Warren Chernaik and Martin Dzelzainis (Basingstoke: Macmillan, 1999), 50–74.

Manogue, Ralph A., 'The Plight of James Ridgway, London Bookseller and Publisher, and the Newgate Radicals, 1792–1797', *Wordsworth Circle*, 27 (1996), 158–66.

Marsh, Joss, *Word Crimes: Blasphemy, Culture, and Literature in Nineteenth-Century England* (Chicago: University of Chicago Press, 1998).

Marshall, Ashley, 'The Generic Context of Defoe's *The Shortest-Way with the Dissenters* and the Problem of Irony', *RES*, 61 (2010), 234–58.

Marshall, Peter H., *William Godwin* (New Haven: Yale University Press, 1984).

Mayton, William T., 'Seditious Libel and the Lost Guarantee of a Freedom of Expression', *Columbia Law Review* 84 (1984), 91–142.

Mee, Jon, *Print, Publicity, and Popular Radicalism in the 1790s: The Laurel of Liberty* (Cambridge: Cambridge University Press, 2016).

Mee, Jon, 'Treason, Seditious Libel, and Literature in the Romantic Period' (2016), in *Oxford Handbooks Online*.

Milhous, Judith, 'Theatre Companies and Regulation', in *The Cambridge History of British Theatre, Volume 2: 1660–1895*, ed. Joseph Donohue (Cambridge: Cambridge University Press, 2004), 108–25.

Miner, Earl, *Dryden's Poetry* (Bloomington: Indiana University Press, 1967).

Monod, Paul, *Jacobitism and the English People, 1688–1788* (Cambridge: Cambridge University Press, 1989).

Monod, Paul, 'The Jacobite Press and English Censorship, 1689–95', in *The Stuart Court in Exile and the Jacobites*, ed. Eveline Cruickshanks and Edward Corp (London: Hambledon Press, 1995), 125–42.

Mueller, Andreas K. E., 'A "Body Unfitt": Daniel Defoe in the Pillory and the Resurrection of the Versifying Self', *The Eighteenth Century: Theory and Interpretation*, 54 (2013), 393–407.

Mullan, John, *Anonymity: A Secret History of English Literature* (London: Faber, 2007).

Mullan, John, 'Dryden's Anonymity', in *The Cambridge Companion to John Dryden*, ed. Steven N. Zwicker (Cambridge: Cambridge University Press, 2004), 156–80.

Neth, Michael J., 'A Committee of One: Shelley's Preemptive Self-Censorships in the Draft Manuscripts of *Laon and Cythna* and Legal Censorship of the Press', in *Publishing, Editing, and Reception: Essays in Honor of Donald H. Reiman*, ed. Michael Edson (Newark: University of Delaware Press, 2015), 215–43.

Newton, Theodore F. M., 'William Pittis and Queen Anne Journalism', *Modern Philology*, 33.2–3 (1935–6), 169–86 and 279–302.

Norbrook, David, *Writing the English Republic: Poetry, Rhetoric and Politics, 1627–1660* (Cambridge: Cambridge University Press, 1999).

Novak, Maximillian E., *Daniel Defoe: Master of Fictions* (Oxford: Oxford University Press, 2001).

Oldham, James, *Trial by Jury: The Seventh Amendment and Anglo-American Special Juries* (New York: NYU Press, 2006).

Orwell, George, 'Politics vs. Literature: An Examination of *Gulliver's Travels*', in *Collected Essays, Journalism and Letters*, ed. Sonia Orwell and Ian Angus, 4 vols (New York: Harcourt, Brace & World, 1970), 4: 205–23.

Owen, Susan J., *Restoration Theatre and Crisis* (Oxford: Oxford University Press, 1996).

*Oxford Dictionary of National Biography*, <http://www.oxforddnb.com>.

Parker, Fred, *Scepticism and Literature: An Essay on Pope, Hume, Sterne, and Johnson* (Oxford: Oxford University Press, 2003).

Patterson, Annabel, 'Andrew Marvell: Living with Censorship', in *Literature and Censorship in Renaissance England*, ed. Andrew Hadfield (London: Palgrave, 2001), 187–203.

Patterson, Annabel, *Censorship and Interpretation: The Conditions of Writing and Reading in Early Modern England*, revised edn (Madison: University of Wisconsin Press, 1990).

Patterson, Annabel, 'Defeating Innuendos: Thomas Rosewell (1684) and Daniel Isaac Eaton (1794)', in *The State Trials and the Politics of Justice in Later Stuart England*, ed. Brian Cowan and Scott Sowerby (Woodbridge: Boydell & Brewer, forthcoming).

Patterson, Annabel, 'Dryden, Marvell, and the Painful Lesson of Laughter', in *John Dryden (1631–1700): His Politics, His Plays, and His Poets*, ed. Claude Rawson and Aaron Santesso (Newark: University of Delaware Press, 2004), 198–216.

Patterson, Annabel, *Fables of Power: Aesopian Writing and Political History* (Durham, NC: Duke University Press, 1991).

Paulin, Tom, *Crusoe's Secret: The Aesthetics of Dissent* (London: Faber, 2005).

Paulson, Ronald, *Hogarth: Art and Politics, 1750–1764* (Cambridge: Lutterworth Press, 1993).

Philp, Mark, *Reforming Ideas in Britain: Politics and Language in the Shadow of the French Revolution, 1789–1815* (Cambridge: Cambridge University Press, 2013).

Pierce, Helen, 'The Devil's Bloodhound: Roger L'Estrange Caricatured', in *Printed Images in Early Modern Britain: Essays in Interpretation*, ed. Michael Cyril William Hunter (Farnham: Ashgate, 2010), 237–54.

Pittock, Murray G. H., *Material Culture and Sedition, 1688–1760: Treacherous Objects, Secret Places* (Basingstoke: Palgrave Macmillan, 2013).

Pittock, Murray G. H., *Poetry and Jacobite Politics in Eighteenth-Century Britain and Ireland* (Cambridge: Cambridge University Press, 1994).

Pollard, Mary, 'Who's for Prison? Publishing Swift in Dublin', *Swift Studies*, 14 (1999), 37–49.

Poole, Steve, 'Pitt's Terror Reconsidered: Jacobinism and the Law in Two South-Western Counties, 1791–1803', *Southern History*, 17 (1995), 65–87.

Poser, Norman S., *Lord Mansfield: Justice in the Age of Reason* (Montreal: McGill-Queen's University Press, 2013).

Price, Leah, *How To Do Things with Books in Victorian Britain* (Princeton: Princeton University Press, 2012).

Rawson, Claude, *Satire and Sentiment, 1660–1830* (New Haven: Yale University Press, 2000).

Raymond, Joad, 'Censorship in Law and Practice in Seventeenth-Century England: Milton's *Areopagitica*', in *The Oxford Handbook of English Law and Literature, 1500–1700*, ed. Lorna Hutson (Oxford: Oxford University Press, 2017), 507–28.

Rayner, Samantha J., *Images of Kingship in Chaucer and His Ricardian Contemporaries* (Woodbridge: Boydell & Brewer, 2008).

Reese, Christine Noelle, *Controlling Print? Burton, Bastwick and Prynne and the Politics of Memory* (University Park: Pennsylvania State University Press, 2007).

Ribble, Frederick G., 'Fielding's Rapprochement with Walpole in Late 1741', *Philological Quarterly*, 80.1 (2001), 71–81.

Ribble, Frederick G., 'New Light on Henry Fielding from the Malmesbury Papers', *Modern Philology*, 103 (2005), 51–94.

Richards, Penny, 'A Life in Writing: Elizabeth Cellier and Print Culture', *Women's Writing*, 7.3 (2000), 411–25.

Ricks, Christopher, *The Force of Poetry* (Oxford: Clarendon Press, 1984).

Robertson, Randy, *Censorship and Conflict in Seventeenth-Century England: The Subtle Art of Division* (University Park: Pennsylvania State University Press, 2009).

Roe, Nicholas, *John Keats and the Culture of Dissent* (Oxford: Oxford University Press, 1998).

Roe, Nicholas, *The Politics of Nature: William Wordsworth and Some Contemporaries*, 2nd edn (Basingstoke: Palgrave Macmillan, 2002).

Roe, Nicholas, *Wordsworth and Coleridge: The Radical Years* (Oxford: Clarendon Press, 1988).

Rogers, Nicholas, *Crowds, Culture, and Politics in Georgian Britain* (Oxford: Clarendon Press, 1998).

Rogers, Nicholas, 'Popular Protest in Early Hanoverian London', *Past and Present*, 79.1 (1978), 70–100.

Rogers, Pat, *Eighteenth-Century Encounters* (Totowa: Barnes & Noble, 1985), 151–67.

Rogers, Pat, 'Nathaniel Mist, Daniel Defoe, and the Perils of Publishing', *Library*, 10.3 (2009), 298–313.

Rogers, Pat, *A Political Biography of Alexander Pope* (London: Pickering & Chatto, 2010).

Rogers, Pat, *Pope and the Destiny of the Stuarts: History, Politics, and Mythology in the Age of Queen Anne* (Oxford: Oxford University Press, 2005).

Rogers, Pat, 'The Symbols in Pope's *One Thousand Seven Hundred and Forty*', *Modern Philology*, 102.1 (2004), 90–4.

Roper, Alan, 'Innuendo in the Restoration', *JEGP*, 100.1 (2001), 22–39.

Rose, Mark, *Authors in Court: Scenes from the Theater of Copyright* (Cambridge, MA: Harvard University Press, 2016).

Rose, Mark, 'Copyright, Authors and Censorship', in *The Cambridge History of the Book in Britain, Volume 5: 1695–1830*, ed. Michael F. Suarez and Michael L. Turner (Cambridge: Cambridge University Press, 2009), 118–31.

Rosenfeld, Sophia, 'Writing the History of Censorship in the Age of Enlightenment', in *Postmodernism and the Enlightenment: New Perspectives in Eighteenth-Century French Intellectual History*, ed. Daniel Gordon (London: Routledge, 2001), 117–45.

Ross, Trevor, *Writing in Public: Literature and the Liberty of the Press in Eighteenth-Century Britain* (Baltimore: Johns Hopkins University Press, 2018).

Rossington, Michael, 'Tragedy: *The Cenci* and *Swellfoot the Tyrant*', in *The Oxford Handbook of Percy Bysshe Shelley*, ed. Michael O'Neill and Anthony Howe with Madeleine Callaghan (Oxford: Oxford University Press, 2013), 299–308.

Rostenberg, Leona, 'Robert Stephens, Messenger of the Press: An Episode in 17th-Century Censorship', *Papers of the Bibliographical Society of America*, 49.2 (1955), 131–52.

St Clair, William, *The Reading Nation in the Romantic Period* (Cambridge: Cambridge University Press, 2004).

Sambrook, James, *James Thomson, 1700–1748: A Life* (Oxford: Clarendon Press, 1991).

Santesso, Aaron, '*Lachrymae Musarum* and the Metaphysical Dryden', *RES*, 54 (2003), 615–38.

Saslow, Edward L., 'The Rose Alley Ambuscade', *Restoration*, 26 (2002), 27–49.

Schwoerer, Lois G., *The Ingenious Mr. Henry Care, Restoration Publicist* (Baltimore: Johns Hopkins University Press, 2001).

Scott, Jonathan, *Algernon Sidney and the Restoration Crisis, 1677–1683* (Cambridge: Cambridge University Press, 1991).

Scrivener, Michael, *Seditious Allegories: John Thelwall and Jacobin Writing* (University Park: Pennsylvania Statue University Press, 2001).

Sedgwick, Romney R., 'Ward, John (d.1755), of Hackney', *History of Parliament Online*, <https://www.historyofparliamentonline.org>.

Seidel, Michael, 'Crusoe in Exile', *PMLA*, 96 (1981), 363–74.

Sharpe, Kevin, *Criticism and Compliment: The Politics of Literature in the England of Charles I* (Cambridge: Cambridge University Press, 1990).

Shoemaker, Robert, *The London Mob: Violence and Disorder in Eighteenth-Century England* (London: Hambledon, 2004).

Siebert, F. S., *Freedom of the Press in England, 1476–1776: The Rise and Decline of Governmental Controls* (Urbana: University of Illinois Press, 1952).

Simpson, Antony E., 'Spectacular Punishment and the Orchestration of Hate: The Pillory and Popular Morality in Eighteenth-Century England', in *Hate Crime: The Global Politics of Polarization*, ed. Robert J. Kelly and Jess Maghan (Carbondale: Southern Illinois University Press, 1998), 177–220.

Smith, Greg T., 'The Decline of Public Physical Punishment in London, 1760–1840', in *Qualities of Mercy: Justice, Punishment, and Discretion*, ed. Carolyn Strange (Vancouver: UBC Press, 1996), 21–51.

Snyder, Henry L., 'The Reports of a Press Spy for Robert Harley: New Bibliographical Data for the Reign of Queen Anne', *The Library*, 5th ser., 22, no. 4 (1967), 326–45.

Solomon, Harry M., *The Rise of Robert Dodsley: Creating the New Age of Print* (Carbondale: Southern Illinois University Press, 1996).

Speck, W. A., *A Political Biography of Thomas Paine* (London: Pickering & Chatto, 2013).

Stevenson, John Allen, *The Real History of Tom Jones* (Basingstoke: Palgrave Macmillan, 2005).

Taylor, David Francis, 'The Practice of Parody', in *The Oxford Handbook of Eighteenth-Century Satire*, ed. Paddy Bullard (Oxford: Oxford University Press, 2019), 353–68.

Taylor, David Francis, *Theatres of Opposition: Empire, Revolution, and Richard Brinsley Sheridan* (Oxford: Oxford University Press, 2012).

Thomas, David, 'The 1737 Licensing Act and Its Impact', in *The Oxford Handbook of the Georgian Theatre, 1737–1832*, ed. Julia Swindells and David Francis Taylor (Oxford: Oxford University Press, 2014), 91–106.

Thomas, David, David Carlton, and Anne Étienne, *Theatre Censorship: From Walpole to Wilson* (Oxford: Oxford University Press, 2007).

Thomas, Donald, *A Long Time Burning: The History of Literary Censorship in England* (New York: Praeger, 1969).

Thompson, E. P., *The Making of the English Working Class*, revised edn (Harmondsworth: Penguin, 1968).

Todd, Janet, *The Secret Life of Aphra Behn* (New Brunswick: Rutgers University Press, 1997).

Tracy, Clarence, *The Artificial Bastard: A Biography of Richard Savage* (Toronto: University of Toronto Press, 1953).

Treadwell, Michael, 'The Stationers and the Printing Act at the End of the Seventeenth Century', in *The Cambridge History of the Book in Britain, Volume 4: 1557–1695*, ed. John Barnard and D. F. McKenzie with Maureen Bell (Cambridge: Cambridge University Press, 2002), 755–76.

Troyer, Howard William, *Ned Ward of Grub Street: A Study of Sub-Literary London in the Eighteenth Century* (Cambridge, MA: Harvard University Press, 1946).

Urstad, Tone Sundt, *Sir Robert Walpole's Poets: The Use of Literature as Pro-Government Propaganda, 1721–1742* (Newark: University of Delaware Press, 1999).

Visconsi, Elliott, *Lines of Equity: Literature and the Origins of Law in Later Stuart England* (Ithaca: Cornell University Press, 2008).

Walker, Jeffrey K., 'A Poisen in Ye Commonwealthe: Seditious Libel in Hanoverian London', *Anglo-American Law Review*, 26 (1997), 341–66.

Weber, Harold, *Paper Bullets: Print and Kingship under Charles II* (Lexington: University Press of Kentucky, 1996).

Wheatley, Kim, *Romantic Feuds: Transcending the 'Age of Personality'* (Farnham: Ashgate, 2013).

Wilcher, Robert, 'Eikon Basilike: The Printing, Composition, Strategy, and Impact of "The King's Book"', in *The Oxford Handbook of Literature and the English Revolution*, ed. Laura Lunger Knoppers (Oxford: Oxford University Press, 2012), 289–308.

Williams, Abigail, *Poetry and the Creation of a Whig Literary Culture, 1681–1714* (Oxford: Oxford University Press, 2005).

Wimsatt, W. K., *The Prose Style of Samuel Johnson* (New Haven: Yale University Press, 1941).

Winn, James Anderson, *John Dryden and His World* (New Haven: Yale University Press, 1987).

Winn, James Anderson, 'The Promise of Dryden's Elegy for Hastings', *Modern Language Review*, 79.1 (1984), 21–31.

Wohlcke, Anne, *The 'Perpetual Fair': Gender, Disorder and Urban Amusement in Eighteenth-Century London* (Manchester: Manchester University Press, 2014).

Womersley, David, 'Confessional Politics in Defoe's *Journal of the Plague Year*', in *Cultures of Whiggism*, ed. David Womersley with Paddy Bullard and Abigail Williams (Newark: University of Delaware Press, 2005), 237–56.

Wood, Gillen D'Arcy, *Tambora: The Eruption That Changed the World* (Princeton: Princeton University Press, 2014).

Wood, Marcus, *Radical Satire and Print Culture, 1790–1822* (Oxford: Clarendon Press, 1994).

Woods, C. J., 'Cox, Walter', in *Dictionary of Irish Biography*.

Worden, Blair, *Literature and Politics in Cromwellian England: John Milton, Andrew Marvell, Marchamont Nedham* (Oxford: Oxford University Press, 2007).

Wright, Jonathan Jeffrey, 'An Anglo-Irish Radical in the Late Georgian Metropolis: Peter Finnerty and the Politics of Contempt', *Journal of British Studies*, 53 (2014), 660–84.

Zall, Paul M., 'Lord Eldon's Censorship', *PMLA*, 68 (1953), 436–43.

Zwicker, Steven N., ' "He seems a king by long succession born": The Problem of Cromwellian Accession and Succession', in *Stuart Succession Literature: Moments and Transformations*, ed. Paulina Kewes and Andrew McRae (Oxford: Oxford University Press, 2018), 60–74.

Zwicker, Steven N., *Politics and Language in Dryden's Poetry: The Arts of Disguise* (Princeton: Princeton University Press, 1984).

Zwicker, Steven N., and David Bywaters, 'Politics and Translation: The English Tacitus of 1698', *Huntington Library Quarterly*, 52.3 (1989), 319–46.

Zwicker, Steven N., and Derek Hirst, 'Marvell and Lyrics of Undifference', in *The Oxford Handbook of Andrew Marvell*, ed. Martin Dzelzainis and Edward Holberton (Oxford: Oxford University Press, 2019).

# Index

*Note*: Figures are indicated by an italic *f* following the page number.

For technical reasons connected with digital access, index entries point to the full paragraph in which an indexed term occurs. On occasion, terms indicated by a two-page span (e.g. 52–3) may appear on only one of those pages.

'Advice to a Painter' poems 31–3, 61–2; *see also* Marvell, Andrew
Aesopian writing 75–6, 82–5, 114–15, 242–54
*Albion's Fatal Tree* 18–19
allegory 62, 70–4, 83–5, 124–5, 148–9, 151–4, 181–2, 232–4, 243–5; *see also* analogy, encoding
amatory fiction 90–1, 157n.2
ambiguity, functional 22–5, 83–5, 99–100, 115–17, 123–5, 127, 242, 260–1, 288–9; *see also* indeterminacy, indirection
American Revolution 161–3, 201–2, 275–6
Amhurst, Nicholas 115–16, 178–9, 186–8
Amin, Idi 18n.37
analogy 39–44, 55–7, 59–60, 70–4, 80–1, 85–7, 110–13, 129–30, 149–54, 197–8, 243–5, 249–53; *see also* allegory
Anderton, William 78–9, 121–2
Angelico, Fra (Guido di Pietro) 143*f*
Anne, Queen 145–6, 166–7
*Anti-Jacobin Review* 266
apophasis 110–13, 128–9
Arbuthnot, John 110
Archenholz, Johann Wilhelm von: *Picture of England* 172–4
Association for Preservation of Liberty and Property 242
Atkinson, Christopher 1–3, 2*f*
Atterbury, Francis 106–7, 178–9
Atterbury Plot 106–7, 251–2
Aubrey, John 35–6, 160n.11
authors:
 executed 64–6, 121–2
 imprisoned 3–5, 19–20, 114, 168n.32, 178–9, 186–8
 negotiating with officials or politicians 23, 79–81, 131–2, 193–4, 198–9, 254–5
 patronage or purchase of 20–1, 78–9, 131–2, 179–82, 192–4, 198–9, 208–9, 240–1; *see also* pensions
 pilloried 3–5, 9–13, 64–6, 69*f*, 89–90, 96–108, 131–45, 133*f*, 135*f*, 136*f*, 137*f*, 139*f*, 140*f*, 141*f*, 159–60, 165–6, 169–72, 226–7
 relative importance of, as prosecution targets 5–7, 32–3, 97–8, 178–9, 205–6
 uncertain about libel law 18–23, 121–5, 238–9

Bacon, Francis 56n.74
Baines, Paul 108
Ball, John 277
ballad operas; *see* dramatic satire
ballads 1–3, 65–6, 95–6, 261–2
Barbauld, Anna Laetitia:
 *Eighteen Hundred and Eleven* 286–7
Barber, John 20–1, 106–7, 109n.65
Barber, Mary 178–9
Barlow, Francis 69*f*
Barrell, John 14–15, 243–6, 250–1, 259–60, 285–6
Barrin, Jean:
 *Venus in the Cloister* 167
Bastwick, John 9–10
Beardmore, Arthur 169–71
Beattie, John 1–3, 167–8
Beckford, William (the Elder) 274–5

## Index

Behn, Aphra 70–1, 78–9, 184
  *Oroonoko* 77–8
  'Pindaric Poem to Burnet' 78–9
Bentham, Jeremy 19–20
Bethel, Slingsby 36–7
Bickham, George:
  *Whigs Medly* 134, 136f
Bingley, Edmund 114
Bishop, Philip 114
Bisse, Edward 164–5
Black, Jeremy 188
Blackburne, Francis 205–6
  *Remarks on Johnson's Life of Milton* 205–8
Blackstone, William:
  *Commentaries* 7–8, 8n.14, 17–19, 94–5
Blake, William 25, 83–5, 243
blasphemous libel 6–7, 10f, 32n.18, 64–5, 73–4, 93–4, 159, 223–5, 227–8, 236–9
Bloody Assizes 153–4
Blount, Charles:
  *Plot in a Dream* (attrib.) 67f
Bold, Samuel 40–1
Bolingbroke, Henry St John, 1st Viscount 93–4, 104–6, 109–10, 118–19, 149–50, 175–6
Bond, John 101–2
book-burning 3–5, 54, 66f, 87–8, 98, 144, 176–8, 245–6
booksellers; *see* book-trade professionals
book-trade professionals:
  clandestine 22–3, 31–2, 168n.31
  executed 16–17, 32–3, 83–5, 154–5, 167–8
  imprisoned 20–1, 82, 95–6, 114, 118, 168n.32, 186–8, 192n.106, 264–5
  pilloried 10–12, 20, 32–3, 37n.31, 64–6, 66f, 104–6, 157–9, 164–7, 172–4, 174f, 176–8, 226–31, 231f
  provincial 6–7, 114, 226–7, 234n.34
  relative importance of, as prosecution targets 5–7, 32–3, 97–8, 178–9, 205–6
Bossy, Peter James 223
Boswell, James:
  *Life of Johnson* 164–5, 206–7, 213–14, 218–19
Bourdieu, Pierre 18–19, 254–5, 285–6
Boyer, Abel 178–9
Bramston, James:
  *Man of Taste* 176–8

Brett, John 213
Bricker, Andrew 125n.113
Brome, Richard 40–1; see also *Lachrymae musarum*
Brooke, Henry 185–6
  *Fool of Quality* 185–6
  *Gustavus Vasa* 185–6, 206–7, 272–3
brothel-keeping; *see* sexual offences
Brown, Tom 37–8
  'Pleasant Dialogue' 134–8
Browne, Joseph 97–100, 124–5
  *Country Parson's Honest Advice* 123–4, 283–4
Buckingham, John Sheffield, 1st Duke of 106–7
Buckingham, Katherine Sheffield, Duchess of 108–9
Bugg, John 260–1
Bulwer, William 240
Burdett, Francis 227–8, 230–1, 234–5, 238–9
Burke, Edmund 1–3, 161–3, 225–6
  *Appeal from New to Old Whigs* 277
  *Reflections on Revolution in France* 242, 270–1
Burnet, Gilbert 77–8, 81, 123–4; *see also* Behn, 'Pindaric Poem'
Burton, Henry 9–12
Bute, John Stuart, 3rd Earl of 171–4, 174f, 183–4
Butler, Marilyn 243, 278–9
Butler, Samuel 159–60
Byron, George Gordon Noel, 6th Baron 271–2, 288–9
  *Cain* 271–2
  *Don Juan* 271–2
  *Vision of Judgement* 284–5

Caligula 238–9, 249–50
Callender, James Thomson:
  *Deformities of Samuel Johnson* 218
Calvert, Elizabeth and Giles 32n.18
Camus, Albert:
  *La Peste* 151–2
Canning (or Cannyn), William 82
Captain Swing Riots 235
Care, Henry 27–8, 32–4, 122–3
  'Towser the Second' 27–8
caricature 266
Carlyle, Thomas 218
carrots; *see* sticks

Carteret, John, 2nd Baron, 2nd Earl Granville 175–6
Castlereagh, Robert Stewart, Viscount 283–4
Cato Street Conspiracy 233–5
Cave, Edward 210–12
Cellier, Elizabeth 3–5, 65–6, 69*f*
  *Malice Defeated* 3–5, 65–6
censorship; *see also* licensing:
  and rule of law? 18–19, 95–6, 175–6, 178–9
  as creative stimulus 21–6, 87–8, 287–9
  as inadvertent promotion 14, 70–1, 206–7, 250–1
  as negotiable 23, 80–1, 131–2, 198–9
  as thought control 209–10, 214–15, 245–6
  constitutive 18–19, 254–5, 285–6
  controls on theatre before 1737 54, 181–4
  decline of 13–14, 21–2, 202, 237–9, 257–8, 283–9
  defined 18–19, 27–8, 92–4
  distributed responsibility for 18n.36, 29–30, 35–6
  hermeneutics of 9–10, 62–3, 216–17, 249
  improvised mechanisms of 13–14, 178n.59
  in Ancient Rome 85–7
  indirect (via copyright or revenue laws) 16–17, 93–4, 240–1, 271–2
  informal (raids, harassment) 20–1, 27–8, 95–8, 117–18, 175–6, 178–9, 257n.101
  in France 23, 87–8, 90–2
  in Restoration England 34–7, 62–71
  persistence of 14–22
  post-publication retribution 3–13, 17–21, 92–3, 95–6; *see also* pillory, punishments
  pre-publication restraint; *see* licensing
  self-censorship 255–6, 258–61, 271–2, 285–6
Chandler, James 286–7
Charles I, King 28–9, 160n.11
Charles II, King 35–6, 45–6, 55–8, 244–5
cheap print; *see* popular print
Chesterfield, Philip Dormer Stanhope, 4th Earl of 184–8

Churchill, Charles 102–3, 171–2, 178–9
  *Author* 170–1
Church of England 97–8, 123–4, 127–31, 134–8, 153–4, 167–8
Cibber, Colley 182–3, 195–6, 214–15
Clarendon, Edward Hyde, 1st Earl of 12–13
Clarke, Norma 157n.2
Clegg, Cyndia Susan 23n.45, 96
Cleland, John:
  *Memoirs of a Woman of Pleasure* 175–6
Cleveland, John:
  *Idol of the Clownes* 274
Cobbett, William 10–11, 21–2, 227–8, 235, 240
  *Political Register* 229–30, 235, 240–1
  *Rural Rides* 235
  'Rural War' 235
  *Soldier's Friend* 272
Cochrane, Thomas, Lord 230–1
Cock–Lane Ghost 171–2, 173*f*
coffee houses 36–7, 64–5, 92
Coleridge, Samuel Taylor 240–1, 259–60, 267*f*, 272, 288n.12
  'Fire, Famine, and Slaughter' 259–60
  *Lyrical Ballads* 254–5
  *Moral and Political Lecture* 263–4
  'This Lime–Tree Bower My Prison' 260–1
College, Stephen 65–6, 285n.4
  *Ra–Ree Show* 65–6, 285n.4
*Common Sense* 188, 213
Congreve, William 110–13
Constitutional Association for Opposing Seditious Principles 284–5
Cooke, Thomas 30–1
Cookson, William 114–15
  *Nero the Second* 113–14
Cooper, Thomas 254–5, 270–1
copyright; *see* literary property
*Courier* 288
Courteville, Ralph 191
Cowan, Brian 92n.10
Cox, Walter 230–1, 231*f*, 233–4, 249; *see also* Finn, Thomas
  *Irish Magazine* 230–3
*Craftsman* 109–10, 115–16, 157n.2, 174–5, 182–3, 186–8, 191n.102, 252–3
  courtroom defence of; *see* Fazakerley, Nicholas

Cromwell, Oliver 28–9, 43–4, 47–9, 136f, 265; see also *Three Poems upon Death of Cromwell*
Cromwell, Richard 43–4
Crook, Japhet 107–8
Crowe, Eyre:
  *Defoe in the Pillory* 138–42, 141f, 218–19
  *Dr Johnson Doing Penance* 218–19, 219f
Crowne, John:
  *City Politiques* 70–1
Culliford (or Colliford), John 64–5, 66f
Cumberland, George 255–6
  *Captive of Castle of Sennaar* 255–6
Curll, Edmund 6–7, 30–1, 103–4, 106–7, 157n.2, 159, 166–7, 176–8, 225–6
Curtis, Jane 65–6

*Daily Gazetter* 188–9, 191
Dalton, Isaac 75–6, 149–50, 164–5
Darnton, Robert 23, 90–2
Davenant, William 101n.44
*Déclaration des droits de l'Homme* 275–6
decoding 29–30, 77–8, 118–19, 150–1, 216–18, 236–7, 242–54; *see also* encoding
defamation 114–15, 125n.114, 171–2, 188; see also *scandalum magnatum*
Defoe, Daniel 3–8, 89n.1, 100–6, 105f, 121–48, 133f, 135f, 136f, 137f, 139f, 140f, 141f, 150–5, 164–5, 179–80, 218–19, 287–8
  *Answer to Question That Nobody Thinks of* 145–6
  *Appeal to Honour and Justice* 153–4
  *Brief Explanation of The Shortest Way* 128–9
  *Consolidator* 7–8
  *Essay on Regulation of Press* 16–19, 121–2, 248–9
  *Hymn to the Pillory* 3–5, 144–5
  *Journal of a Plague Year* 150–1
  *Jure Divino* 132–4, 135f, 153, 287–8
  *Legion's Memorial* 131–2
  *Moll Flanders* 154–5
  *New Test of Church of England's Honesty* 152
  *Original Power of People of England* 131–2
  Petition to Queen Anne 145–8, 147f
  *Present State of Parties* 127–8, 152
  *Reasons against Succession of Hanover* 145–6
  *Review* 103–4, 145–6, 175–6
  *Robinson Crusoe* 100–1, 150–5
  *Serious Reflections* 151–3
  *Shortest Way* 3–5, 126–32, 137f, 152
Delafaye, Charles 6–7, 95–6, 148, 165–6, 174–5, 178–9, 186–8
Denham, John 31–2, 39–40, 160n.11
deniability 22–3, 43, 74, 82–3, 85–6, 116–17, 127–8, 150–1, 212–13, 244–5
*Dialogue between Louis le Petite, and Harlequin le Grand* 97–8
Dickens, Charles 241n.58
Dissenters 126–32, 150–4, 277
Dodsley, Robert 118, 210–13
Domitian 85–6, 244–5, 249–50
Dottin, Paul 138–42, 139f
Downie, J. A. 99–100
Drake, James 98, 122n.100
  *Mercurius Politicus* 98
drama 62–3, 70–4, 181–6, 192–6, 264–81
  censorship of 80–1, 94–5, 181–2, 184–6, 192–3, 209–10, 254–5
  rehearsal plays 194–6
  topical application tragedy: 62–3, 70–4, 80–1, 183–6, 272–81
Dreiser, Theodore 221–3
Dry, Richard 226–7
Dryden, John 27–9, 33–88, 110–13, 149–50, 195, 208–9
  *Absalom and Achitophel* 27–8, 36–8, 41n.44, 62–3, 81
  *Albion and Albanius* 54
  *Alexander's Feast* 227–8
  *Amphitryon* 79n.128
  *Annus Mirabilis* 27–8, 51–4, 149n.161
  *Astraea Redux* 55–7
  *Cleomenes* 80–1
  'Discourse Concerning Satire' 83–7
  *Duke of Guise* 62–3, 70–4
  *Heroic Stanzas* 37–8, 43–4, 47–55, 261–2, 265; see also *Elegy on the Usurper O. C.*
  *Hind and Panther* 37–8, 41n.44, 75–8, 82–3
  *History of the League* 37–8
  *King Arthur* 79n.128
  *Mac Flecknoe* 57–62, 110–13, 134–8
  *Medal* 62–3

## Index

Preface to *Ovid's Epistles* 82–5
Prologue to *The Prophetess* 79–80, 184
Song from *Secular Masque* 33–4
*State of Innocence* 29
*To His Sacred Majesty* 57
'Third Satire of Juvenal' 82–3, 86–7
'Twelfth Book of Ovid's *Metamorphoses*' 75
'Upon the Death of Hastings' 42–3, 48–9
'Upon the Death of Dundee' 82–3
*Vindication of The Duke of Guise* 72–5
Dyer, John 174–5, 178–9
Dzelzainis, Martin 31–2

Eaton, Daniel Isaac 6–7, 10–11, 227–31, 242–53
 *Pernicious Effects of Printing* 245–6
 *Politics for the People, or Hog's Wash* 242–6, 253, 263–5
Egan, James 161–3, 162*f*
*Eikon Basilike* 40–1
Eldon, John Scott, 1st Earl of 246n.71, 254–5, 269–72, 283–5
elegy 39–54
*Elegy on the Usurper O. C.* 51–4, 52*f*
Ellenborough, Edward Law, 1st Baron 227–8, 230–1, 237–8
ellipsis 46–7, 118–19, 120*f*, 190, 233, 260–1
Empson, William 200–1, 213
Emsley, Clive 257–8
encoding 24–5, 43, 75–6, 114–16, 123, 150–5, 176–8, 233–4, 242–53, 260–1, 280–1, 287–8; *see also* decoding, innuendo:
 linguistic and bibliographic 31–2, 38–40, 109–10, 148
engravings 134, 161–3
epic 29, 47–8, 82n.136, 106–7; *see also* mock epic
epideixis 42, 123–4
Erskine, Henry 255–6
Erskine, Thomas 247n.75
Esdaile, James Kennedy 277n.152
Etherege, George:
 *Man of Mode* 66–70
Evelyn, John 48–9
Exclusion Crisis 5–6, 13–14, 36–7, 57–8, 62–75, 82–3, 248–9

*Exeter Mercury* 114
*ex officio* information 20–1, 238–9
Eyre, James 256–7, 278
Ezell, Margaret J. M. 18n.36

fable; *see* Aesopian writing
*Fall of Mortimer* 183–4
false attribution 31–2
false imprints 22–3, 31–2, 110
farce; *see* dramatic satire
Farley, Edward 168n.32
Fazakerley, Nicholas 109–10, 115–16, 212–13, 252–3
Feather, John 15–16, 91
Felski, Rita 25
Ferguson, Robert:
 *Second Part of The Growth of Popery* (attrib.) 64–5
Fielding, Henry 94–5, 158–9, 165–7, 188–201, 288–9
 *Author's Farce* 158–9
 *Champion* 159, 188–93; *see also* Ralph, James
 *Covent–Garden Journal* 159, 165–6
 'Essay of Knowledge of Characters of Men' 192–3
 *Eurydice Hiss'd* 195–6
 *Grub–Street Opera* 192–3
 *Historical Register* 192–5
 *Jacobite's Journal* 198–9
 *Jonathan Wild* 182–3, 197–9, 288–9
 *Joseph Andrews* 191, 196–7, 199
 *Journal of a Voyage to Lisbon* 200–1
 *Modern Husband* 193–4
 *Of True Greatness* 198–9
 *Opposition: A Vision* 199
 *Pasquin* 192–3
 *Shamela* 196–7
 *Tom Jones* 25–6, 116–17, 199–201
 *True Patriot* 199–200
 *Vernoniad* 200–1
 *Welsh Opera* 183–4
Fielding, William 250–2
Finch, Heneage 244–5
Finn, Thomas:
 'Painter Cut' 230–4
Finnerty, Peter 226–7
Firth, Charles 102–3
*Fog's Weekly Journal* 166, 182–3, 186, 217–18

# Index

Foote, Samuel 157–8, 164–5
  *Author* 157–8
  *Devil upon Two Sticks* 157–8
  *Patron* 157–8
forgery 1–3, 7–9, 89–90, 107–8,
  169n.34
Forster, John 142
Foster, John 277n.152
Foucault, Michel 7–8, 204–5
Fox, Samuel M.:
  *Delaware Pillory and Whipping Post* 222f
France; *see also* French Revolution:
  censorship in 23, 90–2
  smuggled print in 90–1
Francklin, Richard 115–16, 157n.2
fraud 1–3, 7–9, 107–8, 169
Frederick, Prince of Wales 196
freedom of expression; *see* liberty of the
  press
French Revolution 5–7, 257–8, 277
Frost, John 225–6
Fuller, William 132–4

Gay, John 182–3
  *Beggar's Opera* 181–3
  *Polly* 182–4
Gaywood, Richard 10f
general warrants 93–4
*Gentleman's Magazine* 206, 217–18
George I, King 60, 113, 115n.79,
  169–70
George II, King 60, 110–13, 116–17,
  208–9
George III, King 171–2, 179–80,
  229–30, 244–5, 262–3, 284–6
Gibbon, Edward 14–15
Gifford, John:
  *Plain Address to People of England* 274–5
Gildon, Charles 178–9
Gillray, James:
  *New Morality* 266, 267f
  *Tom Paine's Nightly Pest* 247f
Gilmartin, Kevin 22n.43
Girling, Robert 177n.56
Glorious Revolution 3–5, 14–15, 75–6,
  78–9, 89–91, 94–5, 277
Godolphin, Sidney, 1st Earl of 123–4,
  174–5, 179–80
Godwin, William 256–7
  *Caleb Williams* 256–7
  *Cursory Strictures* 256–7, 278–9
  *Enquiry Concerning Political Justice*
    256–7
Goldie, Mark 36–7, 92–3, 150–1
Gordon Riots 202
Goth, Lord 171–2
Gould, Robert 54
Grande, James 235
Griffiths, Ralph 157n.2, 199–200
  *Ascanius* 175–6
Grubstreet 5–6, 93–4, 101–2,
  106–7, 134–8, 157–8,
  176–9, 218
*Grubstreet Journal* 176–8
'Gurney defence' 72–3, 250–3
Gurney, John 250–3
Guthrie, William 178–9, 181n.67,
  217–18

Habermas, Jürgen 14, 92
Haines, Henry 186–8
Hall, John 39n.36
Hamburger, Philip 64n.93, 178n.59
Hammond, Paul 59n.78, 60n.81
Hanoverian Accession 92–3, 106–7, 125,
  145–9, 164–5, 167–8
Harding, John 20–1
Hardinge, George 257–8
Hardwicke, Philip Yorke, 1st Earl
  of 175–6, 178–9, 188
Harley, Robert 5–6, 97–100, 131–2,
  146–8, 178–80
Harling, Philip 237–8
Harris, James 199
Harris, Michael 186–8
Harris, Robert:
  *Charlottetown Pillory* 224f
Harrison, Thomas 101–2
Hastings, Henry, Lord 39–41
Hatchett, William; see *Fall of Mortimer*
Havard, William:
  *King Charles* 184, 272–3
Hawkins, John 178–9, 215–18
Hawkins, William:
  *Pleas of the Crown* 125
Haywood, Eliza 100–1, 178–9,
  199–200
  *Letter from H[enry] G[orin]g* 175–6
Hazlitt, William 265–9, 272
  *Spirit of the Age* 269n.131

Henley, Robert:
  *Wat Tyler and Jack Straw; or, The Mob Reformers* 273–4
hermeneutics of suspicion 25
Herringman, Henry 43–5, 58–9
Hervey, John, Lord 115–16
hieroglyphics 118–19, 123
Higgons, Bevil 178–9
history:
  censorship of 169–70
  Tacitean 85
  Whig view of 14–16, 91, 138–42
Hobbes, Thomas 35–6
  *Behemoth* 35–6
Hogarth, William:
  *Times* 171–2, 173f
Holberton, Edward 46–7
Holcroft, Thomas 256
  *Anna St Ives* 256
Holt, John 122–5
Homer 84n.142, 106–7
Hone, Joseph 150n.162
Hone, William 236–8, 269–70, 287–8
  *Right Divine of Kings to Govern Wrong!* 287–8
  *Three Trials* 236–8
Hooton, John 226n.12
Horace 85–6
Hume, David:
  *History of England* 90–1
Hunt, John 234–5, 284–5, 287–8
Hunt, Leigh 284–6
  *Examiner* 225–6, 284–5
Hunt, Thomas 71–3, 74, 144–5
Hurt, William 104–6
Hutcheon, Linda 126n.115

*ignoramus* verdicts 36–7, 66–70, 166
imitation, formal 82–3, 206–13, 262–3
Inchbald, Elizabeth 257–8
  *Nature and Art* 257–8
indeterminacy 22–4, 200–1, 250–2; *see also* ambiguity
indirection 22–5, 83–5, 123, 126–7, 166, 192, 238, 243, 254–5, 286–8
innuendo 103–4, 121–2, 251–3
  legal definition of 122n.100, 249–50

interpretation 25–6, 72–4, 77–8, 83–6, 121–31, 200–1, 216–17, 250–1; *see also* decoding, reading
*Irish Magazine, see* Cox, Walter
irony 47–54, 145–8
  'double irony' 200–1, 213
  prosecution of 99–100, 123–32
  Scriblerian 148–9, 213–18
Ireland, seditious libel in 20–1, 114, 226–7, 230–4, 249

Jacobinism 225–6, 259–60, 274–6, 279–81; *see also* novel, Jacobin
Jackson, John 226n.12
Jacobite Rebellion (1715) 106–7, 157–8, 164–5, 177n.56, 257–8
Jacobite Rebellion (1745–6) 117–18, 175–6, 199–200, 245–6, 257–8
Jacobite verse 113–15, 176–8
Jacobitism 16–17, 78–83, 93–4, 106–7, 110–18, 145–50, 154–5, 164–9, 179–80, 199–200, 207–18, 245–6, 257–8
James II, King 152–3
Jeffreys, George, 1st Baron 64n.94, 153–4, 252
Johnson, Samuel 6–7, 14, 118, 164–5, 178–80, 201–19, 219f; *see also* Boswell, James:
  *Compleat Vindication* 188–9, 213–16
  *Debates in Parliament* 206
  *Dictionary* 205–6, 218
  *Lives of the Poets* 201–7
    'Life of Dryden' 43, 49–50, 54–5
    'Life of Milton' 202–6, 250–1
    'Life of Thomson' 206–7
  *London* 206–13, 211f, 214–18, 261–3
  *Marmor Norfolciense* 207–8, 215–18, 265, 283–4
  'Observations on Present State of Affairs' 201–2
  *Taxation No Tyranny* 201–2
  *Vanity of Human Wishes* 210
Johnson, Samuel 'Julian' 89–90
Johnston, Kenneth R. 258–9
Johnston, William 171–2
Johnstone, Charles:
  *Chrysal* 165–6, 180–1
Jones, William 13–14
  *Principles of Government* 13–14

journalism; *see* newspapers
judges, role of 17–19, 21–2, 121–3, 126–7, 171–2, 175–6, 202, 226–8, 248–9, 270–2; *see also* Fox's Libel Act (1792)
Junius 90–1, 202, 204–5
juries 14, 36–7, 121–3, 126–7, 169, 174–6, 227–8, 236–7, 248–9, 253
   special 109n.65, 175–6, 186–8, 209–10, 216–17, 227–8, 237–9, 278
   *ignoramus* 36–7, 66–70, 166
*Justa Edouardo King naufrago* 40–1
*Just Reward of Rebels* 274
Juvenal 82–3, 85–7, 206, 262–3

Keats, John:
   'To Autumn' 260–1
Kelly, Gary 256
Kelly, John 178–9, 186, 217–18; see also *Fog's Weekly Journal*:
   *Levee* 186, 193–4
   *Pamela's Conduct in High Life* 186
Kemp, Geoff 15–16, 70–1
Kewes, Paulina 70n.105
King, William:
   *Vindication of Sacheverell* 134–8
Kinservik, Matthew 186

*Lachrymae musarum* 39–43, 48–9; *see also* Richard Brome; John Dryden
Lamb, Charles 102–3
   'Reflections in the Pillory' 8–9
lampoons 36–9, 57–62, 66–70, 76, 80–1, 102–3, 134–8, 195
Larkin, Philip 58–9
Laud, William 9–10, 12–13, 28–9
*laudando praecipere* 56–7
Lauderdale, James Maitland, Earl of 225–6
Lee, Nathaniel 62–3, 70–2; see also *Duke of Guise*:
   *Lucius Junius Brutus* 70–1
legislation; *see* statutes
Leonard, John 102–3
Leslie, Charles 85, 138n.142
   *Wolf Stript* 142–4
L'Estrange, Roger 6n.7, 27–8, 30–7, 72–3, 76–9, 174–5
   *Account of the Growth of Knavery* 30–1
   *Considerations and Proposals* 6n.7, 8–9
   *Fables, of Aesop* 25, 75–8, 83–5, 128–9, 243–5
   *Observator* 72–3, 103–4
   *Truth and Loyalty Vindicated* 255–6
libel; *see* blasphemous libel, obscene libel, seditious libel
liberty of the press 13–20, 90–3, 169–70, 186–9, 202–6, 240–2, 261–2, 285–6
licensing 14–17, 63–4, 90–6, 121–3, 184–91, 203–7, 213–15; *see also* statutes (Licensing Act):
   distributed responsibility for 18n.36, 29–30, 35–6
   stage licensing 16–17, 184–9, 192–3, 196–7, 206–7, 209–10; *see also* statutes (Stage Licensing Act)
Lilburne, John 144, 236–7, 262–3
literacy 214–15, 245–6
literary property 16–17, 93–4, 117–18, 265, 269–72
literature:
   as commodity 14, 157–9
   as constrained by censorship 18–22, 87–8, 118–22, 209–10, 240–1, 256–61, 271–2
   as enriched by censorship 22–6, 83–5, 87–8, 150–1, 280–1, 287–9
   as privileged or transcendent category 22–3, 259–60, 285–6
   indeterminacy of 22–3; *see also* ambiguity
   practical immunity of 90–1, 259–60, 285–6
Liverpool, Robert Jenkinson, 2nd Earl of 240–1, 288–9
London Corresponding Society 256
*London Magazine* 203–4
Louis XVI, King 244–5
Love, Harold 58–62
love poetry 90–1
Lund, Roger D. 113
Luttrell, Narcissus 65n.98
Luxford, John 226–7

Macaulay, Thomas 14–15, 91
Macdonald, Archibald 226–7
Macdonald, Thomas:
   *Thoughts on Public Duties of Private Life* 8–9

McDowell, Nicholas 39n.36
McElligott, Jason 15–16
McGann, Jerome 31–2
MacKenzie, John 223
McKeon, Michael 62
MacNally, Leonard 249
Maltzahn, Nicholas von 29–30
Manley, Delarivier 14–15, 178–9
Mansfield, William Murray, 1st Earl of 169–70, 202, 248–9
manuscript; *see also* scribal publication
  circulation of 32–3, 38–9, 43–4, 51–4, 60–2, 82–3, 114–15, 149–50, 176–8, 277n.152
  legal status of 16–17, 32–3, 64–5, 174–5
  newsletters in 174–5
Marlborough, John Churchill, 1st Duke 81, 103–4
Marsh, Joss 285–6, 285n.4
Marvell, Andrew 30–3, 38–45, 64–5
  *Account of the Growth of Popery* 31–2
  *Horatian Ode* 43–4, 50–4, 63n.89
  *Miscellaneous Poems* 44–5
  'Nymph Complaining' 39–40
  'Painter' Poems 31–2
  *Poem upon Death of Lord Protector* 43–4, 47–8, 50
Mason, William:
  *Epistle to Shebbeare* 180–1
Matthews, John 16–17, 154–5, 167–8
Maynwaring, Arthur 81–2
  *King of Hearts* 82
  *Tarquin and Tullia* 81–2
Meal–Tub Plot 65–6
Mee, Jon 14–15
Meibom, Johann Heinrich:
  *Use of Flogging* 167
*Memoirs of the Pillory* 170–1
*Memorial of the Church of England* 97–100
Middleton, John 167–8
Mill, John Stuart 240
Millar, Andrew 203
Milton, John 28–30, 38–9
  *Areopagitica* 16–17, 203–7, 240
  *Eikonoklastes* 28–9
  *First Defence* 28–9
  *History of Britain* 29–30
  *Lycidas* 40–1

*Paradise Lost* 29–30, 49n.60, 227–8, 254–5, 265
*Paradise Regained* 102–3
*Readie and Easie Way* 29–30
*Samson Agonistes* 29–30, 102–3
Miner, Earl 42
Mist, Nathaniel 148, 159, 165–6;
  see also *Fog's Weekly Journal*:
  *Mist's Weekly Journal* 114, 148, 165–6, 186–8, 233–4
  'Persian Letter' 168n.32, 233–4
mock epic 60, 62, 100–6, 106–13
mock panegyric 57–62, 79–80
Monmouth, James Scott, 1st Duke of 57–8, 70–1, 153
Monmouth Rebellion 103–4, 153
Montaigne, Michel de 203–4
Mooney, Thomas 232–3
*Morning Post* 161–3
Morris, Gouverneur 246–8
Muir, Thomas 241n.57, 263–4
Mulgrave, John Sheffield, Earl of 60–1
Mullan, John 109–10
Mullart, William; see *Fall of Mortimer*

names:
  cratylic 210
  gutted or dashed 58–9, 125, 190, 210–13, 259–60, 283–5
  historical surrogates 40–1, 115–17, 210–12, 283–4; *see also*
    Caligula, Domitian, Nero, Sejanus, Tarquin, Walpole, Wolsey
  in anagram 125
  in pictogram 118–19, 125
Nayler, James 9–10, 10f
Nedham, Marchamont 41–2
Needham, Elizabeth, 'Mother' 107–8
Nero 85–6, 113, 115n.79, 234–5, 244–5, 249–50
Newcastle, Thomas Pelham–Holles, 1st Duke of 169, 178–9
newsbooks 40–1; *see also* unlicensed newsbook printing
newsletters (manuscript) 174–5
newspapers 94n.18, 164–5, 186–8, 190–1, 202, 240–1, 265n.125, 288
Northey, Edward 124–5

Nottingham, Daniel Finch, 2nd Earl of 131–2
novels 150–5, 169, 191, 197–200
   Jacobin 255–8
Nozy, Spy 258–9

Oates, Titus 64–5, 144n.151
obscene libel 6–7, 157n.2, 166–7, 238–9
O'Connell, Daniel 232–3
Oldham, John 208–9
   'Thirteenth Satire of Juvenal' 64–5, 82–3
Oldmixon, John 82n.135, 104n.53, 106–7
Ollier, Charles 284–5
orality; *see* seditious words
ornamental headpieces 40–1, 110–13, 112*f*
Orwell, George 209–10, 288–9
   *Nineteen Eighty-Four* 214–15
Osborne, William 95–6
Otway, Thomas:
   *Poet's Complaint of His Muse* 64–5

Paine, Thomas 246–8, 247*f*
   *Age of Reason* 10–11, 227–8
   *Letter Addressed to Addressers* 246–8
   *Rights of Man* 241n.57, 245–6, 254–5, 272, 274–5
Palmer, Thomas 32–3
*Pamela Censured* 183–4
panegyric 54–62, 149–50; *see also* mock panegyric
Parker, Fred 203–4
parody 57–60, 127–30, 213–14, 236–8, 284–5
   liturgical 236–8
   theories of 236–8
pastoral 149–50
patronage, literary 80–1, 179–80, 192–4, 240–1
Patterson, Annabel 9–10, 14–15, 22–4, 32–3, 61–2
Paulin, Tom 153–4
Paxton, Nicholas 118–19, 187n.88
Peacock, Thomas Love 240–1
   'Essay on Fashionable Literature' 240–1
Peasants' Revolt 264–5, 273–4

Pelham, Henry 179–80
*Pendragon* 76–7
pensions 20–1, 179–81, 218, 240–1; *see also* authors: patronage or purchase of
perjury 1–3, 8–9, 161n.13, 167–9, 223, 225–6
*permissions tacites* 92, 253
Persius 86–7
Peterloo Massacre 233–5, 240–2, 260–1, 283–4, 286–8
petitions 89–90, 146–8, 147*f*, 186
Pigott, Charles:
   *Political Dictionary* 246–8
   *Treachery No Crime* 272
pillory 1–13, 20, 64–70, 96–100, 132–45
   abolition of 1–3, 161–3, 221–31
   as book-promotion 12–13, 142–5, 157–60
   as crucifixion or martyrdom 11–12, 138–42, 141*f*
   as disgrace 1–5, 4*f*, 8–9, 100–9, 132–8, 163–4, 218–19, 221–3
   as satirical *topos* 7–8, 64–5, 100–6, 106–9, 134–8, 144–5, 157–9, 171–2, 173*f*, 225–6*f*
   as triumph 10–13, 138–45, 164–74, 174*f*, 176–8, 229–31, 231*f*
   crimes associated with 1–3, 7–9, 64–5, 167–8, 225–6
   *cum papyro* 3–5, 99, 106–7
   deaths in 107–8, 161–3, 162*f*, 167–8, 225–6
   in Canada 223, 224*f*
   in Delaware 221–3, 222*f*
   in Ireland 89n.1, 114, 226–7, 230–1, 231*f*
   locations of 3–5, 11–12, 98–9, 138–42, 144, 167, 169–70, 172–4, 225–6, 229–30
   mob violence in 10–11, 69*f*, 89–90, 104–6, 108–9, 132–8, 160–3, 162*f*, 165–8, 223–5, 229–30
   mutilation in 3–5, 9–10, 10*f*, 11–13, 75, 89–90, 100–3, 114, 160–1, 262–3
   rotation of 2*f*, 229–30
   slang terms for 1–3, 36–7
   women in 1–5, 65–6, 69*f*, 107–8

*Pillory Triumphant* 172–4, 174*f*
piracy 51–4, 52*f*, 62, 107n.59, 132–4, 135*f*, 207–8, 265–72
Pitt, William (the Younger) 248–9, 256–8
and 'Reign of Alarm/Terror' 256–9
Pittis (or Pittes), William 97, 99–100,
 *Heraclitus Ridens* 142–4
 *Hymn to Confinement* 99
 *True–Born Hugonot* 134–8, 144–5
 *Whipping Post* 99–100
playing cards 64–5, 66*f*, 69*f*, 134, 137*f*
politeness, culture of 14
Pope, Alexander 7–8, 23–4, 100–20, 148–50, 213, 227–8
 *Alcander* 106–7
 *Dunciad* (1728) 100–8, 110, 116–17, 132–4, 163, 198–9
 *Dunciad in Four Books* (1743) 107–8, 287–8
 *Dunciad Variorum* (1729) 60, 100–13, 112*f*, 116–18, 132–4, 163
 *Epistle to Arbuthnot* 108
 *Epistle to Bathurst* 23–4, 107–8, 116–17
 *Illiad* translation 106–7
 *Key to the Lock* 148–9, 182–3
 *One Thousand Seven Hundred and Thirty Eight* 117–19, 185n.82, 188–9, 207–8, 213, 286–7
 *One Thousand Seven Hundred and Forty* 118–19, 120*f*, 286–7
 *Rape of the Lock* 148–9
 *Windsor Forest* 149–50
Popish Plot 64–5, 67*f*
popular print 40–1, 93–4, 233–5, 238, 242–8, 254–7, 269–72
pornography 63–4, 157–8, 175–6
preaching; *see* sermons
Price, Leah 58–9
Price, Richard:
 *Discourse on Love of Our Country* 277
Priestley, Joseph 269–70
Prior, Matthew 178–9
printers; *see* book–trade professionals
proclamations 28–9, 89–90, 96, 245–6
 Jacobite 117–18
prophecy 215–18, 230–3
public sphere 14, 92, 176–8
publishers; *see* book–trade professionals

punishment, types of 20–1, 121–2; *see also* pillory:
 execution 16–17, 32–3, 55–6, 64–6, 83–5, 154–5, 167–8, 244–5
 fines and sureties 3–5, 19–20, 98–9, 121–2, 171–4, 179–80, 284–5
 imprisonment 3–5, 19–21, 82, 95–6, 114, 118, 168n.32, 186–8, 192n.106, 264–5
 kneeling before Parliament 43, 96, 213
 transportation 240–1, 263–4
 whipping 3–5, 76, 89–90, 99–100, 103–4, 221–3, 226–7
Prynne, William 9–13, 28–9, 100–1:
 *Histriomastix* 144

Quakers 9–10, 10*f*

Ralph, James 181n.67, 188–91, 237n.43; *see also* Fielding, Henry: *Champion*
Rawson, Claude 106
Rayner, Elizabeth 192n.106
Rayner, William 192n.106
reading; *see also* decoding, interpretation:
 and marginalia 29–30, 51–4, 177n.55
 and partisanship 45–8, 75–6, 127–8, 130
 as creative participation 25–6, 83–8, 146–8, 150–1, 154–5, 200–1, 216–17, 243, 280–1, 287–8
 as seditious act 72–3, 83–5, 212–17, 280–1; *see also* 'Gurney defence'
Reading, Nathaniel 64–5, 67*f*, 68*f*
regicide 28–9, 34–5, 39–43, 54, 77–8, 243–5
*Remarks on The Fall of Mortimer* 183–4
Restoration 27–30, 45–6, 54–7, 254–5
Richardson, Samuel 178–9
 *Aesop's Fables* 78n.125
 *Pamela* 183–4
Ricks, Christopher 208–9
Ricoeur, Paul 25
Ridgway, James 262–5, 272, 277
Ridpath, George 103–6, 105*f*, 124–5
 *Flying Post* 104–6, 138–42
 *Observator* 103–4
Robertson, Randy 63–4
*Robin's Last Shift* 75–6, 149–50; *see also* Dalton, Isaac
Robinson, Henry Crabb 229–30

Roe, Nicholas 260–1
Rogers, Pat 116–17
romance 175–6
Romanticism 10–11, 254–61, 283–9
*Romulus and Hersilia* 70–1
Roper, Abel 104–6, 178–9
  *Post Boy* 104–6
Rose-Alley Ambush 36–9, 51–4
Rosenfeld, Sophia 285–6
Ross, Trevor 13–14, 91n.9
Rossington, Michael 286n.9
Rushworth, John:
  *Historical Collections of Private Passages of State* 12–13
Ryder, Dudley 197n.119
Rye House Plot 66f

Sacheverell, Henry 95–6, 127, 167–8
  *Political Union* 130
St Clair, William 269–72
St John, Henry; *see* Bolingbroke
satire 23–5, 30–2, 57–63, 287–9; *see also* parody:
  clandestine 31–2, 61–2, 212–13
  dramatic 181–6
  graphic 1–3, 171–4, 246–8, 266
  in novels 196–201, 257–8
  Juvenalian 82–7, 208–13, 262–3
  under Queen Anne 96–100
  under Walpole 106–20, 181–4, 188–99, 207–18
Savage, Richard 114–15, 176–9, 218
  *Author To Be Lett* 176–8
Sayer, Charles 171–2
*scandalum magnatum* 38–9, 64n.93, 96, 125n.114
Scott, Walter 236–7, 259–60
Scottish martyrs 241n.57, 263–4
scribal publication 32–3, 60–2, 174–5; *see also* manuscript
*Scribler's Doom* 132–4, 133f
Scroggs, William 5–6, 32–3, 122–3, 178–9, 248–9
Sedgemoor, battle of 153–4
seditious libel; *see also* censorship, statutes, trials:
  abolition of 241–2
  and literary property 269–72
  as commodity 14, 157–60, 176–8, 180–1, 185–6, 269–72
  crackdowns against 5–6, 78–9, 85, 92n.10, 93–4, 96–100, 123, 164–5, 227–8, 227n.14, 235
  decline in prosecutions for 202, 237–9, 257–8, 284–5
  difficulty of securing convictions for 114–16, 166, 175–8, 227–8, 233–40, 242–53
  indistinct definition of 8n.14, 18–19, 21–2, 74, 121–3, 130–1, 238–9, 241–2
  private prosecutions for 242, 284–5
  proxy charges for 6–7, 27–8, 64n.93, 71–2, 95–6, 178n.59, 227–8, 230–1, 236–7
seditious words (speech) 96–7, 114, 164–5, 167–8, 225–6, 226n.12, 240–1, 276–80
Seidel, Michael 153
Sejanus 115–16, 210
Selden, John 144–5
Self, Will 241–2
Senior, Nassau William 271–2
sermons 95–6, 98–9, 164–5, 276–7
Seven Years War 201–2
sexual offences 1–3, 4f, 107–8, 144n.151, 161–3, 226n.11, 229–30
Shadwell, Thomas 34–5, 57–61, 66–70, 75, 79–80, 184; *see also Mac Flecknoe*:
  *Address of Dryden to Prince of Orange* (attrib.) 79–80
  *Lancashire Witches* 63–4
  *Medal of John Bayes* (attrib.) 34, 66–70
  *Some Reflections* (attrib.) 72
  *True Widow* 101–2
Shaftesbury, Anthony Ashley Cooper, 1st Earl of 62–3, 66–70, 90–1
Shaftesbury, Anthony Ashley Cooper, 3rd Earl of 90–3, 99–100
  *Characteristicks* 126–7
Shakespeare, William 186–8
  *Richard II* 187n.88
Shebbeare, John 169–71, 179–81, 225–7, 283–4
  *Marriage Act* 169
  *Letters to People of England* 169–70, 217–18
Shelley, Mary 284–5; *see also* Shelley, Percy Bysshe: *Poetical Works*

*Index* 321

Shelley, Percy Bysshe 271–2
  'England in 1819' 286–7
  *Hellas* 284–5
  *Letter to Ellenborough* 227–8
  *Mask of Anarchy* 283–6
  *Poetical Works* (1839) 284–7
  *Queen Mab* 271–2
  *Swellfoot the Tyrant* 284–5
Sheridan, Richard Brinsley:
  *Critic* 158–9
  *Pizarro* 254–5
Sherwood, William 269–70
*Shift Shifted* 164–5; *see also* Isaac Dalton
Shoemaker, Robert 169
*Shortest-Way with Whores and Rogues* 134–8
Sidmouth, Henry Addington, 1st Viscount 237–8, 283–5
Sidney, Algernon 64–5, 121–2, 249–50
  *Discourses Concerning Government* 64–5, 244–5, 274
Siebert, F. S. 15–16, 91
silence 118–19, 198–9, 260–1
Smith, Adam 5
  *Theory of Moral Sentiments* 163–5
Smith, William (d.1780) 161–3
Smith, William, MP 266–9, 272, 280
Smollett, Tobias 179–80
  *Briton* 171–2
  *History of England* 96–7
  *Humphry Clinker* 158–9
Society for Constitutional Information 202, 256
sodomy, attempted sodomy; *see* sexual offences
songs; *see* ballads
Southey, Robert 12–13, 240–1, 261–73, 267*f*, 268*f*, 275–81
  'To the Exiled Patriots' 263–4
  *Wat Tyler* 264–73, 275–81, 288n.12
Spa Fields Riots 233–4, 280
speech; *see* seditious words
Spenceanism 227–8, 237–8, 280–1
Spinoza, Baruch; *see* Nozy, Spy
Spofforth, Robert 134, 137*f*
Sprat, Thomas 45–7
  *Plague at Athens* 46–7
  *History of Royal Society* 46–7
  'To Happy Memory of Cromwell' 46–7
Stanley, Edmond 226–7

*State Law; or, The Doctrine of Libels* 252–3
Stationers' Register 43–5, 110
Statutes:
  Act of Indemnity and Oblivion (1660) 28–9, 57
  Act of Settlement (1701) 92–3
  Act of Union (1707) 130–1
  Alien and Sedition Acts (USA, 1798) 246–8
  Blasphemy Act (1698) 93–4
  Copyright Act (Statute of Anne, 1710) 16–17, 93–4, 269–70
  Coroners and Justice Act (2009) 241–2
  Excise Bill (1733) 195–6, 273–4
  Fox's Libel Act (1792) 122–3, 227–8, 248–9
  Gagging Acts (1795) 245–6, 260–1
  Indemnity Act (1690) 78–9
  Licensing Act (1662) 13–14, 16–18, 35–6, 92–3, 95–6
    lapse of (1679–85) 36–7, 63–4, 95–6, 122–3, 248–9
    lapse of (1695) 14–17, 91–7, 122–3, 150–1
  Obscene Publications Act (1857) 239n.53
  Pillory Abolition Act (1816) 225–8
  Printing Act (1649) 34–5
  Publications Act (1819) 240–1; *see also* Six Acts
  Reform Bill (1832) 238–9, 284–5
  Seditious Libels Act (1819) 13–14, 238–41; *see also* Six Acts
  Seditious Meetings Act (1795) 245–6; *see also* Gagging Acts
  Six Acts (1819) 16–17, 240–1
  Special Juries Act (1730) 109n.65, 175–6
  Stage Licensing Act (1737) 16–17, 94–5, 184–93, 196–7, 203, 206–7, 214–15, 254–5
  Stamp Act (1712) 16–17, 93–4, 240–1
  Succession to the Crown Act (1707) 16–17, 94n.17
  Theatres Regulation Act (1843) 94–5
  Treason Act (1351) 244–5, 278–9
  Treason Act (1707) 94n.17

Statutes: (*cont.*)
  Treasonable and Seditious Practices Act (1795) 16–17, 245–6; *see also* Gagging Acts
Star Chamber 9–10, 12–13, 89–90, 230–1, 241–2, 262–3
*De libellis famosis* (Pickering's Case) 241–2
Steele, Richard 105*f*, 125
  *Tatler* 103–4
  *Crisis* 125
Stephens, Robert 'Hog' 82
Stephens, William 97–100
Sterne, Laurence:
  *Tristram Shandy* 233
sticks; *see* carrots
Stokes, Benjamin 277n.152
Stubbe, John 262–3
subornation 1–3, 64–5, 225–6
surveillance 35–6, 256–61
Swift, Jonathan 20–1, 23–4, 93–4, 104–6, 185–6, 213
  *Gulliver's Travels* 20–1, 102–3, 181–2, 198–9, 214–15, 251–2, 288–9
  *Letter Concerning Sacramental Test* 106
  *Modest Proposal* 126–7
  *Public Spirit of Whigs* 125
  *Windsor Prophecy* 215
Symonds, Henry 264–5, 272

Tacitus 85
Talfourd, Thomas Noon 223–6
  'Brief Observations on the Pillory' 223–5
  'Modern Periodical Literature' 223–6
Tarquin 81, 244–5, 249–50
Taylor, David Francis 254–5
Taylor, John 159–60
  *Aquamusæ* 159–60
Temple, Richard Grenville, Earl 171–2
theatre; *see* drama
Thelwall, Cecil 242n.62
Thelwall, John 234–5, 242, 259–60, 287–8
  'King Chaunticlere' 10–11, 242–5, 250–3
  *Tribune* 274–5
Theobald, Lewis 103–4
*This Is Not the Thing: or, Molly Exalted* 4*f*
Thomas, Donald 240
Thomason, George 40–1

Thompson, E. P. 256–7
Thomson, James 185–6, 203
  *Edward and Eleonora* 185–6, 206–7
  *Liberty* 206
Thomson, Nathaniel 37n.31
Thoresby, Ralph 114
*Three Champions* 103–4, 105*f*
*Three Poems upon Death of Cromwell* 43–7; *see also* Dryden, John: *Heroic Stanzas*
Toland, John 29–30, 49n.60
Tomkyns, Thomas 29–30
Tonson, Jacob 82
Tooke, John Horne 255–6, 266
translation 37–8, 82–7, 106–7, 208–9
transportation 240–1, 263–4
treason 28–9, 32–3, 64–6, 78–9, 89–90, 93–4, 118–19, 149–50, 167–8, 183–4, 244–5, 256–7; *see also* trials
trials; *see also* judges, juries:
  for seditious libel and related offences 103–4, 109–10, 115–16, 122–5, 233–8, 242–53
  for treason 114–15, 249–50, 256–7, 264–5, 276–9
  publication of 236–8, 248–50
*Trip to the Pillory* 144n.151
Tutchin, John 103–4, 122–3, 134
  *Observator* 103–4
Twiss, Horace:
  *Posthumous Parodies* 227–8
Twyn, John 32–3
Tyler, Wat 264–5, 274–5; *see also* Southey, Robert: *Wat Tyler*
typographic emphasis 63–4, 118–19, 120*f*, 233

*Universal Spy* 186–8
unlicensed newsbook printing 27–8, 64n.93, 95–6, 122n.100
United Irishmen 226–7, 233

ventriloquism 127, 150–1
Vere Street coterie 229–30
*View of Corn Exchange and Mr Atkinson* 2*f*
Visconsi, Elliot 57
Voltaire (François–Marie Arouet) 87–90
  *Lettres philosophiques* 45–6, 87–8
  *Vox Populi, Vox Dei* 16–17, 154–5, 167–8; *see also* Matthews, John

Wale, Samuel 161–3, 162*f*
Walelop, Retrob 206
Waller, Edmund 45–6, 55
  'Upon the Late Storm' 44–6
Walpole, Horace 169–70, 179–81
Walpole, Robert 94–5, 110, 179–84, 186, 192–201, 288–9
  client poets 179–80, 210–12
  literary campaign against 115–16, 118–19, 201–2, 206–18
  sobriquets for 115–16, 206, 210, 237n.43
Walsh, James 258–9
Ward, Edward (Ned) 97, 99–102, 108, 159–61
  *Hudibras Redivivus* 99, 159–61
  *London Spy* 159–60
Ward, John 107–9
Warton, Joseph 118–19
Watson, Richard 45–6
*Wat Tyler, or The State Menders* 273–4; *see also* Henley, Robert
'What Makes a Libel' 114–15, 253; *see also* Eaton, Daniel Isaac
Wharton, Philip, 1st Duke of:
  *True Briton* 186–8
Whitehead, Paul 118, 178–9
  *Manners* 118, 188
Wild, Robert:
  *Dr. Wild's Humble Thanks* 153–4
Willes, John 175–6
William III, King 77–8, 81–2, 149–50, 153, 244–5

Williams, Charles:
  *Poet Mounted on the Court Pegasus* 266, 268*f*
Williams, John 172–4, 174*f*
Wilkes, John 90–1, 171–2, 173*f*, 179–80, 202, 274–5
  *North Briton* 171–4, 174*f*
Wilson, Thomas 118–19
Wilson, Walter 142
Wilson, William 44–5
Wimsatt, W. K. 204–5
Winn, James 42, 72–4
Winterbotham, William 277
wit 43, 59–60, 90–1, 113
Wither, George 45–6, 159–60
Wollstonecraft, Mary 266
  *Wrongs of Woman* 260–1
Wolsey, Thomas 195–6, 210
woodcuts 132–4, 133*f*
Wooler, T. J. 234–5, 238–9
  *Black Dwarf* 234–5, 280
Wordsworth, William 240–1, 258–9, 262–3, 270–1
  *Lyrical Ballads* 254–5
  *Prelude* 258–9
Wrangham, Francis 262–3

Yorke, Philip 202

Zall, Paul M. 270n.135
Zwicker, Steven N. 33–4, 38–9, 44n.47, 47–8